Up for Grabs

Timber Pirates, Lumber Barons, and the Battles Over Maine's Public Lands

Thomas Urquhart

Camden, Maine

Down East Books

Published by Down East Books
An imprint of Globe Pequot
Trade division of The Rowman & Littlefield Publishing Group, Inc.
4501 Forbes Blvd., Ste. 200
Lanham, MD 20706
www.rowman.com
www.downeastbooks.com

Co-Published with Maine Historical Society
489 Congress Street
Portland, Maine 04101
www.mainehistory.org

Distributed by NATIONAL BOOK NETWORK

Names: Urquhart, Thomas, 1944– author.
Title: Up for grabs : timber pirates, lumber barons, and the battles over Maine's public lands / by Thomas Urquhart.
Description: Camden, Maine : Down East Books, [2020] | Includes bibliographical references and index. | Summary: "The story of how over half a million acres of Maine's most beautiful and revered land came to belong to everyone"— Provided by publisher.
Identifiers: LCCN 2020003388 (print) | LCCN 2020003389 (ebook) | ISBN 9781608936861 (cloth ; alk. paper) | ISBN 9781608936878 (ebook)
Subjects: LCSH: Public lands—Maine—History. | Land use—Government policy— Maine—History.
Classification: LCC HD243.M2 U77 2020 (print) | LCC HD243.M2 (ebook) | DDC 333.109741—dc23
LC record available at https://lccn.loc.gov/2020003388
LC ebook record available at https://lccn.loc.gov/2020003389

∞™ The paper used in this publication meets the minimum requirements of American National Standard for Information Sciences—Permanence of Paper for Printed Library Materials, ANSI/NISO Z39.48-1992.

To Amy

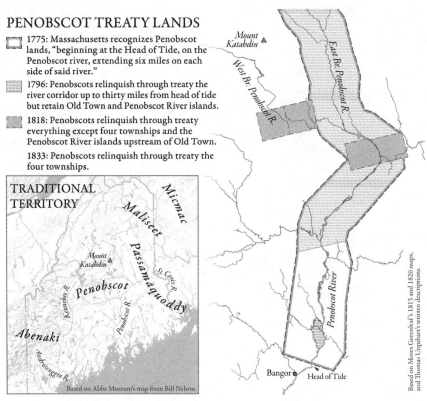

PENOBSCOT TREATY LANDS

1775: Massachusetts recognizes Penobscot lands, "beginning at the Head of Tide, on the Penobscot river, extending six miles on each side of said river."

1796: Penobscots relinquish through treaty the river corridor up to thirty miles from head of tide but retain Old Town and Penobscot River islands.

1818: Penobscots relinquish through treaty everything except four townships and the Penobscot River islands upstream of Old Town.

1833: Penobscots relinquish through treaty the four townships.

Mount
Katahdin ▲

East Br. Penobscot R.

West Br. Penobscot R.

TRADITIONAL TERRITORY

Micmac

Maliseet

Passamaquoddy

Mount
Katahdin ▲

Penobscot

St. Croix R.

Kennebec R.

Penobscot R.

Abenaki

Androscoggin R.

Based on Abbe Museum's map from Bill Nelson.

Penobscot River

Bangor ●   Head of Tide

Based on Moses Greenleaf's 1815 and 1820 maps, and Thomas Urquhart's written descriptions.

Penobscot Treaty Lands (Margot Carpenter).

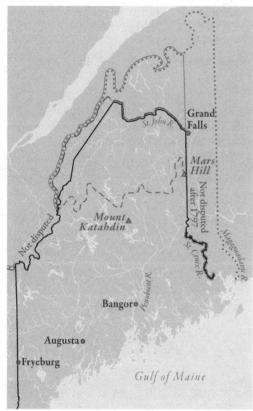

NORTHEASTERN BOUNDARY
1783-1842

The 1783 Treaty of Paris defined the boundary as: "From the North West Angle of Nova Scotia. viz., That Angle which is formed by a Line drawn due North from the Source of the St. Croix River to the Highlands, ...". A description that led to counter claims.

····· **1783**
United States boundary line claim based on Treaty of Paris.

▪▪▪ **1797**
Survey determining the St. Croix River and boundary line.

—— **1821**
United States boundary line claim.

– – – **1821**
Great Britain boundary line claim.

——·· **1831**
King of the Netherlands proposed boundary line.

▬▬▬ **1842**
Boundary line established by the Webster-Ashburton Treaty.

Map based on *Maine Northeast Boundary Settlement* from the Maine Historical Society's *Maine Bicentennial Atlas, An Historical Survey* (1976) and the *Map of the Boundary Lines Between the United States and the Adjacent British Provinces* (1843) drawn by Thomas Jefferson Lee for the U.S. House of Representatives.

Maine's changing northeastern boundary, 1783–1842 (Margot Carpenter).

Attention of the people of Maine has frequently been called to the so called wild lands of the State. It is a matter of great importance and one upon which from time to time much has been written.

—Forest Commissioner Edgar E. Ring, 1908

It's a tale of neglect of responsibility by some state officials and of extraordinary dedication by others. It's a saga that had its beginnings with the first land grants by English kings three centuries ago—a saga that will largely be played out by the end of summer. It's the story of Maine's public lots.

—Bob Cummings, *Maine Sunday Telegram*, June 4, 1984

Contents

Prologue

This Land Is Our Land
(May 4, 1982)

Governor Joseph E. Brennan's words landed like the proverbial tree falling in an uninhabited forest. Which he didn't expect, addressing as he was a more or less full house.

"Welcome, fellow Democrats."

It was a ploy the Maine governor sometimes used to warm up an uncertain crowd. Coming from the leader of the state's Democratic Party and said with a smile, the salutation could be counted on to break the ice, add a little humor, and—at chambers of commerce, for instance—it usually got a laugh. Today, though, the laughs were few and strained. "Stone-faced" was how one person recalled the general response. The audience was not amused.

That they were very likely overwhelmingly Republican wasn't the cause of the icy politeness that met the governor's greeting. The two dozen or so men in the audience were the chiefs of the paper and timber companies of Maine. They were all at the Blaine House—the governor's mansion—by personal invitation, and they had an uneasy suspicion why.

Nine years before, in 1973, representatives of Maine's forest products industry—two paper companies and three private landowners, most of them now sitting in the Blaine House—had filed suit against the state. The state had promptly countersued. In dispute was the wood harvested on certain publicly owned lands, around 320,000 acres, in fact. The paper and timber companies had been cutting them for a hundred years or more without, in the view of Maine's attorney general, any legal right to do so for most of that time.

No one denied that the lands belonged to the state. Since the days when Maine was a largely wild and unsettled part of Massachusetts, whenever a township from the public domain was sold to a private entity, the law required the state to reserve a part of the land.[1] The general assumption was that in private hands, the township would soon bring forth a community, at which point these "Public Reserved Lands" would be handed over to the new town to provide for its religious and educational needs. When Maine became a state in 1820, Massachusetts insisted that the law be incorporated into its constitution. (Soon after statehood, by mutual agreement, support for church and minister was dropped, and the benefits were earmarked for the schools.)

As for the timber growing on the Public Reserved Lands, again, no one denied that the legislature had sold the rights to harvest it long ago. When settlement failed to take root in the northern half of the state, these scattered faraway lots—mostly a thousand acres each—had become an invitation to timber thieves and squatters, which brought the additional risk of fire. Without the resources to watch over the forests—and prohibited by its constitution from selling the land—the government's reasonable solution was to sell the timber growing there before it was lost and let the lumber companies take care of the trespassers.

The legal question boiled down to this: Did the sale include all future forest growth, or had Maine sold the right to cut trees growing *at the time of the sale* only?

The case had been a contentious rollercoaster of a ride. When the forest companies prevailed in superior court, the state appealed. At the end of August 1981, Maine's Supreme Judicial Court—universally referred to as the "Law Court"—overturned the lower-court ruling and found in favor of the attorney general's position. Today's meeting had been called by the governor in anticipation of the conclusion of this legal battle. For the landowners, it promised to be a day of reckoning, likely expensive and painful. Since the court's decision, officials from the State Planning Office and Department of Conservation had been busy crafting proposals for compensation for a century of timber trespass.

David Carlisle and his father, George, president of the forest management firm of Prentiss & Carlisle, didn't know exactly what to expect. They had arrived with Brad Wellman, the head of Seven Islands Land Company, which managed nearly a million acres—over 5 percent of the state's forest—for the descendants of David Pingree, a Salem shipping magnate who had started buying forestland around 1840. The three men could hazard a guess at the meeting's agenda. How it might unfold was another matter.

By virtue of their position as captains of its most important industry, the Carlisles, Wellman, and the others present were among Maine's most powerful citizens. They were the backbone of the state's social, economic, and political fabric. Bangor, the onetime lumber capital of the world, was their stomping ground. It was there they held their meetings until their lawyers advised against it on antitrust grounds. Augusta, the state capital, had never seen such a gathering before.

The Blaine House is an impressive white Federal-period building that sits amid neatly trimmed lawns. On its steps, Richard Barringer, director of the State Planning Office, waited for the meeting to begin, meanwhile enjoying the scents and sounds of a delightful May day. The air was full of the promise of summer. For Barringer, it was full of something else as well: a sense of "great pith and moment," which also brought with it a sense of trepidation. "Will they show up?" Brennan had asked him. Now, as he watched the governor's guests arrive, it dawned on him that this was a truly extraordinary moment in Maine's history.

It was also unprecedented that the governor would consider doing what his natural resource advisors had recommended. His demand of these corporate titans was going to be very aggressive and, in their eyes, even outrageous. But Barringer knew it was Maine's last, best chance to enlarge its public domain, and to do so with the best land possible. This was 1982. Acquiring land for conservation and recreation would not become state policy—in the form of the Land for Maine's Future program—for another five years.

Inside the Blaine House, the distinguished invitees were assembled in the State Reception Room. Nobody had declined the governor's invitation, and the space was not ideal for an assembly of this size. To the Carlisles, it felt like two or three rooms put together railroad style. In fact, it had been two rooms, until they were merged by James G. Blaine—speaker, U.S. senator, secretary of state, and, as presidential candidate, branded the "continental liar from the state of Maine"—who lived there from 1862 until his death thirty-one years later. Its long elegant proportions and antique furnishings may have made it a perfect venue for parties to entertain the late-nineteenth-century Republican elite. On this occasion, however, with folding chairs replacing the Chippendale and the audience tucked about and behind the room's pillars and partitions, Governor Brennan, up front at his podium, seemed a long way off. The younger Carlisle found the setup awkward, and the steel chairs a further discomfort. This was clearly not going to be a meeting so much as a pronouncement. Still, it was the governor's house, which gave the event enough gravitas to outweigh the uncomfortable arrangements.

Thirty-five years later David Carlisle could remember exactly where he was sitting. The mood in the room was cordial but tense, and he thought he detected grim looks on the faces of the governor's staff, as well. Carlisle guessed that he and his colleagues were not the only ones feeling on edge. Doubtless wondering what the landowners' reaction to his proposal would be, even the governor had felt the need to lighten the mood. He was somewhat unsettled when his effort fell flat ("I've used that line about fellow

Democrats a hundred times, and always got a good response," Brennan said afterwards). It was no wonder his officials seemed a trifle ill at ease. This was high-stakes poker, as Barringer was all too aware, and nothing to joke about. Like lawyers going into the trial of their career, a somber demeanor was all that was appropriate.

Conservation Commissioner Richard Anderson had arrived early to make sure the room was set up properly and to put up large maps to accompany the governor's remarks. Attorney Martin Wilk, who had seen the case through the courts practically from the start, was making last-minute adjustments to the podium from which Governor Brennan would speak. His immediate worry was that the three-ring binder containing the notes he had prepared for the governor might slide off the lectern. Annee Tara, Anderson's deputy, was the only woman in the room. She assumed that the members of the audience were crusty old guys who weren't going to show their feelings readily.

At two o'clock, Governor Brennan started speaking. He summarized the history of the case, which the state had won. The verdict, however, had said nothing about damages. Rather than go back to court, he said, he would prefer to settle all claims once and for all, through negotiation. The usual penalty for timber trespass was treble damages; but, said the governor, he was not going to seek financial restitution. Anderson and Barringer had come up with a more creative plan: to ask for land, of which the companies had more than enough, instead.

Maine would seek reparations on a two-acre-for-one basis. At the same time, hundreds of inconsequential thousand-acre plots, scattered all across the state, would be exchanged and consolidated into blocks of a more meaningful and manageable size. As they were, the Public Lots were of little use to the public since nobody knew they were there, nor how to reach them. For the landowners and forest managers, the governor's approach offered the advantage of getting the state out of their hair once and for all. It was his hope that they would work with him in good faith toward a solution that would be acceptable and beneficial all around.

At this point Governor Brennan produced a booklet, handsomely printed like a company annual report and specially made up for the meeting. It contained maps of all the ownerships represented in the room, company by company, with the Public Lots highlighted wherever they were marked on the ground. On the same maps were marked, company by company, the specific lands that the state was asking for in settlement. It was a wish list of some of the most spectacular natural places in Maine.

As the booklets were being passed out, one for each company, Brennan announced that a triumvirate—*troika* was perhaps a better word, some of the landowners may have thought—would handle the negotiations on the state's behalf. They were the same officials who had chosen the places the state hoped to acquire: Barringer, Anderson, and Tara.

A deathly hush fell over the State Reception Room. The general reaction was perhaps most intensely expressed by George Carlisle. He was so aggravated and shocked, several people said, he almost fell off his chair. He and his son were horrified at being asked for what they considered "premiums," the additional value that the state was demanding above a straight exchange of the lots themselves. Nobody could believe what the governor was proposing.

But nobody stormed out. There were a few questions along the lines of "where do we go from here?" Most of the audience was too busy looking at the materials to see which of their properties were on the list. Someone mentioned horse-trading. "Yeah," said the man from J.D. Irving. "And I know which part of the horse we'll be getting." As the meeting adjourned, Richard Anderson watched them file out in stunned silence as if it had been the funeral of a beloved.

"This had never happened to them before," Annee Tara realized. "Nobody knew what was coming, what it was going to be like—and they were completely taken aback." She thought they were surprised at how well organized and intent the governor had been. "So they took their booklets and went home and probably had a drink along the way."

As they got up to leave, the landowners had one more immediate concern. In his remarks, Governor Brennan had suggested it would be in everybody's best interest to keep the negotiations confidential, and there had been no announcement in advance of the meeting. All the same, both Carlisles at least had a sneaking feeling that the press might be waiting for them on the Blaine House steps, wanting to know what they were going to do, and how they might respond. Such fears were unfounded. The meeting was never mentioned in the newspapers.

Over the next three years, the State of Maine took title to over four hundred thousand acres of what would become some of its most cherished natural areas. On the map, they now appear as large green blocks, with names like Deboullie Township, Sugar Island in Moosehead Lake, Duck Lake, Round Pond, and Bigelow Preserve—a far cry from the little dots that previously marked the Public Lots, scattered across the map of Maine's Unorganized Territories like a case of the chickenpox.

How Maine lost and regained this magnificent heritage is an epic tale that began two hundred and more years ago with the hapless—and often ethically questionable—land deals of the eighteenth century.

PART I

Chapter One

"Exhaustless Merchandize"
(1783–1795)

On May 23, 1759, Brigadier General Samuel Waldo, hero of the siege of Louisbourg, stepped ashore near what is now Brewer on the Penobscot River. With an expansive gesture embracing all that the eye could see, he exclaimed, "Here is my bound[ary]." With that, he "instantly fell dead, of an apoplexy," probably a stroke.[2]

Already sixty-three years of age, Waldo had accompanied his friend Thomas Pownall, governor of Massachusetts Bay, on an expedition to deal with the Indians of the region. The French and Indian War was at its height, and the Penobscot tribe had been supporting Great Britain's enemies. Determined to check them, Pownall sent natives ahead with an uncompromising challenge to the sachems: "I am come to build a fort at Penobscot, and will make the land English. I am able to do it . . . and I will do it."[3]

Pownall was quite prepared to fight the "People of Penobscot," if necessary; he had four hundred soldiers with him. "I seek not their favour nor fear them, for they can do me neither good nor harm," wrote the governor, before offering the Indians the protection of the fort he was planning to build if they "become English."

The fort, to be constructed at the mouth of the river, was of particular interest to Brigadier General Waldo. The Penobscot River formed the eastern boundary of a tract of more than half a million acres that had made him the most important of the great land proprietors in His Majesty's District of Maine. Waldo's ownership stretched west to the Muscungus River and extended from the coast north to a line, which had never been surveyed, that "embraced a territory equal to thirty miles square." It was now called the Waldo Patent, and he had acquired most of it not in exchange for money, but as a reward from a consortium of businessmen of which he was a member (as was the president of Harvard College) for services rendered.

A century-old claim that had descended to these men was now in jeopardy. George II had inadvertently awarded the same land to an overzealous surveyor of the king's woods (the man responsible for safeguarding—with the "King's Broad Arrow"—pine trees suitable as masts for the Royal Navy). Waldo was chosen to go to London to represent the consortium at the royal court, and when his tireless lobbying carried the day, its members gave him half the disputed land in gratitude.

Waldo called his demesne Broad Bay and styled himself its Hereditary Lord. Those who came and settled for seven years "either in person or through a substitute," he promised, would own their land forever, "without their having to make the slightest recompense, or pay any interest for it." Soon forty families of the Protestant faith—a condition for accepting his offer—were installed, although it was said that Waldo had not done much for them since their arrival.

In search of more settlers, particularly from Germany, Waldo printed a prospectus of "collected advices and regulations" in 1753. It advertised a healthy climate and a soil

> exceedingly fruitful, since the wood which grows there is mostly oak, beach, ash, maple, and the like, and it yields all manner of fruit as in Germany. . . . Also, there is much game in the woods, and many fish in the streams, and every one is permitted to hunt and fish.

Besides a congenial climate and productive soil, new plantations would have their own churches and schools. "In every such district," Waldo's circular promised, "there shall be given to the church two hundred acres; to the first preacher settling among them, two hundred; to the school, two hundred."

Against all these blessings, however, Indian raids remained a persistent threat. A fort adjacent to his land would be a material selling point in attracting new settlers. With the same formidable energy that won him his property, Waldo had persuaded Governor Pownall to build one. As the first stop on their Penobscot expedition, they found a suitable site—"a crescent crowning elevation"[4]—at the mouth of the river.

With construction of the fort begun, Pownall and his party sailed up the Penobscot as far as their ship, HMS *St. George*, could navigate. Among the governor's effects was a lead plate on which he had had engraved: "May 23, 1759. Province of Massachusetts Bay, Penobscot, dominions of Great Britain. Possession confirmed by Thomas Pownall, Governor." It was to take formal possession of the region in the king's name that Pownall and Waldo had debarked.

Undistracted by Waldo's apoplectic demise, Governor Pownall proceeded to a spot above the falls and "did there hoist the King's Colours which were saluted by the artillery at sunset." The "Leaden Plate" was buried, as Pownall described it, beneath a "Large White Birch Tree, three large Trunks springing from ye one Root. The Tree is at the Top of a very high piked hill on ye East side ye River, about three miles above Marine Navigation." Waldo's body was then taken back to the fort and buried with full military honors. The chief mourner was the governor himself, and "upon the Interment of the Corps, the Guards fired three Vollies over the Grave," reported the *Boston Evening Post.*[5]

The efforts of General Waldo, wrote Maine's second governor, William Williamson, a century later, "hastened the development of the Penobscot Valley by at least a generation. He found the Patent a wilderness; he left it containing ten flourishing plantations." The Waldo Patent would soon become an object lesson on the risks of land speculation in the new Republic.

As part of His Britannic Majesty's colony of Massachusetts Bay, Maine was called the County of Yorkshire, after the great northern shire of the Old Country. It was "early a resort for those with but small regard for creed or church," wrote the authors of the Federal Writers' Project in *Maine, A Guide 'Down East.'*[6] What regard there was, according to author and journalist Colin Woodard's *The Lobster Coast*, tended in the opposite direction to Puritan Boston. A century and a half of life on the frontier had honed a fierce strain of individualism in the inhabitants. To bring this "Wild East" more in the way of law and order, two counties, Cumberland and Lincoln, were hived off from the mother county in 1760 (and the "shire" docked from her name).[7] All three stretched from the ocean north into the uncharted wildlands, covering a far larger area than do their namesakes today.

Settlement was the goal, and the colonial authorities granted large tracts of these empty lands to syndicates of merchants and gentlemen (who were generally their social peers). In the beginning, these proprietors had been directly involved in the nuts and bolts of their villages, often raising families there. By the mid-eighteenth century, however, speculation more than civic purpose drove the land business. Proprietors' shares were "hawked about for anyone who wanted to invest."[8]

To counter this trend, the government in Boston imposed conditions, when granting land to would-be proprietors, that fostered "improvement" of the wilderness, not just private profit: "60 Protestant families" per township had to be settled within six years. Each family was to have a house, "none to be less than eighteen feet square, and seven feet stud," and together, they must put three hundred acres under cultivation. The plans for a settlement by Sir Francis Bernard, the last confirmed colonial governor of Massachusetts Bay, were exemplary.[9] He had received a grant for Mount Desert

Island—recently relieved of the French—as a reward for his distinguished service to the colony.[10]

Here Sir Francis hoped to lay out a town around Southwest Harbor. Starting at the bay's head, lots of five acres were to be counted off on either side, ten at a time, each one facing the water. Besides their home lot, the first sixty settlers would be granted an outlying lot of fifteen acres, and if possible, an additional "five acres of salt meadow to lie in common and to be mowed only and not pastured unless it lies high enough to bear cattle without hurting the land."[11] Of the ten-lot parcels, every other one was to be left ungranted. "In one of these sets of reserved ten lots, I propose to set out lots for a Meeting house and School," wrote Sir Francis, and added that another "and one of the pleasantest sets (in the centre or otherwise) I shall reserve for a settlement of my own."

A revolution later, Massachusetts' General Court would make reservation of land for public use the law, as it sought to sell—either for or in lieu of cash—as much of the District of Maine as it could, as quickly as possible, "for almost every conceivable purpose of trade."[12]

As the Commonwealth of Massachusetts began to enjoy a hard-won peace, it had under its jurisdiction approximately seventeen million acres in Maine, most of them uncharted. Governor Bernard had sent a party into the wilderness to map the Penobscot River in 1763. A dozen years later, Benedict Arnold (before his name became synonymous with *traitor*) hacked his way up the Kennebec in a heroic attempt to capture Quebec City for the Americans. Otherwise, away from the coastline, the "Eastern Lands" were terra incognita.

To John Hancock, Massachusetts' first governor, all this undeveloped real estate was just waiting to be turned into desperately needed funds for the new Commonwealth. The parlous financial condition in which it emerged from the revolution is described in poignant prose, all the more pleasant to find in an official report to Maine's legislature. Forest Commissioner Austin Wilkins quoted verbatim from Moses Greenleaf's 1829 *Survey of Maine*:

> ... her people borne down with the weight of taxes—her treasury empty—her credit that of a bankrupt—her paper currency worth, in the market, scarcely 10 per cent of its normal value—her commerce next to nothing—her utmost exertions barely able to discharge the ordinary expenses of government, in time of peace.[13]

Further taxation was out of the question. Governor Hancock urged his General Court to direct their search for revenue at the "exhaustless merchandize" to the northeast instead. The belief that the Eastern Lands were a commodity that could be parlayed into cash rested on some deeply ingrained assumptions. Ever since their discovery by Europeans, the main sources of information about the new territories had been promoters. In order to lure investors and settlers, they naturally tended to exaggerate the land's attractions as a cornucopia. Confidence in Maine's soils and climate as an agricultural blessing died hard as a result.

At the same time, clearing the forest primeval to make way for a "garden of the north" was, to pious Puritans, a demonstration of moral worth. If virtue was less important to Mainers, there was still heroism in the yeoman working his own fields, an aspiration the colonists had fought Great Britain over. Conversely, state ownership of great swathes of land—the very definition of a colony and the loathed state of affairs in hierarchical Europe—was politically suspect. The republican ideal was to get land, lot by lot, into the hands of the people who would improve it. Once added to the tax rolls, those lots would raise revenue rather than cost the state for their stewardship.

Republican ideals notwithstanding, land tenure in Massachusetts continued broadly to follow colonial models that gave government a say in where the wilderness could be cleared to its best advantage. Townships—standardized to an even square, six miles by six—were laid out as a grid on a map; how they sat on the actual landscape was left to future surveyors.[14] From the township down to individual lots of fifty or a hundred acres within it, a regular, numbered plan allowed development to be systematically traced and the wilderness methodically pushed back.[15]

That the growing community as well as the land be "improved," lots for its future spiritual and educational needs were reserved in every township sold. Thus, a "Report on the petition" of one Samuel Freeman to settle four townships in 1785 stipulated the following:

> . . . four whole rights or sixty-fourth parts, for quantity and quality, in the division of the same, for the following purposes, viz. one for the first settled minister, his heirs and assigns forever; one for the use of the ministry; one to and for the future appropriation of government, and one for the use of a grammar school forever.

Public Lots were conceived as a civic commitment to the twin pillars of Puritan aspiration: the Protestant religion and education. They were dedicated to the two most important requisites for success in a fledgling state: revenue and settlement. At the time, they were at the heart of how a God-fearing Yankee society employed its divinely given natural endowments. The next step was to get a better idea of what the District of Maine's seventeen million acres had to offer.

Despite Governor Hancock's dreams, Maine's far-flung natural bounty was a source of headache as much as funds. The meaningful writ of the authorities had no way of extending to the distant lands, and "trespasses and illegal entries, possessions and encroachments" abounded. It was difficult even to tell the rightful claimants from squatters who had taken advantage of distance and the lack of civil order while the colony was fighting for its life. In 1781, the General Court empaneled a committee to identify as far as reasonably possible what the Commonwealth actually owned beyond the populated, well-explored districts around Boston. Its responsibilities would ultimately concentrate on managing the sale of the Eastern Lands, but at first the committee looked westward to the Berkshires rather than northeast to Maine.[16] York, the eastern county nearest to Boston, was only added to the lands to be explored in July 1783.

Soon surveys were being undertaken with a view to marketing the land, both by township (to proprietors) and by lot (to yeomen). These could be sold either at public auction or privately, whichever the commissioners decided was "most conducive to the public interest." They were also to consider "what lands it may be necessary to reserve for the use of the commonwealth for timber and other public uses."

Taming the wilderness being in everyone's best interest, the committee was directed to offer squatters the chance to purchase "their" land and to "settle and agree with all such who are disposed to settle and agree," at a price the commissioners thought fit. Advertisements were placed in local newspapers to attract those who might avail themselves of "this instance of lenity in government." Those who remained obdurate would be prosecuted.

With Governor Hancock's sights set on the Eastern Lands for badly needed revenue, lots were to be sold "for the most [the committee] can obtain in the public consolidated securities of this commonwealth." The governor drew his confidence from the assumption that Maine's population would continue to grow. Despite the Revolutionary War, it had jumped from thirty thousand to fifty thousand during the previous decade, mostly on the coastal plain, with settlement thinning out the farther north and east they went. With the lure of territories to the south and west to contend with, however, the committee was less sanguine. Its first report stressed the need for "preventing emigrations from this into other states, and accelerating the settlement of the lands belonging to this commonwealth."[17]

The first step was to expand or connect established settlements. An early example was the town of Fryeburg, flourishing on the rich soils of the Saco River some fifty miles inland. To tie it in with communities along the coast, the committee was instructed to lay out the intervening "unappropriated lands" into townships,

> . . . to be surveyed by a surveyor and chainman, under oath; a plan of each of
> which, with the contents and boundaries, the quality of the soil of each, the
> growth, goodness and kind of wood on each, its distance from any settlement, or

navigable river, whether rocky, mountainous, plain, or abounding with brooks or streams.[18]

With the addition of Cumberland and Lincoln counties to the committee's responsibilities, it became obvious that timely completion of all these surveys called for considerably greater manpower. By itself, Lincoln County extended east to the border with British Canada (wherever that was precisely) and northwards up the Penobscot into the unknown. Three months later, a second committee was established for that county alone.[19]

The government wanted to push settlement east and north, and the new committee at once began to lay out townships on the Penobscot River, thirty miles up from the sea. On its eastern shore the surveyors were constrained by lands that had been granted to the Penobscot tribe, as well as existing American settlements. The west bank, however, had room to lay out four townships, running west from the river, more or less parallel with the general trend of the coastline to the south.

Part of the committee's job was to set the price of the surveyed lands when they were ready to be sold. High-end lots were those with access to the river, the most practical means of getting about in the absence of roads. Half of these would be offered in tracts not more than five hundred acres per person, at six shillings an acre. Another six thousand acres adjacent to the water (about a quarter of the township) would be made available in 150-acre lots, the price to be at the committee's discretion. In townships away from the river, three thousand acres were set aside to be given away in hundred-acre lots as an enticement to settle the backcountry. All lots sold had to be settled within a year, "unavoidable casualties excepted." Recipients of land in the backcountry had to clear a minimum of four acres a year for four years, as well.

Geopolitics had to be considered, too. The recent history of Machias showed just how important strategic location could be.[20] Though little more than an outpost, its successful defense during the Revolutionary War was the difference between leaving Maine's—and the nation's—eastern boundary at the Penobscot and making it nearly a hundred miles farther east at the St. Croix River. Leaving the border's western shore to chance now was to invite foreign encroachment by a recent enemy.[21]

To lay out a further six townships along the St. Croix River, the Lincoln committee hired as its "trusty and accurate surveyor" a former brigadier general of the Continental Army, Rufus Putnam.[22] Putnam had worked as far south as Florida and west to the Mississippi, and he was about to set off on an expedition to survey and settle the Ohio territory. As it happened, the Ohio project was in limbo, pending congressional action, which left the brigadier eager for the new assignment. On his first expedition to the eastern border, in 1785, Rufus Putnam laid out ten townships. He also reported that there was much confusion in pinning down exactly where the St. Croix River was, since the names of the different rivers running through the region were frequently mixed up on different maps.

In fact the northeastern boundary was nebulous along most of its length. For want of accurate maps, the Treaty of Paris that ended the War of Independence in 1783 had resorted to vague geographical terms, describing the new country's border as:

> From the northwest angle of Nova Scotia, to wit, that angle which is formed by a line drawn due north from the source of the St. Croix river to the highlands, along the said highlands which divide those rivers that empty themselves into the St. Lawrence, and those which fall into the Atlantic ocean, to the northwestern most head of the Connecticut river.

This was not the only unfinished business from 1783, and much of it was successfully cleared up in another treaty with the British, negotiated by John Jay in 1794. The boundary claims of "his Britannic Majesty, in his province of New-Brunswick," however, were not. Dispute over this border would continue to affect the settlement of northern Maine for almost fifty more years.

As part of Jay's Treaty, the two sides appointed a commission to continue negotiating a more precise demarcation of America's northeastern boundary. Well aware that it was an issue in which "this state is directly and most materially interested," the General Court placed the land committee's records at the disposal of the American government's agent.[23] A British American survey then traced the St. Croix River up to its headwaters. These were found to be a string of lakes, the Chiputneticooks, including Grand and Spednic Lakes. The boundary followed the stream for about five miles farther up to the river's source.[24] Here the surveyors planted "a Stake near a yellow-Birch Tree hooped with Iron, and marked ST and IH 1797," the initials of the men who did the work, Samuel Titcomb and John Harris. Up to this point, the boundary was now agreed. Beyond, the "line drawn due north . . . to the highlands" in the original treaty, unsatisfactory as it was, remained the only guide.[25]

In 1784, the Lincoln land committee was given an office "in or near the State House." Open the first and third Wednesdays and Thursdays of every month, it was to serve "those who may be disposed to become purchasers of any of the said lands." Here the commissioners collected and stored the most up-to-date maps and plans they could find or have made. Once a tract was surveyed, a detailed description would be returned to the office and added to a map at a "scale of not more than three miles to an inch." Also on file were records of the committee's "doings," conducted at a formal meeting held every first Wednesday.[26]

One bit of housekeeping that had to be done was the investigation of colonial grants made prior to the war. The General Court wanted assurance that these were being developed according to their contracts, and that "the quantity by them taken in, [did not] exceed the quantity granted or sold." Smaller claims—half a dozen or so townships—were relatively easy to scrutinize, and several were renewed at between £1000 and £1250 per township. Larger grants in the more distant lands—among them the Waldo Patent and the Plymouth Company's Kennebec Claim, which went all the way back to William Bradford and the Pilgrims—were another matter.[27] They soon had a list, based on "ancient grants and various Indian deeds, etc.," but verifying their "authenticity and extent" took longer.

In addition to their duties in the Boston office, the commissioners were often in the field. They were no longer targeting a couple of townships here and there; the whole territory must be surveyed,

> . . . beginning upon the sea coasts, navigable rivers, and the boundaries of lands already located, (having regard to the lands and islands the most saleable) and proceeding back towards the interior parts of the said counties in a regular manner.

With them went surveyors and chainmen to locate and assess the most valuable lands, "with all convenient dispatch." Quick work was needed if the Eastern Lands were to solve Massachusetts' financial woes. The men were instructed to "run only the outside lines." They must, however, report on the quality of the soil and the general condition of the tracts, and "in the admeasurement of them no allowance to be made for ponds, bogs or meadows."

At the end of its first year of operation, however, the Lincoln land committee had disposed of a mere one hundred thousand acres. Disappointed with the progress in selling off its Eastern Lands, the authorities decided to speed things up.[28]

In July 1786, the General Court directed the Commissary General to supply the land committee with "six barrels of pork, one barrel of beef, and eight hundred pounds of ship bread." Rufus Putnam was going on another expedition, once again to the very east of Lincoln County. This time he had been contracted to lay out fifty new townships, which would be offered at a public lottery in tracts of varying sizes.[29]

The legislative title that authorized the land lottery promised first and foremost to raise £163,000 for the Treasury of the Commonwealth.[30] By means of the lottery, "the debt of this Commonwealth, may be reduced; the burden of the necessary taxes, diminished, and the settlement and improvement of the vacant land greatly promoted," presumably in that order of importance. Putnam's survey data was incorporated to "locate" the land in question, replete with compass bearings, distances in rods and miles, and when in doubt, local markers: "a heap of stones by a rock-maple tree," "a white-pine tree marked," here a "spruce tree," there a "beech-tree."

The bill passed on November 14, 1786, and the drawing was scheduled for the following March. Two thousand seven hundred and twenty tickets— "printed on good paper"—were to be sold at £60 a piece. Each ticket represented a lot of varying size within the fifty townships, so that there were: "one lot or prize of a township, two prizes of half a township each; four prizes of a quarter of a township each," and so on, up to "thirteen hundred and sixty-six prizes of half a mile square each."[31]

To the land committee—"sworn to the faithful performance of their trust"—went the management of the process from beginning:

> ... procure the said Tickets and number and check the same ... lay down in a book and number the townships and lots ... publish the foregoing Scheme of this Lottery, in such of the public news-papers, as they may judge best;

to end:

> ... publish an account of the numbers and prizes ... return to the Secretary the book and plans aforesaid ... list of the numbers and prizes drawn by the respective numbers, in opposite columns ... sign the same book, and annex their seals to their names.

To sweeten the deal, "every State or Continental land tax" on the land was waived for fifteen years. Anticipating that the tickets would be highly sought after, not to say tempting, harsh and various punishments were threatened to anyone caught forging or otherwise tampering with a ticket. They could be: "fined not exceeding one thousand pounds," "imprisoned not exceeding twelve months," "publicly whipped, not exceeding thirty-nine stripes," made to "sit on the gallows with a rope about his neck, for the space of one hour," "branded," or "sentenced to hard labour." They might "suffer all or any of the said punishments, according to the discretion of the said Justices, and the nature and aggravation of the offence."

In reality, the results fell far below the General Court's dreams. Only 437 lottery tickets (not 2,720) found buyers—the state called them "fortunate adventurers in the land lottery." A mere £26,220 was added to the government's coffers, some £137,000 short of the goal.

The leftover lottery townships, already surveyed, became the focus for a new committee set up by the General Court a year later in a further effort to invigorate land sales in Maine. The Committee on the Sale of Eastern Lands (with two additional members) was now responsible for all the unappropriated lands in Maine, and its first priority was to start marketing all the townships ready for sale. Sales were to be arranged "in such quantities, and on such terms as they shall judge most for the interest of the commonwealth."[32] A 2 percent charge on each transaction covered the cost of hiring local land agents as well as the salaries of the commissioners.

At the same time, "unlocated" lands continued to be surveyed, laid out in the usual six-mile-square townships and subdivided into lots. As these efforts penetrated deeper into more or less virgin territory, road-building became an urgent consideration. Maine's great rivers were still the major travel corridors, and they flowed generally north–south. In between, old-timers recalled to one Rev. Amasa Loring towards the end of the nineteenth century, "[t]he lowlands and swamps were miry, and, as the snow usually fell early, they would not be frozen and passable till deep snow obstructed traveling."[33] The Eastern Lands committee was soon laying out roads—"not more than three rods wide"—between the Kennebec and the Penobscot, and between the Penobscot and the Schoodic River on the eastern border.

Unauthorized squatters were still trespassing on Commonwealth land, "presuming upon the indulgence of government, that they shall be quieted in their possessions." Besides another warning from the General Court, the committee hired a Maine judge to actively prosecute those caught in the act.[34] Greater nuance was required where a squatter had "possessed" and "improved," over a significant period of time, land belonging to a major proprietor. Boston was still reeling from the shock of Shays' Rebellion over taxes and foreclosures in western Massachusetts. The last thing the government wanted was its citizens in the Eastern Lands getting fractious, too.[35] Though the commissioners might lean toward the proprietors as their peers—and selling to them was easier and potentially more profitable—it behooved them to recognize a squatter's rights if he had improved the land.

A squatter would be regarded as a settler, the General Court declared, if he had "entered upon unappropriated lands," cleared an acre "fit for mowing and tillage," built a house before the first day of January 1784, and had lived there ever since.[36] Such a person, the court resolved, was allowed to buy—for "five Spanish milled dollars"—a deed for a hundred acres that would "include his improvements, and be least injurious to the adjoining lands."[37] The settler also had the choice of purchasing from the proprietor any additional land he had cultivated, "estimating the same in a state of nature," or receiving a "reasonable allowance" for the work he had done to "improve" it. If they couldn't come to terms, they would choose two "disinterested men"—one each—to decide the case, and, in the event of a further deadlock, would appoint a third to break it.

Natural resource economist Lloyd Irland considered, "The best approach would administer squatter tenures leniently and continue sales to individuals on easy terms."[38] According to others, however, the attempt to accommodate both sides ended up dissatisfying both. "By favoring speculators, Massachusetts antagonized pioneer settlers . . . by protecting squatters, it repelled investors."[39]

During the next two decades, the General Court spawned an almost infinite number of ways to sell or give away the Commonwealth's Eastern Lands, all primarily aimed at settlement. Together they reflect a mosaic of the attitudes and preoccupations during the early days of the Republic, starting with compensation for the veterans of the Revolutionary War.

The original land committee had accepted payment with scrip issued by the treasury to "officers and soldiers of the continental army, which may have or shall become due" between 1784 and 1786.[40] Later, the General Court authorized grants to old soldiers as fitting recognition of men "whose meritorious services in the field so essentially contributed to establish our independence."[41] Another reason, suggested Irland, was the government's hope to keep veterans, whose outlook had been considerably broadened by their wartime experiences, "down on the farm" and out of trouble.[42]

In 1801, the Commonwealth offered two hundred acres of land each to former soldiers and noncommissioned officers from Massachusetts who had served in the Continental Army. As soon as enough requests had been received to make up a township, roughly a hundred, the lots would be laid out at the state's expense. Should anyone sell his lot before he had "brought under improvement" at least five acres, however, his claim would be "null and void." Locating the old soldiers on the extreme northeast border with Canada satisfied a strategic interest, as well.

With a new century came new wars and new heroes to reward with grants of land.

> Whereas in a rising republic it is highly important to cherish that patriotism, which conquers a love of ease, of pleasure, and of wealth, which prompts individuals to a love of their country, and induces them to embrace every opportunity to advance its prosperity and happiness, &c, &c.

Thus honored was William Eaton, victor of the first American battle fought on foreign soil, who received a grant of ten thousand acres (not "located" at the time) in the District of Maine. With "undaunted courage and brilliant service," Eaton had rescued American prisoners from the "chains of slavery" in Tripoli.[43] The Commonwealth's generosity differed sharply from the Jefferson administration, which refused to repay the hero $10,000 he claimed to have spent to front the campaign.

Civilians were compensated for their losses with territorial largesse, too. A group of American sympathizers from Nova Scotia were awarded 9,360 acres. They had lost everything because of the "laudable attachment which they expressed to the American cause" when Jonathan Eddy tried to incite the province to rise against Great Britain. Eddy retreated to Machias, which he successfully held for the colonies throughout the war. He then appealed to the General Court on the refugees' behalf, receiving lots on the east bank of the Penobscot ranging from a hundred and fifty to the fifteen hundred acres given to Eddy himself. (The town became Eddington.)

The "sufferers of Falmouth" were granted two townships. Early in the war, the defenseless town (by now rebuilt as Portland) had been burned in a punitive raid by the British navy, an action so notorious it inspired a line in the Declaration of Independence: "[King George III] has plundered our seas, ravaged our Coasts, burnt our towns, and destroyed the lives of our people." The land was divided among the sufferers "according to their present respective circumstance and wants." To ensure fair play, a committee of disinterested citizens, chosen by vote, did the allotting.[44]

Residual enmities and amities of the recent conflict informed many decisions. Among the lands confiscated from "certain conspirators and absentees" and handed over to the land committee was Sir Francis Bernard's Mount Desert Island. The former governor was dead, but his son petitioned the General Court to reclaim his inheritance. After "ample testimony of the uniformity, consistency and propriety of his political conduct" during the hostilities, John Bernard received half his father's lands. He was, however, unable to make a success of it, according to the surveyor, Park Holland, who bumped into Bernard in the course of Rufus Putnam's first surveying expedition. Bernard's family travails during the war "were said to have affected his reason," Holland reported. "We found him in a small hut of his own erecting, with no living creature but a little dog, for his companion." Bernard said he intended to build a farm, but the surveyors were skeptical. "Poor fellow! we pitied him," wrote the intrepid Holland. "He had probably never done a day's work in his life."[45]

The other half of the governor's land went to a French lady, Marie Theresa de Gregoire, whose grandfather, the explorer Sieur de Cadillac, had been granted Mount Desert Island by Louis XIV. Its "liberality and generosity," the General Court was at pains to explain, were not to be seen as a precedent.[46] It only wished to "cultivate a mutual confidence and union between the subjects of his most christian majesty and the citizens of this state."[47]

Another way to use land was as a path to naturalization. "Any foreigner or foreigners" could buy it if he put a family on a square mile of land within three years. After two years of successful settlement, he would be eligible for

American citizenship, provided that two justices of the peace or three pillars of the community could certify that he had "behaved himself during that time, as a good member of society."

Unappropriated land soon attracted the attention of those interested in encouraging the humanities and natural sciences in the new country. One resolve, dated February 28, 1793, directed the Eastern Lands committee simply to make grants "for the encouragement of literature," without further guidance as to how this might be accomplished. The new Agricultural Society received a township, the proceeds of which would endow a Professorship of Botany.[48] Other nations had botanical gardens, the legislators noted, and not just those basking in the "genial climes of the south of Europe." In Massachusetts, it could display native plants, study the potential of local soil and climate, and test the "ideas of ingenious Agriculturists."

Gifts of land had always been used to support seats of higher learning. The colonial government granted a "sixty-fourth part" (one of the four lots customarily reserved for public uses) of several townships to Harvard. These were reconfirmed in 1790 and a half-dozen lots already reserved for "future appropriation" added.[49] Even a township—or two, as was granted to Williams College—was a painless way to endow a college or seminary "without any burden on the community."[50] The typical formulation read, "Sell, convey and dispose of, in such way and manner as shall best promote the welfare of said academy."[51] For the next few years land was granted to burgeoning academies, including Hallowell, Berwick, and Fryeburg in the District of Maine. And lest Fryeburg need more, the land committee set aside Pleasant Mountain "and all other lands and ponds contiguous thereto . . . in case the said trustees shall apply therefor."

A plethora of land was now owned by cultural institutions, most of them more than willing to sell it. They provided a quick and easy way for investors to purchase a tract or two, especially when in 1795 the committee for the sale of the Eastern Lands had to suspend its sales activities. After a decade of trial and error, it had kept up with neither the General Court's expectations nor its own increasing expenses. From 1795 on, all land sales and settlement decisions were made by legislative resolve, although the committee would not be finally dissolved until 1801.[52]

If they applied to the General Court, speculators had no alternative but to don the "ardor which was then exhibited for the establishment and endowment of literary institutions," wrote Moses Greenleaf when he made a *Survey* of Maine after it became a state. Such applications were "not frequently rejected," he noted. Their number increased accordingly, as did the range of endeavors, including public works projects such as construction of roads, bridges, and canals. "For a time, the Legislature was continually, and, in general, successfully importuned," on behalf of all these efforts, wrote Greenleaf. What followed had been inevitable.

> More purchases had been made with a view to a speedy profit from resales in smaller parcels to actual settlers, than was sufficient to meet the demand of the increasing population; and more families were contracted to be placed, in a given time, on the lands thus purchased, than could easily be obtained. Of course the fever for speculation abated, and the purchasers were left at leisure to employ themselves in improving the value of their property, or waiting until the progress of the population of the country should bring it again into demand.[53]

Eventually, the liberality toward academies led to more critical consideration.[54] Land grants should only be awarded to those institutions with enough capital in hand

> . . . to erect and repair the necessary buildings, to support the corporation, to procure and preserve such apparatus and books as may be necessary, and to pay a part of the salaries of the preceptors.

No new academy should be encouraged unless there was a local population large enough—thirty to forty thousand inhabitants—to support it. Moreover, given that Massachusetts already boasted fifteen "academies," the committee would now recommend grants of no more than half a township each. To add more, even in parts of the state that had most need of them would be very difficult "until the wealth and population of the state shall be very considerably increased."

And then there was religion.

> WHEREAS religion and morality have a direct tendency to promote the interest and happiness, not only of individuals, but of society in general; and it being the unhappiness of many of the infant plantations in the county of Lincoln, to be destitute of public religious instruction.[55]

Thus the General Court introduced its intent to provide a minister for Lincoln county. It was "of the highest consequence, that the earliest foundation be laid in those infant settlements for acquiring the knowledge of, and of being led to the practice of religion and morality." Once again, one is reminded of the reputation the early residents of Maine had earned for being morally somewhat beyond the pale. Acting from a "parental regard" toward the plantations, the court ordered the employment of a "discreet and suitable preacher" and sent him into the wilds of the county for six months.

One preacher, be he never so "discreet and suitable," could not properly serve a county as large as Lincoln. The "60 Protestant families" settled in a handful of townships granted before Independence expected to have their own minister. In reconfirming these grants, the Commonwealth followed the steps of its colonial predecessors. The proprietors would build a "suitable meeting-house for the public worship of God," in each township and provide for the minister's "comfortable and honourable support." To this end, the state would reserve two plots of land—one for the minister and one for the ministry—in every township it conveyed against the day the settlement became a bustling community, which was the unchallenged assumption for every township the land committee's surveyors laid.

As a sine qua non for future settlements, education was on a par with religion. In 1788, the General Court recommended "building and supporting a public seminary of learning." To be located midway between the Kennebec and the Penobscot, a township, six miles square, was appropriated of "as good a tract of land for that purpose, as may be found there." In due course, this became Lincoln Academy. But just as each town would eventually need a minister, it would also need its own grammar school. Reserving a lot in each township was the way to ensure support for education, as well as religion.

Even the fifty townships in the public lottery had specifically reserved "four lots of three hundred and twenty acres each, for public uses." On March 26, 1788, the Massachusetts General Court made it official. Four 320-acre lots would be reserved in each township sold: one for the minister, one for the ministry, one for the schools, and "one for the future appropriation of the General Court."[56] This was the resolve that, nearly two centuries later, would catch an environmental reporter's eye. It would remain the standard formula (with one significant change) even after Maine separated from Massachusetts. They were not always the focus of public or political attention, but the Public Reserved Lands were embedded in the settlement history of interior Maine from the start.

Chapter Two

Sagamores, Speculators, and Statehood
(1795–1820)

In July 1801, a man called Joseph Inman was thrown in jail for murder. The corpse was never found, but the two men—settlers on a plantation that would in a few years become Orono—were known to have had words "under the influence of rum." Five years after its official purchase from the Penobscot Indians, theirs was still a raucous neighborhood inhabited by men who had cleared their patches regardless of legal rights or consequences.

At Inman's hearing, "nearly the whole population of the upper Penobscot" showed up before the local justice of the peace, Jonathan Eddy. They all agreed that Inman was guilty. Most startling was the testimony of his own son William. Young Inman swore he had encountered the victim's ghost—while going to share a pint of rum with a neighbor—and the ghost itself told him: "Your father was the very man who killed me." (The son seems not to have forgiven his father for cheating on his mother and causing their divorce.)

Inman Senior had been some months behind bars awaiting trial when, to everyone's surprise, the "dead" man showed up. He had read of his own demise while traveling out of state and hastened to return to clear things up. By this time, the prisoner had spent everything he owned defending himself, finally selling his landholding for pennies on the dollar. Three years later, acting on the petition of a certain Amos Patten, the General Court authorized the land agent to compensate him with a hundred and fifty acres of land in the "nine townships of land purchased of the Penobscot Indians."[57]

Linked in this nugget of local history are a number of men of importance to the early settlement of northern Maine: Jonathan Eddy, now flourishing in his eponymous town of Eddington, had been the voice of the Nova Scotia refugees. Amos Patten, already a pillar of the Bangor community, would settle the township that bears his name and was one of the first white men to climb

Mount Katahdin.[58] Moses Greenleaf, another signatory on Inman's behalf, published the first map of the State of Maine, as well as the encyclopedic *Survey* of the state. Salem Towne, the land agent, was the future surveyor of Mount Desert Island for Sir Francis Bernard's son. And it was outside the dwelling of Joseph Treat, who would explore the wild reaches of the new state, that Inman's son was accosted by the ghost.

Inman's tale also prompts the question: How did Massachusetts acquire the township from the Penobscots? With its long tradition of negotiating treaties by fiat.

The echo of the "shot heard round the world" had hardly died away over Concord Bridge when Massachusetts appealed to the tribes to join their cause. The smoke from the Battle of Bunker Hill was still in the air when, on June 21, 1775, a delegation of Penobscots sat down with the Provincial Congress in Watertown. The British had never been popular with the Indians—Governor Pownall's contemptuous attitude to them was typical—and Chief Orono responded with a splendid (and famous) speech to his tribe:

> Our white brothers tell us they came to the Indian's country to enjoy liberty and life. Their Great Sagamore [George III] is coming to bind them in chains, to kill them. We must fight him. We will stand on the same ground with them. For should he bind them in bonds, next he will treat us as bears.

Chief Orono promised that the tribe would "aid with their whole force to defend the country." First, however, the painful issue of American sharp practice against the Indians and their lands must be addressed. The Massachusetts government formally recognized Penobscot claims to lands "beginning at the Head of Tide, on the Penobscot river, extending six miles on each side of said river." The treaty banned "trespassing or making waste upon any of the lands and territories or possessions" of the Indians. "Proper and effectual measures" would put a stop to any "fraudulent traffic with them."[59]

The Penobscots were as good as their word, supporting and fighting on the colonists' side. Chief Orono himself took up arms. He also continued to advocate for the struggling Republic with his people. Help them, he said. "They will return good for good, and the law of love runs through the hearts of their children and ours when we are dead. Look down the stream of time."

"The stream of time" did not long reflect Chief Orono's optimism. By 1786, settlers pressing eastward reached the banks of the Penobscot River and the six-mile strip that had been confirmed as Penobscot territory eleven years earlier. If instead the land were available to connect the backcountry homesteads to the river, their value would be increased and further settlement encouraged. General Benjamin Lincoln (Washington's second-in-command during the war) set out to hold another conference with the tribe at what is now Bangor. Among Lincoln's commission was Rufus Putnam, just back from surveying the lottery townships.

In exchange for the Indian lands negotiated at Watertown, General Lincoln offered land farther up the river. The Penobscots were indignant. The general pointed out that as settlement and clearing reached the six-mile-limit, Indian hunting grounds would be spoiled; the territory he offered them was bigger and better. The Penobscots continued to resist. Lincoln "retired" with an implicit ultimatum, "You have our proposals from which we shall not depart." After discussion amongst themselves, the chiefs acquiesced, demanding in addition "350 blankets, 200 lbs Powder, and Shot and Flints in proportion."[60]

By the time a delegation with the blankets and powder arrived two years later, the Penobscots had changed their mind. They had not had a "right understanding of matters," the sachems complained. "We were pressed to make that Treaty contrary to our inclinations." This time it was a minister, the Rev. Daniel Little, who had to "impress their minds with a sense of the authority of Government." They could "expect that Government would abide by that agreement, made by words and witnesses, and expect the same from them," Little told the Indians. Responded one chief, "Brother, ministers ought not to have anything to do with public business." After four hours the conference ended with the treaty unsigned and, Little noted, "not a drop of rum by us or them while in the town."

There the matter rested, with the inevitable result that over the next ten years whites assumed they were allowed to settle, while Penobscots remained equally certain that they were not. In 1796, Governor Samuel Adams appointed a second commission, once and for all, "to fix the Boundaries of such Lots & Parcels of Land as may be necessary to assign for the support of said Indians . . . ; extinguish all [their] right & claim . . . to the residue of the Lands aforesaid."

In Boston, one view held that the Indians had no ownership rights at all, they having acknowledged—in Governor Pownall's time—the forfeiture of "all their lands by taking up arms against the King." Nonetheless, argued William Shepard, a commissioner who had studied the "transactions" between Massachusetts and the tribe, it would be better to deal with the Indians as if they owned the lands in question. The Penobscots agreed to relinquish their territory on both shores of the river from Head of Tide upstream for thirty miles, keeping only Old Town and other islands. When Salem Towne surveyed it and laid it out into nine townships, the acquisition was nearly 190,000 acres. The price was:

one hundred and fifty yards of blue woolens, four hundred pounds of shot, one hundred pounds of powder, one hundred bushels of corn, thirteen bushels of salt, thirty six hats, one barrel of rum, and an annual stipend of three hundred bushels of Indian corn, fifty pounds of powder, two hundred pounds of shot, and seventy-five yards of blue woolen cloth, fit for garments.[61]

This "consideration" may have been more than $24 worth of beads, but nothing near the land's market value of almost $200,000. Wrote one observer, soon to play his own part in settling Maine's wildlands: "The attention of all New England speculators is fixed on these lands and they will sell very high."[62] They were speedily advertised for sale "at public vendue" at a minimum price of a dollar per acre.[63] The settlers—Joseph Inman among them—whose squatting on Indian lands had brought the case to a boil in the first place were "secured in their possessions" and each allowed to purchase another hundred acres. The rest would be sold in parcels no more than a quarter of a township with the familiar reserved lots appropriately downsized:

> one hundred acres for schools; fifty acres for the first settled minister; and one hundred acres for the ministry, each tract to be equal in value with the same quantity of land in the same quarter of a township on an average.

This was hardly the end of land troubles along the Penobscot. Indians continued to lease certain rights (but not others, at least in their minds) to settlers. Settlers continued to trespass on Indian and public lands. The result was more misunderstanding. In 1803, the General Court attempted to get some control over the situation by requiring all leases between Indians and settlers to be approved by the Indian affairs commissioner.

This proved unworkable. Settlers would sell their leases to other settlers. The Penobscots put great stock in developing social ties with those with whom they did business, so this fostered still greater resentment. The commissioner himself had been a poor choice, always complaining of "being at a great distance, bad traveling, & ill health."[64] In 1807, he was fired, and the need for commissioner approval of leases repealed.[65]

As it would be with the Public Reserved Lands 175 years later, the issue was a different understanding of rights and harvestable trees. The Indians believed they had sold the right to cut timber suitable for masts only and only for five years. The settlers, however, claimed the right lasted for thirty years, "cut away all the valuable timber . . . and encouraged others to do the same," complained the Penobscot governor. The Penobscots did not "recognize the part of the bargain which relates to the soil, they say that the thing was not properly explained to them by their agent," wrote the new commissioner, Horatio Balch, in pleading their case.

Balch was more sympathetic to the Native Americans than his predecessor, which only made his job more difficult. Charged with protecting public as well as Indian lands, he was doubly unpopular with settlers. Guards had to be hired to "resist attacks with which [the land agent] is usually threatened." He could only act after the fact, and then it was "extremely difficult to get correct information respecting trespassers," he wrote to Governor James Sullivan.[66] It was an impossible job, "his personal safety assailed, and at the same time exposing himself and family to repeated injuries." After less than two years Horatio Balch resigned. Wrote Sullivan,

> No one man, however able he may be, can perform the duties of a Guardian or Superintendent, over three hundred and fifty miserable savages, spread over one hundred and eighty thousand acres of Wilderness; or protect such a vast extent of Territory from depredations. People in that wide spreading Country, will find maneuvers to deceive and defraud him.[67]

By the mid-1790s, peopling the wildlands had become as much a priority for the General Court as using them as a cash cow. Buyers must have "particular regard to the settlement thereof," it ruled in limiting sales west of the Penobscot to one township per customer. East of the river, land could be sold "in any quantities they may have opportunity for," but forty settlers per township must be installed "within a reasonable time."[68]

Despite these provisos, land, whether sold or granted, was not being settled fast enough. At the same time, with purchasers putting down as little as 20 percent, the treasury was acquiring more credit than cash. Frequent defaults and requests for extensions made the situation even worse. Would-be landowners "now come forward and say, that they are utterly unable to perform their contract." Despite what they had put into "lotting their townships, and clearing roads, &c.," they faced losing their down payment and the abandonment of their settlement. When, in 1791, the Eastern Lands committee asked for guidance in dealing with such cases, all the General Court could advise was to carry on in a way "most likely to expedite the sale and settlement of the public lands, and best promote the interest of the commonwealth."[69]

The other approach to settlement was the siren call of the speculators. Of these the first were General Henry Knox, then Washington's secretary of war, and William Duer, assistant secretary of the treasury under Alexander Hamilton. Their ambition, wrote Frederick S. Allis Jr., was nothing less than to "corner all the wild lands available for purchase down east." They had, moreover, the "sheer nerve" to try to pull it off "with almost no financial resources of any kind."[70]

Henry Knox was a Revolutionary War hero whose transportation of captured ordinance from Fort Ticonderoga across ice and snow had forced the British to abandon Boston. As an impoverished officer before the war, he married the granddaughter of none other than Brigadier General Samuel

Waldo, "hereditary lord" of the Waldo Patent. When her "Colonial Noble-man" father and mother fled with all the other loyalists under the muzzles of their son-in-law's cannon, Knox inherited most of Waldo's land, which at the Brigadier General's death amounted to over eight hundred thousand acres.[71] With it came a taste for speculation, not least because encouraging settlement in Maine could only add value to his new demesne.

Knox had already been involved in a speculation with William Duer, whose Scioto Company was marketing to "unsuspecting Frenchmen" the lands in Ohio that had attracted Rufus Putnam.[72] It was a disaster, doomed by a combination of proprietor incompetence, a Paris agent's dishonesty, and lack of working capital. Leaving the unhappy émigrés struggling in an unfa-miliar wilderness, Knox and Duer moved on to a new venture, the purchase of a "quantity of land, not less than 1 million, or more than 4 million of acres" in the unappropriated Eastern Lands of the District of Maine.

"Four millions of acres well located," they instructed their agents without blushing, "will cover all considerable tracts of cultivable land, in which case the purchase of half would operate as a monopoly of the whole and enable us to fix the price." If the land committee, "from a jealousy of monopoly, and perhaps other causes," proved averse to so huge a purchase, the identity of the real buyers could be hidden by using different names, or as they put it, "different applications varying in some instances in order to avoid suspicion of combination." Every effort was to be made to get the committee to "come into our views." However, if the presumably less malleable General Court had to be involved, now was the time, "as in their present temper they will judge liberal," directed Henry Knox.

Lobbying the committee was one part of the agents' job. Another was to obtain the most up-to-date information on the "quality and situation of the lands," especially townships already surveyed and well situated near naviga-tion or existing settlements. Regarding the lands to which the "Indians have some sort of claim," once the committee had agreed to the sale, they should use that claim "as an argument for lessening the price of the land."

Knox's agent, General Henry Jackson, soon discovered that the land com-mittee was hesitant to sell more than a million acres to any one party. They would have to appeal to the General Court. Fortunately, Knox had been right about its "liberal temper"; the committee was instructed to accept an offer for two million acres. This was only half of what the speculators had in mind, and Knox again urged his agent to use names of other purchasers to get to the total. Jackson, on the front lines in Boston, replied that to go for more would queer the deal, and he and Royal Flint (Duer's agent) signed a purchase agreement for two million acres on July 1, 1791. In addition to the customary reservation of four lots per township, the state kept the rights on up to five tracts of land equaling "six miles by thirty [five townships] . . . for furnishing masts." (This right was never exercised.)

The land lay to the east of the Penobscot River, but the speculators had an option to locate one million acres of it on the upper Kennebec instead. The core of the Penobscot million consisted of the considerable residue of unsold townships from the lottery, none of which were on the coast. Jackson thought this represented a missed opportunity; the ocean would open a "wide door" and increase the value of their lands by 25 percent. He persuaded Knox to buy the half of Mount Desert Island owned by Marie Theresa de Gregoire, the Sieur de Cadillac's granddaughter, and her husband.

But Knox wanted another million acres, in fact everything east of the Penobscot. If the land committee would give the nod to such a sale in principle, he could get the General Court, which was full of his friends, to be responsible for its final approval. The committee, replied his agent, was a "parcel of old women" and would never dare to make so ambitious a deal.

General Jackson's signature on the contract for two million acres was hardly dry when a dying ripple from the disaster in Ohio reached him in Boston. William Duer, who hoped to recoup his Scioto losses with the Maine speculation, had contacted one of the stranded French party's leaders, Madame Bacler de Leval. This forceful woman was scouting out a new life in America for herself and her husband, an idle grandee of the ancien régime whom she had left behind in France. Her recent experience with Duer notwithstanding, she replied expressing interest in his new project. A "veil of obscurity" hung over Scioto, and she was eager to investigate the "more certain prospect of establishing" an émigré colony in Maine. Romantic French attitudes toward the new American republic would assure its success.

A preliminary agreement was concluded in August, and in October, Henry Jackson was sailing Down East with Mme. de Leval and twenty of her compatriots to inspect the lands on offer. Now tour leader as well as lobbyist and promoter, General Jackson was anxious to make a first sale for the proprietors. The party soon got the taste of a very different attitude. When unfavorable winds forced their ship to drop anchor off an island in Eggemoggin Reach, they had to go ashore. A surly squatter appeared as the *voyageurs* were building a bonfire and announced that every tree they cut would cost them three shillings.

They continued to Mount Desert Island, where the Gregoires were a fount of information but not particularly encouraging. Most of the shoreland—the "wide door"—was already taken. On a frost-clear day, they went ashore again in Taunton Bay and got a beautiful view for miles around from the top of Schoodic Mountain. But here too, most of the shore was claimed and expensive; one settler offered them a hundred acres for £500. By the time

Mme. de Leval and her friends picked the townships they wanted, Jackson's patience was wearing thin. However, he promised to buy out anyone already living on them.

A few stout hearts were planning to stay the winter, and Jackson had to buy a farm in Trenton, on the spot, to house them. It was part of the Gregoire land, and the French christened it Fontaine Leval, after "*notre amazone*." While they waited to move in—the farmer required only two hours to vacate the premises—they sang, drank, and danced around the bonfire they had finally built with their own trees. The rest sailed back to Boston, their optimistic mood somewhat dampened by a storm that left "everyone on board sick, even the captain."[73]

Frederick Allis described Mme. de Leval as having a "good business head, a great deal of nagging aggressiveness and perseverance." Upon her return, she outlined her needs in a long letter to Duer and Knox: good land for planting crops, a climate to let them grow, and a way to get them to market. However, the most suitable sites along the shore were already settled, and it was impossible to penetrate the interior, "where certainly the surveyors have not been." The map was useless. "The trees are exceedingly close there, and the small space they afford between them is either crowded by roots or other felled trees." They had found two farms deep in the woods, abandoned almost before they were begun. Lack of access had driven the settlers back to the bay.

However, wrote Mme. de Leval, "a person deprived of being seated on the banks of a river, or on the shores of a Bay, may be indemnified by having an easy communication of good roads." Along the coast, the government had already "caused a road to be traced from east to west." The proprietors must build another one connecting it to a "creek" in the north that was said to connect the Penobscot and Schoodic rivers. She was "convinced that the glory of your being usefull to your country, in settling one of its unhabitted provinces, must equall the pecuniary advantages for you which will result therefrom." This rhetorical flourish at the end of her letter reads—at least in hindsight—as if Madame's tongue were quite through her cheek.

In January 1792, a purchase agreement was drawn up for five townships, plus the land around Fontaine Leval in Trenton. They were to be connected by a road, and two townships were to be cleared for settlers. Knox and Duer also promised to put up funds to promote the settlement in France. He had sold the Trenton parcel to Mme. de Leval at a loss, Jackson later told Knox, "to *stop her tongue* which was very limber, and never idle in proclaiming her difficulties and distress's, [sic] and the causes of them."[74] Nevertheless, so far, so good. Then things went terribly wrong.

In March, Duer's wild financial speculation—based on insider information gleaned while at the U.S. Treasury—brought on the Panic of 1792, the nation's first financial crisis. He himself was bankrupt. On March 23, he was arrested for irregularities uncovered in his treasury accounts. Even his friend Hamilton could not save William Duer. He spent the rest of his life in debtors' prison.

Astonishingly, incarceration didn't stop Duer's wheeling and dealing. He even proposed to buy Knox out, the overwhelming debt that was keeping him behind bars notwithstanding. Whenever Knox lined up a buyer for his share, Duer would balk, looking for a better deal. With his "want of *cander* and *decision*," feared Jackson in a note to Knox, Duer would "sacrifice you and every one else to his own views and wishes." His advice: "Push him to a point and then fix him." Beneath their fine linens, these men were all cutthroats.

Duer's bankruptcy put the whole Maine enterprise in jeopardy. The promised advance to promote the French settlement was now impossible. With Bacler de Leval threatening legal action, it fell to the long-suffering General Jackson to deal with the Amazon. By May, he was fed up. "Madame Leval is yet here," he wrote Knox from Boston. "I wish her gone."

More seriously for Knox, his payments to Massachusetts for the two million acres were coming due. An attempt to broker a deal directly between de Leval and the Commonwealth—which would have passed financial and settlement responsibilities on to the French—was stymied by those "old women" of the Eastern Lands committee. In frustration, Jackson wrote another warning note to Knox: Bacler de Leval and her friends are "*artful* and *cunning*," always ready to "take any and every advantage of you."[75] He backed up his suspicions by showing Knox a letter from a friend in Europe (despite his friend's request, "for God's sake," not to "communicate it to your best friends"). Mme. de Leval's associates in Europe "appear astonished at the boldness of her undertaking and the confidence which the Americans have placed in her." Henry Knox's dream of a bonanza in land speculation suddenly looked very shaky indeed.

The secretary of war's last hope was William Bingham, perhaps the richest man in America. Bingham had spent the war in the French West Indies buying arms on behalf of the Continental Congress and furthering his own business interests at the same time. Back in Philadelphia, he confirmed his impressive social and financial position by marrying the daughter of one of that city's most prominent merchants and politicians.

Knox probably started talking to Bingham about the Maine project during the summer of 1792. By the end of the year, Bingham was ready to commit and had brought on his own agent (another Jackson). Major William Jackson had most recently been President Washington's private secretary.[76] A job with the Philadelphia millionaire had an additional appeal for the younger man: he was courting Bingham's sister-in-law.

Before a final deal could be reached, Duer had to be "fixed." Time was short, and any arrangement with him must be proof against his by now familiar prevarications. Bingham worked with Major Jackson on a contract all one winter night, before dispatching him to Duer's prison the next morning. There the major got the prisoner to sign over all of his shares in the land. At last, for $50,000, William Duer was out of the picture.

Meanwhile, Henry Knox was keeping Bingham in the loop with a barrage of letters. When a survey of the Kennebec tract—prepared for another speculator—was not encouraging, Knox took great pains to rationalize it. Regarding the surveyor, it was "proverbial *that he takes things upon trust*." He might have been trying to guide his employer away from Maine toward other lands.[77] He visited too late in the season. Knox was "not in the least discouraged by this report." And if it turned out the Kennebec lands were a bust, they could buy land east of the Penobscot instead. A follow-up note assured Bingham, on the authority of a veteran of Benedict Arnold's march, that the land and timber were excellent, so good, in fact, that Aaron Burr had wanted a slice of Duer's share.

On the last day of 1792, Bingham signed a memorandum of agreement, taking over Knox's financial obligations to the state and promising him a third of future profits. Early the next year, he was in Boston securing the General Court's approval. Negotiations took longer than expected, in part because of the social stir surrounding so distinguished a visitor. The industrious Bingham was a little put out by the "interruptions to business, occasioned by the excessive hospitalities of this place, which engage a very great portion of my time." He was also gratified: "The governor [John Hancock] has been remarkably civil, and full of attentions."

By the end of January 1793, William Bingham of Philadelphia had title to two million acres in Maine. The investment would be the crowning success of a successful financial career, based on all he had heard. Marketing such excellent tracts, "either in large tracts or at retail," would only require an "energetic system of development and advertisement."[78] For more information on conditions in Maine, the new proprietor sent a questionnaire to General Benjamin Lincoln. Among a wide range of issues were: the population, geography, and suitability for agriculture; the potential for exports, harbors, and ship-building; the fish and game to be found, as well as specialties like seaweed, exotic fruit, ginseng, and bark. Of special concern to Bingham were the forests, how much timber they would provide, and the "mill seats," where it would be turned into lumber.

These were in dire straits, the general warned. It was the old story of trespass, and the state had been "too inattentive."

People have set down on public lands, possessed themselves of the best mill seats, and have cut the timber from any of the public lands where it has been convenient for them, without ever accounting for the same. It is not uncommon for these people and others to take hay on their sleds, when the rivers are frozen and follow up the streams of ice, until they find a good spot of timber near the banks. . . . The timber is cut and thrown into the river, or on the ice, so that on breaking up of winter, the logs go downstream even into the mill ponds, and often when there is a great head of water, they go over the dams into the sea.[79]

Fisheries were another cause for concern, attention to which was "one means by which the Commonwealth of Massachusetts may promote the interest and facilitate the settlement of the District of Maine." The general's comments, written in 1793, are worth noting for their understanding of ecology.

To have a supply of bank [marine] and river fish at all times depends very much on our own conduct, for a supply of the bank fish in our harbours and near our shores depends on the state of the river fish. These nature has pointed to the sources of the rivers, the ponds, and lakes, the quiet waters of which give that security to the spawn necessary for its existence.

Hence it becomes important, if you would preserve those fish, to keep the passages open to the lakes and prevent any unnatural obstruction being thrown in its way. . . . Hence it is important to the proprietors of the inland country to see that the mouths of the rivers, on most of which are mills, are kept open.[80]

Old Benjamin Lincoln's detailed answers—he had been "confined at home by a storm," and it gave him something to do—so impressed Bingham that he had the same questionnaire printed and distributed among the Maine members of the Massachusetts legislature.

One of the witnesses to Bingham's contract with the Commonwealth was a Continental Army veteran turned Massachusetts politician, General David Cobb. Cobb had been familiar with Knox's two million acres since Henry Jackson first started lobbying for it. As speaker, he had helped the General Court towards its positive decision. In March 1795, Cobb, as Bingham's agent in Maine, headed Down East to shepherd the development of the Penobscot lands. His employer expected frequent and detailed reports. "There is no part of the United States that stands so much in need of a helping hand," he wrote, "as the character of this country has been much depreciated by ignorance or design."[81]

Bingham's first order, following General Lincoln's advice, was "to prevent the depredations on the wood and getting possession of the mill seats, so as to command the means of converting the wood into lumber." Another came almost at once. Cobb must "secure every mill seat that was within the bounds of the tract." From those who already owned a mill and were getting their wood from Bingham's land, he must collect "the portion of lumber which I am entitled to, which is one half, by the custom of the country."[82]

Cobb promised to put an end to timber trespass on the lands in his care. However, to take all the mill seats, he cautioned, would make it much harder to sell the land, since these were what the best prospects (wealthy farmers, for instance) wanted to buy. It would also be expensive because Bingham would have to build all the mills himself to accommodate the settlers. Better to reserve a few of the best sites and sell the rest.[83] Bingham replied that he wanted, not to monopolize the mill seats, but to "prevent the depredations on the lumber by depriving the spoilers of the means of turning it to account." If these "lawless proceedings" continued, Cobb must "secure the portion of the lumber, which by custom is due to the owner of the soil, from which the lumber is obtained."[84] A month later, Cobb had the situation in hand. "The fame of my arrival," he wrote, "is *gone forth into all the saw mills*." The operators would cut no more wood. "If they want the logs, they must either purchase and settle the land upon which they grow, or pay for them as is the custom on the Kennebeck River."[85]

There remained the problem of the French connection. As soon as his agreement with Bingham was signed and sealed, Knox suavely referred Mme. Baclerde Leval to the new owner of his Maine lands. She could now, Knox was confident, found her "Colony in the East, which will add to the happiness of the human race." Bingham proved more adept at keeping the Amazon at arm's length than poor General Jackson. Pressure of negotiations, he regretted, had kept them from meeting in Boston where she had pursued him. He had doubtless heard the gossip that Mme. de Leval had "no resources beyond herself, nor any means of making good her contracts but from the lands." When Bingham finally got around to addressing her claims, he ignored the complaints about Knox and Duer, writing to her in businesslike terms (that ought to have raised a blush in those two gentlemen as well):

> You doubtless cannot have undertaken a project, which must necessarily in-
> volve a considerable expenditure, without having formed an association pos-
> sessed of sufficient capital to carry it into complete execution.[86]

Mme. de Leval turned again to an old friend, Colonel Benjamin Walker, who had tried earlier to mediate between Knox and Duer and herself. Walker served as aide-de-camp to Baron von Steuben during the war and was rumored to have been the homosexual Prussian's lover. In March, Walker bought from Bingham on her behalf over one hundred thousand acres in Hancock County, including two "wide door" (or coastal) townships and three from the Penobscot million. The deeds were held in escrow until payment should be completed, several years hence, but without them in hand, Mme. de Leval soon found sales to her émigré clients next to impossible (which was hardly surprising, given the irregularity of the Scioto venture). Without sales, she complained, she could not make her payments. Adding insult to injury, squatters and timber trespassers were running roughshod over her lands.

Bacler de Leval's harassment was taking its toll on even William Bingham's resources. And although the General Court had not yet taken over responsibility for selling the public lands, criticism of the Eastern Lands committee by Maine lawmakers for selling large tracts of the district to speculators could only complicate his plans.[87] Bingham's original intention to develop his land in lots and sell them at retail had to be amended. He realized he needed a sale on the order of hundreds of thousands of acres. As had William Duer with the Ohio lands, he decided Europe was the place to seek such a deal.

In 1793, the Old World seemed ready to implode. In France, the Terror had begun; Mme. de Leval was mourning the loss of "several of my friends and particularly of my sister." For American speculators, on the other hand, there was a silver lining. "The political convulsions of Europe," wrote Bingham to two Dutch bankers he hoped to engage as investors, would "inevitably draw to this country an immense immigration from various quarters, but particularly from Ireland, France, and Germany." It had already started, and as soon as word got back that land could be easily obtained,

the subjects of these kingdoms would certainly wish to exchange the state of oppressed tenantry for that of landholders having property in the soil which will be transmitted to their children.[88]

General Henry Jackson, writing to Knox at about this time, was even balder. "If a revolution should take place in England, Ireland, etc., as there is every appearance, it will be a most fortunate circumstance to our speculation." Accordingly, Major William Jackson was torn from courting his boss' sister-in-law and sailed to Europe in June 1793. He spent two years there dealing with, among others, the murderous Committee for Public Safety in Paris, which he failed to interest in purchasing land in Maine. He reiterated, nonetheless, Bingham's confidence that political turmoil would turn the tide of speculation.

Sober men cannot reflect on the present situation of Europe without alarm both for their property and personal quiet. . . . [T]he safe and happy condition of America hourly increases the disposition to emigrate to that country, and must soon [produce] speculations in every description of property in the United States. Nothing but the dogs of war and watchful shepherds now keep the sheep within their respective folds.[89]

Major Jackson's signal success was in England, where he managed to interest the Baring family, well on their way to becoming among the principal merchant bankers of Europe. No sooner had he returned to the United States in 1795 but Sir Francis Baring agreed to purchase half of Bingham's Penobscot tract. Shortly thereafter, Baring's son, Alexander, arrived to handle the deal. Fifty years later, as Lord Ashburton, Alexander Baring together with Daniel Webster would resolve the question of Maine's northeastern boundary.

Baring spent much of the summer of 1796 with Bingham touring their lands.[90] After an initial shock at the barrenness of the harbor where they made landfall—"I must confess the approach to it made me feel very unpleasantly indeed"—the young Englishman waxed enthusiastic over the lands and waters and people.[91] "In fact the country wants nothing but hands to be made anything of." And for that:

> The New England setlers[sic] are the only I wish for; whenever they are collected together in a small society and the bare necessaries of life are acquired, their first wants are a church and school.[92]

Alexander Baring was by nature an optimist. Far from ruing the amount of land given away to various agents and players in the long saga of the Knox-Bingham-Baring investment, it would, he felt, insure the "exertions and good will of all these people of the first influence." The lottery prizes, "checkered over the whole tract" and fragmenting townships, were "rather an advantage than otherwise. The people are not in our way and must assist us by their exertions if they wish anything of their lands."

Shortly after concluding the deal, Baring sent an admirably concise report of the tangled history of Bingham's "Million Acres" to his employers:

> The original million . . . was bought of the State of Massachusetts by General Jackson and Royal Flint and ceded afterwards to Duer and General Knox at ten cents an acre. General Knox, not having money to make his payments, agreed to join with Bingham in the speculation and to buy out Duer with a proffit of five cents on condition of B's advancing the money. This arrangement included the Kennebec tract. Knox is to have no share in the management of this business, but merely in the eventual proffits when ascertained.

When it came to the Amazon, Mme. Bacler de Leval, Baring allowed an ungentlemanly cattiness to run away with him.

> Madame Leval, who was a mistress of Calonne's[93] and many others in France came over to this country and was connected with Duer, with whom she travelled to the District of Maine, and as a price for her favors these four townships were picked out by her at a certain price and on certain conditions.[94] On the

cession of lands to Knox and Bingham, she failed in performing her part of the contract and it was of course void. But as she was very importunate with Knox and her circumstances were very poor, they at last made her a present of 8,000 acres in the township of Trenton and resold her the four townships on exactly the same terms Mr. Bingham purchased of the state. The payments were to be made in annual instalments of 9,000 dollars on the 1st of May beginning in 1795 and ending in 1800.[95]

This was the land purchased by Colonel Walker on Mme. de Leval's behalf. In the event, she failed to meet her first payment, which allowed Bingham to ignore her endless legal threats and turn his full attention to the Penobscot partnership with Baring.

In the same letter, written just two months before the Penobscots finally sold their land to the Commonwealth, Baring offered his own take—and rather different from their own—on the Indians and their strip along the river.

> When the district of Maine began to settle fast and the State of Massachusetts sold the land in it, it became necessary to make some arrangement with a tribe of Indians that molested them called the Penobscot Indians and it was finally agreed that this strip of valuable land should not be encroached upon but remain their hunting ground. . . . [The Indians] decreased in numbers and at last presented a petition to the State of Massachusetts that they would give them some compensation for their lands and permit them to retire to Canada. The state has consequently appointed commissioners to treat with them, the result of which is not yet known, but they will certainly agree.

He made no attempt to disguise his glee at the prospect of a sale of the townships.

> we shall pick out some that will be of very great service to our lands behind them. . . . I reckon that our back tract worth twice as much when the Indians are removed than before, for it would have been difficult to settle with a wilderness of six miles between it and the finest river.

Nonetheless, the settlers now pouring in beyond the Penobscot seemed to have had no trouble finding their own land without the help of Baring's or Bingham's agents. This was less of a problem for the Barings. Though initial profits did not meet young Alexander's hopes, the business that arose from the American connections he was making (which would include the family bank being the U.S. government's financial agent for the Louisiana Purchase in 1803) made it well worthwhile.

Bingham, however, began to face the fact that the Penobscot million might be a bust. In fact, his million acres on the Kennebec would end up being the more successful deal, but it was many years before the "underbrush of individual claims, legal snarls, and political difficulties" could be cleared away, and the property became profitable.[96] He would not live to see it. In 1801, Mrs. William Bingham died, and Bingham moved to England with his daughter and son-in-law. (His eldest daughter had married Alexander Baring in 1798.) The loss of his beloved wife was a devastating personal blow. His business affairs now dealt an equally catastrophic financial one.

The agreement with the Commonwealth that Bingham had taken over from Henry Knox stipulated a schedule for placing settlers on the land, which added up to 2,500 people in twelve years. His longtime agent, General Cobb, had achieved nothing like that level of settlement, and, according to the contract's Article Ten, he would forfeit thirty dollars "for each and every settler which shall be deficient of the number stipulated at the respective periods." If that couldn't be paid, the land would revert to the state. At the same time, the ten-year tax exemption on his lands was about to expire. (A couple of over-eager towns even levied taxes a year ahead of schedule.) The final injury was a suit brought by the Cabots of Boston over prize money from a neutral ship captured when he was stationed in Martinique during the war. The Cabots won, but by that time, 1804, William Bingham had died in England.

Even before Bingham's death, elements in the legislature were urging the General Court to look into the settler population of Bingham's "Millions." At the time, Cobb argued that the

> public mind will be so compleatly possess'd of the magnitude of your exertions and expenditures, and of your steady perseverance in the best measures for settling the country, . . . that any member of government who should wish a forfeiture from you under such circumstances would be dispis'd.

In 1804, as president of the Massachusetts Senate, General Cobb saw to it that a bill to investigate the number of settlers on the Bingham lands failed in the upper chamber. It was the work of a rising politician named William King. The general was not the most tactful man in the world, and King had a sharp tongue. A public spat between the two ended in a press report that, if the Federalists won the election, they would hang their opponents!

However, Thomas Jefferson's "Democratic-Republicans" were on the rise.[97] Though their leaders were hardly among them, Maine's growing population of smallholders was the party's base. The General Court—once overwhelmingly behind the great land proprietors as the best way to speed Maine's development—was beginning to favor squatters and settlers. It was a tectonic shift. Proprietors "from away" like Mr. William Bingham of Philadelphia were particularly liable to Jeffersonian jabs, and they were none too subtle, if Cobb, a Federalist stalwart, is to be believed.

Cobb had continued to supervise the Penobscot million for the trustees who took over the estate upon Bingham's death. "Partizans of democracy," he fumed, had whipped up dangerous levels of mistrust. Some of "his" settlers had been "artfully persuaded" by Republican agents that their stakes were in peril; Bingham hadn't settled enough people to fulfill his contract, so the Commonwealth could take back all his lands. "If they could only git the Federalists out of office," the Republicans would give the plots they occupied to the settlers. Such "vile insinuations," said Cobb, had incited these "ignorants" to trespass and theft of some of his best timber.[98] For all his disdain—he once wrote of "such rubbish as settlers rights"—Cobb could be persuasive, and his "prudent and regular management" successfully calmed the situation. "[B]eing frequently with these people the last autumn," he reported, "their opinions of their situation are changed." He was confident they would behave themselves in the future.

In 1806, the Republicans did "git the Federalists" out of control of the General Court. When they took the governorship the following year, as well, Maine-born James Sullivan's majority was heavily weighted by Maine voters. As their political fortunes surged, the district's always restive pioneers became still more unruly. "Trespasses committed on the Kennebeck lands are to a great amount and openly done in defiance of any power to controle them," wrote General Cobb as the trouble reached Bingham's other million.[99] When Lothrop Lewis, a surveyor employed by the land agents (who had replaced the Committee for the Sale of the Eastern Lands), went to "run, ascertain and mark the line" of the "Kennebeck Claim," he found "divers persons" threatening the life of any surveyor rather than let him do his job. [100] Men had "assembled in large numbers, and in arms," and had even on some occasions fired on him. The governor threatened to call out the militia to arrest the miscreants.[101]

Ironically, Bingham's million on the Kennebec needed more settlers, no matter how troublesome. Sniffing the looming issue of settler duties, the vultures began to circle. The leader in the Cabots' case against Bingham made an offer at thirty-three cents an acre. The trustees were not averse to selling "this valuable but unwieldy property," replied their attorney, and came back with the "fair and moderate tho adequate price" of fifty cents an acre.[102] The counteroffer was declined. William King—now a senator and "the great instigator" of the legislature's investigation into Bingham's purchases—offered twenty-five cents; "This naturally closed the conversation," wrote blunt General Cobb. Cobb was sure that King's "violent prosecution and rather persecution [sic]," had been part of his strategy.[103]

Charles Willing Hare, the Philadelphia lawyer who was the Bingham trustees' attorney, was more pragmatic. Although "[t]he difficulties attending to it were so numerous and powerful," Hare went to Boston, determined to resolve the matter of the settler duties by any deal he could make with the Republican legislature.[104] He found the key in William King, to whom he offered a bargain: the three most accessible townships in the Kennebec tract for $5,000.[105] In return, King agreed to take over all settlement responsibilities (the deadline for which was extended), and the Bingham trustees received the remainder of the million, free of all obligations to the state. It was "one of the shrewdest pieces of political maneuvering" in a saga rich with them, wrote Allis.[106] Bingham's estate paid a mere seventh of the approximately $70,000 for which it was legally liable.[107]

His apparent hypocrisy didn't trouble William King, but he needed to show he still had settler interests at heart. In 1808, he introduced the Betterment Act, which gave a settler on a proprietor's holding the right to buy his lot at its undeveloped value, or sell it for what his "betterment" had made it worth. The choice was not as clear-cut as it seemed. For example, should a settler pay what his lot was worth when he cleared it (perhaps a dollar an acre) or what the current value of an undeveloped lot would be (four or five times that)? The latter, decided one Federalist amendment. Settlers would have only one year to pay, decided another. Together, they largely gutted the aims of King's bill, which passed by one vote. Two years later, after violence in the backcountry spiked again, the act was amended to allow payment over three years.[108]

William King "had his faults; but he had warm friends and many admirers," recalled John Sheppard, who knew him.[109] Certainly he demonstrated a ruthless nature dealing with old General Cobb. However, despite the pretty story of his beautiful wife naming his verdant pastures Kingsfield, the three townships King got from the Bingham trustees did him little good. "The taxes and costs consumed his property, perplexing contention with town officers and trespassers drove him to insanity," wrote William Allen (who became Maine's clerk of the courts in 1820.[110] But not before King's boundless energy had led Maine to statehood and himself to the governor's mansion.

As early as 1785, the movement to separate the District of Maine from Massachusetts was building steam. An acrostic in the *Falmouth Gazette* that year heralded the movement. The same fall, a number of Maine's leaders foregathered in Portland. Mainly merchants and proprietors eager to be bigger fish in a smaller pond, they were also of the class that had included many Tories. The Commonwealth's government feared it was dealing with an "insurrection" that would welcome back loyalists from Canada, with untold consequences. However, two years later, after Shays' Rebellion had to be put down with private militias, Maine's squirarchy changed its tune. Should a similar uprising take place down east, the landowners' faith was with the General Court. In background and interest, they remained of the same cloth as Boston's nabobs.

Leadership of the independence party fell, briefly, to a fire-breather whose spirited actions in kidnapping a British captain had led to the burning of Falmouth in 1775. Brigadier General Samuel Thompson argued passionately for statehood, but having done so, went off to Boston where he argued equally passionately against ratifying the Constitution. For a while, the drive toward statehood petered out.

The first vote on separation took place in 1792, even as Henry Knox was trying to shore up his faltering speculation. The nabobs were still calling the shots, however, and it was narrowly defeated: 2,524 to 2,074. Four years later, when Alexander Baring traveled around Maine, "the separation of the District from the State of Massachusetts" seemed to him a matter of when, not if, with Portland becoming the capital. Indeed, the next vote, in 1797, favored separation, 2,785 to 2,412. Out of a population of a hundred thousand, however, Massachusetts deemed it hardly a signal of the popular will and ignored the whole thing.

With immigrants moving into its capacious interior, Maine's population was now growing faster than that of Massachusetts. Farmers carving little plots out of the wild were naturally egalitarian and independent, and Boston seemed farther and farther away, a three-day ride or, more likely, a four-day walk for a settler on the Kennebec. As well as distance, underrepresentation in the General Court made laws—such as trade rules that penalized woodcutters in the district's forest—hard to change. Soon enough, the same Republican zeal that mustered against oppressive proprietors blossomed into eagerness to be free of the mother state altogether. Statehood and Democratic-Republicanism in Maine had become politically one.

Despite the pro-statehood party being in power, a third election went in favor of the status quo by almost three to one (9,404 to 3,370). Settler violence (they were presumed to be separatists) made sticking with Massachusetts the safe bet. As important, in 1807, the economy seemed too good to risk upsetting the apple cart.

The good times didn't survive the year. In December, "Mr. Jefferson's Embargo" banned all exports from the United States, wreaking havoc on mercantile Massachusetts. Republicans paid the price for their president's hated policy: the state turned Federalist again. Five years later, "Mr. Madison's War"—the War of 1812—was even more unpopular. When the Commonwealth refused to put its militia at the service of the national army, President Madison retaliated by withdrawing federal garrisons from the state. British troops overran Maine as far west as the Penobscot River and occupied Bangor.

As major general in command of Maine's militia, William King did his best to bolster the defense of the rest of the district. The government in Boston did nothing beyond seeing to its own protection. King saw it as a betrayal. As soon as the war was over, he devoted his considerable political talents to making Maine its own state. "[T]ouching the management of an electioneering campaign, there are many things to be considered," John Sheppard recalled,

> such as newspaper, club-room, caucus, town, county, or state convention, out-runners for candidates, and distributors of circulars and speeches, yet, there must be some master-spirit behind the curtain, like a fly-wheel to regulate all this machinery; and William King was pre-eminently the man for that.[111]

Maine held two votes on statehood in 1816. The first, on May 20, would have been a decisive win for those in favor—10,391 to 6,501—but for the fact that less than half of the district's thirty-eight thousand eligible voters bothered to cast their ballot. A second vote was held on September 2, three and a half months later. This time, the number of votes cast by each side—11,969 to 10,347—failed to give the required margin of a five-to-four victory. However, by using the "whole aggregate majority of yeas, in the towns and plantations in favor" and the same of nays in those opposed, a majority—6,031 to 4,409—was reached that exceeded the 25 percent bar.

The same ticket had elected delegates from Maine's 137 towns to a constitutional convention, in the event of a separatist win, and the convention proceeded to be held at Bowdoin College in Brunswick. Committees were formed to frame a constitution and to apply to the Congress for admission to the Union. All, however, was brought to a halt by the Massachusetts General Court, which found that by basing the Separatist victory on "aggregate majorities," the convention had "misconstrued the act by which their powers were defined." Majority meant majority of votes returned, not "the aggregate of local and municipal majorities." It dissolved the convention and "declared the separation process at an unsuccessful end."[112]

The same year, 1816, saw the publication of Moses Greenleaf's *Statistical View of the District of Maine*. It was an economic and geographic study that, among its many important consequences, would provide fuel for the debate over separation. Greenleaf was a surveyor and almost forty at the time. As a young man running a general store in various towns, he had developed a fascination for Maine's wildlands. In 1812, he moved with his family to Williamsburgh, an unorganized township fifty miles north of Bangor, as agent responsible for settling thirty families on the land. There he became a scholar-farmer, working now in the fields, now in the woods, now in his study, pulling together all the information he could find about the geography and political economy of what would become the State of Maine.

Living far from a library made research challenging. Gaps in the public record and the difficulty of finding material in private hands were constant frustrations. And there were the "peculiar circumstances in the situation and avocations of the writer, and the embarrassment naturally incident to a novel attempt on a hitherto unexplored and important subject."[113] However, in 1813, Greenleaf's studies came to the attention of a committee of the legislature, which posed a series of questions similar to the ones William Bingham asked General Lincoln twenty years earlier: the acreage of the Commonwealth's unsold lands, their location, where their natural market centers would be. Above all, how could the streams of commerce be redirected to benefit Massachusetts' Eastern Lands?

Settlement and transportation, responded the surveyor. Located a hundred miles north of Bangor, a "central point of communication" would open up six and a half million acres of what is now Aroostook County. "Nothing is more necessary than *good* roads & liberal terms of sale," Greenleaf wrote. In this regard "*parsimony* is real *waste*, & an extensive, liberal and vigorous system of improvement the only true economy."[114] Three years later, with a little financial help from the General Court, Greenleaf published the *Statistical View. More especially with reference to the value and importance of its interiour,* its subtitle continued. The tome was "addressed to the consideration of the legislature of Massachusetts."

The *Statistical View* was very critical of Massachusetts land policy and its results. Greenleaf found nothing of the "extensive, liberal and vigorous system of improvement" that he once recommended. Instead, the real estate market was flooded. Impossible settling conditions were being imposed. The efforts of competing proprietors were not being coordinated, leading to a "general laxity in their exertions." Crucially, the land was being bought up as an investment, rather than as a place to live. Motives ranged from hopes of "immense profits from the sale, when the country about them should become improved and peopled, by the exertions of others, without any trouble of their own," to "planting settlements in the wilderness immediately," to setting aside "their surplus property for the benefit of their posterity."

One way or another, very few landowners had done much to improve the land or encourage settlement. This laissez-faire approach had "checked the settling* of the interior."[115] Any profit was hardly "equal to the mischief produced. The illiberal and injudicious conduct of the landed proprietors has greatly increased the evil." Greenleaf presented the General Court with a choice. They could continue what they had been doing, and let the Eastern Lands "be depressed almost to a cypher." Or they could take concerted steps to open them up and direct settlers to them, in which case their value will "be increased to a degree almost beyond calculation."[116]

One generally favorable critique of the book was all but buried in a blistering diatribe against the Act of Separation, which the legislature had just passed.[117] "Perhaps we cannot better prepare our readers to form an opinion on these interesting questions, than by taking a cursory view of the little work of Mr. Greenleaf," wrote the reviewer. [118] He interpreted it as a plea for Massachusetts to hold on to its valuable Eastern Lands.[119] Opinions differ on whether or not this was the author's intention. His most recent biographer, Walter M. MacDougall, makes the case that Moses Greenleaf was by upbringing—and remained by experience—a "determined Federalist."[120] On the other hand, one might assume from his single-minded focus on Maine as a geographic entity in and of itself that Greenleaf supported separation. Certainly, when Maine separated from the Commonwealth in 1820, he was quick to reissue his map of the District of Maine, published in 1815, and rename it as a map of the new state.

Ever since the demise of the old Eastern Lands committee, its responsibilities had been in the hands of two land agents. Early in the year Greenleaf's book appeared, the General Court replaced them with a three-person commission, which became known as the Land Office. One of the commissioners would become the long-time Massachusetts land agent for Maine, George Coffin. The Land Office's surveyor general was Lothrop Lewis.

In addition to its general care and custody, the Land Office's specific tasks were surveying and mapping the public domain, and reporting on the quality of the natural resources it contained. It also supervised the continued laying out of lots for sale and roads to reach them. A later report for the Massachusetts Senate called it the "first attempt to reduce the management of this great public interest to anything like method." In the remaining four years before Maine became a separate state, the Land Office completed extensive survey work, but sales "appear to have been minimal."[121]

The General Court no longer necessarily saw more settlers in Maine as a boon. The district's citizenry—increasingly politicized—had shown what it could do by way of swaying elections. A Maine Republican majority had given the governorship to James Sullivan in 1807. The Commonwealth was once more in Federalist hands, but lawmakers had to wonder if Down East rabble-rousers were worth the trouble or might even be a threat to their majority. Nor was the land as valuable as it had once been thought. 1816 was the Year Without a Summer, which had set off a spell of cold growing seasons discouraging to farmers. Perhaps a two-state solution was best, after all. By this time, Massachusetts was less than wholehearted about holding on to its Eastern Lands.

Meanwhile, William King's political "fly-wheel" had encountered a major obstacle on the way to statehood. The Coasting Act of 1789 put a tax on trade between noncontiguous states. The price of independence would be loss of the free trade that Maine, as a district of Massachusetts, enjoyed with Rhode Island, Connecticut, and New York. For coastal communities, that was a huge sacrifice. In 1819, King went to Washington and convinced the U.S. Congress to repeal the law. When he returned to Maine triumphant, the political pressure to hold another vote was unstoppable.

Articles of Separation were signed by Governor Brooks of Massachusetts on June 19, 1819. Section I of the act outlined terms and conditions that would have to be incorporated into the new constitution. The seventh item ensured that reservation of public lands would continue:

> and in all grants hereafter to be made, by either State, of unlocated land within the said District, the same reservations shall be made for the benefit of Schools, and of the Ministry, as have heretofore been usual, in grants made by this Commonwealth.[122]

A month later Maine voted on the question, "Is it expedient, that the District of Maine shall become a Separate and Independent State?" It was a landslide for statehood: 17,091 to 7,132. Massachusetts set a deadline for ratifying it. Another constitutional convention opened in Portland on October 19 and elected William King president of the convention. By the end of the month, Maine had a constitution, which included the Articles of Separation.[123] Now it was up to the U.S. Congress, where one last wrinkle had to be ironed out.

Since January 1820, Congress had been considering a petition from Missouri to become a state. The year had begun with an equal number of slave and free states, eleven states each. Missouri would tip the balance toward the slave states. Admitting Maine at the same time would make both sides numerically equal again. Maine abolitionists, most of whom favored statehood, had to overcome their horror at being responsible for the addition of another slave state. The debate was furious, but on March 15, 1820, Maine was admitted to the Union, one day before the deadline.

Chapter Three

Timber Pirates and Border Wars
(1820–1842)

On June 2, 1820, Governor William King welcomed the legislature in Portland (Maine's capital for its first seven years) with an exemplary call to the solons to get down to their duties in a spirit of optimism.[124] He spoke of "citizens peaceably and quietly forming themselves into a new and independent State" and their "unexampled harmony and unanimity." Another harmony—a "lasting" one—could be anticipated between Maine and Massachusetts, thanks to the "wisdom and generosity" of the mother state.

The governor's own confidence rested on the commercial enterprises that were already setting Maine on a happy course. Agriculture was thriving as well as anywhere in the country. With "good soil and healthy climate, we owe it to a bountiful providence to do all in our power" to make Maine farmers "alike prosperous and happy." Industry was being spurred with "new energy," not least the waterpower ready to be tapped at a wealth of potential dam sites. If the legislature would exempt from taxes any enterprise that put these to work, the investment would see a generous return in "increase of capital and a large accession of respectable inhabitants." The fisheries—along the coast, in the bays, and up the rivers—"require your particular attention." Present laws were such a conflicting hodge-podge the governor wondered if they were intended to serve the public good, or if the "views of individuals and sections of country have not been too much consulted."

Of equal importance to the future was the vast wilderness in the north, still almost entirely unexplored, let alone surveyed. Despite the best efforts of the Massachusetts General Court, approximately eleven million acres remained in the public domain, of which Maine had just inherited half. Massachusetts retained ownership of, but not jurisdiction over, the other half. Moses Greenleaf's summary for the General Court from seven years back had changed little.[125]

Considering the country in sections, referring to the quality of the good land and proportion, it appears that of the section immediately west of Moosehead lake containing about 276,000 acres, one-third is good land. The whole tract west of this (about 849,000 acres, including that in the county of Oxford) is mountainous, and about one-fourth good land.

Between Moosehead lake and the East Branch of Penobscot, including a tract north of this, about the heads of the Aroostook, about 1,160,000 acres, of which one-third may be considered good land; this tract is generally mountainous, and not so rugged as the tract last mentioned.

Between Penobscot, Schoodic and Mattawamkeag, generally level, say about 640,000 acres, one-half of good land.

North of Mattawamkeag is a tract of low, swampy land, about 300,000 acres of which probably not more than one-fourth is good land, and about 1,400,000 acres of which one-half is good.

In the N. E. corner of the district is a mountainous tract probably 780,000 acres, quality unknown.

The remaining land, about 6,400,000 acres, on the waters of St. John and the northwestern branches of the Penobscot, is a continued body of good land, extending from the eastern to the northwestern frontier of which three-fourths is good land.[126]

Governor King was eager to sketch out his ideas for Maine's share. Past practice, he told the assembled legislators, "has little to recommend it for further experiment." Good Jeffersonian that he was, King laid the "inconveniences and embarasments" suffered by settlers at the door of the great proprietors, long might they be remembered "in order to be guarded against." More progressive policies would bring enough new settlers to fulfill the dreams of even the "best friends of Maine." Parts of the public domain deemed unsuitable for settlement, said the governor, would still be "highly interesting" as forestland.

Unfortunately, timber trespass in the public lands continued to be as acute a concern as it had been when Massachusetts set up its land committee to deal with the problem in 1781. The Commonwealth had ended up giving lots to anyone who agreed to clear them and live there for a mere $5 to cover expenses. Those taking up the offer were often "of such a character as to prevent more reflecting and substantial men, from settling in the same townships," a committee found a decade later, adding that townships settled in this manner were still "diminished in value."[127]

Huge quantities of wood were also being lost as the unanticipated result of moving the Penobscots upriver in 1796. The Indians had continued to lease rights to any settler who would pay to cut timber in their territory, which they saw as reaching all the way north. Cultural misunderstandings on one side and advantage-taking and harassment on the other had continued as well. For

Massachusetts, the important thing was that its wood basket was being raided. In 1818, a new treaty was negotiated.

The delegation from Boston arrived in Bangor on June 24. It was Saint John's Day and the town's Free Masons feted them appropriately. Then they parleyed with twenty-seven chiefs, "rather noble looking sons of the forest and showily dressed." The Penobscots gave up all their rights "above the tract of thirty miles" on both shores of the river (the land sold to Massachusetts in 1796), "excepting & reserving from this sale and conveyances for the perpetual use of said tribe of Indians, four townships of land of six miles square each."[128] They also kept the islands in the river above Old Town. The rest was relinquished through the treaty for an annual payment of:

> five hundred bushels of corn, fifteen barrels of flour, seven barrels of clear pork, one hogshead of molasses, one hundred yards of broadcloth, of blue and red, fifty blankets, one hundred pounds of gunpowder, four hundred pounds of shot, one hundred and fifty pounds of tobacco, six boxes of chocolate, and fifty dollars in silver.

When Maine became a state two years later, Governor King had to reconfirm the treaty. Scarcely a month after taking office, he welcomed a deputation led by the Penobscot lieutenant governor, John Neptune, in Portland. "Brothers," King told them, "our Chiefs no longer reside at Boston; this is a convenience to you, as well as to us." The question of a new treaty partner was probably a delicate one for the Penobscots, for whom longstanding relationships were culturally important.[129]

In August, Lothrop Lewis—the surveyor who ran into trouble with agitated squatters along the Kennebec River—was dispatched to Bangor where he met with the same sachems who had attended the negotiations with Massachusetts. They appeared, "dressed in scarlet coats or robes, ornamented with silver brooches and with beads, after the Indian mode of that day."[130] The negotiation went well, and Lewis presented Neptune and the Penobscot governor a "fine piece of scarlet broadcloth." The other twenty-five chiefs each received a silver breastplate, on which was engraved the farmer and sailor of Maine's recently adopted coat of arms. All these gifts were accepted with "great apparent pleasure."

Whatever harmony was "apparent" did not survive the decade. Fifty miles farther up the Penobscot, Indian lands continued to be invaded. Woodsmen took their trees, hunters and trappers depleted their wildlife, and squatters made free with their plots. Official intervention was little to none. "White people cut the timber & grass on some of [the islands] & pay nothing. Their cattle and sheep eat up all the Indians' plants; thus they are so hurt & discouraged, they think they will never work more," John Neptune complained to the legislature.[131] The legislators' answer to the issue was a resolve in 1829 to authorize the governor "to negotiate with the Penobscot Indians for the transfer of two townships of land to the State." These were the two eastern townships on the Mattawamkeag River. A new road—the Military Road from Bangor to supply the border post at Houlton—went through one of them, and with it came demands for hostelries to satisfy those that used it.

John G. Deane, a legislator from Ellsworth, was appointed to negotiate for the land. As had his predecessors when parleying for earlier treaties, Deane harped on the prospect of "the destruction of [the Indians'] game, and their means of subsistence produced by the progress of settlement and cultivation" as a reason.[132] With "a change in their modes of life," the Indians could aspire to all the benefits enjoyed by white people. The funds from the land sale could make this happen. The tribe refused. In 1830, the Legislature voted— "in the misleading terminology of their political proceedings," in the words of Professor Jacques Ferland[133]—to "authorize" the Indians to sell two of the townships. The proceeds were to be invested for the benefit of the Indians "as the Governor and Council shall direct, but no part thereof shall be paid to said Indians in money, provisions or clothing."[134]

In 1833, a "lumber baron" and a judge undertook an even less transparent, and more heavy-handed, process than John Deane's. By this time, Maine was determined to have all four remaining Indian townships. The new emissaries persuaded a small group of Indians (of which John Neptune was one) to sign a document the full implications of which it is doubtful they understood. The rest of the tribe was outraged and sent a letter to the legislature decrying "a certain deed fraudulently obtained . . . from a few individuals without the knowledge of consent of the tribe." The subsequent debate in the new State House did little credit to Maine's lawmakers. The four townships were taken for the pitiful sum of $50,000, and the ordeal left a permanent schism among the Penobscots.

John Deane himself would be a participant in a number of other important issues connected to Maine's public domain, including the northeastern boundary and the general way in which Maine was disposing of its public lands.[135]

In 1820, in the wake of the State of Maine's first treaty with the Penobscots, Governor King hired Major Joseph Treat to undertake a "tour of discoveries" of the northern part of the state, "for the purpose of examining and ascertaining the quality of the soil and growth on the Public Land in that vicinity."[136] At the time, the farthest American settlement up the Penobscot was Howland, thirty miles north of Bangor. With Treat went John Neptune, the Penobscot's lieutenant governor, as guide and cultural interpreter. Neptune knew the land as well as anyone, having led hunting parties all over the territory. He had known Treat for many years, too, not always harmoniously, given that the major was in the business of selling Indian land. Nonetheless the detail with which Treat returned would have been impossible without the Penobscot's deep knowledge of the country.

At the end of September, the expedition set off in two canoes. Water level in the rivers had been too low to start any earlier. In a five-hundred-mile loop, they traveled up the west branch of the Penobscot, through Chesuncook and Chamberlain lakes, and into the Allagash. Reaching the Saint John River, they followed it south with a couple of detours, eventually rejoining the Penobscot via the Mattawamkeag River. They were gone two months, dragging their canoes over frozen rivers and lakes at the end.

Despite the difficulties, Treat's notes produced the most accurate descriptions and maps of northern Maine that had yet been made. He also confirmed that there had been a lot of illegal timber cutting, notably along the rivers "Aroostook, De Chute, Presquille, and Meduxnekeag." The culprits here were "persons residing in the British Provinces," and their activities had "for many years past been very great."[137] Not for the last time, political circumstances were giving scofflaws a heyday.

Part of the problem, undoubtedly, was the lack of a broadly accepted map of the area, which made it difficult irrefutably to accuse anyone caught cutting illegally. The larger issue was the continued failure of British and American negotiators to agree on the location of Maine's border with New Brunswick north of the headwaters of the St. Croix River. This was the nation's northeastern boundary as well, and with the War of 1812, it had taken on increasing territorial importance for both sides.

The Treaty of Ghent, which ended the war, had put the question in the hands of a joint commission. In 1820, negotiations had been going on fruitlessly for five years. The British argued that the "highlands" mentioned in the Treaty of Paris referred to Mars Hill (about one hundred miles short of the present line). It had been "discovered by them that Mars Hill was the North West angle of Nova Scotia," declared a somewhat sardonic John Deane, referring to the Treaty's locution.[138] (New Brunswick had been a part of Nova Scotia until 1784.) This would have included land Massachusetts had granted to Revolutionary War veterans, and the Americans rejected it.

In his inaugural address, Governor King had to admit that he had no idea where the matter stood nor how long it was likely to remain unresolved. When he forwarded Treat's report of trespass on Maine's "acknowledged territory" to state lawmakers six months later, he could only repeat his frustration. The situation was giving "lawless trespassers" a field day, and they must do whatever they could to save Maine "from a system of pillage countenanced by the claims of pretended title."

The Legislature had its own problem with the border issue, which was stymying efforts to resolve a separate conundrum. Under the Articles of Separation, the two states were to split the public lands lying in Maine "in equal shares or moieties in severalty having regard to quantity, situation and quality." Until the boundary with Canada was determined, no one knew how much land was involved. They respectfully requested that the governor inform President James Monroe of their concern and do whatever he himself could to help address it.[139]

The president forwarded Governor King's letter to the American agent to the talks, who assured him they were close to a final decision. He was meeting the British agent in New York in October. At King's suggestion, Maine's senators, en route to the capital, dropped in on the discussions, only to find none in progress. They "accidentally" came across the American agent. He had been ready to negotiate, he told them, but his counterpart had not shown up. Helpless before this "unexpected and extraordinary delay," King reported that "all reasonable hope of a speedy adjustment seems, therefore, to have vanished."

The problem became more immediate when Massachusetts offered to sell all its remaining lands to Maine. A joint committee (Lothrop Lewis was called on again) soon negotiated an offer and submitted it to the Maine legislature. The bill, not quite $200,000, was more than the negotiators had hoped, given how far away the lands were from Massachusetts, how expensive they were to manage, and "the little benefit she has ever derived from them."[140] But money should not be the only factor to consider, the negotiators urged. Townships owned by another state, they argued, met neither of Maine's land policy goals: to push back the wilderness and to produce income. Nor could anything useful be done with them—putting in a road, for instance—without courting the good offices of the Commonwealth.

On the other hand, acquisition of so much public land would staunch the flow of emigrants and "turn its current towards our own State." Since the Year Without a Summer, Maine farmers had been pulling up stakes and leaving. Settling the interior would set off a chain reaction that would make the coast more prosperous, which would increase the state's population, which would provide a source of revenue that would be "perpetually augmenting." The opportunity might not come again, Lewis and his committee warned. Massachusetts might decide to hold on to the land, banking on its potential to appreciate in value. The result would be "unpleasant and embarrassing." Maine would see the Commonwealth "disposed to profit and speculate at our expense; she would believe us actuated in relation to her, by a similar spirit; crimination would produce recrimination." Buying it now would remove a "perpetual source of collision and difficulty." Certainly "our infant State" must never

be weighed down needlessly with public debt; in this case, however, "greater
and more serious evils would necessarily result" were the offer refused.
Despite such prescient arguments, the legislature turned the deal down.
"[L]ooking upon it from this distance," rued a forest commissioner years
later, the price was "a mere bagatelle. If the lands could have then been
bought it would have saved endless disputes and misunderstandings, and
been a priceless value to Maine."[141]

Shortly afterward, Governor William King resigned to accept a diplomatic
appointment by President Monroe. Maine's energetic first governor had enjoyed the post for a little over a year. A sequence of three interim officials fulfilled the unexpired term, two of them for a matter of days each. Technically,
therefore, it was as Maine's fifth governor that Albion K. Parris addressed the
legislators in January, 1822.[142] It gave him "anxiety to be obliged to inform"
them that given the "disagreement" over the international boundary, "the final division of the lands *owned in common by this and the parent State*, will
necessarily be delayed to a period uncertain."

The two states spent the next decade surveying these wildland townships
and dividing them. Where townships and ranges had been established, the
simplest method was to assume that adjacent townships had equal value and
make a checkerboard of the map, with Maine's squares in blue, Massachusetts' in red. On Maine maps, an "M" in the center of the township indicated
Massachusetts. Starting in 1832, their respective legislatures authorized the
land agents to survey jointly the considerable expanse of terra incognita still
in northern Maine. The two states split the proceeds equally when they were
sold. Ten percent of all sales was set aside for building roads and bridges,
infrastructure that would raise the value of land for both states. Their sales
policies, however, were different. Massachusetts saw its townships entirely as
a source of income. Maine, while welcoming the cash land sales could produce, was looking further into the future: toward settling the wilderness and
bringing as much land as possible onto its tax rolls. The two perspectives did
not sit well together on adjacent townships. With the checkerboard pattern of
ownership, the seeds of future trouble were already sown.

During Maine's first ten years as a state, attempts to husband the public lands
can best be described as haphazard, with rules constantly changing. "It seems
to be conceded," wrote John G. Deane, this time in a report for the Committee on State Lands in 1831, of which it was the opening sentence, "that our
State lands have not been well managed."[143] There had, however, been plenty
of activity.

At its first session, the legislature had appointed a surveyor general. Two
years later, it gave him responsibility for the protection of "timber and grass

on the public lands, or the sale of any part thereof." A year later, in 1823, it repealed that order in favor of a resolve authorizing him to sell "such lands as had been divided and were held in severalty by this State, in lots not exceeding five hundred acres each to actual settlers." The intent, assumed Deane, was to speed development. "If tracts were sold promiscuously, the forests would be broken in upon." In fact, the surveyor general had little power as his every move was at the governor's discretion. When, the same year, the legislature sought guidance from the commissioners under the Act of Separation, they recommended selling to actual settlers at a fixed price, advice that was "entirely overlooked," wrote Deane. "It may in truth be said that there was not any thing which could be called a system before the year 1824."[144]

"At the opening of the year 1824, the management of the public lands had become a subject of absorbing interest in the minds of the leading men of Maine," noted an adulatory biography of one General James Irish.[145] Trespass was still the major concern, and fingers were still being pointed at the laissez-faire attitude of the Massachusetts authorities before Maine became a state. Someone with legal authority was needed to deal with a "class of inhabitants" that considered the state's timber as "lawful plunder"; if they didn't take their share, "they were not living up to their legitimate privileges."[146] With "An Act to Promote the Sale and Settlement of Public Lands," the legislature called on Governor Parris to appoint some "discreet and suitable person" as land agent responsible for the public lands.[147] His duties would include running lines for new townships, dividing them into lots, executing deeds, and selling rights to land, timber, or grass. He was also entrusted with guarding the Public Reserved Lots, heretofore the responsibility of the township's owner.

The governor appointed General Irish, the state's surveyor general for the past two years. Irish had first applied for that position in 1820, suggesting with some foresight that he should be able to run the Land Office as well. He also asked to be put on the commission dividing the public lands with Massachusetts; as an experienced woodsman who could "swing his pack," he might be useful to the city-folk already appointed. Instead, Lothrop Lewis, who had been the Commonwealth's surveyor general, continued at his post in the new state until his death in 1822, at which point Irish succeeded him.

At the same time, the size of the Public Reserved Lot was changed. Instead of four 320-acre lots, a single lot of a thousand acres would support "public uses" as the legislature saw fit for the benefit of the future town.[148] In incorporated towns, a second law vested fee title for the Public Reserved Lots with the inhabitants (instead of the minister) under a board of trustees made up of municipal officers. It was up to the board to sell or otherwise use the lots to benefit the ministry and the school. The legislature reserved the power to alter or annul the trustees' authority "at its pleasure." After another eight years, agreeable bills were passed by the legislatures of both states directing ministerial monies to the schools.

To John Deane, however, the "important and proper innovation" of 1824 was the land agent.[149] At last, there was "a head restrained by certain rules, and not subservient to the discretion of anyone." Erect and dignified, General Irish was the "personification of robust manhood" as could only be gained from "exacting toil of the farm and mill, the exposures and hardships of life in the wilderness . . . in exploration of lakes and rivers, and in locating and surveying townships." In 1825, with a Land Office set up in Portland, Irish plunged into the woods and his responsibilities. Samples of the risks and dangers of the job were not long in coming.

As soon as the rivers were "boatable," he and his Massachusetts colleague, George Coffin, set off to investigate "depredations" that continued to be reported on the public lands. As the Commonwealth land agent, Coffin had already been surveying and selling lands in Maine for five years. On the east branch of the Penobscot, three of Irish's men were sent to deal with a gang of trespassers. The gang, "blacked and armed, who called themselves Mohawks," accosted them, "insulting them and threatening them with death." The trio beat a hasty retreat. Several of the miscreants were brought to trial, but "for want of sufficient evidence to convict," Irish reported with resignation, "[they] were of course acquitted."

Later that summer Irish ordered the sheriff to go after another party cutting hay illegally farther up the river. Unfortunately, word got to the culprits in plenty of time, and they absconded. The sheriff caught sight of a "few armed men dodging about in the bushes," but he was unable to arrest them. To prevent the trespassers from returning for the hay, Irish had it burned. When, two months later, the Great Miramichi Fire scorched six thousand square miles of New Brunswick's wood basket, he was blamed in some quarters for the disaster. Ignoring the accusation in his annual report, Irish stressed that no damage to other property had resulted. More or less simultaneously, though, fire had devastated the forest north of Bangor, turning Indian territory into "a sea of flames." The Penobscots, including John Neptune, were sure it had been deliberately set, either by the land agent's men or someone else, to drive them off the land. Commented Professor Ferland, "As the reputation of a state official was at stake, the testimony of the Penobscots in relation to the fire was bound to be viewed in a negative light."[150]

Near the presumed border, Irish and Coffin learned that New Brunswick had been issuing permits to cut timber in Maine. They paddled to Fredericton to raise the issue with the Canadian authorities. Finding the lieutenant governor away and the province's surveyor general unwilling to give out any information in his absence, the Americans left a polite note pointing out the trespass, "under a mistaken view, no doubt, of the boundary line." As the two land agents continued up the St. John, all the people they met "rejoiced" at the prospect of becoming part of the "family of Maine," Irish reported with delight, the more so because they were "very industrious, civil and hospitable."

On their way home, Irish received news that the government in London had instructed its Canadian colony to cease granting timber permits around the Aroostook and Madawaska rivers, pending a final boundary agreement. Even permits already issued were canceled, which presented Irish with a different dilemma. Many of the permit-holders had already bought their winter stores, which "would undoubtedly, enable them to plunder," permit or no permit. As an exception, he let them cut timber "from our soil" in the current year; discretion was, he decided, the better part of valor.

The same year, 1825, the surveyor Joseph Norris and his son started to run a straight line east–west across the state.[151] It started at the monument erected at the source of the St. Croix River by Titcomb and Harris in 1797 (still the northernmost point of the agreed international boundary) and crossed Mount Katahdin.[152] The so-called Monument Line formed the base for a regular grid that would stretch over northern Maine, with townships running east–west and ranges north–south. It was a cartographical exercise innocent of topographical consequence that left James Irish and George Coffin, as well as the Norrises and other surveyors, to fill in the blanks. Irish and Coffin worked closely together for four years, despite efforts by proprietors and lumbermen to get Irish fired. Before the land agent took over guardianship of the Public Reserved Lots from "pillage and trespass," their "proper custodian" had been the township's proprietor, who was generally loath to forego his free access to the wood growing there.[153]

George Coffin himself would not leave the woods for another twenty-two years, in the course of which time he saw nine Maine land agents come and go. Even with local agents keeping an eye on particular areas, responsibility for such an immense territory with poor to nonexistent roads was a huge challenge. "Hardships, privations, personal peril, and separation from his family" were the land agent's lot.[154] He could be in the wilds for weeks, assessing the state of the roads and the welfare of settlers and woodcutters,

> going sometimes on horseback and sometimes on foot, into settlements the most remote from the great public thoroughfares, at other times meeting at designated places such of the inhabitants as desired to communicate with me upon matters of public or private interest.[155]

In 1826, the limit of five hundred acres per lot was repealed. It had showed a lack of understanding of the "lumber men." They were plundering all the timberland around their lots. Had it continued, wrote John Deane, the sale of "a

lot or two in a township would have destroyed all the timber in the forest."
The size and quantity of tracts sold were left to the land agent's discretion.
The rules changed again two years later. The preceding year, Maine and
Massachusetts between them had sold a record 350,000 acres of the public
domain. The Maine legislature had also granted fifteen and a half townships
for public works (including ten for the construction of the State House in the
new capital, Augusta). The glut had caused the public to become "entirely
dissatisfied," according to Deane. After 1828, only eight timber townships
could be put up for sale in a year, no more than one per customer. There was
no limit on how much settling land could be sold.

The distinction between land for settlement and land for timber had been
evolving since Governor King spoke of land unsuitable for farming as "highly
interesting" for its forest. Deane deemed this trend "very unfortunate and
profitless." It led to the erroneous idea that "much the largest portion" of the
public lands was unsuitable for farming. Deane had reviewed the reports of
the land agents as far back as 1824, and they confirmed that settling land
sold well wherever there were roads to penetrate the forest. Where roadless
tracts went on the market, speculators took over, and the only benefit the state
received was the ready money, a "trifling consideration per acre." Selling
large blocks of timberland was a throwback to that "ancient system" that encouraged "large proprietory [sic] interests." Deane blamed speculators who
"purchased chiefly with a view to selling at an advance, and not for opening
up and settling the country."[156] They were allowed to run rife in the forest
because it was assumed to have no other value.

At Enoch Lincoln's inauguration in January 1827, "our unsettled territory"
was one of the first things to which Maine's next governor drew the legislators' attention.[157] For Lincoln, the public lands were far more than something
to be meted out, township by township between the two states. The surveys
being undertaken by General Irish and George Coffin were gathering data on
geography and topography that would help connect Maine's northern rivers
to the Great Lakes, via the St. John and the St. Lawrence one day. The key to
success was the Penobscot River, which with its tributaries provided a navigable network of hundreds of miles. The simmering dispute over a mutual
border with one British colony did not stop Governor Lincoln from dreaming
of a flourishing commerce with another.

As a self-proclaimed champion of the public lands, Lincoln was apt to
scold the Legislature for disparaging them. It was "a common, but a very in-
discreet and incorrect remark," he said. It made Maine appear "unfit for self-
government, to say that millions of acres of goodly hills and dales watered
by long and boatable streams, are of no value."[158] The forest's contribution

to Maine's economic success was self-evident. With typical literary flourish, Lincoln would write of the still abundant "towering pines":

> Some of them will rise like spires amidst the naval armaments of this country & instead of the sighing of breezes in their tops, the flag of freedom shall gaily & proudly wave over them . . . Others will be compacted into magnificent palaces & be the instruments of comfort & the aide of health.[159]

Lawmakers, he found, tended to worry too much about "conditions as to improvement, residence, and other objects" and a "code of rewards and punishments." Governor Lincoln tried to cut through all this. A system was already in place, simple and based on common sense: sell the public lands "on reasonably long credits," cheaply, and in small tracts. In addition, would-be farmers could work on the roads around the settlement to pay off their debt. In theory, "lines of communication through the forests [would emerge] as fast as the lands should be sold," wrote John Deane a few years later. In fact, he concluded, labor provided in lieu of payment produced no roads, "which have been of any value to the public." They were constructed "in almost every instance where fancy or interest dictated."

Where good land was lying uncultivated, Lincoln, like William King before him, blamed the great proprietors. The constant improvement he envisioned was being driven by courageous and enterprising settlers blazing a trail into the wilderness. They were the de facto owners of the land, and their arduous circumstances deserved the state's "sympathy and support, and much indulgence." Enoch Lincoln's watchwords were "commended by utility and sustained by justice," and he took a pragmatic line toward "unfortunate collisions" that continued to occur in the public domain between woodcutters and the authorities. Though undoubtedly trespassers, the men were more often misguided than malicious. Lumbering was their business, after all. Putting them right by the law would be a commercial boon for the whole region. After a year, the governor announced that trespassing, that "stain on the character of our State, [and] vexatious and pernicious to all concerned," had been eradicated. This might have been true along most of the Kennebec, but far from it on the upper Penobscot and other northern rivers.

Governor Lincoln's conviction that the future lay in the watershed of the Penobscot River left a large swathe in the northwest of the state in limbo. While Maine was still a part of Massachusetts, *The Boston Daily Advertiser*—lobbying for a road between Quebec City and Boston—had touted the development that a highway must bring to the public lands in its path. The paper deplored the "entire want of public patronage in the making of roads into the wilderness." The next year, 1817, the General Court authorized construction of a "great Canada road." A year later, twenty-five miles were open, reported Boston's oldest daily, "two rods wide, and logs turned out and stumps dug up the width of one rod." The paper foresaw an energetic future:

> Suppose ten, fifteen or twenty men with small families should be furnished with the means of moving to the public lands joining upon the road, provision found them for one season, & some pecuniary aid in erecting buildings, they would then be able to shift for themselves, the ice would be broke, the appalling terrors of a new settlement overcome, and swarms of other settlers would voluntarily follow.[160]

Seven years after Maine became a state, a report to its legislature found a very different state of affairs. The great Canada Road was a barely cut drover's path over most of its length. One stretch—once praised by the *Advertiser* as "convenient for passing both with horses and wheels the whole distance"—was found to be totally impassible for anything wider than a horse. As Jules Verne wrote of a somewhat similar situation in *Around the World in Eighty Days*, "The papers were like some watches, which have a way of getting too fast, and had been premature in their announcement of the completion of the line."

The report rallied governor and legislature to action. Three agents were appointed to supervise construction of a new road from Bangor to Quebec. Land agent Daniel Rose sold a township (T1R2 NBKP[161]) to pay for it, and Massachusetts did likewise. Where the route passed through Bingham's million, they reported, the agent for Bingham's heirs swore he'd make that stretch every bit as good as the state's. Despite an unusually hard winter, tools and provisions were transported into the woods on sleds, ready to be put to work come spring. By summer's end, a crew of sixty men and eight yoke of oxen completed fifteen miles of road wide enough for two carriages to pass each other

> and the trees cut and cleared away so that the path may not be hereafter obstructed by windfalls. The ledges were removed or lowered by burning wood upon them instead of blasting with powder; in places where the rocks could not be moved, they were burnt and levelled with sledges and then covered with earth.

One of the surveyors who had worked on the great Canada Road before Maine became a state was Moses Greenleaf. The good old Federalist was still living in Williamsburgh and working as agent for its proprietor. It gave him a very different view to Governor Lincoln's Jeffersonian faith. "The sin of owning, or being agent for a township of land is (with many) one not to be forgotten," he complained. Prejudice against those who did not live in their townships—whipped up as a political issue in the cause of separation—was still so ingrained that

> . . . it is morally as well as politically wrong to sell land in any quantity larger than for the immediate improvement of one man and that it is morally and politically right to frame and execute the laws so as to compel every person who is so unfortunate as to own a township to sell it at any rate and at the lowest prices whether he can afford it or not.[162]

To Greenleaf, the government was constantly putting obstacles in the way of purposeful settlement. In jaundiced letters to Williamsburgh's proprietor, he tried to explain the circumstances that had sent the market for large tracts of land to rock bottom. Government policies had tripled taxes on unimproved land and discriminated against absentee proprietors, as did "the temper of the people." Maine and Massachusetts were both putting land on the market as fast as it could be surveyed. Massachusetts was advertising lots at bargain prices, but many buyers became "sick of their bargain" and tried to resell, only further adding to the glut. According to Greenleaf, some two hundred townships were available in 1825. A good price was less than a dollar per acre; much of it went for "next to nothing." Lots had dropped to around thirty cents an acre in Williamsburgh. Its location, midway between the Penobscot and Kennebec rivers, made the township something of a no-man's-land. As Governor Lincoln had noted, the "current of settlement" was flowing east and up the Penobscot. It was likely to continue that way for years to come, keeping Williamsburgh and the townships around it "rather in the back ground."

Even when settlers were ready to buy, Agent Greenleaf found, they always wanted to pay for their lot in "something not quite so good as cash." But with more land than purchasers, it was a buyer's market; his advice was to take whatever they offered, even if it usually meant taking a 25 percent loss, "either in price, or wastage, or expense of converting to cash." For the moment, the only way a proprietor could hang on was to live on his land or have "an intelligent faithful agent . . . whose interest & feelings are identified with [his] own." Bingham's General Cobb springs to mind. Eventually, Greenleaf reasoned, as the country filled up, the proprietors would own less and less; voters and the government would then feel less compelled to hold prices down and try to make the large owners sell out. But it would be fifteen or twenty years before land in the region caught up to a fair price.

All this time, Greenleaf had continued to gather information to make *A Statistical View* a more complete reference book, seizing on any document or publication he could find, and spending as much time in his library, writing and drawing maps, as he did in the field with his own explorations. He had been methodically pursuing this task for a decade when Governor Lincoln drew the legislature's attention to the "indispensable" need for "a good map and gazetteer, with correct statistical accounts." The Governor singled out for gratitude "one of our citizens for his exertions in this respect," Greenleaf himself. He was just the man to further Governor Lincoln's quest for progress. He shared the governor's optimism and was equally convinced of Maine's potential. As Lincoln noted, settlers from all over New England had found their way to Maine because of "its cheapness, fertility, and the salubrity of our climate." As they thrived, so would the state, which had the capacity to nurture "many hundreds of thousands" like them.

Inspired by Governor Lincoln's enthusiasm, the legislature urged Greenleaf to hurry up and complete his researches. To that end they voted him an honorarium of a thousand dollars and paid for forty subscriptions. Otherwise, the *Survey of Maine* was undertaken at Greenleaf's personal expense, as was the map—the state's first, and an improvement on the earlier version—that accompanied it. Both appeared in 1829. Both were of unprecedented importance, reflecting the interest of a young state's citizens in its physical and political geography. They also added energy to the storm clouds building up in the northeast.

The *Survey's* contents gave focus to the question of how the public domain might be employed to contribute to Maine's prosperity. As Greenleaf had argued in the *Statistical View*, two positions were battling with each other. Some nay-sayers doubted it would ever be possible to settle the public lands or turn them to a profit; to attempt to do so was a fool's errand. Others worried only that the public lands would be developed too quickly and their value increase too fast. Greenleaf was firmly attached to the latter camp.

In the summer of 1829, the year the *Survey* was published, Greenleaf was surveying one of the distant townships owned by Massachusetts when he contracted typhoid. He hung on in semiconscious delirium, deep in the woods, alone, for a week, until his surveying companion returned with medical attention. He survived the ordeal, but his health was never the same. Moses Greenleaf would go trekking into the wilderness no longer.

Instead, he occupied himself lobbying for anything that might bring development to the wildlands and economic success to Maine. In his surveying days, he had discovered an extensive deposit of excellent slate in Monson, near Williamsburgh. To exploit it commercially required a reliable and economical means of moving the slate to Bangor. A rail connection, Greenleaf calculated, would cost $150,000, well worth it considering the resources— lumber as well as slate—that would reach the market. In 1833, the Bangor and Piscataquis Canal and Railroad Company was incorporated with Greenleaf as its president. It was still a distant dream when he died the next year. Years later, John A. Poor, a nephew of Greenleaf's wife—whose ultimate failure was leavened with some success en route—gave Moses credit for inspiring his passion for railroads. He eulogized his uncle in a speech celebrating Bangor's centennial in 1869.

> To great scientific attainments and large practical knowledge, Mr. Greenleaf united a sanguine temperament with enthusiasm which carried him far beyond his contemporaries in comprehending the natural advantages and resources of Maine.[163]

Greenleaf was a passionate amateur, and his goals were magisterial in scope. His lifework was to compile as much hard data as he could, on as many subjects relevant to promoting Maine settlement. Baron Alexander von Humboldt, the greatest scientist of the age, once said of himself, "People often say that I'm curious about too many things at once." The same might equally have been said of Moses Greenleaf. While laying out a stretch of the great Canada Road, he came upon a place identified simply as T6R9. The Abenakis had known it more descriptively as a "place of very fine paint." Having translated the name, Greenleaf discovered the red and yellow ochres the Indians prized and recognized them as the colorful oxides of iron. He dug enough iron ore to smelt it and make a horseshoe, which he sent to the legislature to encourage investors. He would be dead ten years before the "place of very fine paint" became Katahdin Iron Works. Wherever he cast his net, Greenleaf hauled in material that both fascinated him and promised to benefit the state. His misfortune was always to be ahead of his time.

The 1820s had been a decade of "confusion, and consequently waste and loss," concluded the report by John Deane and the Committee on State Lands in 1831.[164] Falling land prices and the flight of buyers from the market were the result. The legislature was to blame. "What," the committee demanded, "have been her systems?"

> It may be answered that she can scarcely be said to have had any, and none which she has pursued for more than a year or two at a time. Such have been the irregularities and confusion, that it is very difficult, and in some instances impossible to trace any thing with certainty in the Land Office.

Recalling the transactions of colonial times and Samuel Waldo, the report considered that "the people of this State have abundant cause to deplore" such a corrupt system.[165] And yet, speculation still seemed to be thought the best way to settle the wildlands. It might be "plausible in theory, but," the committee asked, "does not all the experience derived from former and present systems show its fallacy?" It had slowed rather than stimulated settlement and for various reasons "tended to demoralize the community." The committee added a warning and a moral admonishment.

It is true that shrewd speculators may not wish a change, because it will deprive them of making the same profits out of the state which they have been accustomed to make. It is not the interest of the few, or any particular class which ought to be our guide, but the greater and permanent interest of the whole people.

Rather than to speculators, land should be sold only to settlers and at a fixed price. Timber should be sold separate from the soil. When and where lots were surveyed and sold should serve the state's interests. If legislators didn't "foster speculation," the committee averred, Maine could be settled in a quarter century. Instead, circumstances would combine to convince state leaders that most of northern Maine would be more profitable as a woodshed than a breadbasket. John Deane's prescriptions for a bustling state would have one last hurrah in 1839, when an unusually feisty legislature resolved

that the policy of confining the sales of the public lands to actual settlers would be eminently republican in its tendencies, by checking the dangerous speculation of grasping monopolists, by preventing the formation of a landed aristocracy by increasing the number of our independent yeomanry.

However, the lofty ideal of promoting a land peopled by farmers enjoying the "blessings of a freehold possession of the soil" did not survive the realities of the times.

In 1831, "An Additional Act to Promote the Sale and Settlement of the Public Lands" underscored the responsibilities of the land agent—now Daniel Rose—for the "care and custody" of the Public Reserved Lands "until the fee shall vest in the town or otherwise."[166] He was also given the right to sell "timber of all sorts" on the public lands, but not on the Public Reserved Lots. Rose was authorized to seize any timber cut on these (and any cut illegally on the public lands) and to confiscate the ox teams, equipment, and supplies of any trespassers. Any merchant who sold equipment to a trespasser was considered a partner in crime, and neither was allowed to bid at the public auction where the spoils were sold. However, the proprietors remained as resistant to the land agent's authority as they had been in General Irish's day. He would finally have to seek a legal decision. In 1840, after four years of deliberation, the Supreme Judicial Court found that until a township was incorporated, the state was entitled to the "care and custody" of the Public Lots.

Deane's Committee on State Lands had also recommended "a great road through the wilderness from the waters of the Penobscot to the river St. John." Having pointed out that historically settlement in Maine had followed and then extended from the banks of its great rivers, their report urged the Legislature to build an "artificial" thoroughfare that would

> furnish equal, if not better facilities for spreading a population through the wilderness, and . . . make land valuable, which in its present situation is without any considerable or certain value.

In 1838, land agent Elijah L. Hamlin (the elder brother of Abraham Lincoln's vice president, Hannibal Hamlin) addressed the legislature in no uncertain terms on the subject of opening the wilderness with highways. [167] Where land and lumber were connected to the more settled parts of Maine, their values rose, as did the class of settler. Without such links, Hamlin expected the wildlands would become the preserve of a "vagabond race . . . fleeing thither from the pursuits of justice, rather than seeking voluntarily, happy homes." The northeastern boundary was still unresolved, but wherever it ended up, the land agent pointed out, New Brunswick would be the "natural outlet . . . for trade and intercourse" in the valleys of the St. John and the Aroostook. If nothing were done to penetrate the wildlands with good roads, a foreign country would be the economic beneficiary of the raw materials produced by a third of Maine. The dilemma prompted him to end his report with a jeremiad.

"It is evident that the citizens of our State have not heretofore been fully impressed of the great value of our public domain," he began.[168] Hamlin rehearsed the saga of the lost "golden opportunity" to acquire all Massachusetts' lands. He deplored the government's generally dilatory attitude toward investments that would have made the wildlands bloom. Money for such efforts had been grudgingly granted when it ought to have been demanded spontaneously by a unanimous legislature. If the leaders lacked the "spirit and feeling worthy of our great resources," how could the public be anything but "possessed of doubts and fears, and misgivings"? Without pride and confidence in their state, the people would never summon the resolve to support the investment and energy needed to realize the huge potential of northern Maine. Hamlin went on to make an impassioned plea for a more visionary approach to Maine's future. The St. John Valley must be connected to the Atlantic through the valleys of the Kennebec and Penobscot, "either by canal or rail, or both in part." By directing its commercial fruits to Maine's coast, the state's wealth and population would grow rapidly and advance it to the position in the Union "to which her natural advantages so justly entitle her."[169] Without such a link, Canada would always be Aroostook's market.

Public works of this kind, Hamlin admitted, ran counter to the principles of many, especially when borrowing money was involved. The same objections had been raised about the Erie Canal. Scoffers had called that project "visionary and chimerical, and at least one hundred years in advance of the age." And they had been completely wrong. A well-considered public investment along the same lines in Maine would be just as successful in promoting "settlement and cultivation" in the public lands. However, with the state of the economy in mind, Hamlin understood that the legislature was in no mood to consider really large-scale public works like a train or canal. Perhaps the best to be hoped for at this point was to build more roads. If done properly, the St. John Valley would be settled "with a rapidity unexampled in New England."

Hamlin sketched out the major routes needed to settle the area. The Military Road should be extended along the eastern border with New Brunswick through Mars Hill to the St. John "as soon as practicable." An Aroostook Road should be laid out through the settling lands up to Fort Kent. A road from Williamsburgh (Moses Greenleaf's old home) up to the border with Quebec and the upper reaches of the St. John would be better than the Canada Road, which crossed large sections of what Hamlin deemed "waste land" that failed to promote settlement. He didn't think much more highly of the Military Road, which passed "unnecessarily over highlands." Routes must be laid out sensibly and roads constructed carefully, said Elijah Hamlin.

Early in the 1830s, the value of land had started to recover from the doldrums described by Moses Greenleaf. Doubtless returning optimism had been part of the easy incorporation of his railroad company. By 1835, prices had risen to $1.45 per acre—more than three-fold in two years—and Maine sold nearly 370,000 acres, double the amount in 1833.[170] Bangor, already on its way to becoming the "timber capital of the world," became the epicenter of a boom in timberland. Recalling it years later, former governor Israel Washburn Jr., who had been a young lawyer at the time, painted a vivid picture with his recollections.[171]

> Retired capitalists, merchants, manufacturers, old sea captains, and others, from abroad, had heard of the vast wealth of the Penobscot forests, of the countless millions of timber they contained, and of its marvellous quality. To own the bond of a township was to have an independent fortune, but to possess the title was "wealth beyond the dreams of avarice." . . . About that time wolf skins for sleigh robes came in fashion in this vicinity, and a man's fortune, or the number of bonds he held, was ordinarily gauged by the number and length of the wolves' tails that hung over the back of his sleigh. [172]

Washburn regaled his audience with the story of an Old Town citizen paying his $80 bill at New York's finest hotel with a hundred-dollar note. When the cashier returned the difference, he was "promptly informed that they did not 'take change down east.'" Still more astonishing was the story that reached a faraway Baltimore paper: a pair of paupers escaped from the Bangor almshouse one evening. Before they were caught the next morning, they had each made $1,800 on land speculation while on the lam.[173] Greed and extravagance triumphed over common sense, with lots surveyed by crooked surveyors bought and sold unseen. In 1836, "when people stopped long enough to look at the lands they had purchased," the bubble burst.[174]

Both Maine and Massachusetts held off putting more land on the market, but the damage was done. The following year, the national panic of 1837 made things worse. Money vanished, people left, businesses closed, their possessions knocked down on the auction block. The elderly Israel Washburn could not "even at this distance, look back upon these cruel years without extreme pain." He recalled "a 'drive' of as fine logs as ever floated from the Baskahegan [that] brought to the operators less than enough to pay the bills for manufacturing and running from the mills to Bangor."

In an analysis three years afterwards, a lawyer-turned-journalist wrote that timberland speculation in Maine was "the most extravagant and irrational, and the most ruinous to those engaged in it."[175] After a couple of years of significant payments, timber investors who had bought land at the height of the boom for much more than its actual value—"in the excitement of A.D. 1835," in the discreet words of Land Agent Elijah Hamlin—were faced with bankruptcy and default. The state was faced with the choice of foreclosing on them, which was hardly in its best interest, or settling with them "upon equitable terms." (In fact, many had by this time paid more or less what the land was actually worth.) Hamlin readily admitted that he had refrained from suing these unfortunates, and advised the governor and the legislature that

> [T]here can be no good reason for the State to enforce ruinous contracts against her citizens, and sound policy would seem to dictate a generous and liberal course toward those, whose future usefulness must be destroyed, if the State exacts the full measure of her legal rights.[176]

From the 370,000 acres sold at the good times' peak, land sales plunged to less than 20,000 acres in 1841.[177] Not every lumberman or mill-owner was ruined. The Eaton brothers—Henry Franklin and Joseph Emerson—had been doing well out of the lumber business on the St. Croix River since the early 1830s, well before the boom or the bust that swept it away. With a large saw-mill in Calais to feed, the H.F. Eaton Company owned timberlands in Washington County and across the river in New Brunswick, but also as far away as Somerset, Piscataquis, and Aroostook.[178] Men like the Eatons were already blazing the trail that would lead to most of northern Maine's remaining forestland to be exploited for its lumber by increasingly large business concerns.

When James Irish had chatted with the merchants of Fredericton on his expedition up the St. John in 1825, the New Brunswickers all said the same
thing: With the Treaty of Paris, the United States had "obtained advantage
over them," though they had not realized it at the time. The proposed boundary had physically separated them from lower Canada, a situation that could
not be tolerated. They felt that all the territory northeast of the St. John and
Madawaska rivers must be theirs, either "by purchase or compromise." Seeing so much of their forest go up in flames later that year in the Miramichi
fire only sharpened Canadian concerns about the disputed area and its timber.
As a practical matter, loggers in New Brunswick had little choice but to head
for the forests of the Allagash. Across the border, Governor Enoch Lincoln's
assessment of the situation was no less resolute. "[O]ur landmarks will be
held sacred and our inalienable sovereignty will be respected," he told the
legislature, although he had to admit that negotiations had been "dilatory."

Faced with continued intransigence by both sides, the joint commission
had no choice but to fall back on the last resort stipulated by the Treaty of
Ghent. Should the parties fail to reach agreement, the question would be put
before "some friendly sovereign or State" for adjudication. In 1827, a convention held in London chose William I, King of the Netherlands, for the role.
Maine had been left out of the negotiation, which shook Governor Lincoln's
confidence. The "umpirage" of a foreign power, he thought, was likely to lead
to an "unjust and disastrous" result. Even as their respective nations pursued
a diplomatic solution, Maine and Canada sought to justify their claims with
facts on the ground.

Besides issuing permits to cut on "Maine's" public lands, New Brunswick
was once again handing out land grants, raising militias, and had even appointed a civil magistrate for the contested area. When a Madawaska settler
flew a handmade Stars and Stripes over his home, he was fined and imprisoned until he paid it. "Are we to remain silent and passive spectators," demanded Maine's legislature, even as the British "strip the land of its timber,
persecute and expel our citizens and cause their own settlers to spread over
the territory?"[179]

Governor Lincoln made a polite protest to his provincial counterpart, hoping it was but the "hasty act" of an "unthinking agent." The New Brunswick
lieutenant governor's answer left no doubt in Enoch Lincoln's mind that the
province was deliberately extending its jurisdiction over the whole disputed
territory, and so he informed the legislature. Having earlier urged "prudence
and moderation" on the restive Madawaskans, he now noted with wry deco-
rum, "I cannot but profess to you the disposition on my own part, subject to
your direction, to offer some difficulties against such a course." In an effort
to forestall any rash move by Maine citizens, the federal government sent a

detachment of troops to the border at Houlton, while both sides awaited the results of the "umpirage."

King William of the Netherlands reached his decision in 1831. The original treaty's language was so vague as to render a judgment impossible, he declared. Instead the king suggested splitting the difference and making the St. John River the boundary. This, objected Maine's furious legislators, was a political answer to a simple question of geography. Rejecting it out of hand, they at once sent the ubiquitous John Deane on a mission to survey the populations of the St. John and Aroostook valleys. The Madawaska Settlement (over four thousand square miles of territory) was annexed and given a seat in the legislature. When the new district's citizens gathered to organize themselves into an official town in August, two British militiamen broke up the meeting with "many opprobious [sic] and threatening terms."[180] A troop of soldiers led by Sir Archibald Campbell, the new lieutenant governor, set out after the meeting's organizers. Those he caught were carted off to the Fredericton jail. Others fled into the forest, where they "slept in the woods three nights without fire or covering, and by stratagem have obtained Potatoes from the fields for subsistence."

Maine's "exemplary moderation" in regard to the border dispute had been a source of pride to Enoch Lincoln when he was in office.[181] Taking Americans captive, however, was too much. The state was adamant, said new Governor Samuel Smith, about defending "a territory, which we not only claim, but know, to be within the limits of Maine."[182] When he appealed to Washington, however, Secretary of State Edward Livingston's response was not the one Smith expected. Congress was considering the King of the Netherlands' proposal, and it was President Andrew Jackson's "earnest wish" that Maine do nothing to disturb the status quo. The governor got a lecture on the diplomatic sensitivities he had put at risk. He was left in no doubt that the president was displeased.

Smith's reply was sheepish. From now on, Maine would avoid any "collision" with the British authorities in New Brunswick. He went on to ask that the federal government come to the rescue of his citizens languishing in Fredericton jail. This earned Governor Smith another rebuke from the president via his secretary of state. Madawaska was "de facto in the occupation of the British," and therefore there was never "what you consider as an invasion of the State." President Jackson would try to free the "ill-advised persons who have been the cause of the disturbance," but Smith was not to let the incident be repeated.

The chastened governor was stuck between the Scylla of an irritable president and the Charybdis of a legislature seething with resentment. If there were more British arrests, the "just indignation of their fellow citizens" would be impossible to control, he lamented. At the eleventh hour, Secretary of State Livingston offered a confidential proposal, "in a spirit of reciprocity and accommodation." Would Maine trade its claim to the disputed territory for an equivalent amount and value of federally owned land from the western territories? The government would then be free to negotiate a deal with Great Britain over the land that "may best comport with the interests and honor of the United States," without involving any loss of face for Maine. Although it meant giving up territory, Livingston's proposal recognized that for Maine in those days, the public domain was as much a financial as a territorial asset.

Livingston was fortunate in having on his side a Maine lawyer who had been ambassador to the Netherlands while King William was deliberating. William Pitt Preble had a poor opinion of the king. "In Europe, not excepting England, it was matter of astonishment that the United States should ever have consented" to allow the king to referee the case. Preble was a practical man; his arguments dwelt much longer on Maine's self-interest than on its rights or grievances. He was a good choice for lobbying a suspicious governor. Refusal to compromise would not serve Maine well, Preble advised Governor Smith. If he waited for Congress to weigh the king's proposal, he would be forced to go along with the decision, leaving Maine in a weak negotiating position. Washington's view of the land was very different from Smith's paradise that is "extremely well watered, has a fertile soil, and is covered with valuable timber." The politicians Preble talked to saw it as a "barren, mountainous region, wholly unfit for settlement and cultivation." Smith might hope for it to become a "flourishing and populous" part of Maine; most congressmen thought it didn't amount to a hill of beans—it would certainly never attract significant settlement, and it was not worth risking the peace or jeopardizing U.S. interests.

Given its remoteness and "infancy as a state," Maine had little influence with which to change Congress' mind. By contrast, Preble assured the governor, Livingston's proposal treated Maine with "courtesy and respect," saving its honor as a state while supporting the nation. Furthermore, from a financial point of view it was *"immensely advantageous."* And in a postscript that would be echoed in 1982, exactly a hundred and fifty years later, he added, *"A more ample indemnity could be obtained in land than in money."*

The governor was persuaded and sent the proposal to the legislature. Negotiations in Washington, led by Preble, soon produced an agreement. (Jackson wanted a quick decision, "not to have any diplomacy about it.") The United States would survey and sell a million acres in the Michigan territory, with the proceeds—over $1,000,000—going to Maine. Meanwhile, the Foreign Relations Committee was recommending that the Senate accept the king of the Netherlands' solution. After much debate—with Maine's congressmen lobbying vehemently against the umpire's proposal—the Senate effectively killed it by voting to reopen negotiations with His Britannic Majesty.

For Secretary Livingston, the end seemed to be in sight. Once the disputed land was conveyed to the United States, he assured the British envoy, his country would come to new talks "clothed with ampler powers than it had heretofore possessed." He underestimated Maine's mood. Its legislature voted to put the whole question up to the people. A popular referendum conferred anything but the "ampler powers" the secretary of state had hoped for. He had to tell the British that loss of Maine territory made any line south of the Treaty of Paris' hypothetical "highlands" impossible.

The next several years were relatively quiet along the border. In Washington, Maine continued to be an obstacle to a diplomatic solution. In Augusta (Maine's capital since 1831), successive governors bemoaned the dwindling likelihood of ever settling the issue. In Fredericton, the "firm but temperate" hand of Sir Archibald Campbell did the most to keep a peace "troubled only by the occasional pilfering of timber by both sides."[183] However, the collapse of the land boom in 1837 brought the boundary question to the fore once more. Land sales, on which state finances were heavily dependent, had plummeted, and some of the best remaining timberlands were along the Aroostook River. That summer the legislature sent Ebenezer Greely into the disputed area to take a census. In New Brunswick, the provincial authorities—with some justification—considered it a "jurisdictional" mission and arrested Greely not once, but twice. The second time, he got aggressive, telling his captors that the census would be completed "if it took every military man in the state." Such activities could only end in military retaliation, warned a new lieutenant governor of New Brunswick, Sir John Harvey.

Maine took this as akin to a declaration of war. Our state has been invaded by New Brunswick, announced Democratic governor Robert Dunlap.[184] As it had six years before, Washington again lost patience with its truculent northeastern state. The first time Greely was arrested, President Martin Van Buren moved expeditiously to have him freed. The second time the president was not amused. Once again, Maine's governor was warned to stay out of the troubled arena of international relations.

In 1838, Edward Kent, a Whig, broke the long Democratic hold on Maine's governorship, and for the next five years, he and Democrat John Fairfield leap-frogged each other almost annually.[185] Kent was known as a moderate who hoped that the U.S. government would resolve the border issue for him. However, when the legislature asked for a joint British–U.S. survey of the boundary, Congress refused. Maine then sent its own surveyors, including former land agent James Irish, to explore the American claim. Kent took the precaution of informing New Brunswick, and Sir John Harvey replied courteously that he had no desire to interfere with the expedition if its object was limited to "obtaining topographical information." He would not, however, "suffer any infringement" of British jurisdiction, "until the question of right is decided." The party completed its task uninterrupted and reported its findings on New Year's Eve, 1838. Its conclusion was inescapable.

> It is difficult to imagine a more certain and accurate description of boundaries than that contained in the treaty of 1783, or which, with more certainty, can be applied on the earth's surface. Its monuments are as fixed and certain as the pole and the everlasting hills.

The same day, in the frozen forest 250 miles north of Augusta, the question looked as if it would finally be decided by combat. Ever since the snow started to fall, the Fish and Aroostook rivers had been the site of an international free-for-all, each side claiming the right to defend its trees against the other. Maine's land agent reported that large numbers of men from the Canadian provinces were cutting heavily on "lands belonging to this State." When a party of New Brunswick men started felling trees on the land granted to the late General William Eaton, hero of Tripoli, his family sent out an SOS. From all over northern Maine, woodsmen responded to the call, driving off the interlopers with sheer numbers. On New Year's Eve, the Canadians returned in force. The Mainers grabbed their weapons, but before anyone had time to shoot, a bear mauled several of the attackers. (The bear's presence, out and about, was noted as unusual so late in the season.) The Canadians fired at and killed the bear, but the defenders, assuming the shot had been intended for them, fired back. In the confusion, the Canadians withdrew to tend their wounded—wounded not by American guns, but the teeth and claws of a bear. Thus began and ended the Battle of Caribou.

In January, the new land agent, Rufus McIntire, reported that as many as two hundred Canadians with fifty yoke of oxen were still cutting timber. [186] The loss might amount to $100,000 before the winter was over. Democrat John Fairfield, who had just been elected governor, was more given to rousing rhetoric than his predecessor. These foreign raiders "not only refuse to desist, but defy the power of this government to prevent their cutting timber to any extent they please," he fumed. This was not just a financial matter but one that went to the "character of the State." He sent McIntire with an armed posse to intercept the perpetrators of this "devastation and pillage." Seize their supplies, break up their camps, send them packing, ordered the governor. The posse headed north in February.

Having arrested some "unruly wood thieves," the party used the confiscated timber to build a blockhouse, calling it Fort Fairfield. Continuing on, they pitched camp wherever they were when the sun set. One night, they awoke to find themselves surrounded by a squad of armed New Brunswickers. McIntire and his men were marched off through snow to the Fredericton jail.[187] In Augusta, saber-rattling rose to new heights while in the woods, days later, Maine volunteers captured a military officer and the chief warden of New Brunswick by way of retaliation. The two men were interned in Bangor, though not in the jail but in the Bangor House where, it was noted, they "fared sumptuously."

From Sir John Harvey's point of view, McIntire's posse—thought to be two hundred strong—was an armed incursion into New Brunswick, for which he had received no warning. Across the Atlantic Ocean, the aging Duke of Wellington addressed Parliament's House of Lords about "lawless Yankees" invading British land. Harvey's only option was an ultimatum to Fairfield: If the governor did not withdraw his posse, "I must proceed to take military occupation."

The excitable Fairfield responded by mustering the militia "to meet the troops of Sir John Harvey and resist his insolent pretensions." The Legislature voted an astonishing $800,000 to defend the state. By the end of the month, ten thousand men were on the march to the Aroostook country. To fan the flames of patriotic feeling, the local press kept up a steady stream of news from the front. One newspaper, the *Bangor Whig*, dispatched a war correspondent who sent back stirring accounts of the "'war,' of the hardships which were encountered, and of the soldiers tenting on the melting snow-drifts."

In Washington, Maine's congressmen finally prevailed upon Congress to support their state with $10,000,000 for war expenses and fifty thousand U.S. Army soldiers under General Winfield Scott (War of 1812 veteran and future hero of the Mexican War). The troops inspired confidence when they arrived, but it became clear that Scott's orders were to make peace, not war. President Van Buren's choice of Scott was particularly fortunate. He had been a British prisoner of war in the War of 1812, and Sir John Harvey had been his minder. Their personal relationship allowed Scott and Harvey to defuse the situation, which could have ignited a shooting war at any moment. They negotiated terms of a truce, and on March 25, Governor Fairfield ratified them and withdrew the Maine militia.

A less provocative armed civil posse under the command of the land agent was dispatched to keep order in the Aroostook country. New Brunswick was given Madawaska to administer, pending a final resolution. Harvey agreed to attempt no "military possession" of the disputed area and to accept the presence of Maine's civil posse without trying to expel it. The Aroostook War had lasted only six weeks, and was bloodless except for the fracas around the bear and, some say, a farm animal—a pig or a cow—that found itself in the wrong place at the wrong time.

Whatever strategic aims lay buried in the diplomatic relations between Great Britain and the United States, Maine had been prepared to go to war over what General Scott described as "a strip of land lying between two acknowledged boundaries, without any immediate value except for the fine ship-timber in which it abounded." From the distance of 175 years, historian Michael T. Perry found a deeper meaning floating in the rhetoric of the times. By calling on the concepts of Maine's honor and rights, and the obligation of the national government to uphold them, the Aroostook War helped a distant, underpopulated state define itself.[188] Even at an interval of seventy years, memories continued to warm the heart of at least one Mainer, John Francis Sprague.

> Patriotic sons of the Pine Tree State left their homes and firesides in the most inclement season known to our rigorous climate and marched through the deep snows of a wilderness, two hundred miles, to defend our frontier from foreign invasion, when the Federal government was needlessly procrastinating and turning a deaf ear to the cries of suffering and oppressed pioneers in the upper St. John valley.

The Aroostook War made it clear to both national governments that discussions on the northeastern boundary must be reopened, but it was still two years before serious negotiations began. Meanwhile, as described by William Parrott, the land agent in charge of the civil posse after the truce, turmoil continued in the Aroostook territory. As they tried to seize a gang of trespassers, his men were surrounded by an "armed mob" led by a member of the New Brunswick militia. On another occasion, the local sheriff "replevined" supplies Parrott had confiscated and let the trespassers continue about their business. In response to the lawlessness, the land agent's crew built two new blockhouses, clearing and planting the land around with oats, barley, and potatoes to get a garrison—as many as 350 men—through the winter if need be. In September another skirmish like the Battle of Caribou took place. As Parrott reported it:

> About two o'clock A. M., an attack was made upon our station by a party of armed men from the Province of New Brunswick. . . . From the marks they made in running through the grass and grain, I should judge that there was at least sixty. The night was very dark, and the first knowledge we had of an attack was from the sentinel . . . [when they were] within ten yards of the breast-work. He immediately fired upon them, when they all turned and ran, leaving

behind them two muskets loaded with balls, a number of bayonets, hats, &c, which they lost in their flight.[189]

Having negotiated the end of the Aroostook War but six months before, Sir John Harvey at once dispatched the warden of the disputed territory to investigate the "outrage" by "reckless persons." They had armed themselves by breaking into an arsenal set up for the local militia. The warden took it upon himself to remove the remaining weapons lest the episode be repeated.

In fact, British fears that Maine might move to take over the territory were not without foundation. "Our true policy was to proceed silently and quietly strengthening ourselves," Charles Jarvis wrote in a secret message to Governor Fairfield in January 1840. Jarvis had led a thousand volunteers during the Aroostook War, where his aide-de-camp had been William Parrott. He needed more time, he informed the governor, to build a military road.[190] One more season, and the road would be opened, putting Maine in a position to hold all the territory described in the original treaty. In the meantime, "no blow should be struck until that blow should be decisive."[191]

But even Maine was getting tired of the problem. The longer it remained unresolved, the more uncertain the supply of timber and the worse off their economy would be. Diplomatic moves began in the spring of 1842, and when they did, two old friends found themselves on each side of the negotiating table: America's Daniel Webster and Great Britain's Alexander Baring, now Baron Ashburton, owner of Bingham's Penobscot million. For a second time, a personal relationship would help solve the insoluble. Though Webster had always been of the view that the line in the Treaty of 1783 was "well defined and easily and readily to be found," both governments wanted to put the issue behind them. The fortuitous discovery, during the talks, of a map that purported to show a boundary line drawn by Benjamin Franklin during the Paris peace talks in 1783 helped assuage American feelings. Maine State Historian Thomas Desjardin believed Webster may also have felt generous to the plight of New Brunswick, which had lost so much of its forest in the Great Miramichi Fire. The Webster-Ashburton Treaty was signed in August 1842.

Maine received seven thousand of the twelve thousand square miles in dispute, plus $125,000 compensation. Each side recognized the other's land grants on the "wrong" side of the line. The U.S. government also reimbursed Maine for surveying costs and maintaining the civil posse. Ironically, the state lost a sliver on the northwestern border, which it would have received from the despised king of the Netherlands. But the main thing was that, at long last, Maine had a grasp on the actual extent of its public lands. Never again would investors or settlers have to worry about investing too far north or east. Even timber trespass was reduced; "it was thereafter in the nature of pilferings, rather in [sic] wholesale depredations."[192]

Not everyone was pleased. To the last, the Maine commissioners had been the most truculent. As Lord Ashburton reported to the British foreign secretary, Lord Aberdeen, "I was in doubt whether I might not fail all together, but at last Preble yielded and after signing he went off to his wilds in Maine as sulky as a Bear."[193]

Chapter Four

"Folly of Exaggeration" vs. "Want of Just Appreciation" (1842–1891)

It is the first duty of a people rightly to value the character and capacity of the country they inhabit. While their interests will suggest the folly of an exaggerated estimate of it in these respects, a want of just appreciation of its resources and natural advantages, is equally unwise.

—Governor Lot M. Morrill, 1860

With the last territorial issues arising from American independence settled, an obstacle was removed that had vexed every governor since Maine became a state. International agreement on the boundary with New Brunswick meant that the respective authorities could survey the wildlands on their side, without fear of official challenge or loss to a political stroke of the pen. Maine could sell as many lots, or as many permits to cut the timber growing on them, under whatever conditions it deemed to be in its best interest. The Webster-Ashburton Treaty also affected relations with the state's southwestern neighbor: the process of divvying up the public lands with Massachusetts, as per the Articles of Separation, could finally be completed.

The next ten years saw a number of trends that would shape how Maine's forests looked and were controlled 130 years later when the public lots finally came to the attention of a state unaware and ignorant of their history. As early as 1840, it was widely held that a "large proportion" of the northern townships would never be incorporated. For the Public Reserved Lands, the implications were clear. Though its Constitution insisted that Maine keep them in trust, for most, their original raison d'être had evaporated.

The public domain was now classified firmly as either settling lands or timber lands. The government made some efforts to establish a yeomanry on the one; on the other, however, the immediate need was to convert the timber

to cash. The commercial opportunities that this promised could not but attract larger business interests. It took capital to harness the rivers to serve the
lumberman: to get his logs out of the woods—by making the river passable
for rafts of tree trunks in huge numbers, by creating booms to catch them, by
redirecting a stream from one watershed to another, if need be—and to power
the sawmills at the end of the river drive.

The hub for all this activity was Bangor, still navigable twenty miles up the
Penobscot River and already known as the "Lumber Capital of the World."
In 1840, three hundred mills were turning out one hundred million board feet
a year, and double that by 1848.[194] In resonant prose, Lyndon Oak reminded
his readers how Maine's vast and faraway wildlands were

> covered with magnificent growths of timber, and threaded by streams upon
> which it could be floated to the mills upon the Penobscot, Maine's largest river,
> and manufactured into various descriptions of lumber, and then floated to tide-
> waters ready for distribution to the markets of the world.[195]

Beauty, of course, is in the eye of the beholder. Henry David Thoreau was
more ambivalent. Visiting the city in 1846, he likened Bangor, positioned at
the edge of the wilderness, to "a star on the edge of night"; but when he saw
thousands of tree trunks corralled behind the boom in the river—"Here is a
close jam, a hard rub, at all seasons"[196]—he was less sanguine about the trade
that had built it, literally and figuratively.

> Through this steel riddle, more or less coarse, is the arrowy Maine forest, from
> Ktaadn and Chesuncook, and the head-waters of the St. John, relentlessly sifted,
> till it comes out boards, clapboards, laths, and shingles such as the wind can
> take, still perchance to be slit and slit again, till men get a size that will suit.
> Think how stood the white pine tree on the shore of Chesuncook, its branches
> soughing with the four winds, and every individual needle trembling in the sun-
> light,—think how it stands with it now,—sold, perchance, to the New England
> Friction-Match Company![197]

In 1842, pine was still the lumberman's prize, and Maine was the last place
in the Northeast where it grew in commercially viable stands. They were long
gone from the state's southern forests, but up north woodsmen could find the
immense trunks of old and in wonderful quantity. Only the border dispute had
prevented them from being exploited with confidence.

The same issue had "arrested" settlement of the region. It could be an
Eden, wrote Dr. Charles T. Jackson, who surveyed the geology of the area in
1838. Settlers arrived "poor and destitute, and some seriously embarrassed,"
and after a few years they were living on easy street. Fix the boundary
problem, said Jackson, and "the tide of emigration will begin to flow rapidly

towards the banks of the Aroostook and to the Madawaska territory."[198] Settler and lumberjack alike would find the territory a cornucopia "possessing every advantage."

Heavy timber offers reward to the enterprising lumber dealer. A rich soil . . . offers an ample reward to the husbandman. Inexhaustible supplies of limestone, valuable both for building materials and for agriculture, vast and inexhaustible mines of rich iron ore for the manufacture of the finest kinds of iron and steel— the country presents every natural advantage that might be required to call forth the enterprise and industry of the farmer and manufacturer.

Thus, northern Maine seemed ripe for its geopolitical moment. The Webster-Ashburton Treaty uncorked a flood of optimism that began to reverse the trend in land sales, which had reached a nadir the prior year. The summer the treaty was signed, advertisements for saws, axes, and other woods-related stuff filled the pages of Bangor's broadsheets. George Coffin, the Massachusetts land agent, had already completed *A Plan of the Public Lands in the State of Maine* in 1835, showing the townships that had been "set off in severalty" to each state, Maine's marked with an "M" and Massachusetts' marked with a "C" for Commonwealth. Now Coffin opened up sixteen of the latter for timber cutting. A running announcement in the *Daily Whig and Courier* offered them in tracts of a quarter up to a whole township to anyone "disposed to purchase for lumbering operations."[199] Aroostook County was where the action would be, just as Dr. Jackson had predicted.

As it would again and again throughout the century, the Aroostook heyday lying just over the horizon stalled. The three townships Maine put up for sale that year attracted few buyers.[200] Lack of ready money kept many "from even examining" them, complained land agent Levi Bradley (who succeeded Elijah Hamlin in 1842). In an effort to level the playing field between rich and poor, Maine had limited the size of lots its agents could sell to a maximum of a square mile, less than seven hundred acres. That might not produce enough wood to make the investment worth it, Bradley warned. "Fitting out for a winter's work" on the upper Penobscot or Kennebec could eat up a thousand dollars, with another two thousand to get the wood to market. "He is not a poor man who can advance his three thousand dollars," concluded the land agent.

"Timber"—by which Bradley meant pine—is "seldom found in compact bodies, but is frequently widely scattered." *Pinus strobus* (white pine) naturally grows in strips along rivers or in clusters set in the forest, towering above the other trees. Naturalist John James Audubon described how the "lumberer" would use one as a natural crow's nest from which to scan the horizon for the next stand to cut. "While anxiously looking for 'lumber lands,' they ascended the eminences around, then climbed the tallest trees, and, by means of a great telescope, inspected the pine woods in the distance."[201]

As woodsmen spread deeper into the wilderness, the forest they left in their wake was much more costly to survey accurately. On virgin land, a township's "general character" could be determined by surveying a small part of it. A good lumberman, however, was assumed to have taken "all that is perfect," which made necessary a "much closer examination" of what he had left behind. Increasingly, potential buyers were checking the timber themselves, with cunning gamesmanship often the result. Judicious selection of a few lots could give the buyer a permanent advantage. "Having taken the heart or centre of every good birth of timber, no one else will purchase the remainder," Bradley explained. "He has the key to the whole, and will wait for a favorable time to purchase." The rise of the lumber barons had begun. In 1843, the legislature revived the policy of selling stumpage and timberland by quarter, half, and whole townships. Sales by Maine and Massachusetts reached a record 420,000 acres the following year. Due to a mix of unforeseen events, they fell dramatically the next.

Permits to cut timber in the winter were customarily sold the previous summer. When the auction was held in 1845, the previous season's bumper harvest had yet to come in; when it did, it glutted the market. With their permits bought and supplies paid for, the woodsmen had little choice but to go ahead, hoping that "increased industry and economy" would see them through the winter of 1846. With expenses already higher than usual, nature piled on: a stormy March brought timber hauling to a complete halt a month early. It also washed away the snowpack, so when the rivers thawed, low flows made driving as much as four times as expensive. "The troubles of the lumbermen did not stop here," recorded Levi Bradley. Rising freight costs and sinking prices for timber in Europe made export impossible. The only option was to stockpile it and wait for the market to improve. Even this plan went awry. A freak storm in the fall broke up the rafts of timber where they had been stored at St. John, scattering much of it into the Bay of Fundy.

Realizing that the lumbermen would be quite unable to pay the stumpage prices they had contracted for, Bradley recommended settling with them on "fair and equitable" terms. A commission was dispatched to negotiate these, meanwhile banning further harvests on the St. John to stop the slide in timber prices. An exception was made for harvesting for local consumption. Some twenty mills depended on the public lands around them; it made no sense to compel them to "lie idle," argued land agent Samuel Cony, who had succeeded Levi Bradley.[202] They could be kept busy with "down pine, . . . being the refuse left by those who have heretofore made square timber," which was better than letting it rot in the forest.[203]

Interest in the settling lands, in the wake of the Webster-Ashburton Treaty, started off more positively. The first six ranges from the state's east line—roughly a hundred miles north–south, by thirty-six miles east–west—had ideal soils for farming, as attested by geologist Charles Jackson.[204] Levi Bradley reported that many would-be farmers had looked them over and indicated they would be moving there "as soon as circumstances permit." He recommended that lots be offered only to buyers who would actually clear and farm them, and he urged Governor Fairfield to continue the liberal and far-sighted policy of allowing a settler to put down cash for a quarter the price of his lot, then pay the balance, a quarter a year, by building roads around the settlements. The state had long realized that profit from the settling lands was not in their sale but more long term: a "thriving population" whose productive farms would be taxable one day.

Initially, harvests in the Aroostook country were everything that Dr. Jackson had promised. Thoreau, who visited the region around Molunkus in 1846, found potatoes "growing like weeds."[205] He described how a field was prepared for cultivation:

> The mode of clearing and planting is, to fell the trees, and burn once what will burn, then cut them up into suitable lengths, roll into heaps, and burn again; then, with a hoe, plant potatoes where you can come at the ground between the stumps and charred logs; for a first crop the ashes sufficing for manure, and no hoeing being necessary the first year. In the fall, cut, roll, and burn again, and so on, till the land is cleared.[206]

Land agent Bradley was inclined to take a tolerant view of the newcomers who swelled Aroostook's population that year. Most of them, he admitted, were in fact squatting on unsurveyed land and "making improvements thereon without purchasing." It amounted to a "custom," and although it caused him occasional difficulty with conflicting claims, "yet the State suffers no injury," asserted Bradley.

The farming tracts mostly had little commercial timber to forego, which could create a problem for new settlers. No pine meant no wood to build the "comfortable dwelling house" their settlement duties required. The land agent suggested he be allowed to sell lumber to "our hardy pioneers," rather than have them forage for it. "When none are permitted to cut," he argued, "no one will inform against him who trespasses; but when any one can buy at a fair rate, those who buy will generally expose those who trespass." Where marketable lumber was growing around their plots, settlers were not allowed to sell it while they were still paying off their contracts. Thus a valuable resource was at serious risk from the fires they used to clear their lands. Bradley recommended such lumber be cut and sold as fast as possible to anyone with "good security for the stumpage."

A significant bonus for farmers was the market for their surplus in the lumber camps, and at "richly remunerating rates."[207] Many were relying on this additional source of income when the local lumber business collapsed, and the legislature banned further cutting along the St. John. There would be no further settlement until the ban was lifted and lumber camps could "again afford a vent for the surplus agricultural products of that region." Before that could happen, the harvest itself failed. This was not, the land agent hastened to point out, because "the soil is steril, or season of summer too short for crops to mature and ripen." After a few good years, wheat, once "as certain, and as abundant" as anywhere in New England, had succumbed to the weevil, and potatoes to the rot. It produced "such discouragement, as really to make discreet men talk seriously, of leaving their farms and their homes, and seeking new ones on the prairies of the west." By the end of the decade, the influx of settlers to Aroostook had slowed to a trickle.

The new international boundary presented one unexpected challenge for Maine's land agent. About two thousand French-speaking souls in the Madawaska settlement on the south bank of the St. John—through no wish of their own—suddenly found themselves on the American side and thus citizens of Maine.[208] Surrounded by impenetrable forest, they were completely cut off from the rest of the state, yet were expected to "learn their duty . . . without a knowledge of our language or laws, without any municipal charters or regulations, without magistrates and without roads." Thanks to Bradley, the legislature employed a "competent teacher" to teach them English, using revenue from the Public Lots.

The effort was a success. Two years later, the land agent reported that "hundreds who had never before thought of learning to read" were now literate. The inhabitants themselves supported the schools generously "in comparison with their means," and hundreds would remember the excellent teacher, a Mr. Madigan, "with gratitude for the benefits of instruction they have derived from him."[209] Bradley knew that "prejudices, engendered by ignorance against our people and institutions, are fast giving way," as the people began to feel "the fostering care of a generous government." He urged the legislature to continue funding the project. It amounted to a mere two cents on every thousand dollars of taxable property. "Who will grudge so mere a trifle in aid of the benevolent object of enlightening such a people?"[210]

In addition to education, the Acadians needed contact with their new countrymen. Starting with Bradley, successive land agents would press for funds to build and maintain a road that would embrace Madawaska in the family of Maine. Such an investment would not just benefit the backward residents. The route would pass through the "finest portions of our public lands" and open them up for development. The only major roads approaching northern Maine at that time were the Military Road from Bangor to Houlton, pushed through as the simmering northeast border dispute threatened to boil over, and the Canada Road, still short of its destination, Quebec.

Besides surveying the lands as yet undivided with Massachusetts, infrastructure development was the major preoccupation for the land agents throughout the 1840s. In the untaxable, undivided wildlands, construction crews were hired by the government, with the expense initially shared by the Commonwealth. Where it crossed settled land, settlers worked on the road to pay off the purchase of their lots, not always the easiest teams to supervise.

Road maintenance, even with sensible construction, was a never-ending issue. Horse-drawn wagons hauling wood frequently weighed four tons; six-ton loads were sometimes pulled by a team of ten or twelve oxen, "not *on* the road," as Bradley noted wryly, "but *through* it." A summer's work making a stretch of road "passable" could be undone in a single winter, with the highway becoming a mire again. A botanical expedition in 1847 found that the Aroostook road, "being crossed by innumerable swamps and miry bogs, is only passable for vehicles in winter."[211] The road to Madawaska, once it was built, was a permanent problem; in 1849, its condition was such that travelers had to go north into New Brunswick, then south on British roads before reentering Maine at Houlton, much to land agent Cony's shame. "A proper self-respect," he wrote, required that the situation be rectified as soon as possible.[212]

Bridges also had to be cared for, especially from winter snows and spring freshets. An expensive bridge might have been carried away by the ice, driftwood, and logs but for the courage of a team of men "continually breaking the jambs," reported the land agent one year. He found it a constant worry and recommended putting someone in charge of monitoring each bridge during the most dangerous times of year. Good road and bridge construction cost money, but the expense paid for itself four times over, asserted Levi Bradley, still the Maine land agent in 1846.

In 1842, the Public Reserved Lands—until then the responsibility of the land agent—were placed under the supervision of the commissioner of the county where they were situated. As farms and villages penetrated deeper into the unpopulated reaches of the state, Maine's counties had doubled in forty years, with half a dozen new ones hived off from the old to keep pace with the spreading settlements. Every township sold added another thousand acres to be held in trust for the people of Maine; sharing this ever-growing responsibility among the counties, instead of leaving it all to one land agent, seemed to make sense. Doubtless, township proprietors agreed.

By and large, the experiment was not a success, but it did lead inadvertently to the sale of rights to the grass and timber on the Public Lots. After two years of caring for them, the county commissioners discovered that the job was both burdensome and expensive. For example, they were expected to "run out and locate[d]" any lots held in common undivided interest. This cost $100 per township, complained a group from Washington County, of which they had forty. They proposed the legislature defray the cost of this unfunded mandate (in today's parlance) by selling permits to cut the timber on them.

The legislature obliged, and from 1845 county commissioners held public auctions to sell the cutting rights in the Public Reserved Lands on timber townships. In order to protect smaller operators from being outgunned, each permit was for no more than "one six ox team on any one lot in each year." The proceeds were to be spent on the county's schools, with the financial records kept by the commissioners and produced for inspection when requested.

By 1847, after just two years, these records were found to be so scanty that the legislature called for an investigation. Its findings were unambiguous: "not one shows an account current of the receipts and expenses arising from its management of these lands." One county used the revenue not for its schools but to build a jail; another was repairing its courthouse. Others were paying one township's expenses with funds generated by another. Not only were the finances a mess. With one authority administering the Public Lots and another the public domain, county and state were in "inevitable collision." Local officials engaged in locating reserved lots clashed with loggers with lawful permits from the state. For most of the investigating committee there was a "peculiar fitness" between the land agent and the Public Lots. A minority, however, favored the county commissioners, and Governor John W. Dana had to compromise by appointing a land agent for the Public Lots in each county.[213]

In 1850, after five years of county management, care and custody of the Public Lots was finally returned to the state land agent. On the Public Lots, many had no pine left, and some had "but little timber of any kind." Harvesting permits had been granted indiscriminately, and trespass had flourished, rued land agent Anson Morrill.[214] As a result, it now cost nearly as much to "look after one of these reserves, as would a township." From then on, revenue from the Public Lots would accrue in a school endowment fund against the day it might be claimed by the "authorities provided by law to receive the same when they shall hereafter exist," that is, the new plantation.[215] "This act," wrote Lee Schepps some 120 years later, "established the basic framework within which the State has administered the Public Lots in the unincorporated areas, and the income therefrom, since 1850."

"When money is scarce and cash payments required, the sales may be expected to be very limited," wrote Levi Bradley the year the Webster-Ashburton Treaty was signed. "Whoever chooses to buy at such times, will find very little competition."

The year before, 1841, a shipping magnate from Massachusetts, David Pingree, dipped his toe into the Maine lumber market with a modest purchase of forestland around Rangeley Lake. From this humble beginning emerged the first of those enormous ownerships that still dominated Maine's north woods when his descendant (by marriage) and president of Pingree Associates, Brad Wellman, signed on as a plaintiff in the suit over the Schepps report 132 years later. Known as the "Merchant Prince of Salem," David Pingree had seen the overseas commerce that made him a millionaire reach its peak. Now, he was looking for a fruitful vehicle in which to invest his wealth. In Maine, land and timber values were slowly making a comeback after the crash of 1836–1837. Perhaps the forest would offer a new arena for his commercial exercise. Pingree and his partners were soon major operators at every link in the process, from tree trunk to market.

As a maritime merchant, Pingree was familiar with the concept of common undivided ownership. Investing in a wooden ship and its cargo sailing all over the world was akin to putting all one's eggs in a single basket. Joining with other owners and holding the equivalent in shares of several ships spread the comparatively high risk around. In Maine's largely undivided northern lands, buying "unlocated" fractions of townships, either from the state or from other landowners, provided similar insurance, albeit against fire, especially, rather than shipwreck. Brad Wellman said that "people in Bangor would meet on the street corner, and say, I'll put in so much, you put in so much, and we'll get somebody else too." One deed for timber and grass on a Public Lot, dated December 4, 1850, had the following inserted: "viz. Three fourths of said timber and grass on said reserved lots to said [David] Pingree one fifth of same to said [John] Winn and the remaining one twentieth of said timber and grass to said [Eben S.] Coe."

Nine years before, Eben Smith Coe had been a young engineer dissatisfied with the direction his career was taking. His father sent him to see Pingree, who at once hired him to survey his new land purchase in Maine. Coe urged his boss to buy more, and he did. "The cooperation of all the very individual personalities involved was extraordinary," wrote Richard Wheatland—another Pingree descendant—attributing much of the remarkable rise of Pingree's forest empire to the people he worked with.[216] E. S. Coe was the first and most important of these. The young man had just the skills and education—and, most of all, a love of the woods—to develop a confident sense for the land.

An acute man of business in his own right, Coe was Pingree's right-hand man and partner almost from the start. Between the two of them, they soon had interests in eleven townships around the Allagash River in northern Maine. For the next fifty years, E. S. Coe made constant treks from his office in Bangor into the woods, overseeing the "jobbers" he had hired and "checking and scaling" the cut trees. He was, in today's term, a hands-on manager. Pingree remained in Salem. Their voluminous correspondence, housed in the Phillips Library at the Peabody Essex Museum, occupies 193.5 linear feet.

One of Coe's first tasks was to build a farm to provide food and fodder for their lumber camps in the north. Towards the end of summer 1844, Pingree purchased a township, T7R12, on the shores of Chamberlain Lake. The next year, Coe started to clear it and plant a tract for a farm that would eventually cover six hundred acres. In its heyday, Chamberlain Farm employed "the year round, some six or eight men, a jolly and good-natured set.[217] Woman's society is seldom or never vouchsafed them, and they are catered to by a man-cook."[218]

Pingree's new township was on the divide between the Allagash and the Penobscot watersheds. Logs rafted in Chamberlain Lake, however, flowed into the St. John and thence to the Canadian market. He and Coe needed to find a way to get their lumber to Bangor, instead. Remains of a dam gave evidence that they were not the first to recognize this problem and try to deal with it. In 1839, a woodsman with some engineering skills, Shepard Boody, told the owners of T7R12 that he could raise the level of Chamberlain Lake eleven feet, high enough to make it flow "backward" into the Penobscot watershed. A dam across the lake's mouth would back water up into the adjacent Telos Lake. Telos naturally drained into the Allagash as well, but the dam would put enough water into Telos to flow into Webster Lake, less than a mile away, which drained into the East Branch of the Penobscot. The terrain between Telos and Webster—"A ravine, according to geologists the natural bed of a stream which in antediluvian times connected these two lakes"[219]—formed a natural sluiceway that only needed a short canal to reach it. A second dam at the "new" mouth of Telos could regulate the flow for the lumber drivers.

Boody was hired to build both dams, and in 1841, trees from the Allagash flowed through the Telos Cut, headed for Bangor for the first time. The next year, eight million board feet of pine went down the Penobscot instead of the Allagash. For a few years, a priceless link in the log-driving chain was switched to serve American, not Canadian interests. However, Bangor's new wood basket was only as good as the dam on Chamberlain Lake. It soon fell apart, as did a replacement. Nature took back its course, until David Pingree bought T7R12, and E. S. Coe hired Shepard Boody to rebuild his dam to more lasting specifications.

Pingree had had the chance to purchase the neighboring township, T6R11, as well, but with uncharacteristic lack of foresight he let it go, even though it included the second dam, on Telos Lake. He probably reckoned that the Telos dam would be useless without his Chamberlain dam, and that would be enough for him to keep control of it. He was mistaken. T6R11 was bought by Rufus Dwinel, one of the first and largest lumber barons of Bangor. Enter another "individual personality," although in this case, cooperation was conspicuously missing. Dwinel at once established a toll for using the Telos Canal. Pingree declared his fees were exorbitant, at which Dwinel upped them to fifty cents per one hundred thousand board feet of lumber and posted a posse of armed thugs at the dam as enforcers. Finding themselves outnumbered, Pingree's "jobbers" had to pay.[220] So began and ended the so-called Telos War.

That Eben Coe had just rebuilt Chamberlain dam at some expense made defeat on the field all the more insufferable. Pingree appealed to the legislature, which came down on his side: Dwinel must halve his toll, or they would give his rival a charter to operate the Telos Canal for free. Dwinel chose the former option, reluctantly. His testimony dripped with the withering sarcasm of the born-and-bred Mainer for one "from away":

> This poor man Pingree, worth only one and a half or two millions of dollars, owner of only twenty-five Townships of the best timberland in Maine, on which his agents think he will make half a million dollars or more, is afraid I shall make or receive half a dollar per thousand on timber growing on five townships of his land.[221]

Dwinel's reputation for cussedness lived on in a local legend, according to which his will stipulated that his much younger wife should receive not a cent, once he rested "under the earth." However, his Merry Widow had the last laugh, interring him in the impressive sarcophagus that stands *above* the earth on four stout granite columns in Bangor's cemetery.[222] The unusual monument is the only factual part of the story. Dwinel never married; but he was one tough customer.

The fruit of the lumberjacks' winter labor—filling, sometimes clogging, the rivers on the drive—was an ungainly monster. Not only did it require skillful taming as it flowed on the spring freshet, but logs cut by one company had to be separated from those of another. To do this, the woodsmen organized cooperative enterprises such as the Penobscot Log Driving Company, founded in 1846. The drivers themselves became an elite group, known for their log-driving skill across the nation. So much so that the need for their services in the west constituted a serious form of "brain drain," or rather brawn drain from the state. The description by Robert E. Pike, paying tribute to the most famous of the river drivers, John Ross, cannot be bettered. Ross, he wrote, took

> a piebald lot of Old Town Indians, Canucks, Province men, Irish, and native Yankees and welded them into a body of log-driving bear-cats whose skill with pike-pole and peavey, with calked boot and driving bateau, has never been surpassed.[223]

Before being delivered to the men and machines waiting to turn it into boards, the monster had first to be penned lest it overwhelm them. Booms—heavy logs linked together with chains and moored to artificial islets in the river—would be strung out to corral and feed it to the sawmills, in as orderly a fashion as possible. Positioned just upstream of the mills, these booms offered handsome monopolistic advantages to the entrepreneur.

General Samuel Veazie, a veteran of the 1812 war, discovered such an opportunity, creating a boom on the Androscoggin River. In Bangor, Rufus Dwinel was doing the same thing. When Veazie moved to Bangor, he bought the Penobscot boom from Dwinel. Veazie also purchased over fifty sawmills in the Bangor area, making money every board foot of the way. Eventually, his interests stretched away from the river towards railroads and banks, and in 1847 General Veazie sold the Penobscot boom to David Pingree.

Pingree's other local investments added up: a number of dams, a chain of mills, and the Katahdin Iron Works—Moses Greenleaf's "place of very fine paint." This last almost bankrupted him. Founded in 1841 as the Maine Iron Company, it seemed a good investment, with the surrounding forest to provide limitless charcoal for smelting. Pingree bought it in 1845. The deed included the entire township (T6R9) and all the buildings of what was already a company town. A year later, the legislature authorized the Katahdin Iron Works to construct a canal or railroad to Bangor—just as Greenleaf had tried to do—to get its iron to market. Once again nothing came of it.

Instead Pingree built a road north to Chamberlain Lake. Teamsters packing supplies into the farm could pick up iron at the Iron Works on their return as "ballast," rather like the Canton ware the Merchant Prince might have loaded on his ships returning from China. When the price of pig iron dropped, he built a more advanced refinery, but his iron still came up short in quality. Finally, in 1858, the Iron Works stopped producing altogether though Pingree held on to it in hopes that the price of iron would rise. It did, as the Civil

War ground on, but by that time, David Pingree was dead and Katahdin Iron Works sold.

Before his death in 1863, Pingree had acquired over a million acres of Maine forestland. By 1907, his son had added a half million more. David Jr. made a rule of "never selling, but always buying more and more." The "destiny of northern Maine's vast woodlands," writes Maine historian Richard Judd, was determined in large part by the Pingrees, father and son.

For some twenty years, Massachusetts and its offspring state had managed to sustain most of the harmony promised at Governor William King's inaugural. That the friction anticipated before separation was held in check owed much to the camaraderie between the land agents, who bore the hardships of the wilderness together. The "usual liberality" of the Commonwealth's long-standing representative in the woods, George Coffin, was praised more than once by his counterparts Down East. Should the Massachusetts legislature adjourn without appropriating its share of funds for something, Coffin was on hand to get it done as soon as possible. On the other hand, during the run-up to the Aroostook War, Coffin sold cutting rights to Canadian woodsmen in the disputed territory, undercutting the Maine land agent's authority. Any trespassers he apprehended could claim to have a permit from Massachusetts.

The summer the Webster-Ashburton Treaty was signed, the hazard of the checkerboard pattern by which the two states had divided the wildlands became clear when Coffin put timber on sixteen townships up for sale. Each one of them abutted four Maine townships, a six-mile temptation north, south, east, and west for the lumber operator to trespass. Levi Bradley, the Maine land agent, suddenly had "nearly four hundred miles of exterior lines to look after." His choice was either considerable extra expense to protect the timber, or "considerable risk of losing it." The checkerboard effect had an equally frustrating impact on Maine's efforts to market the best farming lands. Bradley offered to trade or buy all the townships Massachusetts owned in the settling area, but the asking price was "much more than they are worth." His successor, Anson Morrill, tried to consolidate them, to prevent them from obstructing development of Maine's best settling lands and to provide a "better enjoyment of the improvements we are making"—incidentally foreshadowing the officials who were his heirs in the 1982 consolidation of the Public Lots.

As the 1840s progressed, relations between the two states were marred still further by their diverging interests. Maine saw its settling lands as an investment that would pay off when they would, "sooner or later, be settled by a population of valuable citizens" paying taxes.[224] Massachusetts had little interest in "selling the soil"; it wanted immediate income from timber growing and regrowing on the same plot of land. Resentment burst out when Massachusetts refused to share the costs of roads and bridges, on which Maine was appropriating and spending large sums of money. At one time, it had contributed "somewhat liberally," and in Bradley's day, he would have been confident that George Coffin could convince the Commonwealth to "continue to do justice to herself and to us." Eight years later, and agent Morrill protested that Massachusetts had contributed "not one dollar," even though it had as much to gain as Maine did. With the policies of the two states so "widely and entirely different," was the Commonwealth waiting for Maine's solo improvement effort to increase the value of its lands before selling them? "It may with much force be asked," wrote the exasperated Morrill, "would it be honorable—would it be generous in Massachusetts to adopt such a course?" The reviewer of Greenleaf's *Statistical View* in 1816 turned out to be prescient after all:

> [T]he townships held by each state must unavoidably be unconnected and lie in promiscuous disorder among each other. It will be impossible for either government, therefore, to do much, by way of improvement, without the consent and cooperation of the other. Is it very probable that the legislative bodies of the respective states will agree as to the manner in which improvements may be made, the measures to be taken and the sums to be laid out?

Governor John Hubbard took up the cry of the state's "able and faithful land agent."[225] Calling on the legislature "to guard sedulously and defend sternly our own rights," he regretted to have to say it, but

> Massachusetts, reaping, as she is, a rich harvest from our soil, under conventional rights, is not in my judgment, pursuing that just and liberal policy towards us . . . , which is due from one state to a sister state.[226]

Under terms of the separation agreement, Massachusetts' share of the land could not be taxed by Maine.[227] Selling timber rights on long leases, therefore, indefinitely postponed the day when Maine could collect. Even when a township was sold, it did not owe taxes to Maine until "the last dollar of the last payment is made." Governor Hubbard was probably justified in thinking that in some cases Massachusetts was purposely delaying that day by allowing the purchaser to withhold a few dollars from the final payment. He was as disappointed as his land agent at this egregious lack of fair play. Massachusetts had made some $2,000,000 off its holdings in Maine; it could "well afford to be generous in the future management of these lands, and throw them open for settlement." If it continued to behave so ungenerously, Governor Hubbard warned, the legislators would have to take steps. They could levy a tax on what he called these "recusant lands," or on timber "as personal property, after it is separated from the soil."

The squabble came to a head in 1851 when Massachusetts instructed its land agent to sell timber harvesting permits only, and "in no case, to sell and convey the soil."[228] As a result, lands owned jointly by the two states, which were almost all timberlands—"almost the only [lands] that have a cash value," Governor Hubbard thought—were off the market for Maine as well. With no legal authority to sell them, Anson Morrill turned to the legislature, which gave Massachusetts two weeks to work out a solution before it took action. The more diplomatic Hubbard was appalled at this ultimatum. It was no way to treat "a *sister State*." It disturbed him that the legislators had focused on the settling lands to the virtual exclusion of the timberlands, which were particularly vital to the "application of our industrial energies, and to our financial resources." And he was aggrieved personally that they had usurped a "subject of absorbing interest" to him, one that he had "bestowed not a little thought and labor on."

Although not impressed with Governor Hubbard's objections, the legislators authorized him, on April 3, 1852, to do anything he deemed "expedient." He wasted no time in sending Morrill and John A. Poor (now immersed in his final and most ambitious railroad scheme) to Boston to negotiate. After hearing their arguments, the General Court's public lands committee delivered a report "not very complimentary at least, to Maine." It then recommended that the Commonwealth wash its hands of the whole thing and sell all its lands in Maine to "some individual or corporation upon liberal terms." Managing land in the back of beyond was expensive what with maintaining bridges and roads, to say nothing of timber trespass. A well-timbered acre might be worth $2; otherwise it was less than half that. Why hold out for settlers? The committee posted an advertisement for the sale, among other things offering tax exemption for twenty-one years. The deadline for sealed proposals was December 20, 1852.

Hubbard had little choice but to take action himself. Aware that he was going out on a limb, he pitched it strong to his legislators. What would happen if all the land owned by Massachusetts was purchased by "private speculators," he demanded. Did the lawmakers think that out-of-state capitalists who could meet exorbitant Massachusetts land prices expected to make their investment back "by any fair business process"? Was it not obvious that these people sought to control government policy "for their own emolument"? They were going back to the discredited bad old days of the great proprietorships, Hubbard warned. In fact, it was an even "more odious form" of ownership; at least the proprietors of old had intended to settle the wilderness. These latter-day speculators just wanted "to realize the greatest possible amount from the timber without regard to other considerations." These men deliberately discouraged, even prohibited, farmers from settling. "In their eagerness to possess the land," Anson Morrill testified, large landowners "had 'elbowed out' a very worthy though less fortunate class of men," forcing further afield "that energy so essential to the prosperity of the timber interests of Maine."

Massachusetts' permitting practices, the governor went on, had allowed speculators to gain control of perhaps a third of Maine's public domain, its most valuable timberlands included.[229] These lands should be managed to benefit Maine citizens, who would maintain the resource with "prudent husbandry." Hubbard, a good Democrat, sounded positively socialist as he railed of workers' wages "reduced to the lowest practicable pittance."

> Capital or credit controls him that toils and imposes its own condition—the right of all to participate in the free gifts of the soil is monopolized by the few—the humble but enterprising are disheartened, and men of this class are fast leaving us for regions where greater inducements are presented.

As for the idea that timberland was "utterly worthless for agricultural purposes," it was nonsense, "a most palpable misrepresentation!" Timber and settling interests should complement each other. "Like the rest of our State these two descriptions of land are so intermingled and arranged as to render their interest one and inseparable," Governor Hubbard advised the legislature.

To his Massachusetts counterpart, George Boutwell, Hubbard added a dire forecast:

> [If] your lands are sold to individuals, gloomy indeed is our prospect for future growth in population. . . . Maine may despair of [her lands] being occupied by farmers; for the proprietary interests in lumber are well known in practice to be adverse to settlers; and if perchance, when the timber is removed, there should be any value left, any inducement offered for farming purposes, that value will be used for the benefit of the proprietor, and to the oppression of the cultivator of the soil.

Negotiations dragged on from April to December 1852, but on Christmas Eve, Governor Boutwell tendered an offer, and agents Poor and Morrill accepted it immediately. It was less than the private offers, but certainly more than Maine had hoped to pay. In 1821, the Commonwealth had offered eight million acres for less than $200,000, or about four cents an acre. Thirty years later, Maine paid Massachusetts nearly twice as much money, $362,500, for a mere 15 percent as much land: 1,200,000 acres at thirty cents an acre, payable in annual instalments until 1872.

Nevertheless, the legislature approved it "with a vote nearly unanimous."[230] It secured "the most amicable relations between Maine and Massachusetts forever," gushed Morrill and Poor. The chairman of Maine's special legislative committee, Josiah Titcomb, was more circumspect. At last having control of its lands, regulated by its own laws, Maine could put away forever an issue that "has caused no little annoyance and vexation during the whole period of our existence as an independent state."

That was perhaps overoptimistic. Many tracts on which the Massachusetts land agent had sold timber rights before 1853 had yet to be cut. These permits were still valid, many held by nonresidents who treated the lands as if they owned them at the same time as they claimed tax exemption. They also continued to be hostile to attempts to cultivate the soil. Untangling such situations took considerable tenacity, diplomacy, and time on the Maine land agent's part. (About half of Maine's public lands were compromised by permits, grants, and sales, inadvertently overlaid on each other over the years.) He usually gave these lumbermen a season to harvest their wood after a township was subdivided for settlement.

Starting in 1850, selling grass and timber rights on the Public Reserved Lands until they were all gone was official state policy. Land agent Anson Morrill drew up a standard form to be used in each conveyance.[231] Rights on unlocated lots—those existing as a fraction of the township rather than a surveyed plot—were offered to the proprietor at the same rate he had paid for the rest of it, after a "reasonable deduction for the soil."[232] This seemingly good deal was nonetheless oftentimes ignored by the owners. Isaac R. Clark, the land agent in 1855, was not surprised.[233] So long as the state didn't claim its fraction, the proprietor had no need to purchase what he "annually pocketed" anyway.

The conveyance contract always included the key condition that the timber and grass rights expired when "the said township or tract shall be incorporated or organized for Plantation purposes." A township "organized for plantation purposes" was a kind of proto-town. It enjoyed limited self-government and could be created when the population reached two hundred. A second type of plantation, "organized for election purposes," was mainly a mechanism to allow settlers scattered over a considerable area to exercise their right to vote. Many were transients working in lumber camps. These plantations were somewhat vague, initially covering any number of townships, but after 1859 limited to just one.

Legislative documents did not always keep up with these distinctions. The Revised Laws of 1857 made no mention of plantations for election purposes; did that mean that when such a plantation was organized, the proprietor continued to own the timber and grass rights? The land agent in 1869 appealed for legal guidance, and the attorney general threw his hands metaphorically in the air. This area of law, he confessed, was "entirely unknown" to him.

"There are townships unincorporated, townships organized into plantations and townships organized with plantations for election purposes." They were all provided for under different parts of the legal code, and he would "sooner rely" on the land agent's judgment than his own.

It took a decision by Maine's Supreme Judicial Court after several proprietors sued land agent Parker Burleigh who had "seized the logs in behalf of the State . . . as trespass timber."[234] The justices had to admit that over the years the law's interpretation of what was a plantation had varied, "according, it would seem, as the influence or interests of the settlers, or of the lumbermen controlled the action of the legislature."[235] Cutting through the politics, in 1871, they declared that a plantation of whatever kind was a plantation, but by then the legislature had abolished plantations for election purposes. Rights to timber and grass would be extinguished only upon the incorporation of a township into a town. Regardless, the land agent continued to use the old conveyance form, which referred to "organization" as well as "incorporation." Throughout the middle decades of the century, a policy to deal with the grass and timber growing on the Public Lots was a work in progress. Many jumps and starts sowed a crop of contradictions for lawyers to debate a century later.

Looking back on the previous decade in his address to the legislature in 1860, Governor Lot M. Morrill (land agent Anson's younger brother) characterized it as a period of "vague apprehension" that times had been better. Despite unsurpassed natural endowments, Maine had made "but slow advances in population and wealth"—a change from the days when it grew at the national average and "far beyond the other New England States."[236] Instead, gains in population, agriculture, the lumber trade, and fisheries had given way to a "comparative decrease" in population, with "larger increase in commerce, navigation, manufactures and mechanic arts, and in works of internal improvement."[237] Governor Morrill chalked up the disappointing 1850s not to Maine's deficiencies but to the perception that "real or supposed attractions elsewhere have been stronger."

Events beyond Maine's borders undoubtedly helped shaped this retrenchment. The discovery of gold in California in 1849 added a decisive edge to the perennial lure of the American West. In 1857, the world endured its first international economic crisis, an event that influenced the thinking of Karl Marx. A third calamity—the outbreak of the Civil War—marked a decisive end to the 1850s. At the start of the decade, however, all had been optimism. The sale of over a million acres in 1850 netted $150,711.60 for Maine's treasury, although, warned Governor Hubbard, they were the state's "very best timber lands," and nothing like it could be expected in the future.[238]

In the settling lands, too, "better days are dawning," wrote Anson Morrill. Enviable harvests the past two years suggested that "seasons of productiveness" had returned. He was referring in particular to the Aroostook country whose rich soils had for so long occupied a special niche in the pantheon dedicated to Maine's future by land agents and governors alike. In addressing the legislature for the first time as governor in 1850, John Hubbard employed the usual superlatives regarding the public domain. It was of "paramount importance" from every point of view, "political, pecuniary and industrial." To the familiar list of blessings found in Aroostook, he added that its latitude and climate were the same as "the most populous portion of bread-growing Europe." The lost lumber camp market would soon return, he assured the lawmakers; and the pest "is now passing away" so that crop failures would soon be a thing of the past.

Would-be settlers, however, had little in the way of cash to take advantage of the turnaround, despite the state's "liberal" terms. Even a small down payment of cash was likely too much for "that class of our fellow citizens who would be most likely to occupy these lands," Governor Hubbard feared. With the lure of emigration so strong, Maine must do everything it could to keep "our people" at home. "It is a common remark," he continued, "that it would be better for us to give away our lands, than to suffer them to remain unoccupied. Would it not be well to make the experiment?"

From then on, a bona fide settler could purchase up to two hundred acres of public land for fifty cents an acre, all of it payable over three years with labor on the township's roads. After that, he had two years to make the lot his residence, and a further four to build a "comfortable dwelling house." By that time he should also have cleared fifteen acres, ten of them "well laid down to grass." Morrill and Hubbard waxed enthusiastic about the promise of this new liberality for the future. It was "judicious and wise." The governor extolled upon "the fostering care of government and the toil of a hardy yeomanry." Once they thought about it, wrote Morrill, "our young men" would see how much better off they were in Maine. The climate out West was unhealthy, and the society "not that of New England, but a promiscuous community of adventurers and strangers, congregated from different nations." Even so, the influx of homesteaders was regrettably slow throughout the first half of the 1850s. That, and the Western competition on which it was blamed, were leitmotifs that flowed out of both Land Office and Governor's Mansion throughout the decade.

Though it did little to encourage farmers to head for Maine's settling lands, the gold pouring out of California made the early 1850s prosperous years for the nation as a whole, and lumber operators made the most of the boom. Encouraged by that liberal policy Governor Hubbard so deplored, they purchased all the timber and land they could get their hands on. Maine's "true policy," land agent Morrill allowed (without any of the customary "if-I-mays" of a land agent reporting to a governor), should be to sell the timberlands until they were all in private hands. Much of the 1,200,000 acres just added to the public domain from Massachusetts was distant timberland where nothing, not even "utmost vigilance," could keep the trespassers out. Privately owned, it would be less prone to thievery, Morrill argued. The "disposition, or, I might say, determination" to trespass was far less on land owned by individuals than on land owned by the state.

On the settling townships conveyed by the Commonwealth, the land agent continued with his predecessors' recommendations. Many held timber of considerable value, which was going to get cut, legally or not. Morrill recommended that he sell permits to harvest it, being sure to leave enough for settlers—whenever they arrived—to build their farms. As another argument, he pointed out that land and timber sales would help defray the state's cost of purchasing the land. Altogether, Anson Morrill saw a bright future based on the symbiosis of lumbering operations and settlements in the "vast" forests of the Allagash and St. John. Settlers who "desire to labor during the winter season" could become woodcutters; woodcutting operations needed locally produced supplies. With such a liberal and dependable flow of cash, any new settlement would be uncommonly lucky.

Then the flow of gold began to dwindle. Speculators found themselves "in years of unusual severity and depression" struggling to pay back the debts they had taken on during the boom times. The situation "deranged all calculations" of their profits, wrote Isaac Clark in 1855. The legislature had no choice but to extend the terms of payment, which straitened the Land Office's circumstances. However, the land agent was optimistic. Timber was where the value was, and timber was still growing. It would still be there when prosperity returned, ready to be harvested and pay every debt with interest.

Before that could happen, however, a national boom in railroad stocks collapsed and, combined with simultaneous events in England, became the Panic of 1857. Not only did respectable financial institutions fail. The crisis "touched the springs of labor, paralyzed the activities of ordinary pursuits, and leaving thousands of our fellow men . . . without employment and the means of support," lamented Anson's brother, Governor Lot Morrill.[239] It was, he sniffed, an "anomalous spectacle of want and distress in a nation blessed with unexampled general prosperity, and wholly free from any great public calamity."[240]

Governor Morrill's view was that this, too, would pass (and, indeed, come round again). He rejoiced in his estimate that there would still be two million acres of public domain—three-quarters of it settling lands—when the economy revived. The timber on the remainder would generate enough revenue, the governor hoped, "under a judicious system of annual permits and occasional sales," to pay off the public debt. He was confident that its vast forest would see Maine through, providing "lucrative employment" as well as a major commodity for export. The legislature must continue to prime the pump of settlement—"in a spirit of enlightened liberality," even in these parlous times—with better roads. Nothing would encourage northward migration more quickly than improving the highways. For years, they had been built and repaired, directed by a legislative resolve here, dealing with an emergency there, now and then furthering a land agent's priority. Results of this scattershot approach were all too apparent. Fund the "great thorough-fares" and make them first rate, the land agent, George Getchell, had advised in 1855.[241] Byroads could be left to the settlers; they would "speedily and cheerfully" complete them.

In 1860, a good portion of land agent B. W. Norris's report was devoted to congratulation and celebration.[242] In the last three years, the population of Aroostook had increased to the extent that it had nearly doubled since 1850—from 12,533 to 22,489. Norris credited his predecessor, Noah Barker.[243] In 1858, Barker had compiled all the information he could find on the "quality, situation, and extent of our 'settling lands'"—information on soil, climate, transportation, markets, and so forth—into a *Circular*, which he had distributed to the "laboring classes," the people he thought would gain most from it. "While the increase in population is thus gratifying in *quantity*," wrote Norris, "a still larger field of congratulation is found in the *quality* of the people who are settling there." Nowhere in the country could "a more intelligent and enterprising class of men" be found. Nowhere were they more equal to the pioneer life or more able "to establish the institutions, which are at once the distinguishing mark and the ornament of a New England community." His panegyric's conclusion exuded confidence.

> The people of Aroostook feel every assurance that their agricultural products will never be without a good market, and that, in this respect, they are far more eligibly located than those who are settled in the distant Northwest.

The date was November 30, 1860. Four and a half months later, General P. G. T. Beauregard attacked Fort Sumter, and the Civil War began.

Migration to the Aroostook country did not dry up immediately. During the first year of the war, enough lots had already been purchased to keep settlers moving in at a rate "fully up to the recent ratio of increase." However, few new tracts were sold, and Norris had to admit that he expected immigration rates to slow again. For the timberlands, the war's impact was immediate. "The prostration of the Lumber trade was so sudden and so

total," wrote the land agent, that he had been unable to collect on the previous year's stumpage. Although the region's progress and development
was suffering the same "delay and depression" as the rest of the country,
Norris tried to maintain that optimism characteristic of land agents. The
harvest was a cause for great satisfaction, in spite of the "calamity having its origin elsewhere." For the duration, his efforts would be directed
toward maintaining roads and bridges and surveying for settlement against
the day when peace should return to the nation.

By the second year, the war was taking its toll. The lumber business was
being deprived of manpower by the army, which drew "largely upon the stalwart men of that county." In Aroostook, land sales were minimal. Not only
was there a war on, but President Lincoln had signed the Homestead Act in
May 1862. One silver lining, Norris noted, was that the remaining settlers had
"mastered their position" and were diversifying their agricultural endeavors
with stock-raising, to considerable success.

The year 1863 brought a sudden surge of interest in the settling lands,
all the more surprising because the army continued to drain northern Maine
of young men to fight in the war. B. W. Norris had moved on to become
a paymaster in the Union Army.[244] The new land agent, Hiram Chapman,
ascribed the change to a number of familiar factors: the growing reputation
of Aroostook's rich soil and healthy climate, as well as the improving lines
of communication and increasing number of mills. He also credited popular
confidence that "ere long the advantages of railroad communication" would
reach the area. There was also the cheapness of the land thanks to the state's
liberal settling policy.[245] This "excellent homestead feature" particularly
makes the settler feel secure—here Chapman grew lyrical—leading him to
"improve his lands and buildings, to ornament his grounds with trees and
shrubs, and his garden with flowers." The same sense of security, he noted
sententiously, did "much to allay that uneasiness and desire to change places
and business which is the bane of American society."

In a bid for a pay raise, Chapman spelled out his responsibilities, which
gave an indication of how the land agent's duties had grown over the years.
Ever more roads and bridges had to be maintained; the forests under his care
were "now mostly on remote waters"; and always he had to fight against
timber trespassers. In the settling lands, forty townships were now open for
sale, and he was supervising thirty-five local agents. In Bangor, he noted,
the Land Office was open from "the adjournment of the Legislature until it
meets again."[246]

Whatever had caused the uptick in settlement petered out the next year.
Aroostook County continued to answer the call of the national armies, a grim
Isaac Clark informed Governor Samuel Cony (himself a former land agent).

"And while no murmurings have been heard in the performance of this patriotic duty," he feared a backlash would soon be inevitable. Clark, who had
been land agent in 1855, was at his old post once again after Chapman fell ill
and was "removed from his earthly labors."

Although land sales had been negligible, throughout the war the legislature
continued to grant lands or the timber on them in support of educational institutions, although the results could be disappointing. In 1864, five academies
shared the timber on one township that was "supposed to be as valuable as
any belonging to the state." Two years later, with the war over, it was still
unsold; the land agent had been unable to get a price "sufficient to meet the
charges on it." Evidently, the legislators had "exaggerated opinions" of land
values, observed Governor Cony ruefully. "The general enhancement of
prices has not affected that of timber lands, thus far."

With the coming of peace, Maine's leaders had to reckon once again with
the fate of the public domain, of which the best guess was that some 950,000
acres remained. In his first postwar address, Cony made it plain that Maine's
leaders were eager to be rid of the public lands and let someone else have the
task of settling them. They would, he said, continue to diminish, especially
if the European and North American Railway Company "shall so far comply
with the conditions of the contingent grant made to it, as to secure it absolutely." The grant in question was almost 750,000 acres of public land.

Ever since Elijah Hamlin's rousing plea, hopes for rapid settlement of
the wildlands had become linked more and more with dreams of a railroad
system. In 1858, the legislature considered "An act to aid the Aroostook
Railroad Company, increase the value, and promote the sale and settlement
of the public lands." The railroad, connecting Bangor with Aroostook, was
an enterprise driven by Moses Greenleaf's nephew, John A. Poor. His uncle's
dream of a railway between Monson and Bangor was just the beginning of
Poor's obsession with the railroad.[247] Three years later, on the eve of the war,
the legislature voted to sell all the unencumbered public lands in Aroostook
and Penobscot counties (in fact, most of Maine's remaining public domain)
for the benefit of the Aroostook Railroad.

Anything that led to the "rapid and profitable sale" of the public lands was
every land agent's dream. The "conceded influence" that a railroad would
have in increasing their value made notice of the vote "an appropriate feature
of my report," wrote B. W. Norris. The Civil War had intervened, but he
was confident so beneficial an enterprise, though it might "from great public
misfortunes, suffer postponement," would in the end "overcome all obstacles
and be accomplished." Norris continued to make frequent reference to the
legislature's "very favorable and liberal grant" of the public lands. The grant,

however, was contingent on the financial participation of Bangor. It lapsed in 1862 when that city voted down the loan as too risky.

With the Aroostook Railroad defunct, John Poor turned his energies toward switching the grant of public lands to the European and North American Railway, for which he had procured a charter in 1850, while still promoting the Aroostook Railroad.[248] In 1865, he petitioned the Massachusetts legislature to discharge the remaining debt for the public lands purchased by Maine in 1853; Maine's legislators would then transfer them to his new railroad. Compensation was also sought from the federal government for lands given up in the Webster-Ashburton Treaty and for claims dating back to the 1812 war. All would be put at the disposal of Poor's railroad company. Construction began in 1867.

In 1868, Governor Joshua Chamberlain, the hero of Gettysburg and an avowed railroad enthusiast, signed the law giving all the remaining public lands, 734,942 acres, to the European and North American Railway.[249] That these were mostly in Aroostook, which the route (from Bangor to Vanceboro on the Canadian border) scarcely touched, stirred great local resentment. The grant of "certain lands to aid the construction" of the railroad was also causing prospective settlers a "degree of alarm," wrote land agent Parker Burleigh, despite the fact that its framers had made clear that settler interests—or rather the state's interest in settling the land—were "paramount." The legislature stipulated that the railway must sell its designated settling lands to actual settlers only; and it must mount an advertising campaign and employ an agent to encourage immigration. Curbing the railroad's heavy-handed dealings with people already on the land took a number of lawsuits by lumber operators and settlers alike.

In October 1871, the European and North American Railroad reached Vanceboro and linked up with the Canadian line to St. John. John Poor had died the month before, but President Ulysses S. Grant and the governor general of Canada led the celebration on the international bridge across the St. Croix River. The Railway's troubles, however, were not over. Nationwide, railroads were the major victim (and partial cause) of the financial Panic of 1873. The European and North American defaulted, having sold less than a third of the lands granted to it. Much of the rest was auctioned off, mainly to lumbering interests, to pay the company's debts.

When he turned over the last of the public domain to the European and North American Railway, Governor Chamberlain had appointed a commission to devise the best means of populating the settling lands, once and for all. Three commissioners set out for Aroostook in October 1869, although for want of a passable road they had to make a detour into New Brunswick. Back in Maine, however, they reported in lyrical terms, "Broad fields smile with abundant harvests on every hand, and huge barns give even surer evidence of the prosperity of the settlers than the neat houses in which they dwell."

The commissioners described a map of the settled areas as resembling a scythe, its handle running along the eastern boundary, and its blade the St. John Valley in the north. Within this "imaginary scythe" was an empty quarter, "larger than the State of Massachusetts, whose virgin soil awaits the real scythe and plow of the settler." Its very emptiness testified to the inadequacy of "spontaneous, un-assisted growth," a policy that had been tried long enough. The time had come for an aggressive program to attract immigrants from abroad.

One of the commissioners had spent the war in a junior consular post in Sweden, and it was to this energetic and well-connected Svenskophile that the commission owed its almost exclusive focus on emigration from that kingdom. In the opinion of William Widgery Thomas, "honest, pious, plodding Swedes" would be a good counterweight to the "fickle, merry, light-hearted Irish" coming to America in ever greater numbers.

"Some great isothermal law," Thomas maintained, led people from the Old World to seek a similar place in the new, and Aroostook's climate would make a Swede feel at home. In fact, its milder and shorter winters would make him feel better off and "keep him contented." Swedish immigrants were already settling in Minnesota and Iowa, following their friends and neighbors. A successful colony in Maine could be seeded by bringing in twenty-five families together. After that, success only needed an agent meeting every steamship from Europe and flagging the road to Aroostook.

In 1870, Thomas personally escorted fifty immigrants across the Atlantic to Aroostook. The commission, which included Parker Burleigh, the land agent, had already recommended a site, T15R3, in the heart of the settling lands—"fertile, well watered, healthy"—with room to expand into neighboring townships. Many of the Scandinavian newcomers found themselves working on John Poor's railroad to fulfill their settling duties. In a few years, the community had increased to six hundred. Thomas turned their care over to land agent Burleigh, who reported that as a result of abundant harvests, "they are in consequence feeling greatly stimulated and happy."[250] In 1876, the township was organized into the plantation of New Sweden.

In 1878, with less than four hundred thousand acres left of its public domain, the Land Office organized a series of auctions, public and private. The timberlands quickly sold, and when settling lands didn't move, the legislature declared them "unfit for settlement," and they were snapped up by lumbermen, as well. Four years earlier, a legislative resolve had tried to abolish the office of land agent. It had to be repealed the next year after it was discovered that the land agent was a constitutional officer and thus beyond the legislature's command.[251] The constitution was then amended, but the position was not actually discontinued. "The time when the office might be permanently discontinued seems never to have arrived," observed Forest Commissioner Neil L. Violette fifty years later.[252]

Parker Burleigh had protested that the legislature made no "specific provision for closing [the Land Office's] business or transferring it to any other department." If the measure was to be reenacted, he wrote, it would be very important "to determine how the want now supplied by that department shall be served in future." He listed his major obligations: the Public Lots, unsold lands, the settlers and settling lands, and the "multifarious duties which a half century of legislation has gradually imposed upon the office to perform."

"Bring all unsettled business to a termination," the legislature insisted. Burleigh was "to turn over to the Governor and Council all records, moneys, and other property of the State to be administered by them until otherwise provided." In 1878, Burleigh's son, Edwin, was wrapping up the final details of the Land Office "as speedily as the public good would allow."[253] He had done everything he could to advertise the remaining settler opportunities, via circulars, the press, and "private correspondence." He had investigated titles, closed outstanding contracts, and completed settling duties. All that remained had been some ten thousand scattered acres, mostly "lands not taken up by settlers in townships appropriated for settlement." They were all sold by the end of the year, "thus leaving the State devoid of all its once rich and extensive landed possessions."

It had taken less than a hundred years, starting when it was a province of Massachusetts, for Maine to dispose of the entirety—some fifteen million acres—of its public domain. Or almost the entirety: there still remained several hundred thousand acres of Public Reserved Land, held in trust for a future that in most cases had become far from clear. In 1891, the legislature passed "An act creating a forest commission and for the protection of forests," which in effect turned the land agent into the forest commissioner. With the Public Lots all that was left of the public domain, his priority shifted from sales and settlement to the health of the entire forest.

Forest Commissioner Austin Wilkins would compile the following specifics in his 1963 report:

Sold by Massachusetts (1783–1853)	6,752,987 acres
Granted by Massachusetts (1783–1853)	1,686,712 acres
Sold by Massachusetts and Maine in common (1820–1853)	1,750,605 acres

Sold by Maine (1820–1878)	3,573,323 acres
Granted by Maine (1820–1878)	1,968,285 acres
Total	**15,731,912 acres**

The land sold by Maine (3,573,323 acres) brought in $2,014,221.66, an average of 56.4 cents an acre. Slightly less than a third of the total land granted by Maine went to the European and North American Railway.

Chapter Five

Trouble Brewing

"A Tremendous Issue Regarded from any Point of View" (1891–1931)

In December 1903, readers of *The Machias Union*, a Down East weekly, heard from a new correspondent, Stephen A. Douglas Smith, a patent plow and harrow salesman. Smith's travels around the state gave him the chance to talk to all the good old boys of Maine's dominant Republican establishment. The party chairman, F. Marion Simpson, was one of those with whom he had been fraternizing, and Smith gleefully reported on his conversation in the *Union*'s pages, his tongue resolutely in his cheek.

On top of all his political duties—lamented Simpson to Smith—he had recently been appointed state assessor. Already being treasurer of the American Realty Company—a subsidiary of International Paper and therefore a major wildland owner—made it an awful "trying" combination, poor Mr. Simpson confided, never more so than when he had to assess the value of a township "just at the time when his company was dickering for it." The stress made F. Marion quite long for the days when he kept a country store; the days, the plow salesman interjected, of "giving fourteen ounces of sugar to the pound and never selling less than thirty-four inches of calico for a yard."

The Machias Union's roving correspondent was actually named William R. Pattangall, until that time an obscure though eloquent state legislator. He had just become the weekly's editor, and his reports from the political trail would make him a statewide figure.[254] "Have you seen Patt's latest?" became as common an utterance in the State House as a comment about the weather, according to Raymond Fellows.[255] By this time, Republicans had been so long in power that Maine was generally considered a one-party state.[256] Pattangall had recently turned Democrat, and writing under the Smith alias, he delighted in skewering the "awful pleasant crowd" of pols he found in Simpson's Bangor office. One of them, Charles Oak, as land agent, forest commissioner, and commissioner of fish and game, was drawing three salaries simultaneously, "Smith" alleged.[257]

A few years later, in *Maine Hall of Fame*, Pattangall put a still blunter spin on F. Marion Simpson's path to the post of state assessor.

> The wild lands of Maine were beginning to enhance in value and the taxation thereof was becoming a vexed question. It was necessary, therefore, that a tried and trusty servant of the ring should be placed upon the board of state assessors. The public need and F. Marion [Simpson]'s needs coincided. He needed the salary. The public needed a state assessor to stand between it and the wild land owners and prevent it from taking the wild land owners' money.[258]

By 1900, many people were regretting Maine's careless disposal of its public lands.

> The State has unwisely parted with all its wild land. It is now largely held by private owners, in immense tracts, often comprising one or more townships. These owners clear no land, and sell no land, thus obstructing its settlement and the making of roads.[259]

Half the state remained unpopulated, while large companies—many controlled from other states—reaped the exclusive rewards of its greatest natural resource, the forest. Across the border, Canada had found a very different way, as an editorial in the *Portland Daily Press* pointed out. The provincial governments were not "squandering [their] heritage"; they retained the land and sold licenses at public auction to cut the timber.[260]

Austin Cary, then an assistant professor of forestry at Harvard, blamed the state government.[261] Its priority had always been luring farmers to the settling lands, while selling the timberlands for cash. "The value of permanent forest," wrote Cary, "was not understood." It was too often considered an administrative headache, to be got rid of. Maine had been "weak against individual interest and push" by powerful landowners, and "through a succession of land agents this great resource was sold at ridiculous figures, practically given away."[262]

With dawning seller's remorse came awareness that the forest was forever changed. The bell started tolling for King Pine in 1845 when, though hardly noticed at the time, the first spruce logs were driven down the Penobscot. As the prized merchantable pine stands became fewer and farther between, lumbermen had to resort to other species: birch, maple, hemlock, and more and more, spruce. The markets that developed during the second half of the nineteenth century ensured that "large, ancient trees" would never again be seen in a Maine forest.[263]

Species that had been worthless when the rights to cut "timber and grass" on the Public Lots were sold were now being harvested, considerably expanding what was included in the term "timber." In a case from 1900, the court interpreted the word to signify wood "suitable for building houses or ships or capable of being squared and cut into beams, rafters, planks and boards" at the time of the conveyance.[264] This definition mainly referred to size. The state brought suit to ascertain whether "beech, maple, birch and other trees, not suitable for any purpose but for fire-wood" counted as timber under existing law. Failing to get a definitive answer from the court, the legislature declared that, as regards rights to the Public Lots, "timber and grass" meant "all growth of every description."[265]

The significance of the transition from pine to spruce was well illustrated in an anecdote told by a nonagenarian attorney to James Elliott Defebaugh, the chronicler of the American lumber industry, at the turn of the century. Back in 1845, he had hired a surveyor to assess a bankrupt estate. Based on the standing pine, the surveyor recommended selling it for a dollar an acre. Was there any other timber, inquired the lawyer. "Oh, yes," said his surveyor, there was so much spruce that if it was all cut down "a man could go all over the town by jumping from one stump to another without ever touching the ground." But it was only a nuisance; the land would be worth more without it. So the estate was sold for a dollar an acre. In 1905, when the attorney related his story, the despised spruce had increased the value of the land four-fold.[266]

Behind this staggering increase was a new commodity that could be extracted from the forest: paper. By the end of the nineteenth century, thanks to scientific inventions in Europe, paper was being produced from wood pulp instead of rags, the basic raw material since the Middle Ages. Spruce, initially harvested for sawlogs, turned out to be especially well suited for making high-quality paper because of the wood's long, strong fibers. Even better, for the forester, the size of the trees used—and therefore the years it took to grow them—was immaterial. A regenerating forest could be harvested for pulp without waiting for the trunks to grow to sawlog size. Lastly, the market for paper had become insatiable. This new industry, however, required capital-intensive construction, facilities, and machinery. New levels of up-front investment were needed. It would take new types of owners and favor even larger patterns of ownership in the forest.

Well into the second half of the nineteenth century, enterprising young men could still put together significant ownerships, lot by lot, and become rich as a result. One of these was J. P. Webber, great-great-grandfather of Charles Cushing, who, almost a century later, signed onto the Public Lots lawsuit with Seven Islands and the paper companies. Webber accumulated almost five hundred thousand acres of forestland. Dr. Cushing, by then a retired dentist, recalled his forebear's tale in the cadence of a born Maine storyteller:

> Right after the Civil War, J. P. Webber ran a wagon from Corinth, Maine to Boston, and he made friends with a merchant in Boston. The merchant in Boston, after some trepidations, allowed him credit and filled his wagon with goods. And J. P. Webber came back to Maine, and he sold his goods, and he took some of his money to get more goods, and some of his money for land. And as he went back and forth to Boston and brought products back to Maine, he made more money, and he bought more land. He bought it from all over. If somebody owned timberlands, he would talk them into selling it. If somebody was selling timberlands, he'd run over to buy it. He felt that land was a commodity that wasn't going to go away, and he kept his eye on it. It was an investment because we're not making any more land.

By 1885, J. P. Webber had moved to Boston, where he was recognized as "unquestionably" the city's leading timberland dealer. "Mr. Webber is an excellent and experienced judge of timber lands, and any blocks of these lands purchased from him will prove of great value," stated the handbook of Boston's leading businessmen that year.[267]

Roger Milliken, president of Baskahegan Company, told a similar tale—"a classic rags to riches story"—about Henry Harrison Putnam of Houlton. Putnam put together what, under Milliken's grandfather, became the core of the company's landholdings. "Putnam used to run the stagecoach between Calais and Houlton," according to Milliken, "and from that seat he knew everything that was going on in that region of the state.[268] There were also rumors that he would sell whiskey at 10 cents a swig to the passengers," he added wryly. Putnam settled in Danforth, the midpoint on his route, and by the time he died in 1921, he owned four sawmills, a gristmill, and a hundred thousand acres.

By common consent, Putnam had sharp elbows. Roger Milliken guessed that he acquired much of his empire by wearing down the previous owners, the Prentiss family of Bangor, who owned the timberland around Danforth. To get their logs to Bangor, the Prentisses counted on the spring freshet on the Baskahegan Stream, and they impounded its headwaters to be sure they had a good run. Putnam, on the other hand, needed the stream's steady flow to power his mills in Danforth.

"So he didn't want all that water to get flushed down in April," said Milliken. "And they had these fights where he would go lower the gates on the dam on Baskahegan Lake to keep the water there to power his mills through the summer; and then the Prentisses would have to send somebody in to open it. So there was this feud going on back and forth, and ultimately you get the impression that the Bangor people just said, 'This guy's too hard to deal with.

We'll just sell him the land.' And so Henry Putnam, starting out with nothing, ended up being a pretty big deal in eastern Maine."

The landholdings accumulated by J. P. Webber and Henry Putnam, like David Pingree and a few other old Maine families, are still intact. Their owners in the 1970s were deeply involved in the court case against the state over the Public Lots. These "nonindustrial" landowners tended to manage their forests for a higher-value product than paper. The larger trend, however, was in the opposite direction.

Asked when the pendulum swung from cutting trees for saw logs to producing pulp and paper, Brad Wellman pinpointed the year quickly and succinctly: "1900. International Paper Company." Between 1900 and 1905, the economic value of the paper industry went from third to *the* "most important single manufacturing pursuit" in Maine. In Wellman's view, paper saved the state. The days of the great pine drives were long gone. The need for timber for shipbuilding had been eclipsed by the arrival of ironclad vessels. The long-log business had not quite vanished, but it was nothing like it had been. Pulp and paper was the future, and the paper companies would forge it.[269]

Even before 1900, "great quantities of softer woods are consumed in the manufacture of paper pulp," wrote a pair of contemporary historians.[270] The first to do so was the newly incorporated S.D. Warren Company, in 1867. Just before the Civil War, the company's founder, Samuel D. Warren, had built a paper mill on the Presumpscot River, at the same falls where Samuel Waldo had established one in 1734. (In Waldo's time, it was in the town of Falmouth; in Warren's and today, it is in Westbrook—named, ironically, after Waldo's partner in the mill enterprise, whom he beggared financially.) Warren started out making paper in the age-old way, but after 1867 more and more wood fiber supplemented the rags of yore.[271] During the next decade, paper mills sprang up all over the southern half of Maine. By the century's turn, thirty of them were either grinding wood into pulp or using a chemical soda or sulfite process. Maine had become the third-largest paper producer in the country.

It was a publisher of tourist guides—their pages brightened by the latest in scenic photographs—who pioneered the model of the integrated industry that came to dominate Maine's wildlands for the next hundred years. Stopping by woods on a snowy evening in 1882, Hugh J. Chisholm sat in his sleigh, awestruck at the sight of a run of waterfalls on the Androscoggin River. What stirred him as much as the natural magnificence were the possibilities it opened to the keen entrepreneur. At Rumford Falls, the river drops 180 feet in a stretch of half a mile. He had already built two paper mills farther downstream, but the water tumbling past him, Chisholm saw, was the largest source of power "east of Niagara."

Acquiring a tract of 1,100 acres—the land "considered necessary to control the falls and give the necessary flowage rights"—took eleven years.[272] Chisholm used the time to mature his plans for "the best possible development." He saw to it that the Portland and Rumford Falls Railroad was extended so that his paper could get to market. His Rumford Falls Power Company dammed the river to make an impoundment above the falls big enough to hold fifteen to twenty million feet of logs. By 1893, the Rumford Falls Paper Company was up and running. Five years later, it became the lynchpin of Chisholm's new company, formed by amalgamating seventeen such mills in northern New England, New York, and Canada: the International Paper Company.

Soon enough a Bangor engineer with local business connections was reproducing Hugh Chisholm's integrated model. The Bangor and Aroostook Railroad—a revived version of the stillborn Aroostook Railroad—had finally made it to Houlton, crossing the west branch of the Penobscot River near the falls and rapids between Quakish Lake and Shad Pond. Unlimited hydropower plus dependable transportation, Charles Mullen saw, made it the ideal situation for a paper mill. He set about purchasing the surrounding land for the plant and a village for his workforce.

The Great Northern Paper Company was incorporated in 1898. To build the company—and to raise the capital for it—Mullen hired an executive, Garret Schenck, away from International Paper. The Millinocket mill began operating in 1900, Schenck himself sawing, barking, and sending the first log into the grinder, according to Maine historian Neil Rolde.[273] It was the world's largest paper mill, every day turning a bit of Maine's forest into 240 tons of newsprint, 120 tons of sulfite pulp, and 240 tons of ground wood pulp.[274]

A year later, the legislature gave Great Northern responsibility for the annual log drive down the Penobscot. It was a fiasco. Many lumbermen lost part or all of their harvest. Great Northern blamed the river's low level of water. Because the company had drawn too much to power its mill, retorted the lumbermen. They filed suit for their "logs being 'negligently and wrongfully' driven."[275] In London, *The World's Paper Trade Review* reported that "plaintiffs seek to recover damages for 1,140,330 feet of logs valued at 17,239.95 dols., which were lost by going to sea."

Despite this, Great Northern was allowed to run the drive again the next year and, in 1903, to set up the West Branch Driving and Reservoir Dam Company, its board loaded with company executives and investors. The legislative hearing for the bill incorporating the company was as charged inside the chamber as it was closely watched from beyond. According to a Bangor newspaper:

> The great fight on the Millinocket bill begins next Tuesday, that is the open fight. The scheme has been talked and talked during the past several weeks by more than a score of lobbyists but it has been done in the quiet of boardinghouse rooms or in out-of-the-way places about the state capital.[276]

The outcome was a victory for Great Northern. The West Branch Driving and Reservoir Dam Company was granted the power of eminent domain to take "all the dams, real estate, piers, booms, wing dams, side dams and steamboats now owned by the Penobscot Log Driving Company," as well as all its "powers, rights and privileges . . . pertaining to the driving of logs and the improving of the West branch of the Penobscot river." In the process, Great Northern had also gained a tight relationship with political power in Augusta and permanent lobbying clout in its halls.

Great Northern's coup was a sign of the times. Cooperation had given way to competition, shared organization to corporate domination. For many, it represented progress. One judge testifying in favor of the "Millinocket bill" had looked into his crystal ball and seen the Penobscot River "not a mere highway for logs but instead a highway between a chain of prosperous manufacturing centers."[277] Three years later, Schenck added the first link in the "chain," the mill in East Millinocket.

Schenck, Mullen, and Chisholm all had that "individual interest and push" of which Austin Cary had written. They had the genius to establish control over the entire process of papermaking, from growing and harvesting the raw material to delivering the finished product. Where they found the resources (wood for pulp, water for power), they bought them up and exploited them. They bent rivers to their wills and controlled their use. They built railroads for transportation. Where a link in the chain was missing, they created it, including whole towns to house their workers.

One after another company town sprouted around its mill like a "magic city in the wilderness."[278] Millinocket is still called "The Magic City." Before 1898, its only settlement was a farmhouse with a barn and a few outbuildings. By 1903, the newly organized town had three thousand people. In Rumford, Hugh Chisholm turned "a sleepy hamlet in a farming community" into a bustling town with streets lit by electricity, water mains, and sewers, not to mention churches, schools, and shops, almost overnight.[279] The rise of Rumford and Millinocket, gushed a reporter, "reads more like romance than reality."[280]

The mill workers who lived in these towns enjoyed one particular perk. They had free access to great swathes of company land for hunting and camping. It was a right bestowed by "our forefathers of the seventh and eighth generations," wrote Austin Cary at the time. As a social contract between workers and the companies, public access to private land became part of the mystique of the Maine woods.[281]

Maine had been attracting visitors come to revel in its wild lands (as opposed to those looking to invest in them) since long before the Civil War. John James Audubon passed through on his way to Labrador in 1833. In Dennysville, he picked up a young man to join his expedition, Thomas Lincoln, General Benjamin Lincoln's grandson. It was he who procured (i.e., shot) the little bird that Audubon would name Lincoln's finch (now Lincoln's sparrow). Thoreau famously made three expeditions to the Maine woods; in 1846 he stopped at the farm that was Millinocket.

In 1853, Frederick Church painted his first picture of Mount Katahdin. Two years later, he canoed down the East Branch of the Penobscot into Katahdin Lake, where some twenty years later he bought land and built a camp. By that time, a hunting trip to the Maine woods was as much a part of a young man's education as trekking in Nepal would be a hundred years later. In 1871, a Harvard undergraduate, Louis Shreve Osborne, wrote a light-hearted poem, possibly commemorating his own experience, which began,

> Riding down from Bangor, on an eastern train
> After weeks of hunting, in the woods of Maine
> Quite extensive whiskers, beard, moustache as well
> Sat a student fellow, tall and slim and swell.[282]

Just as the paper industry was industrializing the forest, the Bangor and Aroostook Railroad was finally fulfilling its backers' dreams of opening up northern Maine.[283] Going one way, BAR trains brought the pulp and paper industry's product out; going the other, they brought "sports" in—as many as possible. A 1911 newspaper article congratulating David Pingree Jr. on becoming the largest landowner in Maine described his lands as a "mysterious forest wilderness" where "hundreds of sportsmen beat its trackless woods every fall"; it was "the best hunting ground in the eastern part of the United States."[284]

Forestland owners were quick to point out how this use of their land was contributing to state coffers. It was one of their "stock arguments," for instance, against increasing taxes on their holdings. The forest was becoming a giant game park for hundreds of thousands of tourists, bringing in millions of dollars to Maine, all without even asking the landowners' permission.[285] What would happen, they asked—"some of them put it in the form of a threat"—if instead of cutting "so as to preserve the forests," they were forced to "make a clean sweep of their woods in order to escape what would amount practically to confiscation?"[286]

Taxation levels became one of the first ways proponents of extractive and nonconsumptive practices squared off against each other. The explorers and sports of the nineteenth century would become the hikers, hunters, and nature lovers of the twentieth. Their numbers would increase exponentially, as would their influence. By the last decade of the twentieth century, one pillar of the argument for conservation of the Maine woods would be the fact that they were within a day's drive of sixty million people.

In 1907, the Chicago journalist and occasional poet Frank Putnam spent a month in Maine on assignment for *New England Magazine*. His editor wanted a series of articles on "What's Wrong with New England?" After talking to people all over Maine, from Governor William T. Cobb on down, Putnam answered the question with his title: "Maine: A Study in Land-Grabbing, Tax-Dodging and Isolation." Putnam diagnosed ten problems that kept Maine stagnating, despite possessing "natural resources surpassed by those of few American States." Four in particular prevented the state from benefiting from the northern lands as it should. The first problem was the state of the forest: "hundreds of unorganized and practically unpopulated townships" owned by "six hundred individuals, firms, and corporations," paying minimal taxes: a mere three mills on a valuation of $90,000, which should have been twice or even three times higher.

Those six hundred owners—together with the railroad moguls and manufacturers—had a stranglehold over the government, which kept their taxes low even as their profits went out of state. Equally culpable was the political order itself, concealing its "land-grabbing, tax-dodging, tariff wall-building operations" behind the smokescreen of prohibition.[287] Finally, the press, controlled by this unholy alliance, was letting them get away with it. Though many other things shocked Putnam—the paucity of public education, the abuse of child labor, the lax corporate laws that made Maine a haven for disreputable out-of-state companies (a "Queer Business for a State to Engage In")—he saved his particular outrage for the wildland owners and politicians.

> I should require, not a month, but a year, and should need to be, not a reporter, but a detective, in order to trace in detail the processes by which the State of Maine, through successive administrations, alienated her forest wealth.

Of one thing Frank Putnam was convinced: the story "would be shadowed throughout by treacherous graft." Many of the proprietors were in official positions when they obtained their titles. "What Maine needs worst of all is a Hughes to uncover their rascality and a free independent newspaper press to scourge them out of public life."[288] Prison was the place for them, and it was too bad they would never get there. Putnam's sentiments ran parallel to those of William Pattangall, the *Machias Union* columnist who famously wrote of one of these rascals, "he will pass into history unwept and unhonored and (because of the lenity of our laws) unhung."

Little could be done to restore its forestlands to Maine, but at least they should contribute fairly to the public weal. At the moment, almost half of Maine's land mass was generating a mere 10 percent of total state taxes. Assessing the wildlands at their proper value would nearly double annual tax revenue—just shy of a million dollars in 1907—and provide enough to fund important functions that were now being short-changed: roads, education, the needy, and "struggling small communities."

One man had entered the lists against the wildland owners on this score, a "contemporary and peer of Thomas B. Reed and one of the 'noblest old Romans' in the State." So Frank Putnam introduced Liberty B. Dennett to his readers.[289] Dennett, a Portland attorney, was pursuing his crusade "single-handedly, practically without aid or comfort from politician or press of any party." Stalwart Republican though he was, his disgust at the landowners matched the nothing-if-not-partisan Democrat, William Pattangall.

"This wild land issue," Liberty Dennett declared, "is a tremendous issue regarded from any point of view." The same year Frank Putnam's story was published, Dennett was advancing his campaign with an article a month for the *Pine State Magazine* under the title "Maine's Wild Lands and Wildlanders." Only by properly taxing the wildlands could Maine afford to support its public schools as they deserved without overburdening the municipalities.

Dennett had fired his opening salvo in 1890, unveiling an "amazing fact" in the pages of the *Portland Daily Press*. "By far the most valuable single property" in Maine—nine million acres of "thriftily growing trees"—produced a mere $30,000 in taxes each year. Maine's "good overtaxed" citizens would surely be amazed if they knew, but the large landowners paying this pittance had "ever so successfully and for so long a time kept [it] secret." Dennett intended to expose these "wildlanders"—"by which name I shall call these enemies of our state"—and let the public know what was going on in the State House, "in whose lobby are some of the most expert liars and seductive tempters this side of Tammany Hall."

It took the wildlanders no time at all to raise an outcry "against the publication of such damaging, such extraordinary, such condemnatory facts!" Editors and public servants (of both parties) who had initially lined up with Dennett were "silenced, hushed, admonished, by the crack of the republican party's whip." Dennett's polemical style rose to the occasion magnificently in portraying the effect of his efforts.

This, then, little black but very ominous political cloud in the west, not "larger than a man's hand," but laden with forceful and rapidly accumulating indisputable facts, and flashing the sharp lightning of publicity, and rising higher and higher upon the horizon, and spreading wider and wider, immediately attracted, and has constantly held the apprehensive attention of this Czar of all the wildlanders.[290]

The "Czar" was Llewellyn Powers, one of Maine's leading politicians and a man "colossal in fortune" and "dictatorial and triumphant in party caucus." By 1907, the assessed value of the wildlands had risen from $9 million to $36 million. Though paltry, it was enough to make "the wild-land barons and their political vassals hate [Dennett] with an unholy hatred, dub him crank and nuisance, and angrily refuse to discuss him or his agitation." When Frank Putnam asked Governor Cobb about the matter, his answer was typical. "If you mean old Dennett's talk, I don't care to say anything about it," Cobb snapped.[291] It was about this time that Dennett was taking the governor to task for not firing F. Marion Simpson, the state assessor, for conflict of interest.

The Victorian charm of the black-and-white sketch that headed each of Dennett's articles in the *Pine State Magazine*—woodsy lakeshore with mountains in the background—belied the incendiary tone of the diatribes that followed. The wildlanders, in Liberty Dennett's saga, were "a distinct and autocratic political aristocracy" that, starting in the earliest days of statehood, had wrested away "the people's patrimony" until they owned half of Maine.[292] He condemned them with a deep-seated outrage.[293]

> They have from the beginning strangled every attempt at legislation which had for its object the preservation for the people and their posterity any portion of the vast empire of forests which in law and in equity and by absolute right belonged to them.

For his readers who had never heard of John G. Deane, Liberty Dennett revived that wise man's memory. Had Maine listened to him back in 1874, the entire state might have been developed before the Civil War. Only settlers would have bought land; timber companies would have been sold only permits. Instead "stupid legislators" had allowed iniquitous landowners to continue to ply "their favorite vocation of helping themselves to vast areas of wild lands at most trifling prices." As a result, three-quarters of a century later, Maine was still but half-settled. So it would remain, "until the wildlanders are compelled to take their greedy, grasping hands from the throats of the people."

A last-ditch attempt to save what was left of Maine's public domain, a pitiful seven hundred thousand acres in 1874, was made by the "great and patriotic" governor, Nelson Dingley Jr.[294] He could do nothing to "correct the wasteful policy" of the past, he told the legislators. "Yet much may be done to remedy evils that arise from locking up large tracts of settling lands which would otherwise be improved." They answered him, wrote Dennett, with "the exercise of that sly and cunning legislative art, of which they are consummate masters."

According to Dennett, a committee, heavily stocked with forest interests, was appointed to "inquire into and report at an early day" whether or not to abolish the Land Office. The committee duly recommended doing so, despite it being a constitutional office and therefore beyond the whims of the legislature (see chapter 4). When the bill had to be repealed the next year, the legislature amended the constitution to get control over the land agent. A second resolve directed him to sell the remaining public lands at public auction. Once again, behind all was "that learned lawyer and intellectual leader of men," Llewellyn Powers. When the deadline for selling the wildlands was extended from April 1 to December 31, Liberty Dennett assumed "not all the necessary combinations and conventions among the conspirators could be made as soon as April 1st." He was likewise sure that the public auction was underadvertised deliberately to favor the landowners. When prize lands had to be withdrawn because of title questions, he quoted Robert Burns with an almost audible cackle, "The best laid schemes of mice and men gang aft agley."

Governor Dingley should be absolved for signing the bill that abolished the Land Office, wrote Dennett. He was distracted by more immediate issues and could not see what the legislators were up to. They continued such end-runs around succeeding governors until they hit upon a more reliable tactic: to organize the choice of chief executive themselves. The Republican candidate needs none of the customary qualities, mocked Dennett. "No! No! Not such an [sic] one; he must be pledged and well informed as to their cunning methods so he may be well equipped to safeguard the interests of the wildlanders." The usual process started in the House from whence the chosen one could climb "to its speakership, then to the Senate and its presidency, then to the chief magistracy."

The first of these was Edwin Burleigh, son of the land agent who in Dennett's eyes sold the Land Office down the river in 1874.[295] To be fair, Parker Burleigh raised many questions about the wisdom of abolishing the Land Office, expressing particular concern for the settlers and settling lands. "What is to be done with this most vital interest?" he asked. "That it should be abandoned after so long a season of effort, at a time, too, when yielding its richest harvest, would seem to be a folly too great to be for a moment entertained."[296]

In 1903, Liberty Dennett persuaded a Representative from Portland to introduce a bill to raise the tax rate in the wildlands to fifteen mills. (He noted that the man took care "to state that he did it as a favor to me, and not because he favored it.") Dennett testified at the bill's hearing, and the taxation committee sent it to the full House marked "ought to pass." That such a thing should have made it this far in the legislature was unheard of. The landowners, who had easily shut down Dennett's earlier efforts, were thrown into a panic.[297] They turned to the attorney general.

The AG—elected by the "wildlander" legislature, Liberty pointed out—thought the bill unconstitutional. He sought an opinion from the Supreme Judicial Court. The court unanimously agreed; all eight justices voted even though four of them owned or were otherwise connected with the wildlands. "Judges concerned for their honor" would have recused themselves, wrote an appalled Frank Putnam.

> It speaks volumes for the perfection of the political machine that dominates Maine that none of the four judges interested in the wild lands was visibly troubled by any scruple against sitting in judgment upon a question in which he had a direct pecuniary interest.

If wildlands taxation was a constitutional issue, then amend the constitution. Dennett got over fifty of Portland's most distinguished lawyers, doctors, and businessmen to sign a petition for just such an amendment that would tax the wildlands at a rate of fifteen mills, which was the average rate for Maine's municipal taxes. The measure would go to the people for a vote, but first, two thirds of the legislature had to approve it.

"A moose, of experience with hunters, is not quicker to scent danger than this tyrannical landed aristocracy." Thus spoke Liberty Dennett as, catching wind of his amendment, the landowners sprang into action. A committee of the Maine Lumbermen and Landowners' Association was formed—its work to be "kept within our own circles"—to defeat the bill. Its chairman, Joseph P. Bass, put out a call to all members for financial support.

They would not be "safe with a smaller contribution from the timberland owners than one-eighth of a cent an acre," wrote Bass. This was cheap at the price, his appeal made clear, since it was a "certainty that the people would vote this measure" if it ever reached them. However, if the association could afford the services of "the very best of the legal fraternity," Bass was confident they could kill the bill. Bass's letters were all "confidential." However, one recipient made it public as soon as he received it, much to Dennett's delight.

It made no difference. The bill "received scant courtesy"; nor was there the "remote possibility that the legislature, as at present constituted," would ever pass anything that would tax the wildlands equitably.[298] He had been defeated, said Dennett, "by methods which no honest man can approve." When faced with a bill such as his, the wildlanders and their brethren "combine, conspire, threaten, entreat, seduce, bribe, lobby, dodge, defer, lie, drink, eat and merrily dance," anything to stop the question going to the people for a vote.

The other way to increase timberlands' contribution to the general fund was to assess their value more accurately. As Dennett saw it, the landowners were deliberately starving the State Assessor's Office to keep prying public eyes out of their thousands of acres. The office was given a mere $2,500 a year for exploration of the wildlands, an "intelligent but tyrannically contrived method" of holding back the tide. "Old Dennett" calculated that the cost of "cruising" an acre was one cent, and that at the rate the assessors were going, exploring the wildlands would take ninety years. The fact that an initial effort, tired as it had been, increased the valuation of the land to $4.73 an acre, brought out a classic Dennettian onslaught. If it could make a net profit of $4.72,

> on an investment of a single coin of the very smallest denomination known to our laws, it seems to me, that a Legislature which would let so good an opportunity to serve the people of the State go by, to final adjournmeet[sic], unimproved, except to the pitifully small extent of $2,500, must have been an aggregation and full assortment of all round ineffable fools of that class that cannot help it.

There was, however, one movement that Liberty Dennett's powerful foes dared not stop, much as they would have liked to. Not least because of the minimal taxes being paid by the timberland owners, Maine people had become disgruntled with the legislative process and were demanding a more direct voice in government.[299] In 1907, after a five-year struggle, the legislature unanimously passed the Initiative and Referendum Act, which gave citizens the means to initiate measures outside the legislative process. When it went to the people for a vote the following year, they approved it two to one.

The link between the "initiative and referendum" bill and Dennett's was not lost on Frank Putnam. After three-quarters of a century of having "their own sweet will," the landowners had a new political force to contend with, whose members "embrace a vast majority of the electorate." They would be the arbiters of how much taxation justified "slaughtering their forests." The idea of "'the greatest good to the greatest number,' though long dormant in Maine," Putnam predicted, might "be invoked to save the rights of the majority in the State's forests, despite the attitude of their private owners." If the landowners were crying wolf—as time and again has proved to be the case—the people of Maine now had a vehicle to counter them. A similar sentiment would be reawakened in 1972.

While Pattangall and Dennett were hurling brickbats at the wildlanders over their political corruption, others were going straight to the heart of the matter—the health and future of the forest. When he heard that Great Northern was building its first paper mill, Manly Hardy—a hunter and fur buyer and no Thoreauvian dreamer—wrote to his son,

> You will live to see that pulp mills have been the greatest curse this State ever saw. . . . This pulp mill feed is not like old-fashioned logging. It will just destroy all our woods. . . . These pulp mills mean prosperity to the railroads and a tuppenny gain to Bangor, but they mean death to all our woods industries in a few years. . . . I feel as I can imagine the Wood Nymphs do.[300]

Within a decade, a billion feet of wood was being taken from the forest each year, mostly from the watersheds of the Androscoggin, Kennebec, and Penobscot rivers.[301] Relatively little pulpwood had yet been removed from the northern half of the wildland region.[302] Nevertheless, with railroads opening up the whole area and the ever-increasing demand for paper, Frank Putnam predicted that spruce's "supreme adaptability for paper pulp marks it for destruction unless State laws shall be interposed to save it."

Heavy cutting in the northern forests was not just about the trees. Industrialists in the southern part of the state were worried about the erratic spate of the rivers that powered their mills and factories. On bare hillsides, explained one forest commissioner,

> water is discharged as soon as it falls, causing floods and erosion of the soil. If the water-shed of a stream is forested, the discharge of water is gradual and the flow of the stream consequently well regulated and of pure water.

"An impression grows," wrote Putnam, that the situation might warrant legislative action. The legislature saw no need to impose legal limits on timber cutting, but it realized that the forests needed attention. Since the land agent became forest commissioner, his priority had evolved into promoting sound forestry, for example, "the wisdom of cutting no trees less than ten inches in diameter, breast high." Enterprises like the Pingrees', Great Northern, and International Paper were also aware that even Maine's vast forest could not last forever without help. Their self-interest called for setting size limits below which trees were not to be cut and enforcing it in the contracts with their loggers.[303] "Conservative methods of woodland cutting and management" were taking root in Maine. It was a major shift in norms from the previous frontier mentality of cut-and-move-on-to-the-next-patch.

Much of the credit belongs to Austin Cary, who has claim to being called America's first forester. After graduating from Bowdoin College, Cary took to the North Woods, carrying out research on forest growing cycles. Impressed by forest practices in Germany, he tried to put them into practice in America. In 1898, he was hired by the Berlin Mills Company in New Hampshire, becoming the first company forester in the country. There, wrote Jamie Lewis for the Forest History Society, "began a lifelong battle to persuade industrial forestland owners to embrace and undertake long-range planning of cutting, planting, and land use."[304]

In a paper for the State Board of Trade, Cary defined three public values that came from forests. They contributed to the land's "general habitability and prosperity"—what we would now call ecology although at that time, Cary admitted, "science has not fully mastered" the subject. Secondly, they were matchless places for recreation and human inspiration. "Forest rests soil and forests rest men," he wrote, before embarking on some imaginative metaphysics.[305] "The slow growth of the tree is the best tie between the restless human spirit and the patient, exhaustless forces of nature." Finally, forests produce raw materials that contribute to "comfort, wealth and national independence."[306]

In his conclusion, Cary speculated on "Forests as a Public Possession." He had known the Maine Woods inside out "as a boy and man." They were not "a private interest alone, but a public one as well." Owners and people alike had rights *and* obligations. They included access for hunting and fishing and camping, and responsibility for protecting against fire. Forest practices, said Cary, were a thornier issue, but one that "as conditions change, the people, as a whole, must have their say about." And people were already engaged. "Popular interest is awakened, is seeking light and guidance, and this is a tendency to be heartily encouraged," said Cary. The public's "perception of large interests, their amenity to reason, their willingness to exercise self restraint" boded well for "handling other problems relating to our forests as they may arise."

All concerns over possible loss of Maine's forest were met with stout denial by the papermakers. "Alarmists everywhere" were making him and his cohorts out to be "public enemies," complained Hugh Chisholm.[307] The pulp and paper industry was causing no decline in spruce. Forest Commissioner Edgar Ring himself had stated that "saw mills and pulp mills combined are not consuming more timber than the total annual increase."[308] It stood to reason, wrote Chisholm, that no one could be "more vitally concerned" for the forest than the men who made their money out of it. "Fire and fungus" destroyed as much forest each year as did all the paper mills.

Fire had always been the greatest threat to the wildlands and the greatest fear of their owners. Fires used to clear settling lands were one source of the old antipathy between farmers and timber companies. The army of sports invading Maine's forest was a more recent worry. "The campfire of the heedless hunter and fisherman has been the cause of many a conflagration that has meant enormous loss," wrote Hugh Chisholm.

The same legislation that established the post of Forest Commissioner had set up a statewide system of forest fire prevention, and it soon became his major preoccupation. Starting in 1903, Maine appropriated $10,000 a year to hire fire wardens, supplementing the landowners' funds for the same purpose. Spring to fall, these wardens kept a constant watch over the forest from various high points around the state. Six years later, to further improve fire prevention in the unincorporated forestlands, the legislature created the Maine Forestry District.[309] It included, under the forest commissioner's "care and custody" (to use an earlier term), all the unorganized towns and some of the plantations, and it was paid for by a tax of 1.5 mills on its nine and a half million acres. While tussling with Liberty Dennett, the forest owners had held a bargaining chip in reserve. Should they have to negotiate, they would "submit to a small tax" for fire prevention on their lands.[310] It now funded the "prevention, control, and extinguishment of forest fires" within the Forestry District.[311]

The fight against "fire and fungus" increasingly overshadowed all but the most basic concerns about the Public Reserved Lands. "Our forest commissioner" drew high praise from Hugh Chisholm for his fire prevention efforts.[312] The relationship between the large forest landowners and the forest commissioner grew increasingly symbiotic. For the first nine years, the post was held by International Paper's Charles Oak—for which he was needled by William Pattangall (see above)—after which he became the Maine Lumbermen and Landowners' Association's clerk and treasurer. Oak's successor was Edgar Ring, a regular at the association's meetings, who held it for the next decade.

By 1911, the only township left in state ownership was Indian Township in Washington County.[313] That year, Forest Commissioner Frank Mace reckoned he had responsibility for about ninety thousand acres of public or "school" lots.[314] He issued twenty permits to cut timber on them, taking care to find trustworthy men who would be mindful of "the future growth." It was a small part of his job, but a certain amount of housekeeping always had to be attended to: tracking down some three thousand acres that had not come to the state when a township was organized, and when one was deorganized again; supervising the incorporation of three plantations (and making the moneys collected over the years available to the new towns). In general trespassing was down—sometimes it was "clearly a mistake," Mace concluded—and the state's policy was "not to work any great hardship" on squatters.

And so it went year after year: stumpage permits, campsite rentals, trespasses, insignificant compared to the annual struggles with forest fire, and recently, the spruce budworm and the white pine blister rust. In 1915, the Public Lots produced not quite $40,000 for the Reserved Land School Fund. In 1920, the highlight of the Public Lots report was negotiating the location of the Public Lot in T3R11 with Great Northern. Some years there was nothing to report.

Since 1918, the annual appropriation toward the Public Lots had been a munificent $500, specifically to "retrace and define exterior lines." When he took up his post at the end of 1922, Forest Commissioner Neil Violette calculated that he was supposed to be managing 53,000 acres in fifty-five townships, plus the grass and timber rights on another 393,000 acres.[313] It couldn't be done with the resources he was being given, Violette complained. Five hundred dollars was "hardly sufficient" just to maintain the boundary lines, some of which had not been checked for fifty years or more. And on top of that, he was expected to supervise timber sales, lease campsites, and discourage trespassers. He didn't always have time to inspect a tract before it was sold, still less check out a proposed campsite. As for trespass, it was running "practically unchecked" again.

The situation, wrote Violette, was untenable. The Public Lots were not public in the sense that they were open to one and all. They had one purpose, and that was to provide financial support for the area schools. Any irregular activity—in land sales, camp leases, trespassing, and squatting—directly detracted from this purpose. If land was sold to farmers (Violette affirmed that state policy was to sell lots in the Public Reserved Lands to bona fide settlers only), they should pay the going rate. "Any other course would virtually deprive the schools, for the benefit of private individuals, of funds intended exclusively for their use."

The commissioner recommended that the appropriation title be expanded from "Retracing and Defining Lines" to "Administration of the Public Lands," and that it be increased to allow him to hire a full-time forest engineer and a seasonal forester for the summer. Only that way could the Public Lots be managed so that they "yield continuously the revenue they should." At stake, added Violette, was Maine's reputation.

His appeal fell on deaf ears. The annual appropriation remained as it was, although the legislature changed its title to "Administration of the Public Lands" in 1929. It was all still spent on retracing and defining lines.[316] The commissioner's report on the public lands for the next biennium (1931–1932) was virtually identical to the previous one: $500 appropriation for retracing and maintaining boundaries on about fifty thousand acres in fifty-five plantations, and so forth. One new heading, however, stood out: "State Park." It began:

In March 1931 the Hon. Percival P. Baxter, former Governor of Maine, presented to the State a large tract of land in the northwest corner of Township No. 3, Range 9, Piscataquis County, which included the greater part of Mount Katahdin, highest point of land in the State.

The actual facts were a little bit more complicated, not least because at that point Baxter had only purchased a three-eighth interest in the land.

The story of how Percival Baxter bought Baxter Park bit by bit with his own funds is well known.[317] Mount Katahdin had been the prize of various development proposals at least since 1856, when Shepard Boody (the engineer of the Telos Canal) obtained a charter for the Mount Katahdin Road Company. Inspired by what was happening on Mount Washington in New Hampshire, Boody wanted to build a road from Patten, on the Aroostook Road, to the top of Maine's highest mountain. The route was surveyed in 1858, but nothing came of it, probably in the first place because the Civil War intervened. When the war ended, said Earl Raymond, himself a surveyor, the capital required to do anything in so remote and forbidding an area was already flowing out West. Moreover, Raymond noted, the railroad didn't reach Patten until the 1890s.[318]

Dreams of grand mountain hotels continued, but as the new century moved into its second decade, they were overtaken by a different kind of dream: preservation of the fast-dwindling "forest primeval." An attempt at giving Mount Katahdin the status of a national forest in 1913 failed in Washington. A few years later, Baxter, a state representative and then senator, tried to make it into a state park to celebrate Maine's centennial in 1920. Unfortunately, much of the land around the mountain was owned by Great Northern Paper Company, and to that company's leader, Garret Schenck, Baxter was anathema.

One of the issues over which Baxter and Schenck had clashed was the Kennebec Reservoir Company.[319] The Kennebec Reservoir Company's purpose was to create a storage reservoir to regulate the Kennebec's flow for the benefit of mills and hydropower downstream. All the major industry interests along the river were involved, including Great Northern. The company's charter was approved by the legislature, but now-Governor Baxter vetoed it. When his veto was overridden, Baxter accused the lawmakers of throwing away the people's rights and called for a referendum the following year. The legislature insisted that the referendum be held at once. It was an election year, 1924, and the lawmakers did not want Percival Baxter running for a third term on the water power issue.

As the two sides geared up for a showdown, the governor announced that he had negotiated a compromise with the power companies. They would lease the two Public Lots—the center of the controversy (although the forest commissioner made no mention of them in his report that year, 1923)—where the dam was to be built for $25,000 a year for forty years. The legislature was "amazed," reported *Paper, A Weekly Technical Journal for Paper and Pulp Mills*. Garret Schenck denied having anything to do with such an agreement.

Walter Wyman, another incorporator and the founding president of the Central Maine Power Company, went so far as to introduce an alternate bill under his own name, even though he was not an elected lawmaker.

The legislators "evidently felt that they were not being consulted and were disgusted with the whole matter," reported *Paper*. The Kennebec Reservoir Company's charter was repealed. With such a "sensational finish," it was "one of the least satisfactory sessions of the Maine legislature ever known."[320] There the matter rested until 1927, when—with Baxter no longer governor— the legislature approved a bill that was essentially the compromise the former governor had tried to work out.

It found no immediate takers.

Only after Schenck's death, in 1928, and the crash of 1929 did Great Northern express any interest in selling land to Percival Baxter. The township in question was T3R9, in which Great Northern owned a three-eighth undivided interest. The company agreed to sell Baxter 5,760 acres in the township's northwest corner, which included Mount Katahdin. The only fly in the ointment was that the other five-eighth interest was held by a former state legislator, Harry Ross, who was as antagonistic as Garret Schenck. He was determined to hold out and spoil Baxter's dream.

The former governor called Ross's bluff by donating his share to the State of Maine, as recorded in Neil Violette's report. Ross filed suit against Baxter and the state. Eventually, the land was divided, some said favorably to Ross. But Baxter got Mount Katahdin, and Maine the beginning of Baxter Park, to be forever wild against a time that "yet may come when only the Katahdin region remains undefiled by man."[321]

Chapter Six

Crash, War, and Recovery

Muddling Through (1931–1972)

For much of the world, the 1930s were dominated by economic catastrophe; for most of it, the 1940s were overshadowed by war. Maine was no exception, escaping the trials of neither misfortune. In 1933, the pitiful appropriation for managing the Public Lots won in 1918—$500 per annum—was reduced to $100 as the Great Depression forced state government to slash budgets across the board. The sum was not enough to maintain even minimal operations. To locate a Public Lot—"establishing its metes and bounds"—cost on average five times that amount. With lines needing to be redrawn on lots not surveyed in some cases for over fifty years, there was little left for pursuing willful trespassers. On top of all this, the forest commissioner was responsible for selling grass and timber on fifty thousand acres for the benefit of fifty-five plantations not yet incorporated.

Perhaps inevitably under such conditions, plantations began treating the income from their Public Lots rather casually. Plantation assessors were selling stumpage themselves, and the receipts were being spent for general municipal purposes rather than being delivered to the Maine treasury for the benefit of future schools. In some cases, "all record of it has been either lost, or overlooked," despaired a report from the superintendent of public schools. It actually dated from 1898, but the renewed need to address "gross irregularities" prompted its recirculation to remind school and municipal officials of the "importance of scrupulously guarding the 'permanent school funds' of their towns." They could be spent on schools only. No town, admonished the Education Department, had "ever had the right" to use the money for anything else. Whether misapplied "intentionally or carelessly," these funds must be paid back in full. Henceforth, each school superintendent would be responsible for giving account of the exact balance in the town's school fund, how it was invested, how much income it generated, and "such other details as will give a complete history of the original funds and disclose their present amount and condition."

Even as funds for managing the public lands dwindled, visitors were arriving each summer in greater numbers than the last, putting a new strain on the Public Lots and all of the state's forest. Maine's place as "The Playground of the Nation" would be impossible without its forests, stated Neil Violette in the forest commissioner's report for 1925–1926; "the demand for recreational uses of the forests is increasing annually." Ten years later, his successor, Waldo Seavey, wrote plaintively:

> There is coming to Maine every year an increasingly large body of independent vacationists who carry all travel and camping equipment with them. They travel far from the more popular resorts and desire to camp by themselves in remote sections.[322]

Since 1921, the Forestry Department had constructed campsites and "lunch grounds" in the wildlands as a way to reduce the risk of forest fire caused "by inexperienced campers building fires in unsafe places." The sites—typically a small tract near a spring or running water, outfitted with a fireplace, tables, and benches, and a lean-to—were cleared and constructed by forest wardens and (after it was established in 1933) the Civilian Conservation Corps (CCC). They soon became popular features for hikers and canoers. By 1936, some ninety-three campsites (and thirty-three lunch grounds) in the Maine Forestry District were scarcely keeping up with demand. Somewhere along the way, a fire-prevention tactic had become a tourist program, a responsibility with which the Forestry Department felt ill equipped to deal.

"In no way is the Department seeking to draw people away from the regular motor camping grounds maintained by private individuals," Commissioner Seavey protested; but more and more camping sites were needed, ever deeper into the woods. It was not just the campers that had to be accommodated. "Automobiles with elaborate trailers are appearing on the highways," and they required better parking facilities. By the end of 1940, over a hundred campsites were facilitating a hike into the Maine Forestry District.

Maine citizens, as well as folks from away, were part of the groundswell in demand for outdoor recreation. To satisfy its constituents, the legislature created a commission to establish a state park system in 1935. Its first creation was the Aroostook County State Park, a gift of one hundred acres by the Merchants Association of Presque Isle. The next year, four more parks were acquired on long leases from the Soil Conservation Service, another federal response to the Great Depression.[323] In his report for 1941–1942,

Forest Commissioner Raymond E. Rendall wrote enthusiastically, if somewhat imprecisely,

> The income from the recreational use of State Parks has shown the following increases:
> 1939 Normal; 1940 85% increase; 1941 221% increase; 1942 30% increase.

Rendall's next report was more sober, reflecting an America that had been at war for three years. Maine's five state parks were still open, but limited personnel allowed for only the most basic maintenance. Visitors were limited, too, to "those who could avail themselves of the facilities under gasoline rationing."

The Second World War stopped another forestry initiative—this one at the federal level—in its tracks. The heavy cutting of America's forests had become a matter of public concern nationwide, and in 1938, President Franklin Roosevelt responded by urging Congress to consider what form forest practices regulation might take. A Joint Congressional Committee was appointed to study the question, while the U.S. Forest Service looked at the issue's silvicultural aspects. The Joint Committee's report appeared in April 1941. Bills were prepared and introduced. Aware of the national mood, Maine's Commissioner Rendall began discussions with landowners on how "to meet the challenge of federal control." Not surprisingly, their response was strong and negative. As summarized by Rendall, "Federal regulation is not desired. State regulation, although not desired, is preferable, but [private] self-regulation should be adopted for the best interest of public and private good." Eight months later, the plunge into war put all else on hold. Bills evaporated as Congress adjourned after the attack on Pearl Harbor.

"Since then the demand for forest stumpage in our war effort has precluded all else," wrote Rendall.[324] In his next report (1943–1944), he noted that he was "admonished by law" to look into the impact of "wasteful cutting" on forest health, and to "ascertain as to the diminution of the wooded surface of the land." The war years "tried the mettle" of the men of Maine's Forest Service. In addition to the tribulations brought on by the war itself—"curtailment of much needed equipment, loss of men, increased costs, war regulations"— the year 1944 was exceptionally dry, making for "extreme fire hazardous weather." The absence of the CCC—terminated at the war's outbreak—was particularly keenly felt that summer. The lost manpower in the woods was filled, to some extent, by Axis prisoners of war. Four POW camps would be located in northern Maine, and from 1944 to 1946, one or other housed some four thousand German prisoners of war.

A Maine paper company led the way. Hollingsworth and Whitney happened to be the nation's only manufacturer of tabulating cardstock, used by the U.S. Army in great quantities for record keeping. The first POW camp was established on the company's land in Hobbstown, near Spencer Lake above Jackman (T4 R6). The camp held two hundred prisoners, mostly from General Rommel's Afrika Korps. In two years, they cut thirty-four thousand cords of pulpwood. (Hobbstown was the site of the only breakout from a POW camp in Maine: three prisoners escaped but were recaptured five days later.) Other prison camps were established at Seboomook, where Great Northern rebuilt its old company farm for the purpose; in an old CCC camp in Princeton, Washington County, a joint venture by several paper companies (including Hollingsworth and Whitney)[325]; and in the army barracks at Houlton airport, where some prisoners were hired by farmers to help in the potato fields, as well as woods work.

In his book, *Ten Million Acres of Timber*, Austin Wilkins collected some interesting reminiscences of Maine's POW camps. For the most part, wrote Norman Gray, a forester for Great Northern, the prisoners only wanted the war to be over. Some were even "frank in admitting that if to cut pulpwood well might help in their return to their homeland they would wish to remain right in the woods." This was perhaps less surprising, given that they were treated well and sometimes fed better than their forester supervisors. One of Wilkins's correspondents recalled lunchtime for the Houlton POWs at their forest worksite.

> Big steaming kettles of vegetable and meat stew, hot home made bread and German pastry—the best of good plain food—was trucked out to the operation site every noon where the prisoners gathered around a woods fire and apparently enjoyed themselves. Our Company foremen pulled a peanut butter, or canned corn beef sandwich out from the back of their shirt and were lucky if they had tea to wash it down with.

As the tide turned in the Allies' favor, a Post War Planning Commission began to consider where financial grants might encourage "some needed planning for future public recreation in 'Vacationland.'" The forest commissioner proposed nine "ready-to-go" projects, starting with a statewide forest survey. Among the proposals, boundary line surveys and upgrades as State Forests were a couple of modest efforts that benefited Maine's Public Lots.[326]

World War II was still being fought in the Pacific when the legislature appointed a committee to "investigate and study" the Public Reserved Lands. The "legislative interim committee" report two years later opened with the familiar history from before Maine became a state up to 1850, when the land agent was given authority to sell the timber and grass rights. It reiterated the equally well-known stipulation:

Pursuant to that law the timber on many of our school lots was sold and the purchasers were given the right to cut and take away the timber until the townships became organized as plantations or incorporated as towns.[327]

The report's comments on the status quo were succinct. Out of "approximately" 395 unorganized townships in Maine, 161 had never had its Public Lot "surveyed or set aside." Thus, assuming a thousand-acre lot per township, there were 161,000 acres on which the timber—as well as the land—belonged to Maine "for school purposes." Where the timber and grass rights had been sold, the land still belonged to Maine. The committee members concluded there was no need for "court action" to test the titles obtaining in either situation. (It did not have the funding to do so, anyway, they admitted.) Foreshadowing a court ruling thirty or so years later, they noted:

The wisdom of previous legislatures which authorized these sales might be questioned in the light of present and future values, but that should have no bearing on the legality of the titles, or sales.

Stumpage prices and leases on school lots, however, did "seem to deserve attention." Before harvesting began in undivided townships, the committee recommended that stumpage prices be agreed between the forest commissioner and the private owners; if there was disagreement, it must be settled by arbitration, and harvesting would have to wait. Owners should receive written reminders of this, "periodically, or even annually." As to leases—whether located or undivided; if the stumpage rights were sold or not—the forest commissioner should review them to ensure that the state was getting its fair share.

The report's final recommendation broke new ground. Wary though it was of "embarrass[ing] the State in future court action," the committee considered the way the state tax assessor came up with a value for a Public Lot on which timber and grass rights had been sold might be worth looking into. At the moment, a value was put on the soil and on the standing timber, the value of the latter being generally about the same as what the land would sell for. "Possibly a third factor" should be considered, the Legislative Interim Committee suggested gently: the rights to future growth. Not that the amount "apparently escaping true valuation" was large; "still an inequity seems to be there, and the committee suggests that a formula should be devised to correct it." Further consideration had to wait for the next decade.

The Great Fires across Maine also occurred in 1947. They devastated some of the state's settled areas (particularly Mount Desert Island and York County), but the Public Lots—and the Maine Forestry District as a whole—got off relatively lightly. There had been "about the same weather and ground conditions" prevailing all over the state, wrote then-Deputy Forest

Commissioner Austin Wilkins in a special report devoted to the disaster. He attributed the Forestry District's fortunate escape to "better organization and preparation" of the Maine Forest Service, which had total authority for fire control in the area. By the next biennium, a forest fire program for the whole of Maine was in place.

The reappearance of an old fire control problem from before the war was another reason for an "aggressive" new protection program. The return of peace and a civilian economy was bringing tourists, especially canoers, deep into the forest once again, and in ever-increasing numbers. "There are several agencies in our state that are putting forth their best efforts to advertise our forest area as a vacationland," wrote Albert Nutting, the new forest commissioner, with thinly veiled resentment. They had been most successful, but no comparable thought was being given to how to cope with "this influx." Such campsites as existed were built and maintained at the expense of the Forest Service, and there were already not enough of them. The legislature had appropriated nothing to pay for more, nor had those "several agencies" set any funds aside for this purpose.

The legislature's attempt to respond to the issue was something of a fiasco. A bill was introduced with the sensible intention of prohibiting anyone from "pitching a tent" in any state campsite for more than a week. The campsite would thus be open for the use of a greater number of visitors. But, noted a frustrated Commissioner Nutting, the law was "stripped of all its teeth" before it was even passed, rendering it "useless." The penalty to enforce it was removed. Thus, on the Allagash River, for instance, local guides continued to occupy the most popular campsites for the whole summer to be sure they had them for the fishermen that were "booked for the future." Nutting predicted that the problem could only get worse with the continued surge in hiking, fishing, camping, and hunting, to say nothing of "shorter working hours permitting longer weekends" and better roads. The Maine Turnpike reached Augusta in 1955; the interstate got to Bangor four years later.

The same postwar boom that brought the summertime influx of tourists to the forest was driving demand for more and more wood products. In 1948, Nutting reported a "large number of stumpage sales" on the Public Reserved Lands. "Timber on school lots has been in great demand," he wrote in 1950. In 1952, demand was "very active," and so it continued through 1956 when stumpage sales peaked. For the Maine Forestry District as a whole, that year was "among the very best on record," with less than usual losses due to fire, insects, or disease. The next biennium (1957–1958) the cut was half that, "due to the inactivity of markets and the stockpiling of previous years' cuttings."

The clash of tourist and industrial demands was a "double whammy." Over the next forty years, it would spawn increasing conflict over legitimate forest uses, and even the rights of private forest ownership. Hostility smoldered throughout the 1960s and 1970s, and grew ever more acrid in the eighties. It climaxed in 1996 with a referendum to ban clear cutting.[328]

To get the most out of the Public Lots, Nutting made a conscientious effort to develop management plans for those unfettered by long-term cutting leases, assigning the task to one department forester.[329] This might have worked well enough, but the man resigned after a year. From then on, management of the Public Lots was delegated to those "regular personnel" working in their immediate vicinity, mostly during fall and winter, when their number one priority—threat of forest fire—could be assumed to have diminished. This proved to be an efficient use of the department's limited resources, allowing more time for monitoring timber permits, checking camp lot leases, and warding off the ever-present threat of trespass. With such a "large number of small scattered areas," however, it was never easy. "Only through close coordination with other forestry work can any reasonably economical program be worked out," wrote Nutting.

As part of a "best possible program of management" for Public Lots, the Forest Service started to introduce a new step in the harvesting process. Before ax or saw was applied, the trees to be cut were marked. The U.S. Forest Service's Northeastern Forest Experiment Station marked the first school lot in 1951, free of charge.[330] This sensible innovation quickly ran into opposition in organized plantations where local assessors were used to cutting everything in sight with no thought to future growth. It was a "real complication"; some plantations considered their rights went "far beyond what the law provides" for managing Public Lots. They were selling stumpage, even deciding who got the timber, regardless of bids, the kinds of behavior the Education Department's circular had intended to quash before the war.

"The department is very glad to have their suggestions, but when they go beyond that point it makes it difficult to sell the timber and administer the areas properly," wrote Nutting. He looked forward to the day when marking would be the rule on all Public Lots. Before that could happen, however, two major problems had to be solved: "joint responsibility and widely scattered areas." The handicap of being "so widely scattered over the state" became a regular refrain in his reports, as was the need for forest fire personnel to manage them.

Toward the end of the 1940s, a couple of dams were on the drawing board that would submerge Public Lots upstream. By far the largest was the long-stalled effort to control the flow of the Kennebec River for the benefit of electricity generation downstream.[331] Its forerunner was the Kennebec Reservoir Company project that sparked the feud between Governor Percival

Baxter and the paper and power companies. After they had fought each other to a draw, and Baxter had left the Blaine House, the legislature offered more or less the same proposal that Baxter himself had sprung on the lawmakers at the battle's height: to lease the land for a dam at the Forks, where the Dead River flows into the Kennebec.

A lease was not an attractive option to CMP's Walter Wyman. He found an alternative situation farther up the Dead River, at Long Falls, and began buying up the land as early as 1930. It took almost twenty years, but in 1947 and 1948, the Forest Service was undertaking "considerable survey and cruise work" on two Public Lots that would be part of the flowage. These were leased to CMP for thirty years for $25,000 annually. The gates of the new dam were closed the next year, and by 1950, the village of Flagstaff—where Benedict Arnold planted the eponymous pole on his trek up the Kennebec—lay beneath eighteen feet of water at the bottom of Flagstaff Lake.

In the mid-1950s, Forest Commissioner Nutting turned his attention to the issue raised by the 1947 Legislative Interim Committee: the distinction between timber standing on the Public Lots when the rights were sold, and subsequent growth. "The present timber is growth," he argued and likened it to the interest generated from capital. The revenue from the original harvests had gone into the treasury's education fund, from which the annual interest was distributed to schools in the wildlands. Revenue from the sale of "present" timber represented the interest from the first harvests and as such should go directly to the schools instead of the education trust fund. Nutting cited other states and Canadian provinces where this was the rule and recommended Maine do the same, in cases of "timber harvests under good management." He undertook to study the issue further, and various reports went to the legislature, but no action resulted.

By 1960, there was nearly $2 million sitting in the Public Reserved Lands Fund. That year the new forest commissioner, Austin Wilkins, announced that the public lands would be harvested on a "sustained yield basis for the perpetuity of growth for the purpose the Public Lots were reserved—for schools in the Unorganized Territory."

Timber was never the only material resource with potential for extraction in the Maine woods. Moses Greenleaf's discovery of the "place of very fine paint" led to the construction of Katahdin Iron Works. A Maine Mining Bureau was originally established in the early years of the twentieth century, with the land agent one of its appointed three members. In 1908, however, it was found to exist "in name only," for want of an appropriation. The bureau was revived in 1955, and in 1957 it proposed a "workable procedure" for mining on state lands, including the Public Lots. The law gave the forest

commissioner authority to negotiate long-term leases with "competent organizations." If a claim was developed, Maine would receive rental and royalty
payments. By 1958, 135 claims had been staked on the Public Lots. Although
"state-owned mineral lands administered by the Mining Bureau have never
been precisely compiled," Nutting guessed that as many as 320,000 acres of
Public Reserved Lands could be of interest.[332] (Other state-owned lands that
were of some interest to the bureau for their minerals included institutional
lands, minerals beneath great ponds, and minerals beneath tidal waters.) The
following year, two long-term leases were signed that, with other license fees,
brought in $2,200 to the state coffers, "the largest sum ever received."

In 1961, the legislature requested another report on the Public Lots. Forest Commissioner Austin Wilkins was to look into their "history, location,
size and use" and "whatever other information the commissioner may deem
desirable." The expense—not more than $3,500—would be paid out of the
Organized Townships' Fund, but only after the $10,000 for "managing and
improving the growth of Public Reserve Lots" was allocated.[333] As to why
another report was needed at all, the best explanation the reporter who would
"rediscover" them, Bob Cummings, could come up with was that "someone
in the Legislature heard mention of them somewhere and wanted to know
what happened to them." There must have been "a little flurry of concern
in the Legislature"—his hands made a fluttering motion—just as there must
have been in 1945 when the previous report had been ordered. Cummings
said he "searched and searched the files," but he couldn't find anything written about either.

This report would be broader in scope than any similar effort heretofore,
"an ambitious attempt . . . to compile a record of helpful information that will
serve the purpose of a valuable reference," as Wilkins wrote in its Introduction. It would be "the most up to date record of the reserved lands." He and
his staff descended into the bowels of the Forestry Department to the steel
vault where the original documents related to the Public Reserved Lands were
stored. In the 1870s, when the Land Office was about to be abolished, land
agent Parker Burleigh had made a priority of preserving all the old maps, field
notes, and records. They were too valuable to be "estimated or compared with
gold or silver, for these can never replace them if once lost or destroyed,"
he wrote. By 1878, Burleigh's son Edwin confirmed that all had been "carefully arranged, repaired, and neatly bound." Constant use over the years had
led some of the older documents to crumble, and they had been microfilmed
about ten years before Austin Wilkins's review.

Dating back to Maine's first years as a state, it was truly a historical trea-
sure trove, of which commissioners' reports never failed to boast: 114 books

of field notes, 38 volumes of deeds, and 49 boxes full of "other valuable records" such as certificates from the Revolutionary War and Bingham's millions, applications for land grants from educational institutions and academies, and much else. The field notes in particular excited Austin Wilkins's admiration. The penmanship of the early land agents and surveyors resulted in "fine examples of Spencerian style of writing" as they described the hardships they encountered: crossing paths with "friendly and unfriendly Indian parties," being at the mercy of the elements, running out of provisions (Park Holland nearly starved to death surveying Bingham's millions), or foundering on the appalling roads. "There are even humorous accounts," wrote the commissioner, and he included a selection of colorful extracts as an appendix.

As had his precursors, Wilkins borrowed freely from past reports; the history was "so well documented that it is needless to attempt a rewrite." Instead, he tracked down and verified "every single acre of the reserved lands." Every township's reserved lot was listed, by county, with the date it was sold, for how much, and whether it was unorganized or a plantation. Each entry also included the legislative authorization for selling the timber and grass, a fact of which the commissioner repeatedly reminded the legislators. "From the time Maine became a State in 1820 to the present time, the State has never parted with a single acre of land, except under legislative authority."

Report on Public Reserved Lots was published in 1963. Beside the historical background, the guts of the report were statistics, and the data Wilkins collected was presented in a masterpiece of tabulation.[334] In 1963, the Public Reserved Lands could be divided into the following categories:

Timber & Grass Sold	318,890 acres (a little more than half located)
Plantations (State Administered)	48,412 acres (mostly located in 55 plantations)
State Owned	26,873 acres (mostly located)
Tax Delinquent (State Administered)	3,372 acres
Total	**397,547 acres**

Included in the report's findings was one minor surprise: four lots that had never been conveyed by the state. Totaling all of 1,269 acres, these were all that remained of the expanse of forest once inherited by Maine from Massachusetts. "It is not known just when it was discovered that the State of Maine still held title to a portion of the original public domain," Wilkins wrote. The best he could say was that at some time in the 1930s, the lots had been incidentally "uncovered" in the course of an unrelated title search.[335] He went on to comment rather quaintly that since the state had so little public land, "there is no plan to dispose of this acreage from the standpoint of its unique history."

Excluded from the forest commissioner's term "original public domain" were the nearly 50,000 acres of Public Lots held by the state for the fifty-five plantations over which they were spread.[336] Nor did he include 320,000 or so acres of Public Lots where rights to the timber and grass had been sold. The distinction between the thousand-plus acres to which Maine still "held title" and the hundreds of thousands of acres where timber and grass—but not the land—were "privately owned" is a measure of the prevalent assumption: a Public Lot without grass or timber had little value with which the state should concern itself.

Somewhat ironically, Austin Wilkins's report was probably the document that would put a conservation sleuth on the trail of Public Lots in the first place.

In the wildlands, the 1960s saw the creation of the Allagash Wilderness Waterway, arguably the first time citizens all over Maine mobilized over a conservation issue. Preserving the special wild character of the Allagash River was not a completely new concept. The Maine State Park Commission had suggested acquiring it in 1956, and the National Park Service considered the same thing a year later. Aware that Mainers were unlikely to welcome a national park, U.S. Supreme Court Justice William O. Douglas—a passionate wilderness advocate—appealed to Percival Baxter to include the Allagash under the Baxter Park Authority. Nothing came of the idea, but the justice's instincts were right. In 1963, the U.S. Department of the Interior proposed an Allagash National Riverway, while the Maine legislature established the Allagash River Authority. The real struggle had begun.

Following Justice Douglas's reasoning, the Allagash River was a "major recreation resource" of national significance, the department declared. Private ownership offered "no real assurance" that it would not "eventually be encroached upon by diverse industrial demands."[337] The "private" owners were Great Northern, International Paper, and the heirs of David Pingree. They and the other landowners opposed the recommendation in no uncertain terms, accusing the federal government of "arrogant disregard for the rights of State Government and private property owners" and "politically-inspired government ownership of forest resources." But they overplayed their hand.

The landowners demonstrated "little desire to talk over the substantive aspects of our recommendations," Interior Secretary Stewart Udall wrote to Governor John Reed on the last day of 1963. Although they repeated "over and over again" that they were "perfectly capable of preserving the area," a number of specifics "shook my confidence in [their] good faith." Only public ownership and management would ensure adequate protection of the Allagash, "and I stand firm on this position." Udall was open to either federal or state ownership. In 1965, Maine's Allagash River Authority proposed a compromise based on suggestions from the major stakeholders. It would protect 145,000 acres of land and water surface between Allagash Lake and the St. John River. The alternative, warned the *Lewiston Evening Journal*, among others, was "almost certainly . . . imposition of federal control." The next year, with the support of Governor Reed, Maine's legislature enacted a bill authorizing the "Allagash Wilderness Waterway." That November, Maine voters approved—by over 2 to 1—a bond issue of $1,500,000 "to develop the maximum wilderness character of the Allagash Waterway." It was matched by the federal Land and Water Conservation Fund. At the same time, Senator Edmund Muskie added an amendment to the National Wild and Scenic Rivers Act, which allowed Maine to manage the Allagash Wilderness Waterway within the Wild and Scenic Rivers Program, the first state-administered project in the federal program.

The Allagash Wilderness Waterway was officially dedicated in July 1970, the ceremony taking place above the Allagash River where it flows out of Churchill Lake. Three years later, land acquisition was completed. Using the unlocated Public Lots in the townships through which the Allagash ran might have lessened the price tag, but Attorney General James Erwin refused to allow it. He cited the old rule that a Public Lot must be "average in quality, situation and value" with the rest of the township. "Anyone familiar with . . . the Allagash knows that the shoreline for long distances may be nothing but flowage, grass, swamp or other land of such character to be economically valueless," he wrote.[338]

As the 1960s picked up momentum and headed for the first Earth Day in 1970, Maine was living up to its motto, *Dirigo*, "I lead." Attorney Harrison Richardson, who was majority leader in the State Senate at the time, liked to refer to the opening paragraph of a ruling by Judge Ronald Russell on one of his law cases (Portland Pipeline, 1973), which concluded, "Our Maine Legislature has been in the forefront of those seeking to control, and where necessary abate, threats of environmental destruction." "We were already addressing environmental issues in the Maine Legislature in a very far-sighted way," Richardson later recalled. "It was like a movement, it really was. There was an impetus, a thrust that said, 'We have to act, and we have to act now.'" It had become obvious that "if we didn't learn from the experiences of the megalopolis to the south of us [the Boston–Washington corridor], we were going to lose important resources." Not just economic resources, but the foundation of the values that are "so much a part of who we are." Maine needed to wake up and protect them. Thanks to a "happy confluence of events and good leadership," he said with a grin, the legislature enacted some "pretty progressive" environmental bills.[339]

The Public Lots themselves played little part in the decade's environmental-conservation crescendo. In 1962, one of the Public Lots provided the Christmas tree for New York City's Rockefeller Center. Scott Paper had the honor of cutting the sixty-seven-foot monster spruce on Squaw Brook near Greenville, now Little Moose Public Land. Otherwise, forest productivity was the goal. In 1960, an additional appropriation of $5,000—a 50 percent increase, taken from the "interest on the cumulative principal" of the two school funds—created "conditions favorable to a program of extended management practice," reported Austin Wilkins, just starting out as forest commissioner.

The first step was to systematically resurvey all the Public Lots, still ignored for so long that their boundary lines were vanishing. John Walker, who would work for the Bureau of Public Lands, headed an eight-man field crew of experienced woodsmen who during the summer were assigned to the Forest Fire Control Division. They cleared and spotted disappearing boundary lines, locating them "by compass line and distances. Lot corners are remarked with a hewn post, scribed on 4 sides, and properly witnessed." Public Lots where mineral rights might be valuable to the state were given particular priority. Rerunning the boundary lines was completed in 1968. Wilkins calculated that this "intensive effort" had dealt with 126 separate lots involving timber, grass, or mineral rights and reestablished 242 miles of boundaries. One result was the commissioner's discovery that many Public Lots "lie isolated within a township." Would it not be better, he wondered, to tie each lot into its respective township line?

In 1965, the "widely scattered" factor had prompted a further "decentralization of authority." Responsibility for the Public Lots was transferred to the Maine Forestry District. Commissioner Wilkins's aim was "to obtain the highest standards in forest management of Public Lots and the greatest economic benefits for the Townships' School Fund." The shift addressed the need for "intensive management, better distribution of limited appropriated funds, and closer supervision of management activities."

John Walker continued to advise and assist on all related field activities, acquiring an unsurpassed knowledge of the Public Lots that would prove invaluable in the future. After the boundary lines were all resurveyed, he and his crew devoted their attention to supervising harvest operations—continuous check-scaling and timber marking—as well as investigating cases of timber trespass, none of which jobs had gone away while they were surveying. Demand for camp lots was also on the increase, which the department met with a concerted effort to utilize "all shore frontage." The need to lay them out, as well as the paperwork involved in arranging leases, meant the work never lessened.

And then, a certain journalist working at the state's paper of record wrote "a simple little feature for a slow news weekend."[340] It would turn out to be the snowball that started the avalanche. Maine's Public Lots were about to step into the public eye for the first time in a hundred years.

PART II

Chapter Seven

"A Tale of Giveaways and Neglect" (March 1972)

In 1958, Bob Cummings, a twenty-nine-year-old journalism graduate from the University of Illinois, came home to Bath on the midcoast of Maine. Located on a tidal stretch of the Kennebec River, Bath's reputation as the "city of ships" was based on a heritage of shipbuilding, exemplified today by Bath Iron Works. Lanky and with a craggy demeanor even then, Cummings soon found a job at the local newspaper, *The Bath Times*, a small daily with a circulation that hovered around three thousand. In various incarnations, its lineage could be traced back to Maine's earliest years as a state. When Cummings got there, "The entire news staff was essentially me and a series of part-time society reporters."

In Bob Cummings's voice, the Public Lots story begins with an almost saga-like lilt. "There was a fellow by the name of White Nichols who lived on a hillside in Wiscasset, on property owned by a relative. He lived in a one-room camp with his wife and teenage kid. He had drifted out of the habit of earning a living, but he was into preserving things." Among other things, Nichols was the enthusiastic founder of the Benedict Arnold Expedition Historical Society. Herb Hartman, who later became a long-time director of the Maine Bureau of Parks and Recreation, went hiking with Nichols (and Cummings) on the Benedict Arnold Trail and remembered him as an Elmer Fudd–ish gentleman. "As soon as I arrived in town," continued Cummings, "White started showing up in my office at least once a week with ideas for stories." One of the first was how a dam was blocking Atlantic salmon from swimming up the nearby Sheepscot River. Cummings wrote the story, and largely as a result the dam was notched to facilitate fish passage in 1960.

Another Cummings story led to Maine's first Clean Water Act. It was really a statewide story, but with two of Maine's major watersheds—the com-

bined Androscoggin and Kennebec rivers—draining through Bath and bringing waste from "all the towns up and down the two rivers plus six or seven
paper mills," the reporter realized it had a local hook. He wrote front-page
stories day after day, sending copies up to Augusta to be put on the desks of
legislators and, especially, the Water Improvement Commission. "We were,"
he claimed, "the only paper in the state that gave it any serious coverage." He
didn't expect it "to go anyplace," but Cummings became personally invested
in the Clean Water Act, even when friends and colleagues told him it was a
dream—it would never pass. When it did, he was reluctant to take credit for
it. "Who knows why it passed?" was as far as he would go.

Then one day in 1963 Nichols appeared with a new cause. Somewhere
he had picked up a copy of Austin Wilkins's report on the Public Reserved
Lands, which had come out that year. Write something about the "Public Lots," he told Cummings. "And I said, 'What are the Public Lots?'"
Cummings recalled. "And Nichols laid it all out." Since the Revolutionary
War—starting with Massachusetts before Maine became a state—every time
a township in Maine was sold, the state had reserved a portion of the land, to
be held in trust until a town was incorporated. There were still approximately
four hundred thousand acres of these "Public Lots," owned by the state but
essentially absorbed by the timber companies. Cummings was building up a
formidable track record as an environmental journalist who could clap onto
an issue and get political results. But this one sounded too far-fetched for a
small local daily. Its readers, "mostly BIW employees," were unlikely to take
an interest in an issue nobody had heard of, hundreds of miles away in the
North Woods. Cummings didn't follow up on the idea just then, but "filed it
away" in the back of his mind.

At about the same time, a big rough-and-tumble man of the woods named
Ed Sprague was also getting exercised about the Public Lots. Like Nichols,
Sprague was a man on many missions, and he had developed a reputation as
something of a gadfly. He was a regular fixture at public hearings on legislation or rule-making—any meeting to which the public was invited—and he
was known for being very direct, not to say outspoken. He had what Richard Barringer later called an "intrepid insistence that injustice needed to be
righted," but that didn't make Ed Sprague easy to deal with.

"Mostly in a challenging mode" was how diplomatic Annee Tara remembered Sprague. He was convinced that "he had a clear view of the public
interest that was clouded in most of the rest of us [public officials] by something else, like politics or who knows." When she saw him coming, she didn't
say, "'Oh boy!,'" Tara confessed. "It was mostly, 'Now what?'" She was
working in the office of Governor Joseph Brennan the day Sprague came
in with a plan to stop hunters setting out bait for bears by prosecuting them

under the antilittering laws. "He had these ideas." She paused. "And some of them were better than others."

By far his best idea—the one for which he will be remembered—was that Maine must start paying attention to its Public Lots again. Growing up and working in the woods, Sprague had heard about them all his life, but he never really knew what they were. What he saw happening around his camp in remote Chain of Ponds prompted him to find out. The state had leased part of a Public Lot on Natanis Point (named after a Norridgewock Indian who joined Benedict Arnold's march on Quebec) to a paper company which turned it into a commercial campground. By a stroke of the pen, Maine people would now have to pay to camp or hike on what had once been theirs—and in Sprague's view should have been still.

"Ed was outraged at what he saw the state doing with the Public Lots," Barringer explained. Like many others were beginning to do when faced with an issue that needed airing, Sprague took his beef to the *Maine Times*, a relatively new player in the game of Maine politics and the environment. Started in 1968, the *Maine Times* was by this time a critical part of the dialogue about natural resource use in the state. It was thoroughly a product of its time, the 1960s, and it very consciously brought advocacy journalism to Maine. An unabashed point of view regularly challenged the political and economic powers in the state. For legislators, *Maine Times* was a must-read. Every Thursday early afternoon—it was a weekly—a copy would appear on every lawmaker's desk, fresh from the printer in Belfast. Business in the chambers would stop while they all read it to find out what was going on. "Leaders could not *not* read it," Barringer recalled. Indispensable to policymakers, the paper affected other environmental reporting in Maine, as well. Peter Cox, one of the founding editors, used to say that Bob Cummings got to write the environmental stories he wanted to cover by holding the threat of a *Maine Times* scoop over his editors' heads.[341]

In his interview with the paper, Ed Sprague was characteristically blunt. The problem was people "land-grabbing for their own greedy interests." Maine had to get serious and develop an actual policy toward the people's land, instead of "squandering" in a "haphazard manner," as it had been doing for over a hundred years.

Next Sprague went to enlist the help of the Maine Audubon Society. At the time it was led by Richard Anderson, who, as conservation commissioner, would play a major role in the final fate of the Public Lots. In 1972, as its first real environmentalist director, Anderson was guiding Maine Audubon's transition from the fusty natural history society of Henry Wadsworth Longfellow's day into a major force on behalf of the state's environment. The organization was housed on Baxter Boulevard, the Olmstead-designed necklace around Portland's Back Cove, in a building more generally identified as the showplace for an oriental rug company.

When Sprague cornered him, Anderson was headed for a meeting, and he soon began to feel like the Wedding Guest button-holed by the Ancient Mariner in Coleridge's poem. "He's telling me this story, and he's kind of a rabid guy," Anderson remembered. His advice was to talk to Bob Cummings, who was now with the Portland newspapers, having left the *Bath Times* in 1967. With the first Earth Day just around the corner, Cummings's beat was the environment, and he generally had a feature on one issue or another in the *Maine Sunday Telegram*, Maine's major Sunday newspaper.[342] Sprague and Cummings, mused Annee Tara: "Two crusty guys; together they must've been quite a pair."

Cummings was an "extraordinarily thoughtful and analytical reporter," said Jon Lund, who, as attorney general, would start the court case to reclaim the Public Lots. From his days as a state senator in the 1960s, Lund remembered watching Cummings at the back of a legislative hearing room, "sort of hunched over in a corner," quietly making notes and just occasionally asking questions.[343] He was one of the few environmental reporters "who could put things together and connect the dots."[344] Lund had grown up hunting and fishing in the Maine woods, which gave him his own perspective on what was at stake if the government didn't take steps to protect its wildlands. Maine may have been dubbed "Vacationland" as far back as the nineteenth century, but setting aside open space for public recreation was never a priority for state officials. With the paper companies letting people hunt and camp and fish on their huge ownerships, legislators saw no need to own—and have to manage—much land.

Just how shortsighted a policy that had been was suddenly becoming very clear. By the late 1960s, a number of factors—the opening of the interstate, for one—were fueling a boom in second-home development in Maine. As officials strove to make up for lost opportunities, the state was paying for the delay in inflated real estate prices. In that context, it seemed mistaken to be so casual with four hundred thousand acres of land already belonging to the people of Maine.

Such was the thrust of Bob Cummings's front-page article about the Public Reserved Lands in the *Maine Sunday Telegram* on March 12, 1972. "Public Land Sold And Given Away" was the banner headline. "Maine is pondering the disappearance of its coastline to out-of-state developers and speculators," the article began. It was struggling to buy what was left of its undeveloped lakeshores so Maine people could enjoy them. And all the while, "the recreational potential of some 400,000 acres the public already owns continues to be neglected, sold and given away." Those Public Lots—scattered all over the state, mostly in tracts of about a thousand acres, and invisible to the public—represented a potential prize far exceeding a mere windfall of acres. These lands "straddle mountain tops and slopes, encompass miles of lake, pond and riverfront, and include within their environs hundreds of free flowing wilderness streams," wrote Cummings. "This is the amazing story of the state's little known, and little understood Public Lots—a vast legacy of public domain dating from colonial times."[345]

It was exactly 184 years—less a fortnight—since the Resolve of the Massachusetts General Court had first codified the Public Lots.[346] After two centuries, wrote Cummings, their tale was "one of giveaways and neglect."[347] It's doubtful that he realized immediately what he had started. "I was short of an idea for a story one week," he remembered. Casting about for an issue, White Nichols's tale came to mind. "I told my editor, Let's do a story on the Public Lots. He'd never heard of them, as nobody else had. But I did the story." Having convinced his editor that it was a story, Cummings went and "fished around" the State House. He interviewed Austin Wilkins, the forest commissioner who had written the report on the Public Reserved Lands ten years before.[348] Wilkins's position was that when the state sold the rights to cut trees on the Public Lots, they had included the surface rights as well. Since about 1870, all the state owned were the minerals under the soil.

Like a good, skeptical reporter, Cummings dug deeper. "I read the deeds," he insisted, "and they didn't say anything about owning only minerals under the soil. And I just speculated that if there was more than a thousand acres [in a lot], there was a lot more that you could do besides cut trees on it. You could camp on it, you could walk on it, you could hike on it, do all kinds of things on that soil. And that was the basis of my first story."

For the first time that anybody could remember Maine's Public Reserved Lands were attracting serious attention in the press. The story made headlines not just on that Sunday, but for nine years after that, at times almost weekly. He might not have foreseen it at the time, but Bob Cummings had launched the largest land conservation effort Maine had ever seen. As a result of his article, the lands that the state would ultimately reclaim added up to twice the acreage Governor Percival Baxter bought up around Mount Katahdin to create the iconic Baxter State Park.

Chapter Eight

Wanted

Some Astute Horse-Traders (April–June 1972)

Until Bob Cummings's article appeared in March 1972, scarcely anyone other than the landowners who were cutting them knew anything about the Public Lots. Not Maine's governor, Kenneth M. Curtis, certainly; nor most of its legislature.[349] One of the few people in government who did was Austin Wilkins, the forest commissioner. At the age of sixty-seven, Austin Horatio Wilkins was winding up a distinguished career. As a graduate working on his master's degree in forestry at Cornell, he had visited Germany, where he absorbed the legacy of Carl Schenck, considered one of the fathers of American scientific forestry. (It was also while he was in Europe that he found himself at the aerodrome in Le Bourget when Charles Lindbergh landed in the *Spirit of St. Louis*.) Wilkins worked for the Maine Forest Service for forty-four years, the last fourteen as its commissioner.

Anyone who has devoted their working life to a single institution may be forgiven for getting set in their ways. In the course of his long career, Wilkins had been part of tremendous advances in how Maine managed its forest resources. But in the early 1970s, "the times they were a-changin'." Concerns over water quality were putting an end to the log drives on Maine's rivers; combatting an epidemic of spruce budworm was overtaking fire prevention as the major task of the Forest Service; the service itself was about to become a bureau within a much larger natural resource agency. And then came Bob Cummings's story in the *Maine Sunday Telegram*, "Public Land Sold And Given Away," opening Pandora's box.

The Guy Gannett newspapers quickly made the Public Lots their cause. "Startling" was how the *Telegram*'s editorial described the revelations the following Sunday. The author was the legendary Bill Caldwell, whose "unabashed love for Maine made him one of the state's most popular and influential columnists."[350] Their reporter's digging, wrote Caldwell, had shown that the public lands were being "either ignored or misused." The paper was accusing no one of "deliberate wrong-doing," but it looked as if somebody in government was "asleep at the switch." That somebody could only be Forest Commissioner Wilkins. His "drowsiness on the job," the editorial went on archly, was likely to end up depriving the people of Maine of "their legal heritage." In neglecting the potential of the public lands, Wilkins was "missing the chance of a lifetime." The editorial ended with a call to its readers. "Let's wake [these state officials] up to the opportunities and get some action now. Time is running out."

The salient feature of the Public Lots—and one that made their situation unique from the start—was that there were about four hundred of them, mostly parcels a thousand acres in size, and they were dispersed throughout Maine's ten million acres of wildlands. Cummings had realized at once that these tracts would be much more valuable to everyone if they could be consolidated into fewer, larger blocks. His newspaper went a step further: Wilkins and Lawrence Stuart, the Parks and Recreation director, should consider "parlaying these 400,000 wildland acres into 100 new State Parks of 4,000 acres each." All that was needed to realize such a worthwhile goal, it argued, were state officials "with an astute ability to engage in some good horse-trading."

Alas, such men seemed to be in short supply. When the private developer of a ski resort, Squaw Mountain, wanted a thousand acres of "spectacular mountain top land," the state had exchanged it for a woodlot instead of holding out for recreation land of comparable high quality. Actually, "bad swaps" were only the half of it. Companies with cutting rights were leasing lands with the greatest potential value to the public—stream and lakeshore sites with beautiful views—to private individuals for seasonal camps at nominal rates.

When the Public Lots began to make headlines, Governor Curtis was preoccupied with a massive reorganization of state government, streamlining 185 separate "departments" in the executive branch. He was just beginning his second term, and the sudden public criticism of his forest commissioner caught him off guard. In fact, for letting this state of affairs develop "under [his] nose," Caldwell had taken Curtis to task, as well, calling for his "immediate correction" of the way state officials managed the public's lands.

"And Curtis, who had never heard of the Public Lots, did the obvious thing," recalled Cummings. "He appointed a committee of state department heads to investigate what the hell these things were." In fact, the governor had established the Interdepartmental Committee on Public Lands the previous June with an executive order titled "State Acquisition and Sale of Land." Chair and secretary were, respectively, the directors of Parks and Recreation and State Planning; members included the commissioners of Forestry, Inland Fisheries and Game, and Highways, and the executive director of the Land Use Regulation Commission, usually known by its suggestive-sounding acronym, LURC. As part of Curtis's reorganization, and pending legislative approval, most of the agencies were slated for incorporation into a new Department of Natural Resources.

The committee had a broad mandate. A review of how state agencies were dealing with the sale and purchase of Maine's public lands would provide the basis for future policy on land sales or trades in the Unorganized Territories. At the same time, towns, conservation organizations, and individuals would be encouraged to set aside land for recreation, and to work together to resolve the inevitable conflicts between public and private rights, and between conservation and development. The problem was that in nine months, the committee had not yet met. It was time it did.

Meanwhile, Governor Curtis consulted his forest commissioner. Wilkins's review of the Public Lots had been comprehensive, and it was only ten years old. To him, the Public Lots were curious and inconvenient vestiges of forestry issues past. No one was very interested in them anymore. Already on the defensive, Wilkins drew particular attention to "a quote frequently found in the records: 'From the time Maine became a State in 1820, to the present time, the State has never parted with a single acre of land, except upon legislative authority.'" Why then were the Public Lots suddenly in the news? And why was he in the crosshairs? As far as the forest commissioner was concerned, there was nothing more to be said on the matter.

Still, to a governor always ready to listen and think in new ways, the idea of consolidating all these little tracts into several state parks had some merit. The problem, Wilkins told Curtis, was that Maine had unrestricted claim to only twenty-six thousand acres, or about 5 percent, of all the Public Lots. On the remaining 95 percent, nothing but residual rights to the soil and the minerals under it were left to the state. The rest had gone with the grass and timber rights when they were sold to the timber and paper companies a century ago.

Getting out his slide rule, Cummings countered with a more precise figure: the Public Lots owned outright by the state amounted to 26,873 acres. An additional 4,372 acres in tax-delinquent lands would make it forty-eight square miles, or "a pretty big chunk of land," claimed an editorial in Portland's *Evening Express*. Less diplomatic than their colleagues at the *Telegram*, the *Express*' editors wound up with a provocative reflection on things past.

It will be well to keep in mind that Maine's timber resources, during the nineteenth century, were being looted and stolen by private interests—in other words, the people of Maine have been robbed blind. There ought to be some way to make productive use of what is left.

From that point, and for the next ten-plus years, the shadow of an ancient wrong that might finally be righted loomed increasingly large over the state's policy-makers.

The *Telegram*'s "wake-up call" was answered by hundreds of letters to the editor. Public interest flared up, and the issue was quickly—if only briefly—adopted by Maine's burgeoning conservation movement. By chance, the fourth Environmental Congress was about to be held at Bowdoin College. Its agenda was hastily expanded, and when the three hundred or so participants arrived on campus the fate of the Public Lots received a thorough airing. Having never heard of them but three weeks before, the environmentalists focused on Cummings's original point: that the state was letting private interests acquire its own land for a song, even as it paid top dollar to buy other lands for state parks.[351] The conference formally called on Governor Curtis to halt all selling and leasing of lots until further investigation could bring greater clarity to what was at stake.

Commissioner Wilkins, meanwhile, was smarting from being put on the spot by the *Maine Sunday Telegram* over what still seemed to him to be a tempest in a teapot. He found it "difficult to remain silent on the recent editorial," he stated in a response to the paper that was a paradigm of long-suffering, professorial patience. There were "several inaccuracies," and he was especially nettled by implications of "wrong doing or mismanagement of the State's Public Reserved Lands."[352] He offered the *Telegram*'s readers a tutorial on the subject that went into considerable detail.

"Public Reserved Lands"—the official name for what the news stories had been calling "Public Lots"—existed in every unorganized township in Maine, Wilkins explained. The state "reserved" these tracts against the time when the township might be incorporated. When this happens, title to them is transferred to the new town as a resource for the support of the school. The forest commissioner has a guardianship role until then. He is required to generate income from "stumpage sales, sand and gravel, leasing of camp lots, utility lines, etc.," to be invested for the potential future needs of the township. Interest is paid out in a lump sum to cover the costs of existing schools in the Unorganized Territories. Thus, the Public Reserved Lands are "in a sense a trusteeship and not areas which the public can use at will." Scattered as they are over northern Maine, Wilkins admitted, "administrative management presents a difficult problem."

With regard to the sale or leasing of public land, Wilkins noted once again that the legislature decided such transactions, not the Forest Service. The paper had given a "false impression" about their extent; they were insignificant. (At that time, there were 389 leases—most of them an acre or so—laid off along a lakeshore or a road; rental income was shared, fifty-fifty, by the state and the company holding the timber rights.) To the criticism that Maine should make more if it was going to sell or lease its land, Wilkins responded that fees and prices were based on comparables in the area; and that at this time, rent controls imposed by the "Presidential freeze" prevented him from boosting them. (On August 15, 1971, President Richard Nixon had frozen prices and wages nationwide in a bid to stem unemployment and inflation.) But, the commissioner gently pointed out, the revenue would not look quite as paltry as Bob Cummings had suggested if his arithmetic were corrected: at 11 cents a square foot, the state gained closer to $5,000, not $500, an acre.[353]

The idea of consolidating the Public Lots into a hundred state parks showed Austin Wilkins to be the very model of the well-meaning, successful, and quintessential bureaucrat: raise questions, form a committee, and play for time. Such a "unique idea," he averred, would represent a major shift in policy. It would certainly require special legislation, possibly a constitutional amendment. A "long series of field studies, meetings with landowners and public opinion hearings" would be needed. In short, it would "create problems." As a first step, the commissioner suggested the governor convene the Interdepartmental Committee as a way to "clarify some of the so little known facts about this interesting subject."

Wilkins pointed out one further twist that would bedevil popular conceptions of the issue to the end. The Public Reserved Lands had only been surveyed and marked so that they might be found on a map in about half of the townships. In the others, they existed only as a concept—a "common and undivided interest" shared with the township's owner, usually a family or company engaged in large-scale forestry. In these cases, the state owned an undesignated twenty-fourth of the land area, a typical Public Lot being a thousand acres in a twenty-four-thousand-acre township.[354] This turned out to be hard for the public to grasp and created much confusion as the case unwound.

In light of the revelations about public lands, the interagency committee's failure to meet began to look like further official incompetence. Chairman Lawrence Stuart was quick to explain the delay. As Parks and Recreation director, he had been too busy creating a Department of Natural Resources in the new government plan. (It was not Stuart's fault that the legislature had voted down this particular part of the reorganization.) On April 11, 1972, the Interdepartmental Committee on Public Lands convened at last, the governor presiding. The rediscovered Public Reserved Lands were at the top of the agenda.

Progress at the meeting was overshadowed by the forest commissioner's refusal to halt the sale or lease of land in the public domain. The Natural Resources Council of Maine had followed up the Environmental Congress' resolution with a last-ditch plea for a moratorium. Second-home development, it pointed out, was the "current greatest threat" to Maine's wildlands.[355]

Wilkins was defiant. "As far as I know the leasing of camp lots is legal and I know of no reason why it should be halted," he told Cummings in an interview. Absent word to the contrary from the attorney general, his obligation was to "manage these lands to provide maximum income." That included leasing lots for camps.

Curtis provisionally backed his commissioner's position, but he gave Wilkins—together with James Haskell, executive director of LURC—the task of digging once again into the origins of the Public Lots. "Wilkins Gets History Assignment" was Cummings's headline. He also directed the committee to formulate a clear policy for reviewing and handling the Public Lots in future. "We must," said the governor, "make clear our willingness to use scarce land resources better." He would make the policy the basis for a governor's bill to be submitted to the legislature the next year.

Curtis's snappy response to the situation—the committee met exactly a month after the *Telegram* story came out—generated support from a surprising quarter. In his editorial, Bill Caldwell had blamed Curtis as well as Wilkins for mishandling the Public Lots. Now "the paper companies, who hated Ken Curtis, wrote letters defending him." To Bob Cummings, that meant he might be on to something big. He had his "first inkling" that the story was more than just a "typical Sunday feature."

The president of the Paper Industry Information Office—informally known as "P110" (pronounced P-One-Ten)—Morris R. Wing spoke at the Interdepartmental Committee's meeting in June. Wing was a classic rough-hewn Maine forester—"a substantial human being," as Richard Barringer remembered him, for whom a handshake was enough to seal a deal. As regional woodlands manager for International Paper, he knew every inch of the woods. He was also rarely happier than when in a sulky, training his trotters.

Wing's testimony followed much the same line as the forest commissioner's: praise for the status quo and support for any change so tepid and hesitant as to hardly merit the word.[356] Managing small areas embedded in large private ownerships, he admitted, could cause problems and extra expense. "If forest lands owners had their druthers, I'm sure they'd like to have no Public Lots or divided interest lots," he allowed. In that sense, consolidating thousand-acre lots into larger tracts might be useful. But swapping land must be carefully thought out to be fair. There were "many intricate factors to be resolved," warned Wing. "A considerable amount of thought [should] be put into the subject before we shift horses."

Of course, if Maine people want to "undertake a new concept of public lot use, they are within their rights to do so," Wing assented to the panel. But it was surely a complicated issue that would take some time to straighten out. Preserves for recreation were all well and good. However, the merits of setting aside "vast areas of land" that would only be used during a "very short summertime" by people on vacation, many of them from away, must be weighed against the many benefits offered by healthy timberland. "It gets to be a very lopsided comparison of values at times," Wing opined, especially in a state like Maine, where the public had access to millions of private acres—that same "good growing timberland"—for free. Morris Wing's testimony recalibrated Emperor Augustus's famous motto, *Festina lente*—"Make haste slowly."

At this point, Cummings was using the committee to keep his story alive until the public would take up the cause, or the political and legal reflexes cranked into gear. "So I wouldn't let that committee cross the street without doing a story on it." Besides chasing down its activities, he used his considerable investigative skills to set its agenda. Burrowing into state records, he dug up hidden inconsistencies that had never seen the light of day. "A surprising aspect in the continuing bizarre saga of Maine's public lands prompts several questions," wrote Cummings in mid-April. Why, when it sold public land near Sugarloaf Mountain to a group of camp owners, did the state hand over $665 per acre from the proceeds to the J.M. Huber Corporation? Huber didn't own the *land*, only the timber rights, which the Taxation Bureau valued at $14 per acre. It prompted a larger question, too. What portion of an acre's value was in the cutting rights, the only rights the state had sold?

Finding himself in the spotlight again, the embattled Austin Wilkins had to defend his actions once more. "I think I did very well for the state on this," he protested. "I feel rather pleased." Huber was paid a third of the price, not the usual 50 percent. As to Cummings's question about values and rights, this was the way it had always been done. With leases, Wilkins suggested that the committee might consider buying back the cutting rights before leasing a campsite. Given that camp owners wanted sites that were less than ideal for timber operations—lakeshores or mountainsides—that shouldn't be very expensive.

Aided and abetted by a "deluge" of letters to the editor, the *Telegram*'s bloodhound continued to press his case with questions that leapfrogged Wilkins's myopia. The Public Lots were a completely unexpected bonanza, he insisted. Maine should use them to its best future advantage; what was that? As they were currently being used, was Maine getting the most value out of them? Cummings doubted it, so long as the forest commissioner was ignoring their value to the public. Parks and Recreation, meanwhile, was paying through the nose to purchase suitable parcels, while Wilkins sat on—or more or less gave away—four hundred thousand acres of public land, much of it ideal for outdoor pursuits. As one environmental leader observed, "Many people looking at the State House from the outside and jarred at the prices being demanded for potential state park and other lands, have come away wondering whether the left hand was aware of the right hand."

Catalyzed by the environmental awakening of the 1960s, attitudes toward natural resources had changed since Governor Edmund Muskie appointed Austin Wilkins to head the Maine Forest Service fourteen years earlier.[357] (They had changed even more from 1783, when Massachusetts Governor John Hancock deemed Maine's forests "inexhaustible.") The North Woods were clearly finite; now they were diminishing just as more and more benefits and services were being demanded of them. Any given acre might provide for a multitude of uses other than cutting the trees that grew there for timber. Different constituencies started pressing for greater accountability from the powers that be, both public and private. It wasn't long before the Forest Service's leasing program—that other "area of misunderstanding"—came under fire again.

Once again, Commissioner Wilkins played down the extent and effects of leasing campsites on public lands. No Public Lot had ever been sold in toto. Such sales as there were came to seven acres out of five hundred here, twenty out of a thousand there, and always executed "by act of legislature." What was the problem?

And once again, the editors of the *Maine Sunday Telegram* joined the fray. In the face of the continuing public outcry, suggested a sly editorial, Wilkins's refusal to stop leasing campsites could only mean that he was deaf—deaf to the public he was paid to serve, with its overwhelming support for a moratorium. "We are baffled by the ailment in hearing which apparently affects the Forest Commissioner," wrote the editors. "Now Commissioner Wilkins is a fine and gentle man," they went on; one who would never "kick in the teeth the citizenry. . . . So for sweet charity's sake we must assume that [he] is a little hard of hearing as the result of the sudden uproar about public lands—an item that had been long tucked so quietly away in the corner, when this newspaper woke it to strident life." In other words: stop selling or leasing the public's land.

Wilkins's argument—to the public and to the Interdepartmental Committee—was that his activities had to be, and were, approved by the legislature; and that short of an injunction from Attorney General James Erwin, he saw no reason to stop. If he imposed a moratorium on his own initiative, he might even hear a complaint from Erwin. In the aftermath of the committee's meeting and this latest attack, he asked the attorney general for an opinion.

Erwin punted: leasing the public lands was a question of policy not law; it was up to the governor to decide. As chair of the committee, Lawrence Stuart announced that all future requests for a lease would be reviewed. Any that interfered with potential recreational or other public uses would be rejected. Existing leases (most of which were annual), Stuart admitted, would be renewed; but he expected they too would eventually come under his committee's review. It was a moratorium in deed, if not in word, while the department heads wrestled with the larger issues surrounding the future of the Public Lots. "For all practical purposes," concurred Governor Curtis, "I would expect there would be no land leases for some time." Better not to issue any new ones until the standing of the Public Lots had been cleared up.

To that end, Curtis issued an executive order for a study of the Public Lots, using two student interns to gather information for the committee. Attorney General Erwin also committed his office to an "in-depth study of the procedure in leasing public land since Maine separated from Massachusetts." It would begin once he had decided who to run it. Bob Cummings had indeed set off an avalanche. In the three months since that first headline on March 12, the Portland newspapers had already devoted over a dozen articles—mostly by Cummings—and hundreds of column inches to the Public Lots. The attention had borne results. The Interdepartmental Committee on Public Lands had sprung, Phoenix-like, to life and initiated a study of future options. Before the summer began, Erwin appointed a young assistant attorney general, Lee Schepps—who had served as the attorney for Stuart's committee—to review the legal twists and turns that had accrued to the Public Reserved Lands since Maine became a state. Forty years later, it's hard to imagine a newspaper having the ability to have such an impact so quickly.

Chapter Nine

Suppressed

"An Honest Report by a Competent, Conscientious Young Lawyer" (June–December 1972)

Maine, as everyone knows, is "Vacationland." Even in the halls of government, official business slows between July 4 and the Labor Day weekend. Those who can, head for their camps on the state's many lakes, ponds, rivers, and streams, or out to their boats on the coast and islands. For two men, however, the summer of 1972 was different. Assistant Attorney General Lee Schepps and Tom Gibbon, an intern from the University of Maine Law School, never got away from the capital, Augusta. Instead, they bounced between the attorney general's office and the Maine Law Library, digging into the arcana of the constitutional history of Massachusetts and Maine as it pertained to the Public Reserved Lands.

Schepps, a Texan, had fallen in love with Maine while doing his active duty in the Naval Air Reserve at Brunswick Naval Air Station during the Vietnam War. His passion for environmental causes was kindled by a maverick waging a solo war to protect a nearby river from the Army Corps of Engineers. Schepps volunteered for him after hours from his day job at a big private law firm in Dallas. "I became his Sancho Panza," he chuckled. At his office, the high-voltage work already left little time for a personal life. The offer of a promotion to partner in the law firm provoked an existential crisis. Lee Schepps needed a change in lifestyle. In 1971, he found a job that combined his legal expertise, his environmental avocation, and his love for the Maine landscape: he joined the environmental protection division in the Maine Attorney General's Office.

Maine was, at the time, one of the few states to have such a division (even though the position of attorney general itself was still part-time). The two environmental lawyers who were already there had divvied up the prime cases, so Schepps picked up responsibility for a slew of natural resource agencies:

149

forestry, parks, inland fisheries and wildlife, agriculture, geology—Schepps reckoned there were fifteen or twenty of them. (A single Department of Conservation was still in Maine's future.) Schepps's "little division" had already chalked up some impressive successes: a site location law, Maine's innovative Land Use Regulation Commission, shoreland zoning. He or his colleagues had written the legislation for them all. The Texas lawyer had come aboard at a very exciting time.

When the papers started asking questions about the Public Lots, it was only a matter of time before Attorney General James Erwin had to step in. He had tried to put off Austin Wilkins, when the forest commissioner asked for an opinion on leasing campsites, saying it was not a matter of law. But eventually, Lee Schepps was certain, someone—either from the paper companies, or large landowners, or, indeed, Commissioner Wilkins on their behalf—"went to Erwin and said: We need you to clear this up; there is nothing crooked going on here; this is all above board, and these newspaper articles are very destructive of our interests." Erwin tapped Schepps to research these Public Reserved Lands, whatever they were, and get back to him with a report. It was generally agreed that the AG picked this relative newcomer because he wouldn't have an axe to grind. At a time when students were protesting and demonstrating all over the country against the war in Vietnam, this clean-cut young Texas lawyer who wore three-piece suits to the office was just the person to calm the jitters of the forest industry. "I was a good bet. I wasn't a barnburner; didn't come across that way," Schepps said with a grin. He was also acutely aware that assistant AGs had no civil service protection at that time, and he had a young family to feed.

Shortly after he was given the task, Bob Cummings offered to take Schepps to Baxter State Park to show him the kind of land that was at stake. With them went Herb Hartman, another connoisseur of Maine's outdoors. The expedition was a "baptism by fire for this young greenhorn from Texas," recalled Schepps with a groan. They were going up Hamlin Ridge trail when it began to snow. "Hartman and Cummings reach in their pockets, put on gloves and some sock hats and a little pocket kind of windbreaker. I had none of that: no gloves . . . it was a beautiful early June day! We keep going and going, and I'm literally falling and slipping over the boulders; my hands are freezing, my ears are freezing." Finally he had to cry uncle. They turned back. "I hated to be the weak link in the chain," but, he had to accept, it was the only option. This did nothing, however, to put off the self-styled "city boy" from his love affair with Maine.

The Public Lots study took Lee Schepps and Tom Gibbon three months to research and write. Gibbon, the intern, did most of the research, spending eight-hour days in the law library. Schepps would review the results and suggest points that needed further casework. "So back to the stacks I'd go." This, Gibbon pointed out, was before the days of digital research, and gradually the cases he was consulting were spread out all over the tables in the law library. As a law student, Gibbon was thrilled. He was digging back in time, "using the law as it is supposed to be used."

From time to time, Cummings would phone Schepps, always with the same question: "Where's the report?" And Schepps would give the same answer. "I'm working on it; I'm doing the best I can." On top of the Public Lots, he was still responsible for his regular workload, and in the Maine Attorney general's office, the lawyers of the environmental protection division had a heavy caseload. As Schepps remembered it, they did something almost nobody did in state government those days: they worked weekends.

When he and Gibbon started, the case was a tabula rasa. Neither of them had any idea whether or not the state could recover its Public Reserved Lands. As the summer went on, the possibility started to take shape. Every week, there would be what Gibbon called a "Eureka moment." Nobody guessed how explosive the conclusions would turn out to be when done. The two of them had kept it completely under wraps. On September 12, the assistant AG presented his completed work to the attorney general. A few days later, Erwin called him into his office and asked if he had made any copies. He had, he said: one for himself and one for the law librarian, Edith Hary, who had been particularly helpful and had taken an interest in his study. "I want all those copies back right now," Erwin snapped. Schepps knew straightaway that his boss' instinct was to suppress the findings of the report.

Meanwhile, Labor Day had gone by; then Columbus Day came and went; and still the attorney general had said nothing about the Public Lots. With the early enthusiasm of his editors waning, Bob Cummings was feeling isolated. After their initial excitement at the Environmental Congress, the state's conservation groups weren't paying much attention—it was not an environmental issue, declared the Natural Resources Council of Maine. No one else was watching, either. "The idea that the state could misplace 400,000 acres of land [seemed] absurd. My editors and most readers treated the story as almost a joke," wrote Cummings in his own obituary. But he was dogged in his persistence, and he gave as good as he got. Bob, one of his editors related, was a "cranky cuss" who wrote "blistering complaints" about how his stories had been edited.[358] Forty-five years later, at the end of a life packed with achievement on behalf of Maine's woods and waters, Cummings took the greatest pride in the Public Reserved Lands. For him and for his editors, they were the "biggest story" of his life.

So he kept on calling Schepps, and one day, his persistence paid off. Schepps's reply wasn't, "I'm working on it," but, "Talk to the boss"; and he did. Looking back, Schepps said it was after that conversation—whatever was said—that Cummings's suspicions were really aroused. "What had been questions being raised now looked like there was a bunch of smoke coming out of the State House, that indeed there were things to hide."

Another reporter was on the scent. The week before Halloween, the Associated Press' Phyllis Austin asked Erwin the obvious question: what was Lee Schepps doing?[359] The attorney general was evasive. Schepps's brief was to look into the history concerning the Public Lots; what powers government had over them; the state's legal relationship with the grass and timber rights holders; and the legal status of the owners of the townships where Public Lots had been located on the ground. It was "an excellent resumé of the history, fact and legal consequences" of the Public Lots, but the work was still "incomplete," Erwin told Austin. Schepps had been too busy with other things. The study had reached no "significant conclusions." To make it public as it was would be "counterproductive," Austin quoted the AG as saying. "We don't want anyone making their own interpretations on the law research done." It was "just a working tool," he told her, and he doubted it would be finished before he left office in January. In which case, the decision would be up to his successor.[360]

Austin remained unconvinced. According to informed sources in the State House, Schepps had completed his task in September and Erwin was "sitting on it purposely." One went so far as to suggest it was a delaying tactic to ensure that no Public Lots bill could be drafted in time for the next session of the legislature. When she put this to Erwin, he told Austin she was barking up the wrong tree. "I have a responsibility to be right," he retorted loftily. "I don't want this thing coming out of my office with any implications that may later turn out to be wrong."

Erwin was keeping not just the public in the dark. Schepps was under explicit orders to share or speak about the report with no one. Lawrence Stuart, chairman of the Interdepartmental Committee on Public Lands, got half an hour to discuss it with the attorney general in his office. The other members of his committee were invited to submit their questions. When these didn't materialize, Erwin, who was already circling the wagons, commented sourly, "I guess they prefer to ask their questions through the press." The department heads were understandably frustrated at Erwin's stonewalling. They had been charged by Governor Curtis to find a way to deal with the Public Reserved Lands, and Lee Schepps was their legal counsel. If he couldn't find outside funding for the committee's own study, Stuart announced, he would ask the governor to recommend an appropriation in his new budget. Curtis hadn't seen the report, either.

Soon a professor from the Maine Law School weighed in. "Bereft of wisdom, common sense and good judgment" was Orlando Delogu's judgment on Maine's attitude to its public lands. The state had allowed itself to be "systematically ripped off—not just for a few years, but literally for decades," he told the *Maine Sunday Telegram*. To the extent he needed standing to comment, Delogu—no stranger to controversy—was Tom Gibbon's professor. The study was being suppressed, Delogu declared, because "it shows a course of official misconduct that borders on the criminal." He had not actually seen or read it, but his own research into the public lands made him confident in the accuracy of these assertions.

Bob Cummings had found a feisty ally. He quoted the professor at length. "Erwin clearly doesn't want the report out because it is personally embarrassing to him and because it reveals self-dealing and misconduct that will touch any number of people that are still in Maine government." Schepps had brought to light a "link between vested interests and political interests inside and outside of government." His report "attempts to establish the legal capacity for the legislature to undo some of this, in effect to recover for the people of Maine a bit of their lost resource." Putting off its release would delay the legislature from doing just that, Delogu told Cummings. "This is an honest report by a competent, conscientious young lawyer. That's why it's being suppressed."[361]

Not surprisingly, Erwin bridled at these accusations. They were "completely untrue and completely unfair," "unconscionable." The report was intended to clarify opportunities for the future, not to dwell on any alleged wrongdoings in the past. Delogu's tirade, however, led to an actual glimpse into the contentious document in the form of Schepps's transmittal memorandum to Erwin, which he now released. It started by indicating what the one-hundred-page report was not. "No treatment is given to the manner in which the Public Lots have been administered by the state. No treatment is given to the particular situation of any particular Public Lot in a particular township. The focus is exclusively on the rights and powers of the state, not on the details of how that power has heretofore been exercised."

The memorandum was essentially an executive summary of Schepps's findings, and it underscored the following conclusions:

- The legislature had the power to use the Public Lots for other than their original intent, notably for "park or other public purposes"; it could also authorize their "sale or exchange . . . to assemble large contiguous quantities of land."
- In townships where the Public Lots had not been located (on the ground), the state was a tenant in common, sharing "all sources of common income . . . , the right to common possession and the right to prevent waste of the common property."

- When the cutting rights were sold, timber might have signified a certain size and purpose, and might have excluded species like beech, maple, and birch.
- It was a "distinct possibility" that only the "growth of timber in existence at the time of each conveyance" had been sold, which would mean that the rights had expired.
- Whenever a township was organized into a plantation, grass and timber rights on its Public Lots were terminated.
- The state was entitled to use a Public Lot in any way that did not "unreasonably impair" the timber company's right to cut and carry away.
- The state could prevent cutting methods that damaged the land, even if those methods were acceptable on private land, for example, "clear cutting and the use of skidders and similar heavy equipment."

Over the following weeks, these questions were picked up, one by one, in the public discussion. They defined the debate over the Public Lots from then on.

A few days after Delogu's attack, James Erwin found himself under fire from another quarter. His assistant AG had carefully refused all comment on the controversy. Under no such compulsion was Tom Gibbon. The fallout from the Watergate break-in the previous June was still in the air, and Gibbon, as a student, felt no particular sympathy for "The Man." He knew how complete and thorough his and Schepps's work had been and that there was no need for more research. Since Erwin wouldn't release the report, the only way it was going to do any good was if it got leaked to the press. After debating long and hard with himself, Gibbon contacted Cummings and categorically denied the attorney general's repeated assertion that the work was unfinished.

It had needed nothing but a final review and to be typed up when he went back to law school in early September, the intern insisted. In his excitement, he assumed it would be made public as soon as this had been done. "This was so amazing," he said, "I was sure we were going to do something. I was sure everyone would want to act." Erwin's reticence baffled Gibbon. If a lawmaker wanted to address the Public Lots with a bill when the legislative session opened in January, he would need more than the "key conclusions," and he would need it now. "There might be a reason for keeping the report secret if you work for the big land owners," he told Cummings provocatively. "I can think of no reason if you are working for the people of Maine." It was the public's land, and the public had a right to know what the AG knew. Over forty years later, Gibbon remained certain he did the right thing. "I was young and dumb at the time. But even today, from a mature lawyer's point of view, [withholding the report] didn't make sense."[362]

Once again, James Erwin was left sputtering defensively. Gibbon's statement was "patently ridiculous." "This thing is getting to the point where a lot of stuff is being tried in the press," fumed the attorney general, making no secret of how objectionable he found the news coverage. But Gibbon had forced his hand, and Erwin agreed to let Cummings interview Lee Schepps in his presence, although he continued to withhold the report. In response to the reporter's direct questions, Gibbon's version of the study was basically verified.

What jumped out at Cummings right away was that cutting rights on Public Lots reverted to the state if or when a township was organized. All the legislature would have to do to regain full control was to turn a township into a plantation, the first step toward becoming an incorporated town. Admittedly, present law required a population of 250 before this could occur, but the law in question had not been on the books when the timber and grass rights were sold. All that was needed was to repeal it. This, in Lee Schepps's opinion, would not be difficult. Once done, the Unorganized Territory could be divided up into plantations, automatically restoring the Public Lots to the people of Maine.

Schepps also dealt a blow to the long-held assumption that whatever revenue the Reserved Lands generated had to be held in trust for the education of the children of settlers. "This," he said, "just isn't so." It was based on a literal interpretation of a provision in the Articles of Separation that had never been accepted by the courts. "Public lots and the income from Public Lots," he stated categorically, "can be used for any public purposes."

His interview in the AG's office confirmed what Bob Cummings and his paper had been saying all along: the Public Reserved Lands could be used for "public parks, recreational areas or any other public purpose the legislature designates." Laws made "in accordance with the land needs of the late 1700s and early 1800s can be changed according to the land needs of 1972." Maine could recover what it had lost a century before, and use it as it pleased. Reading between the lines in his story, it's fair to infer that Cummings couldn't resist needling the attorney general by suggesting that stories in the press (primarily from his newspaper) had galvanized the state into taking action. Erwin rose to the bait. "I reject that idea completely," he responded. "That this report was written had absolutely nothing to do with any newspaper stories. It started out when it occurred to me that this is a subject this office didn't know much about. I thought we might have a lot of questions that we weren't then prepared to answer."

Still, the *Press Herald/Sunday Telegram*'s reporter could take considerable pride in how far the issue had come in just over six months. "If translated into legislative action, the Schepps study would restore to public control some and perhaps most of the vast remainder of the eight-million-acre public domain that Maine inherited from Massachusetts when it became a state in 1820," exulted Cummings. The claim was overblown, perhaps even misleading, since the "vast remainder" was about a twentieth of said public domain.

Nonetheless, Maine stood to receive the four-hundred-thousand-acre windfall. "Not too many states will get . . . the chance to decide the fate of that much land they don't have to pay for," crowed Tom Gibbon in an extensive interview shortly afterward. Legislators had been handed an "incredible responsibility and an incredible opportunity." Gibbon cast their options in stark contrast. "They could really blow it . . . [and] sell it all off. Or they could sit down and really try to be creative." The Law Court could have the last word on the legal question once the legislature had spoken. However, the "important thing is to get the report before the public so it can be debated and discussed, and people can begin deciding the proper steps to take."

Gibbon also addressed the practice that had come under early fire from the conservation community, leasing campsites on public land. He questioned the state's custom of splitting lease fees with the owner of the timber rights. The companies had no right to compensation unless their cutting operations were impeded. Since most camps were on a lake or on a mountaintop, they had a minimal impact on timber harvesting. And yet, with an acre of forest producing on average a buck and a half's worth of wood a year, the state was giving up $100 from a lease for a camp that might be measured in square feet? "This has to be a figure that someone just pulled out of the air," Gibbon concluded.[363]

Particularly incensed at being denied a glimpse of what was now known as the Schepps report had been James Haskell, the executive director of LURC. Now he got a little of his own back. Erwin had been surprisingly casual in communicating with Governor Curtis about the report. "I have offered to sit down with the executive department," he told a reporter. "Whether I give the governor a copy depends on if after our discussion he wants one and on how he and I decide the matter should be handled." Curtis asked for a summary, which Erwin put into a three-page letter. He refused to share its contents with the press but sent a copy to members of the Interdepartmental Committee, which included Haskell, who promptly shared it with the Portland papers. No one had told him not to, he said.

Given the fears that had been gathering around the Schepps report's future, the attorney general's letter was reassuring. Erwin allowed as how the cutting rights might have run out, and that the legislature had the power to direct their future. "Prudence suggests," he counseled the governor, that the question be put to the Supreme Judicial Court since the constitution was involved. For Cummings, this was a "major new revelation." On November 5, his almost weekly headline ran, "Public Lots: Cutting Rights May Be State's After All."

Cummings was still fueling the public discussion more or less single-handedly. Now he raised a new specter. What if all of a sudden interest in the Public Reserved Lands led landowners to cut all the timber while the cutting was good? If they felt their rights could be truncated at any moment, it would be the prudent decision from a business point of view. The price for legislative dawdling, he warned, could be "a barren wasteland of clear-cut stumps."[364] No journalist in Maine had more experience of—or written with greater love for—the state's wild places than Bob Cummings. Rattling off a list of gems at risk, he sent a chill into the hearts of hikers and campers and nature lovers all over Maine: Gero Island with the "most magnificent stand of big pines remaining in northern Maine"; the scenic summit of Coburn Mountain; Long Lake, at the north end of the "spectacular" Barren-Chairback Mountain range.

"A Maine forest industry that is about to cut the equivalent of 16,000 acres in Baxter State Park," he wrote, "isn't likely to show restraint when threatened with the loss of public lands it has treated as its own for more than a century." The reference was to a deal between Great Northern and the Baxter Park Authority made by James Erwin, who as attorney general was one of the triumvirate that made up the park's governing body. When it sold the land—in the park's southeast section—to Governor Baxter, Great Northern retained the right to cut it. When it came to exercise that right, "there was a lot of wailing about the fact that there was going to be cutting along the road that people drove in on," Jon Lund remembered. Erwin arranged to switch Great Northern's harvest area to part of the park reserved for scientific forestry. However, a "massive cutting operation" yielding 109,000 cords in two years could hardly be called "scientific forestry."

Cummings could be confident that his readers would take notice when he told them that deciding the fate of the Public Lots was "probably the most pressing environmental decision facing Maine's elected and appointed officials." But first, the chainsaws must be stilled. A state senator from rural western Maine was quick to echo his concerns. The paper companies would cut "like mad" unless something was done, warned Republican Senator Elden H. Shute from Farmington in rural western Maine. He was drafting a bill to impose a four-year moratorium for harvesting on the Public Lots. Shute, like everyone else, had concluded that the courts would decide whether the grass and timber rights had been sold in perpetuity or not. Four years should leave enough time for the case.

Two days before Thanksgiving, in response to the attorney general's letter, Governor Curtis reconvened his public lands committee. The new session of the legislature was only six weeks away, and Curtis directed them to "create the machinery to unravel the Public Lots question."[365] Maine, said the governor, was running out of open lands, and "may want to put the [Public Lots] to other purposes." But in such a tangled case, Erwin was quite right to proceed slowly and cautiously, he said, carefully straddling the incipient feud between conservationists and the attorney general. The committee also turned its attention to the use of the Public Lots for purposes other than cutting timber. In townships where they had not been located, the government seemed never to have collected its share of the resulting revenues, which, based on an approximate size ratio, should be one twenty-fourth. Such uses included extraction of gravel or minerals, as well as leasing camps.

Schepps raised another question, obscure but arresting, from his report. When the rights to cut timber on the lots were sold between 1850 and 1875, what kind of wood were the timber companies actually buying? What did the legislature think it was selling? The answer was: sawlogs. At the time, the best trees for sawlogs were large spruce, oak, and pine. That, Schepps attested, was what "timber rights" was assumed to mean. The legislature changed the definition to "anything that grows" in 1903—long after it sold the rights—after the industry shifted to cutting spruce for pulp and paper. Few trees grew big enough for sawlogs anymore. Change the definition by repealing the 1903 law, and the state could insist on being paid stumpage for the hardwoods. That would be the first time the Public Lots had earned money in more than a century, commented Cummings.

The first draft of the bill the committee was preparing for the approaching legislative session included authorizing a pilot project to organize half a dozen townships into one or more plantations. With their timber rights thereby returned to the state, the feasibility of various futures for the Public Lots could be tested. Any that were held in common undivided ownership would be laid out for maximum public benefit. The bill also repealed the 1903 "anything that grows" law to test Schepps's theory.

Of the several ways of dealing with the Public Reserved Lands, extinguishing grass and timber rights by "organizing" one or more townships was the most contentious. As Stuart's committee grappled with the idea, it smacked to some of subterfuge. Others worried that the people living there might have no wish to be burdened with self-government. Organization should be a boon, countered Lee Schepps. Hundreds of thousands of acres of land would be added to the tax rolls. With big enough plantations, "you won't create burdens but tremendous benefits," he asserted. Claimed one observer, in a sumptuous metaphorical mishmash, "Once the word spreads around, everybody will be so hungry to get their olive out of the jar, they may create a traffic jam. The squabble will be over who is to get their slice of the pie first and how much."[366] Cummings addressed the second concern by making the first more transparent. Towns can be deorganized just as townships can be organized, he wrote enthusiastically. "The beautiful part of the plan is that if it doesn't work, you can go back to the original and still keep the public lands as a bonus."

Such a gambit, however, was not likely to come from a committee of department heads made shy by ghosts of legislatures past.[367] When Haskell, the outspoken LURC director, suggested the Unorganized Territories be clumped into one big self-governing "Unorganized District of Maine," Stuart reminded him what happened when another report suggested a similar move: giving the townships responsibility for educating their children. It had seemed like a good idea at the time but "got clobbered in the legislature."[368] The large landowners, opposed to paying school costs, killed it, wrote Cummings.

Instead, the committee ratcheted back its recommendations to organizing only the twenty-three thousand acres still owned, rights and all, by the state, a mere 5 percent of what was at stake. "A way to get a foot in the door" without stirring up a political hornet's nest, was how Chairman Stuart tried to spin the retreat. But even this modest proposal went too far for some. At its final meeting on January 2, only two members voted in favor; two were opposed; and two made their support conditional on approval by the residents of the townships. This was unlikely to be forthcoming, as the committee discovered earlier when it tried to develop two case studies on Public Lots possibilities.

"We just happened to pick these two," Stuart told the *Maine Times*. Sinclair was an unincorporated village in the far north of Aroostook County, with a popular recreation area and the most children of any township in the Unorganized Territories. Rockwood Strip, on the west side of Moosehead Lake, had the makings of a forest preserve and deer wintering area. In both places, the residents were "vigorously opposed" to terminating the cutting rights. Nothing came of either study. In the end, the committee could only recommend that the forest commissioner be permitted to "sell, trade, or relocate" the state's twenty-three thousand acres. For the rest of the Public Lots, they adopted the consensus view: its intent when the legislature sold the timber and grass rights a century ago would have to be divined through the courts.

All this time, James Erwin's defenses had been crumbling. With little more than a month before leaving office, he allowed the governor's committee to read, in his office, what he liked to call "Schepps's memo to me." As to making it available to the public, the AG stood by his decision to keep it under wraps. He had not had time to reach his own conclusion about "all the things specific as well as implicit" in Schepps's work, so he would leave it to the new attorney general to initiate any action. It remained his view that "in this whole area of wildlands use" (including the Public Lots), a court case was inevitable, and the state would base its brief on the study's points of law. They shouldn't be publicized beforehand. "I am not playing games with the Right to Know law," Erwin protested. "Neither am I concealing anything material from the public."

Though not directly related—nor completely separate either—environmental crusader Ralph Nader was simultaneously preparing to release his organization's report on the pulp and paper industry's impact on Maine.[369] "Power and the abuse of power derives from people with names," wrote the author, William C. Osborn, pinning most of the blame on the men at the top.[370] And he promised to name them. Under the headline "The Nader Study," the *Portland Press Herald* nodded approvingly, also urging Osborn to consider the unintended consequences of having a citizen legislature, "an honest enough body which wants to do right by Maine." The report described that body as having "a kind of 19th century belief in amateurism and non-professionalism that is as much the legislature's enemy as are the big power blocs." The *Press Herald*'s editors concurred: "The legislature, with its touching faith in the power of its own good intentions, has allowed itself to remain understaffed, under-informed, and dangerously reliant on lobbyists and industrial representatives." This, as much as naming names, was what needed to be addressed. The piece read like a barometer of Maine people's changing attitudes: toward the forest, and to their relationship with government and the industry. A new era was beginning.

Nothing so clearly symbolized the passing of the old than the graceful retirement of Austin Wilkins on January 1, 1973. As Maine's longest-serving forest commissioner, Wilkins had had a remarkable career dedicated to what he considered best for the state's forests. His close relations with the forest industry—the executives of P110 and the Maine Forest Products Council—had achieved great things for Maine. However, when the "Age of Aquarius" caught up with Maine's North Woods, and especially the Public Reserved Lands, it was not something with which he could come to terms. The penultimate sentence of his farewell essay, "44 Years of Public Service in Retrospect 1928–1972," read: "Purposely omitted has been any reference to some current issues which may or may not have a future impact." The truth was that Austin Wilkins was too close to the trees to see the woods. The public wanted more daylight between the two, as well as transparency—and even a voice—in managing the land, all of which would have been unthinkable even ten years before.

In *Ten Million Acres of Timber: The Remarkable Story of Forest Protection in the Maine Forestry District (1909–1972)*, his history of the Maine woods he had loved and served so meticulously, Wilkins called Lee Schepps's report an "excellent and thorough historical perspective," but he declined to examine it, noting curtly that "[a]vailable material before the cut-off date of 1972 is considered to be not within the scope of this particular study."[371] Elsewhere in his final annual report as forest commissioner, he did include a section, "Recommendations for the Public Lots," somewhat oddly titled because it contained no real recommendations. They had been ignored for a long time, wrote Wilkins, but would be no longer.

> At the end of this reporting period there is much activity relative to the Public Lots. A Legislative Select Committee on Public Lands is making a wide ranging review of all public lands. It is considered likely an interium study will be made with recommendations to the next session of the Legislature.
> . . . With increasing land values and more interest by the public in any public land rights remaining it appears these policies will be thoroughly reviewed during the next biennium.

They were indeed: in the next biennium, and the next, and the next, as they moved from the executive branch, to the legislature, and finally to the judiciary. For now, however, Bob Cummings was pessimistic. The Interdepartmental Committee had essentially washed its hands of the matter. After nine months of Cummings's own relentless effort, his headline on the last day of 1972 read: "Public Lots May Be Lost Again, This Time By Inaction."

Chapter Ten

Public Lots Report

Likely Ammunition in the Spring
(January–July 1973)

The new attorney general, Jon Lund, took a very different view of Maine's forests and public lands than had his predecessor. They were both Republicans, but Erwin, at least in Lund's opinion, was "sort of a good old boy" who didn't want to offend the paper companies. This was why he had sat on Lee Schepps's report. Public land—or rather Maine's lack of it—was a burr that still nagged at Lund over forty years after leaving public office. Why hadn't the state acquired more in the years—the 1940s, 1950s, 1960s—when it was going really cheap?[372] It had always frustrated him, never more so than when Lawrence Stuart, the director of Parks and Recreation, no less, had boasted that the state "hadn't spent a cent [to acquire] any state park." During his first year as a state legislator, Lund had approached Stuart about floating a bond for land acquisition. Lund was "stunned" to find that the director had no ideas, let alone plans, for any new parks at all. It was, he felt, symptomatic of the state's attitude: "We don't need parks, we can get all this wonderful land for free," thanks to the timber companies. In the end, the young senator pulled a dollar figure for his bond out of thin air.

Lund had made no secret of the fact that he would release the Schepps report as soon as he took office as Maine's top lawyer, in January 1973.[373] Anything that helped increase Maine's woefully small public domain had his blessing. Although there were only a few copies—this being before the days when copiers were found in every office—someone had leaked its contents to him in the fall. His assessment was that "Schepps was a very bright and capable guy, and I thought his report made sense." Ironically, Lund's father had come over from Sweden in the thirties to run the Cushnoc Company paper mill in Augusta; and his father-in-law owned the log-driving company on the Kennebec River. "They probably thought I was a 'traitor to my class,'" Lund mused, smiling at the thought.

On January 23, 1973, the banner headline in the *Portland Press Herald* was "Ex-President Lyndon Johnson Dies." Below LBJ's photograph on the front page, there was just room for the beginning of another article by Bob Cummings, "Suppressed Lots Report Is Released." Further embargo of the Public Lots report, Lund said, served only to muddy an issue already confusing and complicated enough. His predecessor's fear that to release it would be to tip the state's hand in any future court case was far outweighed by the benefit of replacing wild conjecture with informed discussion. That could only be done by getting the whole report into the public's hands, and quickly. The new attorney general had been in office less than a week.

In releasing the Schepps report, Lund drew particular attention to two of its conclusions. The four hundred Public Lots (mostly a thousand acres each) could be used in any way the state saw fit. The legislature had established a critical precedent in 1824 when it changed the beneficiaries specified in the Articles of Separation—ministry, church, and education—to education alone. What it could do then, it could do again in 1973.[374] In fact, it could go further and sell or exchange the lots to make large contiguous public lands, like the forty ten-thousand-acre parks that Bob Cummings had conjectured from the start.

The second point was far more explosive. The rights to harvest timber and grass on the Public Lots might have expired. It was not an "unqualified opinion," the report hedged, but Schepps put forward several issues that might be tested in court. The deeds—from the second half of the nineteenth century—were silent about the timber that would grow there in the future. That the lumber companies continued to cut for a hundred years was a function of "time and history" and not the unequivocal intent of the state. Circumstantial evidence hinted that the intention was not to sell more trees than stood at the time: cutting rights on a Public Lot sold for a similar amount as the ten-year cutting rights in the rest of the township. In sum, wrote Schepps, the deeds were so indefinite about their duration as to mean anything.[375] He was confident of one thing: the value of the timber harvested on any given Public Lot over some hundred years "far exceeds, by any measure, the consideration received therefor by the State." The average annual income from an acre of productive woodland in 1973 was three dollars; from 320,000 acres of Public Lots, it came just short of a million dollars a year. Figures being tossed around for the value of the land itself were in the region of $30–$40 million. The stakes were high for both sides.

In the past, Schepps's findings might have made at most a ripple, to be quickly calmed by the lumber bosses in Bangor. But not in 1973. A new attitude was abroad, not just in Maine but across the nation. "The times they are a-changin'," as Bob Dylan had proclaimed ten years before. Whether it was civil rights, the war in Vietnam, or Earth Day, the people wanted to have a more direct say in what their government did in their name. Asserted *Maine Times* reporter Lucy Martin, referring specifically to the interest the Schepps report had stirred up, "The public has a long overdue role to play in any evaluation of the way in which public assets are used and administered."[376]

Democratic Governor Kenneth Curtis, whose committee had been bird-dogging the Public Reserved Lands for almost a year, took up the issue a week after the report's release. The centerpiece of his annual legislative message to the Maine House and Senate was how the Public Lots could "better accommodate the needs of the people." The time had come, said Curtis, to clarify what the state could and could not do with these lands. First, the law of 1824 must be repealed. The expectation that new towns would emerge from the wilderness was no longer realistic. Therefore, holding a Public Lot in trust against that possibility made no sense either. The governor then grabbed the nettle that his committee had in the end refused to touch.

Maine's unorganized townships, about ten and a half million acres of wildlands, should be turned into one or more plantations, the first step toward incorporating them as towns. This would give self-government to the people who lived there and extinguish whatever rights private owners had over the Public Reserved Lands. The income they produced would go straight into the Maine treasury and no longer be left as "a windfall to the incorporators of each new town." The solons should then use their discretion and earmark Public Lots for recreation. To test the legal possibilities, at least one should be turned into a state park or forest. If the justices decided that the state could put the Lots to any public use it chose, the governor would instruct the Bureau of Public Lands (BPL), a proposed agency in the new Conservation Department, to come up with a list of the various opportunities.[377]

That the question—who owns the Public Lots?—should dominate the legislative session was the symptom of an environmental awakening that had begun before Bob Cummings wrote his first article, even before White Nichols and Ed Sprague commenced their agitating. It was set off by waters that poisoned and air that choked, neither of which could be morally defended, even if that was what the industries responsible at first tried to do. Land, however, was more complicated. Public interest collided head-on with America's most fundamental article of faith, the sanctity of private property. Could it be that benefit to the many mattered as much as the private desires of the few, when it came to what to do with or on their land? Or that its value for tomorrow might sometimes outweigh the profits it brought in today? In Washington, these questions were being taken up with legislation like the Federal Land

Policy and Management Act, an attempt to define multiple use on the vast public lands of the West.[378]

By contrast, most of Maine's forest was privately owned. The old compact between the large forest owners and their workers that had opened the land to hikers, campers, and sportsmen was being stretched as more and more of those filling the woods were coming from farther and farther away. That many of the "vacationists" came from "outside the state" was one reason P110's Morris Wing, the previous June, had urged the original public lands committee to discount them and weigh in on the industry's side.[379]

The new population of outdoor enthusiasts, however, was not going away. Instead, they were insisting that they, as well as the owners, had a stake in how the land was treated. The companies harvesting its trees could no longer treat the forest as if it was a factory belonging to them alone, even if the land had their corporate logos all over it. The resulting struggle pitted old assumptions against new, conservative ideas versus progressive, and again—as earlier in the history of Maine's wildlands—great proprietors against the people. More than just a symptom, the Public Lots would become a catalyst in sorting which of the bundle of rights attached to the land were appropriately public and which private.

An exchange in the *Maine Times* offered a snapshot of the human side of this divide. The paper, the advance guard of progressive Maine, had sent out a series of questions about the Public Lots matter to all the paper companies and large landowners. As president of Seven Islands Land Company, John Sinclair, a man respected by all sides, was one of the recipients. Before responding, Sinclair went to the trouble of reading enough back issues to gain a sense of the paper's politics. Then he politely declined to pursue the request further. He and the *Maine Times*, he decided, were "a long way apart in our thinking"; the latter had no respect for private rights, private ownership, and maybe even the forest industry.

Most of the other companies responded with quite extensive, written answers.[380] Release of the Schepps report—with legal chapter and verse that directly questioned their "ownership" of four hundred thousand acres of forest—had not gone unnoticed. Their basic position was summed up in a couple of succinct statements in two missives. One was, "We bought a perpetual cutting right in good faith." The other: "If something belongs to someone, you don't just take it away." Taken together, a clear consensus emerged. The Public Reserved Lands were in good hands, theirs. Their management not only kept the forest healthy, it provided good jobs and useful, even essential, products. The general public was getting a great deal: enjoying company land to camp, hunt, fish, and hike without having to pay for it; and benefiting from the taxes it brought in, to boot. Even the unpaved logging roads the companies were putting in were a "happy compromise," providing public access with a minimum additional change to the environment. This "best of both worlds" offered Maine a sound economic future mixed with tremendous social benefits.

As for the alternative, to manage Maine's forest for recreation or conservation alone would be a "shameful waste of a precious resource." And where was the advantage of replacing private with public management? The *Maine Times* itself, noted one land manager, did not seem too impressed with what the state was doing with the Allagash Wilderness Waterway or Baxter State Park to mention but two examples. In his opinion, a "wise and all competent bureaucracy does not exist." Other companies offered similarly judgmental advice. Bureaucrats should try to respond to real needs, not the wants of a few vocal constituencies. Until Maine developed a comprehensive set of land-use plans, "all headline-making ideas for a change here or a change there" should be strongly opposed. Scott Paper's Robert LaBonta, who would become Maine's conservation commissioner fifteen years later, admitted that there was no "pat answer that would be totally fair to the general public and to the landowners"; but regardless of ownership, the highest and best use of the Public Lots was growing and harvesting trees.

As the paper industry position, a sole commitment to forestry was true only up to a point. State Senator Horace "Hoddy" Hildreth Jr. had been a junior partner at Pierce, Atwood, Scribner, Allen, and McKusick, the Portland law firm that traditionally handled the paper companies' business.[381] There he had lobbied for several paper companies on labor and social issues. However, he was uncomfortable with what they were planning for the forest and steered clear of "environmental stuff." With Maine becoming ever more popular as "Vacationland," it was obvious to Hildreth that the private landowners and paper companies were getting ready to cash in on the hundreds of lakes with beautiful shores and views on their lands. "Not that they were doing anything illegal at all," he recalled later, "but it was very cynical, really." He was sure it was only a matter of time before they started selling off lakeside lots for second homes. "They were very circumspect about it—but it was clear that this was going to happen." In fact, the Huber Lumber Corporation was already laying out a "designer community" on the east side of Moosehead Lake called Beaver Cove.[382] The village was "to have a little bit of everything" and "to provide something to fit every taste." Huber's method—large lots "plotted out to compensate for having less desirable non-waterfront land"—was reminiscent of the efforts of Maine's earliest surveyor-developers like British Governor Bertrand, Moses Greenleaf, and Eli Towne.

It was a striking sign of the times that so much of the pressure on behalf of progressive land use was coming from the government itself. Maine's environmental groups were neither as strong, nor as active, nor as numerous as they would become in the next dozen years or so. In 1973, the engine for environmental change was the state legislature, "the people's house." Consciously or not, enough lawmakers had taken Bob Dylan's words to heart—"Come senators, congressmen/Please heed the call/Don't stand in the doorway/Don't block up the hall"—to start a revolution. And it was a bipartisan effort, with Republicans like Jon Lund, Harrison "Harry" Richardson, and "Hoddy" Hildreth leading the charge.

It was Hildreth's idea to create the Land Use Regulation Commission to guide development in the Unorganized Territories, those parts of Maine where there was no municipal government to make and enforce local ordinances. (In fact, the same part of the state Governor Curtis was now suggesting could be organized into plantations.) When LURC, as it was soon known, was established in 1971, such an approach had never been tried anywhere else before, and it "has never been far from controversy" since.[383] Even as the forest industry was mustering against whatever Kenneth Curtis might put forward regarding the Public Lots, they were also launching an attack on LURC as unconstitutional.

Maine's natural resource agencies—still scattered over half a dozen separate agencies but most on the way to being consolidated within larger departments—had the task of implementing LURC and other groundbreaking laws such as the Site Location for Development law and Maine's early clean water act. They were starting to inventory the state's uninhabited islands and (in a more political "stakeholder" process) its mountains. The State Planning Office was thinking in terms of a "computer analysis system" to store data on all Maine's natural resources and to guide decision-making regarding their use and management. It would be expensive, Maine's first planning director, Philip Savage, acknowledged, but no forward-looking land-use policy could be devised without it.

Backlash was inevitable. Any hint of land-use planning, let alone regulation, was instantly assailed as an attack on free enterprise. "Black helicopters" were just beginning to be discussed in militia circles, so data-gathering was immediately suspect. Rapid change in the forest for the first time in a century made attitudes volatile. On top of planning, said Savage, his main job was to "convince Maine people that they're not giving up their freedoms."[384]

LURC aroused the special ire of the same people who were most suspicious of any alteration in the status of the Public Lots, the residents of the Unorganized Territories and the timber companies. The commission's opinionated director, James Haskell, made it still more controversial. He saw Maine's wildlands as a tabula rasa, and he framed the options for their future in blunt terms. They could either be paved over and developed into a second

New Jersey, or left as the largest wilderness park on the eastern seaboard. Or, anything in between. It was hard to know what trade-offs Mainers were prepared to make in the unfettered use of private land.

With the upswing in outdoor recreation, the State Parks and Recreation Commission had been striving to catch up by acquiring more parks. For Maine's sesquicentennial, in 1970, it put out a brochure that boasted:

> Rockbound coast . . . sweeping beaches . . . scenic views . . . offshore islands and ragged peninsulas . . . mountains . . . lakes and ponds . . . forest covered wilderness, as far as the eye can see. Much of the natural beauty of Maine is displayed in an expanding network of state parks—and Maine is opening new ones every year.

Since his first conversation with State Senator Jon Lund, Parks and Recreation Director Stuart had developed a less passive approach to his agency's mission. Lund's bond issue for land acquisition had ended up at $4 million, with which the department bought thirty-eight pieces of land. They mostly met the needs of day-trippers, still predominantly from in-state, and showed a decided bias toward the coast; the order in which the "150th" brochure proclaimed Maine's outdoor wonders was telling. Acquiring land farther inland, Stuart thought, was only a hedge against the future. Some long-term acquisition planning would be a good idea, he admitted. It would "help to know where to place a park and not be faced the next day with a smokestack next to it." But Stuart still took the paper companies at their word: they just wanted to grow trees, so what was the problem?

Neither so sanguine nor as satisfied, Bob Cummings kept his drumbeat going. "Now we watch in frustrated dismay as our coastline is chewed away by out-of-state developers and land speculators. And we struggle through our state Parks and Recreation Department, to preserve at least minimal public access to our remaining lake and mountain country."[385]

Leaks and trickles in the weeks before Christmas had revealed the Schepps report's broad outline and stoked public interest. The details essential to any legislation on the Public Lots had now been released. By the end of January, both sides were off to the races. Early on in the session, the legislature created a special joint committee, the Committee on Public Lands. It had a budget of $10,000, an office on the top floor of the State House, and instructions to report back with its own recommendations on the matter. The senate chair was Majority Leader Harrison Richardson, who forwent a permanent committee chairmanship to do it. The rest of the committee was equally prestigious, including legislative leaders of both parties.

The questions were familiar: what was the Public Lots' legal status, what rights to them did Maine people have, and what could they be legally used for. Richardson knew what the answers should be. "If what I hope comes to pass, Maine will be in the unique position of having almost 400,000 acres of land that it can put to public use," he announced. The chairman was not inclined to take a limited view. "Who knows?" he said. "The concept of 'public lands' might well include all the land in Maine."

The immediate job of the Committee on Public Lands was to be a combination signal box and traffic cop for the plethora of bills concerned with what Richardson considered "the number one public environmental issue." Various legislators had their own ideas about what should be done. The most practical, not to say modest end of the spectrum was LD 34, Elden Shute's moratorium on harvesting in the Public Lots until a court decided who owned the rights.

Another Republican, Representative Roswell E. Dyar from Strong, also in western Maine, filed three separate bills on different aspects of the question. Having done some sleuthing around the state treasury, Rep. Dyar was sure that "somebody has not paid their fair share of what they've taken off the [public] lots," and he was incensed. His most radical bill would organize all the townships for forty-eight hours; this would allow the state to grab the Public Reserved Lands, after which they could be deorganized again, leaving residents free of the burden of town management. (Bob Cummings could have written this bill himself.) His second bill would "locate" the Public Lots—almost half of the total four hundred thousand acres—that existed only as fractions held in common, undivided interest with the private owner. (In the public's perception, these were the acres that the state had not only lost but couldn't find on a map, which added considerably to the confusion.) A commission would negotiate with the owner of the township to lay out an equitable thousand-acre tract; if they failed, it would be up to the courts. The final bill from the representative from Strong was a little bit of local protectionism. In something of a repeat of history, Canadian companies had been cutting in Maine's forests and trucking the wood back across the border to process it, essentially outcompeting their Maine brethren. Dyar's bill restricted the sale of stumpage from the Public Lots to individuals or businesses in the same county.

Roswell Dyar sponsored one more bill, LD 70, related to the state's wildlands, though not the Public Lots directly. The issue was public access, and the bill's remarkable trajectory in Maine's House of Representatives was one more signal of just how mercurial feelings about Maine's woods had become. Alarmed that more and more land was being put off-limits to the public, Dyar proposed taxing owners of five hundred acres or more $3 for every acre they posted. As he stood to introduce his bill on the House floor, he had no illusions about its odds of success. The judiciary committee had already voted "ought-not-to-pass" by 12–1. But here was the chance to speak his mind, and he did. Rich people from out of state were carving private kingdoms out of Maine's undeveloped backcountry, excluding more and more Maine people, and someday, legislators would have to do something about it. He hoped they would take action before the whole state had a No Trespassing sign on it. To Dyar's surprise, his cause was taken up, first by the lonely "aye" vote from the judiciary committee, and then by the powerful leader of the House Democrats, John Martin. After an energetic debate, a bill that had come in facing certain death was passed by one vote, 71–70.[386] The fact that it died in the Senate made the short life of LD 70 no less remarkable. Maine's "exhaustless" forestlands were no longer to be taken for granted.

Thus, at the end of April 1973, four legislative bills were before Harrison Richardson's Public Lands Committee. Besides Shute's and Dyar's bills, a fourth, LD 837, would repeal the 1903 "timber is anything that grows" law. The hearings were spirited. Shute's proposed moratorium raised serious legal and constitutional issues, said the paper companies' attorney, Gerald Amero. Repealing the 1903 law about tree species would not "make an ounce of difference," said Scott Paper's spokesman; the courts would decide. Since when could the legislature take away a right acquired by contract, asked Great Northern's attorney, Lynwood Hand, echoing the industry's basic position.

Dyar's "forty-eight hour" remedy—organize the townships, take the Public Lots, de-organize the townships again—struck Chairman Richardson as a "sham," aimed only at depriving timber owners of their property rights. Dyar found the committee more sympathetic to his effort to ensure that Maine's woodsmen get first crack at wood cut on the Public Lots. "It is justifiable," stated the bill, "that Maine people should benefit when cutting operations take place on our Public Lots."

Stories of abuse and malfeasance—either with the consent of the Forest Service or beyond its ken—accompanied all these bills. Ed Sprague, one of the original pair of Public Lots advocates, knew of a township on the northwestern border with Quebec where the Public Lot had never been located and the whole township cut for ten years. The state, the co-tenant, had seen not so much as a penny, and it had been cut in the most dreadful way, leaving the soil a mess of holes and gashes. The loss to Maine, not only in income but in damages, was "unbelievable." From the chair, Richardson asked Sprague if he had reported this to the Forest Service. "Many times," was the curt reply.

Other stories included a Canadian fin and feather club that had leased land for years in Chain of Ponds Township without Maine being paid its share.

Public Lots were being moved around to a company's advantage, without letting the Forest Service know. He had heard of the same thing happening in his district, Eagle Lake in Aroostook County, Rep. Martin joined in. "This is so bizarre," exclaimed Richardson. "I don't understand it." As the hearing drew to a close, there was a "residual feeling of something rotten at the State Capitol," wrote *Maine Times* reporter Lucy Martin. She quoted Senator Shute, who in his own bill had entrusted oversight of the moratorium to the Department of Environmental Protection rather than the Forest Service. "The public has a feeling about the Forestry Department being in bed with the landowners," said the man from Farmington.

On May 3, the so-called governor's bill, LD 1812, "An Act to Organize the Unorganized and Deorganized Territories of the State of Maine and to Provide for Management of the Public Reserved Lands," was introduced by its House sponsor, Democratic Minority Leader John Martin. Coincidentally, the same day in Washington D.C., the Senate Watergate Committee subpoenaed White House counsel John Dean. Since March, while the Public Lots were ruffling Maine's established political order, the Watergate hearings had been doing the same in the nation. Dean's testimony on the break-in would start the avalanche that eventually buried Richard Nixon's presidency. The actual burglars had already been convicted, also coincidentally on the day Governor Curtis delivered his legislative message about the Public Lots.

The "long awaited" bill, Bob Cummings announced, would "restore complete public control over nearly 400,000 acres." It proposed creating a Commission on Unincorporated Territory to organize northern Maine into traditional plantations, which would "consist of one or more townships, existing plantations, . . . and be located in a single county." Each plantation would have a minimum of twenty-five year-round residents, which could be achieved by amalgamating any number of townships. The commission's task was to prepare a boundary plan to accomplish this—including number and layout of plantations—in time for the legislature to consider it at its next regular session. Organization would automatically cancel all private rights to the grass and timber on the Public Lots, which could then be used to provide public benefits other than education—recreation, for instance. Schools in the new plantations could use the income from the revenue the Public Lots had generated over a century; it was a relatively paltry sum.[387] The principal would become a fund with which to manage the Public Lots. The governor's bill also confirmed the state's power to exchange, sell, or relocate them as it saw fit; and it instructed the forest commissioner to start collecting the state's one-twenty-fourth share of revenue from things like camp leases and gravel extraction on unlocated Public Lots.

As the hearing got going, LURC director James Haskell ensured that it would be exciting by declaring, "Hopefully, this bill will end the days of industry ripping off the public lands." Less provocatively, Lawrence Stuart praised the bill as "completely reasonable, not radical." Not so Attorney Gerald Amero, who saw nothing but problems. The Public Lots, he said, "belong to future inhabitants of the wildlands." This last point was problematic, and Rep. Martin pounced. One of the things, though not the only one, that had prevented timberland townships from being settled was the paper companies' policy of keeping people out. When a landowner like International Paper leased or sold an acre or so for a campsite, it included a provision prohibiting the lessee or buyer from using the camp year-round, Martin pointed out. This was true at the moment, Amero admitted, adding somewhat lamely that the company might change its policy. Still, no honest woodlands manager would ever attest to anything other than that having people around their harvesting operations—be they residents, seasonal visitors, campers, or hikers—"was nothing but a [expletive] nuisance." People on the land were at the heart of a paradox inherent in the whole Public Lots saga, one that had always entertained Bob Cummings. His very first article ended with the philosophical observation that

> It may be one of the ironies of history that these lots set up to insure eventual civilization may become a major tool in preserving one of the scarcest commodities of the final decades of the 20th century—natural areas and wilderness.[388]

As the debate over the Public Lots progressed, that paradox was becoming a shade less haphazard. Northern townships had failed to attract settlers when growth was a priority, noted Cummings. "It is not in the best interest of the state [that they] be settled now."

That the companies gave up their right to cut grass and timber when a township was organized was never in question. Owners and land managers had seen it happen. For example, when the Huber Corporation's one-time "designer community," Beaver Cove (population: ninety-five adults and ten children), organized itself in the mid-1970s, it included a small tract with a reserved lot managed by Prentiss & Carlisle for the owner. The timber and grass and the income from cutting it reverted to the town (held in trust by the state). "No problem," reflected David Carlisle. He always knew it was a possibility, and the company had kept separate accounts. It just wasn't a big issue. But that had been one small village, organizing on its own, in its own interest, and requesting the legislature to designate it a town. Would a wholesale organization of the Unorganized Territories initiated in Augusta fly? Was anyone speaking for the inhabitants and their interests? No one seemed quite sure which was the tail and which the dog.

Other issues were clearer, at least to their partisans. Richardson wanted his committee to report out LD 1812 to the full legislature and then ask Maine's Supreme Judicial Court for a ruling: could the Public Lots be used for recreation or forestry? Could the state reclaim the cutting rights it had sold so long ago? Asking the justices was a risk. It was by no means certain that they would agree to give an opinion. As described by the State of Maine Judicial Branch,

> An opinion of the justices is issued when the Senate and House propound questions to the justices of the Supreme Judicial Court involving important questions of law in circumstances that present a solemn occasion.[389]

The Law Court would first have to decide that this was a "solemn occasion." They might also choose to answer one question but not the other, preferring to take on constitutional issues rather than property rights. The chairman's problem was that the membership of his committee was so high powered and busy that it was hard to get them all together to make the necessary decisions.

Having got his committee together, Richardson asked Attorney General Jon Lund to have his office draft a question to put to the Law Court for their review. Assistant Attorney General Lee Schepps did the drafting, first the Resolve of the Legislature declaring it a solemn occasion, and then the formal request that the justices rule on LD 1812's constitutionality. The Statement of Fact outlined the evolution of the Public Reserved Lands from when Maine was still a part of Massachusetts. It quoted the Articles of Separation (which still constituted Article X of the Maine Constitution, though seldom printed anymore). It noted that legislatures past had felt free to make changes: the size of each lot to a thousand acres in 1824, the transfer of ministerial funds to schools and teachers in 1831.

To help his Senate colleagues understand the ten-page document, Richardson gave them a brief precis of the need for an advisory opinion. The aim, "very simply stated, is to determine the scope of the state's sovereignty over the Public Lots." Under its Constitution, must Maine use them for school purposes? Must the income from them be kept forever in the treasury, "or until the wildlands become towns"? Must the Public Lots remain scattered across northern Maine, or can they be consolidated "for more functional and, I believe, a more 20th Century use." Finally in locating those that were still undivided, must they consider only timber and minerals, or could the scope be broadened?

Richardson stressed that the committee was seeking an opinion on purely constitutional questions, not property rights. In his personal opinion, "private property rights, including grass and timber rights owned by the several major paper companies, should be determined in a full-blown adversary proceeding, and not through the course of an advisory opinion." Some senators were still uneasy, but Richardson had the last word.

> The public lots have been smoldering, or I should say molding, for 152 years under consultory and fragmented management, and I think it is high time the legislature got under way. I think that this request for an advisory opinion is a perfectly lawyerlike and appropriate method to follow.

On May 25, the Senate formally petitioned the justices for their opinion.

Meanwhile, the landowners and paper companies had taken their own legal steps. The Public Lots issue, they said, was too complex to be dealt with in an advisory opinion. If the legislature insisted on going through with "the governor's bill"—the whole idea of which they opposed—its legality would have to be determined through a court challenge. On May 15, three corporations—Great Northern, International Paper, and Prentiss & Carlisle—and two individuals—Seven Islands's president, Brad Wellman, and Charles Cushing—filed a Complaint for Declamatory Relief in Superior Court in Kennebec County. Attorney General Lund and Forest Commissioner Fred Holt (who had just succeeded Austin Wilkins) were named as defendants. The state, the plaintiffs claimed, was planning to implement the Schepps report's findings, and the controversy generated by the Public Lots bills was interfering with their ability to manage their lands. It remained their opinion that it was all a "subterfuge to illegally regain property the state had sold." They asked the Superior Court to rule on the status of their rights to continue to cut timber on the Public Reserved Lands.

"We tried to create as broad a range of applicants as we could put together," Wellman later recalled. "Great Northern and IP were obviously the lead corporations. [We wanted to] show to the court that it was not just the corporations that were involved and affected by the controversy." To represent the lower end of the ownership scale, they picked Cushing, a member of the Webber family. [390] "The Webbers did not own that much, but they were a big family; so the individual's ownership was relatively small." Cushing always assumed the choice was made alphabetically. "Cushing begins with a C. I was the tiniest landowner of all. I think at the time I owned a couple of thousand acres maybe, 4,000 acres at the most."

Richardson was furious at what he considered a gross breach of faith. "These same people," he said, had been participating in the work of the committee, arguing at its hearings for a cautious and deliberate process. A legal suit did exactly the opposite. With any luck it would not deter the justices from issuing an advisory opinion, but in Richardson's opinion "these people are insensitive enough to the public interest to try to do this." Harrison Richardson's outbursts were legendary.[391] Paper companies—"these same people"—were often on the receiving end. At the hearings that produced LURC in 1971, he declared: "The paper companies and the big owners, with their usual head-in-the-sand attitude, fought the original bill every inch of the way, and they will fight [this one] with their usual total disregard for the public's interest. They have consistently taken a position against any attempt by the people of this state to protect these lakes and these lands, and they have done so even when it was squarely contrary to their own best interest."[392]

In response to Richardson's displeasure over his filing suit, Seven Islands's Brad Wellman said he saw no reason why the two legal appeals shouldn't proceed at the same time. "Questions have been raised that only the courts can answer," he said smoothly, "and the suit is designed to get answers." Nevertheless, some lawmakers were likely to argue, with some justification, that their consideration of the "governor's bill" should be delayed until the court made a declarative judgement on the case. Whatever the final result, delay was very much in the timberland owners' financial interest. "There is a built-in incentive for the large landowners to maintain the status quo as long as possible," wrote Cummings, whose "rabble-rousing" was by this time part of the story.

Some saw still more to it. Although he had yet to announce his candidacy formally, it was well known that Harrison Richardson had his eye on the Republican nomination for governor the next year. One of the paper company lobbyists and Great Northern's attorney, Lynwood Hand, told Rep. John Martin, the House minority leader, that "one of the overriding reasons the suit was filed was to prevent Senator Harrison Richardson from running for the office of governor on the Public Lots issue." Martin made a sworn affidavit to this effect. A *Maine Times* headline said it all. It was a "Spiteful Suit."

Attorney General Lund immediately filed a motion to have the case dismissed saying that the plaintiffs had no standing and there was "no justifiable controversy" for the suit. Citing Martin's affidavit, Lund argued that it "constitutes an abuse of the judicial process and has been brought in bad faith." The landowners had, in legal parlance, "unclean hands."[393] Among other things, the motion continued, the attorneys who brought the suit were registered lobbyists for the paper companies and "have been and are now actively lobbying" for their clients against the Public Lands bill in the legislature. They clearly had a financial stake in the outcome, and therefore a conflict with the process. "It seems apparent that this suit has been brought in an effort to interfere with the legislative and political process of the State of Maine . . . or that it has been brought to prevent or to inhibit the exercise by the Legislature of its constitutional power to submit important questions of law to the Justices of the Supreme Judicial Court."

Jon Lund, also a Republican, had already made himself as much persona non grata with the landowners as had Richardson. Having succeeded James Erwin, Lund had taken the AG's seat on the Baxter Park Authority, and he had already brought an injunction against Great Northern to stop its lumbering activities in the park's northern townships. "They got a very lucrative swap there; but they weren't practicing scientific forestry," he found when he went up and looked at it. He also sued the authority for making such a loose contract. Looking back, Lund remarked dryly, it all "endeared me no end to the forestry industry in Maine." It was no coincidence that the Pierce Atwood lawyers representing Great Northern in that case were at the same time representing the landowners in the Public Lots case, as well as in the suit to have LURC rules declared unconstitutional.

Regardless of the landowner's suit, the Supreme Judicial Court agreed to render an advisory opinion on the governor's Public Lots bill. On June 20, it did so—and solidly in favor of LD 1812. The justices found that in stipulating the beneficiaries of the reserved lands, both the Articles of Separation (and therefore the Maine Constitution) and subsequent legislation had used education and the ministry to *illustrate* appropriate public purposes, not to *limit* them. Therefore, the state could use the Public Reserved Lands for anything that benefited the people of Maine. Furthermore, it could configure them at its discretion, even to the point that a Public Lot need not end up located in every township. However, they could not be sold or given away since the state had "removed the 'public lots' from its dominion as an absolute proprietor and has denied itself *an authority to convey the premises to any other person or corporation.*" Where private parties already owned much or all of a township, the court held that reclaiming the Public Lot would not be a violation of due process, but cases should be decided on their own merits—and compensation would probably be a good idea.

"It's a marvelous ruling," exulted Harrison Richardson, describing it as the "cornerstone" of what his committee wanted to do. Among other things, the Public Lots bill significantly broadened the criteria the forest commissioner could use in equitably "locating" unlocated lots. The justices had agreed that these included not only timber and minerals but also proximity to other public lands or population centers, recreational opportunities, accessibility, the needs of state agencies, scenic quality, and protection of significant natural, recreational, and historic resources. One value shift Richardson saw as particularly momentous. Land was no longer just a commodity to be bought and sold. It was "the fundamental ingredient of what we think living in Maine is all about." Yes, the Public Lots were worth a lot of money, but it was, he thought, "of secondary importance." Think instead, he urged, of "numerous mini-Baxter Parks" or extending the Allagash Wilderness Waterway. Or, suggested U.S. Representative Peter Kyros, a preserve for campers and canoers along the Upper St. John, Maine's other premier wilderness river.[394]

For technical reasons of legislative protocol, LD 1812 had been reported out of the Public Lands Committee "ought not to pass" while the justices were weighing their opinion. Now the action had returned to the State House. Legislators took up the "governor's bill" again at the end of June. It faced "Plenty of Snags"—so ran a Cummings headline. The law left too many loopholes, thought Roswell Dyar, the representative from Strong. Nothing prevented landowners from "completely stripping and annihilating" unlocated Public Lots, he said. Dyar was quite certain it was happening already. In the last two years, townships in Franklin and Oxford County "have become barren deserts because the company, which is an out-of-state company, knew full well that this state was going to take some action." The bill should have included a provision to "locate these Public Lots as fast as possible," or for "a moratorium on cutting or removing anything" from such townships.

Minority Leader John Martin, LD 1812's sponsor, tried to reassure him. The bill stipulated that the forest commissioner and the new BPL receive a management plan before they "sell out or transfer or exchange" any land. A moratorium would be "very, very difficult" especially where Public Lots had not been laid out. However, he hoped that no landowner would try to take advantage of the ninety days before the law took effect, and if they did, that "this state would seriously consider imposing some sort of restriction."

By the time it came to a vote, the "governor's bill" had lost its two most important provisions. One was the commission to delineate the new plantations; the other was the power to assemble large contiguous public lands through sales and exchanges. The first was essential to extinguish the cutting rights, the second to parlay four hundred scattered tracts into blocks of real public value. The loss of the so-called boundary commission particularly raised concerns in the governor's office, as well as with the legislative leadership. Moments before moving enactment of LD 1812, Richardson ventured an explanation. He assured the chamber that it remained the intention of the Public Lands Committee to put together "a comprehensive statutory scheme for . . . the public lots, including their location, collection and management." However, based on discussion with the attorney general, he didn't think it "appropriate to try to do this at this time." Thereupon, the bill was enacted.

What seemed like a volte-face was reasonably interpreted as political maneuvering inside the committee. Harry Richardson was nothing if not a versatile politician, and his public statements on the bill's various aspects were not always consistent. In justifying removal of the "boundary commission," he had also declared that organizing the wildlands to reclaim the cutting rights was a "simplistic" formula. "You can't solve this problem by just saying 'Hooray! Hooray! We have named another commission,'" he later told Bob Cummings. But a commission was just what he had wanted to consolidate the Public Lots.

As activity in Augusta slowed for the summer, the two sides were left outstaring each other. Each had scored an early point. For one, the justices had endorsed Lee Schepps's findings. The other was going to have its day in court. The next legislative milestone would be the special session, starting early in the coming year.[395] Cummings had good reason to predict that it would "embroil the Public Lots in election year politics." Besides Richardson, two other members of the Public Lands Committee were considering gubernatorial runs, and another wanted to replace Edmund Muskie in the U.S. Senate. Meanwhile, the Committee on Public Lands would continue to hold hearings, fine-tuning options for the Public Lots.

At a value of $40 million, the landowners were not going to give them up without a fight. Their feeling was well described, in retrospect, by John E. Mcleod, a long-time Great Northern executive:

> The 400,000 acres or so of wild land in public lots scattered all over the state sat there giving nobody any trouble until they were discovered in 1973 by certain politicians who wished to raise the state flag over them.[396]

Brigadier Samuel Waldo (Courtesy of Bowdoin College Museum of Art, Brunswick, Maine).

General Henry Knox (Collections of Maine Historical Society).

William Bingham (Collections of Maine Historical Society).

John Neptune, Lieutenant Governor of the Penobscot Tribe (Courtesy of the Maine State Museum).

William King, Maine's first governor (Courtesy of Patten Free Library).

Moses Greenleaf's map of Maine, Maine's first official map, 1820 (Courtesy of the Osher Map Library, University of Southern Maine).

Telos Lake, showing the Telos cut or dam (Courtesy of Patten Lumberman's Museum).

"The Main Question"—a cartoon by H.R. Robinson satirizing the incipient Aroostook War. On one side Queen Victoria and the First Duke of Wellington; on the other U.S. President Martin Van Buren and Maine Governor John Fairfield. (Courtesy of Maine State Library).

Rights to grass were vital to feed horses and oxen during the winter cutting season. The simple sleigh was called a pung. (Courtesy of Patten Lumberman's Museum).

Mounts Katahdin and Turner from Lake Katahdin, Maine, *1855–1860 Frederic Edwin Church* (American, 1826–1900); graphite, brush, and oil paint on paperboard; 30.7 x 51 cm (121/16 x 20 1/16 in.); Cooper Hewitt, Smithsonian Design Museum; Gift of Louis P. Church, 1917-4-643; © Smithsonian Institution.

A typical Maine sporting camp, circa 1900 (Courtesy of Aroostook County Historical and Art Museum).

Logs of the Great Northern Paper Company floating down the West Branch of the Penobscot River to Millinocket, Maine (Courtesy of Special Collections, Raymond H. Fogler Library, DigitalCommons@UMaine).

Great Northern's paper mill in Millinocket, Maine, circa 1904 (Courtesy of Special Collections, Raymond H. Fogler Library, DigitalCommons@UMaine).

A raft of lumber on the Penobscot River (Courtesy of Bangor Public Library).

Rumford Falls—here the Androscoggin River drops 180 feet in a stretch of half a mile. The power it generated became the linchpin for Hugh J. Chisholm's International Paper Company. (Courtesy of Special Collections, Raymond H. Fogler Library, DigitalCommons@UMaine).

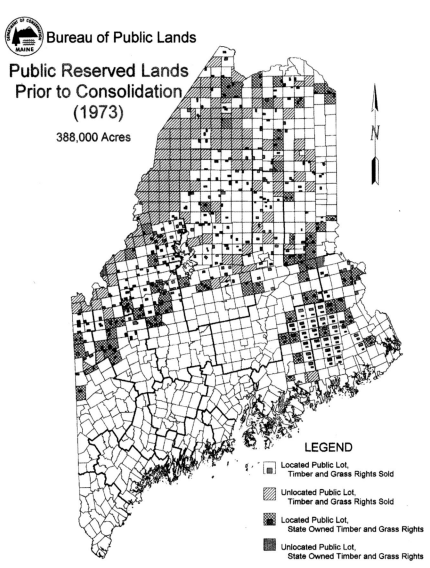

**Public Reserved Lands
Prior to Consolidation
(1973)**

388,000 Acres

N

LEGEND

Located Public Lot,
Timber and Grass Rights Sold

Unlocated Public Lot,
Timber and Grass Rights Sold

Located Public Lot,
State Owned Timber and Grass Rights

Unlocated Public Lot,
State Owned Timber and Grass Rights

Map of Public Reserved Lands Prior to Consolidation, 1973 (Courtesy of Maine Bureau of Parks and Lands).

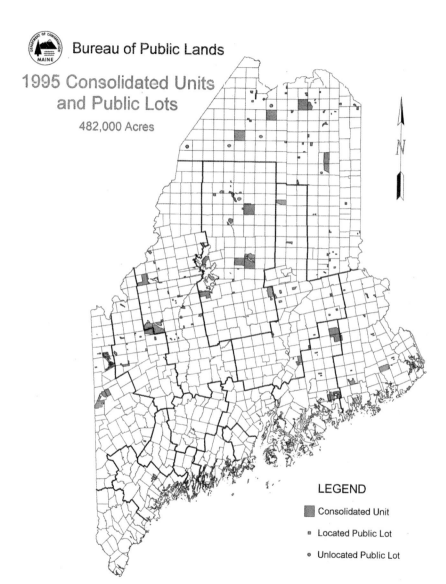

Bureau of Public Lands

1995 Consolidated Units
and Public Lots

482,000 Acres

N

LEGEND

■ Consolidated Unit

▫ Located Public Lot

○ Unlocated Public Lot

Map of Consolidated Units, BPL, 1995 (Courtesy of Maine Bureau of Parks and Lands)

Bob Cummings, the environmental reporter who rescued the Public Lots from a century of oblivion. Later, he hiked the Appalachian Trail, telling his family he would take the train to Georgia "and walk home" (Courtesy of Cummings family).

Lee Schepps, the young assistant attorney general who researched and wrote the report that became the legal basis for the State's case for reclaiming the Public Lots (Courtesy of Lee Schepps).

Martin Wilk, the deputy attorney general who led the legal battle for the State, and then became its master negotiator with the landowners (Courtesy of Martin Wilk).

The Final Deal with Great Northern Paper Company, finally accomplished. From left to right: Richard Anderson (Conservation Commissioner), Donald Perkins, Sr. (Attorney, Pierce Atwood), Martin Wilk (Attorney for BPL), Annee Tara (Deputy Conservation Commissioner), Richard Barringer (State Planning Director), Paul Sterns (Attorney General's Office), Paul McCann (Public Information Director, Great Northern), Robert Gardiner (BPL Director); seated, Governor Joseph E. Brennan (Courtesy of Richard Anderson).

Tumbledown Mountain, a new Unit that could be "loved to death." (Wilfred E. Richard).

Screw Augur Falls, Grafton Notch State Park, established in 1963 with 3,000 acres. After consolidation, state-owned land around Grafton Notch totaled 27,600 acres, with 23 miles of the Appalachian Trail running through it. (Beth Comeau).

"The backside of Bigelow," across Flagstaff Lake. The lake was created by Central Maine Power's Long Falls dam for which the company leased two Public Lots that would be part of the flowage. (Christopher Ayres).

Bigelow Preserve (Wilfred E. Richard).

John Walker (right) re-
surveyed the Public Lots and
marked their boundary lines.
Walker, recalled Richard
Barringer, "was one of those
old-fashioned Maine people
who could do anything"
(Courtesy of Maine Bureau
of Parks and Lands).

Map 26

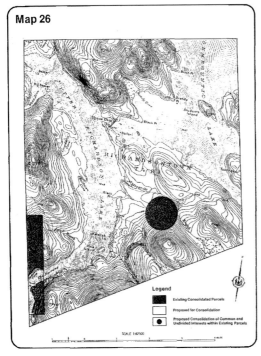

Governor Brennan's 1982
Consolidation Proposal
included "substantial frontage" on Richardson and
Mooselookmeguntic lakes
(17,000 acres). One of the
most sensitive pieces of the
entire proposal, it was the
heart of David Pingree's
empire. "They'll never give
that up in a million years,"
said Richard Anderson when
he saw it on the BPL's wish
list. (Courtesy of Maine
Bureau of Parks and Lands)

Chapter Eleven

Grand Plantations and Grand Negotiations (September 1973–December 1974)

In September 1973, after a summer of breathless Watergate watching, Mainers with an interest in the future of the Public Reserved Lands found little to encourage them. In a long article, "Public Lots Revisited," the Sunday after Labor Day, Bob Cummings summarized the story so far. Readers only had to look at his subtitle to get the gist. "We don't seem to be making much progress." Return of the Public Lots to the public domain seemed as far away as ever. Taking the Schepps report's position that deeds to the grass and timber had expired, Cummings warned that "the 'temporary' rights have become permanent, and will remain so unless the Legislature or the courts intervene."

The previous session's "governor's bill," LD 1812, had been the legislature's first attempt at intervention, and it was stripped of its two most consequential provisions before being passed. There was no boundary commission to define new plantations; nor were there provisions for conglomerating helter-skelter thousand-acre tracts into something big and worthwhile for Maine. On the other hand, bolstered by the justices' opinion, the act:

- Recognized that Public Reserved Lands could be used for public purposes other than education and schools. Besides timber and minerals, their value included "preservation of significant natural, recreational and historic resources, including wildlife habitat and other areas critical to the ecology of the State";
- Charged the forest commissioner, who had their care and custody, "promptly" to prepare a management plan including use of the Public Lots for "outdoor recreation, timber, watershed, fish and wildlife and other public purposes";

179

- Reminded the commissioner that where the Public Lots remained unlocated, Maine must receive a "proportionate share of common income" from the township; and
- Allowed the possibility of exchanging Public Lots or selling them to purchase other land that could be so designated.

It was a first step, though for Cummings only a "tenuous" one.

In the meantime, Harrison Richardson and his Public Lands Committee had hit the ground running. Their ultimate task was to study the deleted "organizational aspect of LD 1812" further and make recommendations that could be incorporated into a new bill.[397] They planned to spend two months holding public hearings around the state, with additional field trips into the wildlands. Richardson intended to keep the committee busy through November. That would leave time to develop a position paper and a bill for the special session of the legislature starting in January.

At this point Richardson had half a dozen staff, many of whom would go on to play significant roles in Maine's environmental politics. Nancy Ross had just returned to the state, after working on public relations for the Massachusetts Audubon Society. Herb Hartman, who from his own experiences hiking and canoeing in Maine's wildlands knew more about the nature of the Unorganized Territories than anyone in Augusta, was employed as a "dispersed recreation consultant."[398] For most of them, it was their first chance to work in government, and they relished brainstorming with the chairman how the state might claw back its Public Lots.

"They said, let's organize all the Unorganized Territories into Grand Plantations," Richardson later recalled. Ross thought the idea was originally meant more as a threat or a last resort. The Public Lands Committee was generally agreed that something had to be done, but the idea of carving out grand plantations was, at least for some of them, going too far. It would be anathema to the large landowners and paper companies. "That's when they called me a 'Banana Republic dictator,'" Richardson chuckled years afterwards.

The other interested party was the Unorganized Territory's population itself. Did those who actually lived there want self-government? Some, if not most, were certainly happy to let the state take care of their municipal needs. A great deal of research would have to be done before asking their opinion. How much taxable timberland would a plantation need? How many people? What would each plantation require in the way of roads and schools? These questions had to have answers in order to create a civic entity that made sense. Nancy Ross remembered spending hours in the archives. First she had to look up the original deeds of all the grants; then she reviewed every statute that the new legislation would affect and that would have to be revised. Nonetheless, that she was helping to "really do something" inspired Ross.

While Chairman Richardson and his staff had their eyes fixed on grand plantations as the prize, other issues were emerging to complicate the committee's efforts. There was still the risk that the timber companies, reading the writing on the wall, would start cutting "their" trees before anyone told them the trees weren't "theirs" to cut. Fred Holt, the new forest commissioner, thought such fears misplaced, but he agreed that the status quo—Maine owning the land while private landowners owned the trees—was still a "very unsatisfactory proposition." The state, he believed, should be "a good citizen" and buy back the Public Lots. The obvious problem was the cost, which could be anything from $15 million to $30 million. Holt, who had been Austin Wilkins's deputy before succeeding him, retained much of his predecessor's traditional loyalty to the large landowners.

"Unlocated" lots were another issue. Lots that didn't exist on a map confused the general public. They were the lots the state couldn't find, a source of incredulity and even ridicule. "Locating" them all at once seemed like an easy, positive first step. It was Holt who pointed out why it would be a mistake and what problems would result. The cost would be prohibitive. A survey to locate a thousand-acre Public Lot would cost $10,535, and there were a hundred and fifty of them. To spend $1.5 million just for location's sake, without considering where or what a Public Lot could be, was a recipe for waste.

Leaving them unlocated, Holt reasoned, had other advantages. When the township was organized (and the owner's rights to the timber and grass lapsed), Maine would receive a twenty-fourth of the income generated by the whole township instead of a cut-over thousand-acre tract. Future negotiations—over creating a public recreation area, for instance—would be unencumbered by previous, possibly irrelevant decisions. And as forest commissioner, Holt could say that the landowners were probably managing an undifferentiated "lot" as part of their lands better than the state could afford to at present. The best policy, he advised, was to have a blueprint ready so that they could be located knowledgably when the time was ripe. Richardson agreed: location shouldn't be done "pin-the-tail-on-the-donkey style." As Neil Rolde, Democratic representative from York and a member of the committee, put it, the issue was too complicated to "go thrashing around without a lot more information." Hasty decisions would make finding a solution harder.

Meanwhile, the attorney general's legal proceeding against the large landowners was drawing attention to a different aspect of the timber rights on the Public Lots. Lee Schepps's research suggested that the practice at the time the land agents issued the permits was to consider standing timber, not future growth. Therefore, on the reasonable assumption that everything standing would have been cut, any trees growing a century later would not be included in the original permit. If this was the case, 320,000 acres of public land were simply waiting for the state to reclaim them. Legislators, Cummings noted, had been "strangely reluctant" go that route. To do so would require some brave politicians ready to withstand the landowners' wrath. Whether the legislature acted on its own or asked Jon Lund to file suit, a court case would be inevitable.

As fall began and the Committee on Public Lands was finalizing its schedule, one more issue, nittier and grittier, was thrown into the mix for its members to address. Bob Cummings had spent the summer poking around camps on public land that either the paper companies or the state was leasing to individuals. The question of leasing public land for private camps had been fraught from the beginning. Cummings's new investigations made it obvious just how poorly these sites were being managed. His story broke a week before Richardson's committee was scheduled to hold its first hearing.

His visit to eleven-mile-long Aziscohos Lake—stretching along the New Hampshire border, just below the boundary with Quebec—had been an eye-opener, wrote Cummings. It was a beautiful Public Lot, wrapped around the southern tip of the lake, just a stone's throw from US Route 16: Could any location be better suited for a public beach? he asked. Instead it was "an appalling cottage slum, no other words properly describe it." The shoreline of the entire Public lot had been divided into eighty-one campsites, seventy-five by one hundred feet—as recommended in the Forestry Department's "all shore frontage" policy—with no concern for the streams, swamps, or steep slopes that were in the way. There were no sanitation standards, nor guidelines for how or where any structures should be built. The result was that makeshift cabins with names like "Kwituworri" were sliding into the lake, dragging the shoreline with them. For $50 a year, the owners of these shanties had bought the privilege of blighting one of Maine's great natural gems.

The sites on Aziscohos Lake had been laid out in 1966, a year after the legislature officially allowed camps to be leased on public lands. Austin Wilkins, the forest commissioner, had seen them as proper fulfillment of the "Public Lots trust," in light of the trend of outdoor recreation that was sweeping the nation. He had permitted hundreds of leases all over the Unorganized Territories, and having been confirmed in the recent Public Lots legislation, the practice was continuing. Quite apart from the "cottage slum" aspect, Bob Cummings asked, how did the state square one department "privatizing" public shoreland for a song, while another was spending millions to acquire more of the same? The answer, he thought, was obvious, but "no one who follows public affairs in Maine will bet that the obvious answer will be chosen."

The Public Lands Committee's first hearing was in Augusta to solicit ideas from state agencies about the Public Reserved Lands' future. First some of those same agencies had to explain the abysmal condition of camps like the ones on Aziscohos Lake. The burning issue when Governor Curtis's interagency committee debated camp leases the year before had been privatization of public land. Now, it was environmental degradation, and the discussion was fiercer still. Once more, a forest commissioner struggling with a new reality found himself in the hot seat as the committee peppered him with questions.

No, Commissioner Holt admitted, his department neither set standards for lease-holders, nor had it ever followed up with any inspection. He wasn't sure what good that would do; the lease had little to say about environmental issues such as erosion, or even sewage disposal. Most of the camps had been built before the new environmental rules. Any change to the leases would be inappropriate without legal or legislative direction. Lease-holders counted on "the good faith of the state" to renew their leases each year, Holt protested. The regulations should be waived, even for those who had not yet built on their sites. It didn't seem fair to burden them, still less to threaten them if they did not comply. Sensing the committee's drift, Fred Holt prevaricated: "This sounds like you want me to take someone's property away illegally."

Chairman Richardson was quick to disabuse him of that notion. "You not only have the right, you have an absolute duty" to ensure that no harm comes to the waters or the land, he told Holt. If he had any question, he could ask the attorney general. Richardson was perfectly certain what the answer would be. The state had an "absolutely unquestionable right" to prevent anything that "wastes the public's resource."

It sounded like the Forestry Department knew it had made a mistake but wouldn't do anything about it, growled James Ezra Briggs, a Republican representative from Caribou and a member of the committee, once hailed by the *New York Times* as "the last courtly member of the Maine legislature." By this time, Jim Briggs was hunched over and walked with two canes, but he was still living up to his well-earned reputation for being cantankerous when the environment was threatened. "Just because nothing has been done before, doesn't mean that nothing can or should be done now," he snapped, when Holt admitted that the leases, though only good for a year at a time, had never been canceled. Briggs was adamant. "This irrevocable loss" to the State of Maine and its people must stop, he said. Holt should cancel all leases until he had some creative solutions to the problem. Another issue vexing Briggs was the matter of the state splitting the lease fee—a paltry $50, if that—with the landowner. The camps were not depriving the company of any income since zoning regulations limited tree-cutting within a hundred feet of the lakeshore, which was also the standard length of a campsite. It had no right to "skim off" any of these funds.

By the time the committe finished grilling him, Fred Holt was in no doubt as to its stance on campsites: "Clean up or get out." The state was not obliged to license environmental nuisances. He could start, suggested Edward Lee Rogers, the assistant attorney general assigned to the committee, with an official letter warning leaseholders of new sanitation standards and giving them a chance to comply. Holt agreed to undertake a full review of all existing leases. Meanwhile no new ones should be issued for the next season. Almost with a sigh of relief, he invoked the new Department of Conservation, which was to come into operation the next month, noting that "I may no longer be in charge of the public lands."

As had his predecessor's in 1972, Holt's performance drew a rebuke from the Portland papers. It was "another instance of the close links prevailing between the pulp and paper industry, the big timberland owners and the Forestry Department." Some people, the editors wrote, returning to the familiar refrain, had difficulty recognizing that

> these lots belong to the people of Maine, that their legislators have the authority to terminate timber and grass rights granted a long time ago, and that camp leases are not granted in perpetuity.[399]

Austin Wilkins testified at the hearing as well. Perhaps the cutting rights had lapsed, the former forest commissioner allowed, but even so, it would be "only fair" to compensate the landowners who had paid taxes and cared for the lands all these years. His forgiving vein did not sit well with Representative John Martin. The landowners had in all probability taken two or even three harvests from public lands for which they paid a nickel an acre a hundred years ago, he shot back. They had made a killing!

For Donaldson Koons, Governor Curtis's nominee to head the new Conservation Department, the hearing was an opportunity to elaborate on his ideas for the Public Reserved Lands. Koons had served on the Board of Environmental Protection and its predecessor the Water Improvement Commission. He was also the long-time head of the geology department at Colby College in Waterville, and he brought with him a refreshing scientific perspective. The Public Lots should be managed for multiple uses, including recreation, conservation, and forest products, said Koons. His first priority would be to inventory them for all their natural resources. With this information, a Public Lot could be located—or relocated—to include the greatest mix of values. (Relocation, said Koons, shouldn't be a problem since he had heard that paper companies did it all the time.) He would use a youth corps, like the New Deal's Conservation Corps, to gather data in the field.

Two weeks later, the forest industry had its turn with the Public Lands Committee. They had felt left out of the loop during the previous legislative session, the woodsmen said, although others thought they had had quite enough influence, among other things dropping the key provisions in LD 1812. Richardson, however, knew that they would need the industry's cooperation "to sort this mess out" and made a point of scheduling a meeting for them in the Bangor area. When they arrived at the University of Maine campus in Orono on September 28, "cooperation" was hardly the word for describing the landowners' attitude.

Once more, Morris Wing, president of the Paper Industry Information Office, led the charge. The paper companies owned the rights to the timber and grass until such time as the township was organized in response to the will of the people who lived there. Where were these people? he asked. That most of the townships had few permanent residents was in large part due to the landowners, whose efforts to discourage settlers went back to the lumbermen of the mid-nineteenth century. One after another, company executives made no bones about the fact that this was their policy, and they had been very successful. People don't mix well with forestry. They "clutter up" the roads used for hauling logs and complain of noise and ugly cut over areas. They had a "restrictive influence on logging," said Brad Wellman, the patrician head of Seven Islands. "Selling lands opens up great, big problems," agreed Arthur F. Steadman, Scott Paper's chief forester. On top of the campsite issue aired at the first hearing, here was another strike against the public's ability to enjoy its land.

One absolute right retained by the state was the "right to prevent waste of the common property," according to Lee Schepps. This applied to the undivided lots where Maine was a co-tenant, but also to the soil where the lots had been located. As the committee considered the impact of forestry operations on the Public Lots, erosion was of particular concern. They had never seen serious erosion, said the foresters with bland self-assurance.[400] As to harvesting trees for pulpwood before they grew large enough to produce sawlogs, Maine was growing all the sawlogs it could sell, said the pulp and paper companies.

They were incensed at the war Richardson and his committee were waging on them in the press and before the legislature. "Let's get from the courts a determination of our rights," said P110's Morris Wing. The paper companies and landowners had been criticized for going to court but "in a matter of this magnitude" it was the proper thing to do. The crusty curmudgeon from Caribou rose to the occasion once more. "You won't hesitate to come back to us if you can't get what you want from the courts," Ezra Briggs told Wing. "You will want us to give you what the courts won't."

Next, the Public Lands Committee headed for the hills of west central Maine. Unlike the Unorganized Territories, many of the towns in the area had been incorporated, with the reserved lots returned to full state control. It was a busy couple of days: two public hearings, one in the morning in Stratton, the other in Rangeley, twenty miles away, the same evening. In between, members got a glimpse of several Public Lots from the air. The next day, a Saturday, they visited Aziscohos Lake to see the "cottage slum" for themselves. Four nonprofit organizations were specifically invited to testify. The Rangeley Guides Association, the Maine Mountain Planning Commission, the Maine Outing Club (to which Donaldson Koons had been an advisor), and the Natural Resources Council of Maine. The committee received the endorsement of another nonprofit at its hearing at the University of Maine at Portland-Gorham (now the University of Southern Maine) in mid-November.[401] The Appalachian Mountain Club, through its Maine chapter, supported anything that would increase opportunities for summer hiking and canoeing, or winter cross-country skiing and snowshoeing. The AMC also offered volunteers to help collect data on the public lands.

While the Public Lands Committee crisscrossed Maine, the world was plunged into a potentially cataclysmic international crisis. On October 6, Egyptian and Syrian armies invaded Israel. When the United States resupplied its ally with arms, the Arabs placed an embargo on oil sales to America. By the end of October, the so-called Yom Kippur War was over, but the energy crisis of 1973 had only just begun. With a cold Maine winter ahead, Maine people were especially vulnerable to interruptions or price hikes in heating oil.

The energy crisis would go well beyond that, testified economist Geoffrey Faux at the committee's last public session. Tourism and recreation would be affected, too. The forests, always the lifeblood of Maine, would be more important than ever. With the economy expected to decline in the next few years, the time had come to move the conversation about the Public Lots from recreation to economics. We must "squeeze every last drop of employment and income from our forest resources," said Faux. This was no plea on behalf of the paper companies. National or multinational companies took their profits to their corporate headquarters, in New York or Philadelphia, leaving Maine without the benefits of its own natural resources, like a Third World country. Faux called for a shift to Maine-owned and Maine-operated businesses. Four hundred thousand acres of public land would be an ideal place to start the transition.

Another speaker, Robert "Bob" Lawrence, was a professional forester. He urged the committee to use the Public Lots to produce quality wood products—"from railroad ties to structural grade plywood"—all made in

Maine. With investment in an "extensive system of small modern sawmills," Maine could be the lumber supply for construction all over New England, he said. Both Faux and Lawrence were taking leaves out of *A Maine Manifest*, a thoughtful exploration of innovative development strategies for Maine, written by an economics professor at Harvard's Kennedy School, Richard Barringer. Barringer summered in Maine, and he had written a report on a proposed oil refinery in Searsport. It had come to the attention of veteran journalist and editor of the *Maine Times*, John Cole.

Cole was frustrated with the mind-set of government that seemed to be endlessly pursuing "the next big thing" that would save Maine's economy. One megaproject after another had dominated development thinking in the 1960s: besides the Searsport oil refinery and another in Machiasport, there had been a massive investment in processing sugar beets in Aroostook and an aluminum smelter in Trenton—all on the coast. Cole suggested Barringer take a look at some alternatives that might extricate Maine from this spiral of natural resource waste and despoliation and move it into a sustainable future. Geoffrey Faux had been a member of Barringer's research team.

A Maine Manifest appeared in July 1972, just after Bob Cummings started stirring up the Public Lots hornet's nest.[402] Maine's future, Barringer wrote, "will turn at precisely the point where land development and environmental protection meet." His premise was a kind of economy-ecology Möbius strip. Thoughtful growth was essential for Maine to afford to protect its natural resources, without which it would have no growth. To Barringer, "economic development is good ecology, and environmental protection is good economics."

That economic development had become part of the Public Lots debate was apparent in Cummings's own broadening perspective. Hiking and canoeing in Maine's wildlands might be where his heart was, but as the grand plantations idea advanced toward legislation, his articles connected it to a more diversified Maine-owned forest products industry as well. A bill, he urged, should provide "the leverage Maine needs to bring competition back to the woodlands, to provide the raw materials for new businesses and manufacturers."

Eighteen months after *A Maine Manifest* was published, Governor Curtis appointed Richard Barringer to be the first director of the Bureau of Public Lands (BPL), part of Commissioner Koons's new Department of Conservation.

On January 2, 1974, Governor Kenneth Curtis called the legislators into special session. Special sessions, he reminded them, once reserved for emergencies, had of late become a standard practice for wrapping up the regular session's unfinished business. This year, there was a real emergency: the energy crisis and the effect it might have on Maine citizens, from heating their homes to driving to work. The governor's address made minimal mention of the public lands. On natural resource issues the session should address, he first recommended a register of critical natural areas. He also invited the legislature to establish a commission to review the operations of Maine's forest products companies.[403]

This was at the request of the attorney general. The forest industry's habitual complacency—assuring the Legislature that their critics did not know good forestry when they saw it—had begun wearing thin on Jon Lund. A public commission on the Maine woods was also one of the Nader report's recommendations, released the previous year. It had been highly critical of the paper industry for pursuing the lowest quality forest product—pulp—and doing so wastefully, taking advantage of the vastness of Maine's forests. To which charge "industry has been virtually silent," the attorney general noted. If the report was correct, he wanted the details "ferreted out and rectified."

At the end of the natural resources part of his address, Governor Curtis made this modest announcement: "In addition, I will support legislation clarifying the powers of the State with respect to the Public Lots."

Two weeks later, its staff presented the Public Lots Committee with a broad outline of the legislation it was recommending. The odd thing about it was that the Public Lots were not mentioned. Instead, eight grand plantations were to be created to bring self-government to ten thousand souls living scattered over some nine million acres of Maine. These people had been deprived of local government—"a basic privilege of citizenship"—for too long. The drafters were at pains to make civic responsibilities in the new plantations as burden-free as possible. An elected council of seven members (it was subsequently reduced to five or three) would appoint a plantation manager to be "clerk, constable, registrar of voters, treasurer, census taker, keeper of records." He would also be the liaison for the numerous agencies in Augusta a town must deal with. The council would also serve as a school committee. Schools would be overseen by the plantation, not the state.

Of the plantation manager's various hats, that of census-taker held particular interest. Amid the flurry of assumptions accruing around the Public Lots debate, the population of the Unorganized Territories was frequently stated to be 10,000, although the census number was 5,622. There were disparities, too, in the figures generated by different agencies. The Education Department showed students getting tuition support in townships where the census found no one. Other townships turned out to have no full-time residents, contrary to the census numbers. An accurate head count would be possible, at last.

Senator Richardson scheduled a public hearing on the "Grand Plantations" for February 14. Depending on how the recommendations fared, his committee would report them to the legislature as a bill. Asked how the Public Lots might be affected by legislation focused on local governance, the chairman would not speculate. "The question of whether this bill terminates any alleged private cutting rights is a matter for the courts to decide," he said. Harry Richardson was a master tactician, and pragmatic to the core. He knew he must keep the two issues separate. His opponents were equally determined to link them and deliver "a karate chop at a bill they feel certain will influence [the court's] decision against the timber takers," wrote *Maine Times* editor John Cole.

That the bill's first hearing was on Valentine's Day had a certain irony. It was no lovefest. Every paper company and major landowner was there ready to fight for their rights. As Richardson gaveled the session to order, there was standing room only in the hearing chamber with the overflow crowding the corridor outside. There was little chance of keeping the debate focused on bringing self-government to the wildlands. Spokespeople for the Department of Environmental Protection and the State Planning Office stressed how grand plantations would improve their dealings with communities there. Otherwise, the debate that unfolded remained firmly fixed on the Public Lots.

In a rare appearance before the legislature, Attorney General Jon Lund made no secret of his desire to see the people's land returned to them. The last time legislators debated an "issue of these dimensions" was in the 1920s, he said, when "Governor Baxter fought many of these same private interests over the ownership of the water resources of the state." Then as now, the issue was private profits *from*, versus public rights *to* the "people's land." Was the state better served, asked Lund, if these lands were managed "for the benefit of all the people of Maine or for the private benefit of primarily a handful of giant corporations?"

One government agency, the Land Use Regulation Commission, testified against the bill. Its director, James Haskell, was on record calling the grand plantations a "can of worms." The landowners and industry were even less complimentary. The bill was a "sham"; it "breaks faith" with the proper stewards of the forest, said J.M. Huber Corporation's David Semonite. Practicing sustained-yield forestry as they did, said Stephen Wheatland, one of the Pingree heirs, "we are an asset to the state." "A completely improper way to proceed," thundered IP's Morris Wing. As an obvious attempt to steal private property rights, it was part of Maine's "anti-business political climate," howled the head of the Forest Products Council, Lawrence Robbins. "It would bring preservationists and socialists to the woodlands!"

It was totally predictable, countered Jon Lund, that "private vested interests, particularly giant out-of-state corporations, would strongly oppose this measure." Structured as they are to make profits for their investors, "their reaction is entirely consistent with that purpose." After a long, contentious session—John Cole described it in terms of a "shoot-out" with "black hats" and "white hats"—the Public Lands Committee adjourned to consider its options: to send or not to send a grand plantations bill to the legislature.

The paper industry and private landowners immediately mounted a full-court press. Either his bill went no further, or Harrison Richardson's chances of becoming governor would vanish. They were already on better terms with his opponent, James Erwin, the former AG who withheld the Schepps report when it was first written. The industry pulled out all the stops. Lobbyists flooded the State House. Harry Richardson was used to jousting with lobbyists. At a press conference, the committee chairman was blunt. The large landowners were engaged in a "Gargantuan" effort to prevent the legislature from even debating the issue. "Every member [of the committee] I have talked with," he told reporters, "has been approached by someone claiming to own the Public Lots." Richardson, now in full campaign mode, knew the impact the grand plantations bill might have on his chances of becoming governor. The paper companies had tried to use the issue to spike his candidacy the previous spring, before it had even begun. The candidate responded defiantly. "I have no intention of surrendering my view on the public lands or the integrity of the legislative process to a handful of people who own these lots or who have taken the position that they think they own them."

Industry influence was not confined to the corridors of power. At a pair of last-minute hearings in Aroostook and Washington counties in the heart of the "paper plantation," it transpired that corporate executives had been contacting local people, many of whom worked for their companies.[404] International Paper, for one, charged Ezra Briggs, had inquired if area residents were planning to attend the hearing. What was the matter with that, asked some of his Republican brethren on the committee. He never said it was wrong, Briggs responded, just that it had been "interpreted as threatening," a subtle suggestion that the company would cancel the leases of anyone speaking in favor of grand plantations. Richardson added that several people had told him they were afraid to testify publicly. All they had done was urge citizens to attend the hearing, said the chief attorney/lobbyist for the paper companies, Donald Perkins. Even the committee staff had done the same.

As the special session picked up steam, the tenor of the discussion in Augusta was not to the advantage of Richardson's bill. A straw vote revealed that even his own committee had so far only three votes in favor, against seven nays. On top of the inherent complexity—always a negative factor in political calculus—surrounding the Public Lots, the concept of a grand plantation had accrued its own stumbling blocks.

Confusion started with the word, *plantation*. In most people's minds, they were the home "of southern belles, Scarlet O'Hara and Rhett Butler," Cummings pointed out, not million-acre-wildernesses in the north country.[405] Large landowners were not the only ones fighting against the bill; many wildland residents wanted nothing to do with government, although the committee staff had done its utmost to make it attractive. (An amendment was added to allow residents to "deorganize" after three years, if the system didn't work.)

The ever-thickening plot around the coming election for governor was another curveball on both sides of the aisle. A vote for the grand plantations bill, whether from a Democrat or from a Republican, was a vote for Richardson, who was widely believed to be the only Republican able to beat the likely Democratic candidate, George Mitchell. Considering so many complicating factors, it was a tough call. To vote against the bill was the easier option.

Only vox populi could overcome that. Massive public support for creation of the Land Use Regulation Commission had overcome lobbying by the same interests that was just as intense. Where was that support now? Lest the public lose sight of its stake in the Public Lots, Bob Cummings convinced his editors at the Portland papers to let him provide a retrospective. Eight front-page articles, some of them above the banner, appeared consecutively from Sunday to Sunday. The last one appeared on the second anniversary of the story that launched the debate. Little in them was new, and in some the padding showed a bit. However, Cummings's aim was to keep his readers focused on the Public Lots every day for a week and encourage them to show their support. "Maine may soon be faced with the happy problem of finding wise public use for 400,000 acres of land—some 625 square miles—that two years ago it didn't know it had," he wrote, with justifiable pride.

Finally, Richardson called a vote. To his surprise, given the poor result of the straw poll, the committee voted 6 to 4 "ought to pass." L D. 2545, "An Act to Organize the Mainland Unorganized and Deorganized Territories of the State into Grand Plantations," was sent to the full Legislature. No one thought that its path would be easy when the Senate took it up two days later. The bill's difficulties were immediately apparent in the position of Senate President Kenneth P. MacLeod, a Republican and hitherto one of Richardson's staunchest allies on the committee. He firmly believed, MacLeod said, that the cutting rights should be terminated; he hoped they would be; but not by "this sham of a bill," designed "to steal back what was stolen from us in the 1850s." Two wrongs don't make a right seemed to be the implication. Having voted for the bill in committee, he switched his vote, giving it a divided report.

"The Senate President is grievously inaccurate," declared an outraged Richardson. MacLeod's position was "nonsense." Harsh words followed. MacLeod said his decision was based on a letter from Erwin, when he was Attorney General, stating that possession of the timber and grass rights was tantamount to ownership of the land. Richardson doubted such a letter even existed and demanded that MacLeod produce it. The idea that the courts, not the legislature, should decide the case, was "the ultimate cop-out," said Richardson. The legislature had the right and duty to "pass legislation in the public interest."

As the debate dragged on, one distinguished senator doubtless spoke for many. "I thought the issue was black and white," said Bennett D. Katz, Republican from Augusta, "but it's only the tip of the iceberg we see today." He could hardly be blamed, listening to Senator Richardson fume that the grand plantations bill was "just good government" that would have passed easily but for the grass and timber rights, and in the next breath promise, "We are going to get this land back regardless of whether we have the courage to do it today."

This time, Bob Cummings's attempts to stir up public support fell short of the mark. One committee member said the only letters he had received in favor of the grand plantations came from Cape Elizabeth, one of Portland's high-end suburbs. Given the rural-urban tension, editorials from the major newspapers in the bill's favor backfired. "The issue is not whether the Senate should buckle under to the big landowners, but whether we will buckle under to the press," said one senator. Wildland residents were also very persuasive, testifying that they neither needed nor wanted government services forced on them. (A few months later, Barringer couldn't help delighting in the irony when a man who had been particularly vocal appealed for more police protection after some violence in his township.)

After another unusually long debate, the Senate voted the grand plantations bill down, 19 to 7. One of those who voted in favor of the bill was a Democratic senator seeking his party's gubernatorial nomination. He had to wait another four years, but as governor, Joseph E. Brennan would play a major role in the eventual fate of the Public Reserved Lands. On this occasion, he issued a strongly worded statement. "This Senate will go down in history as the senate that rejected the public interest in the wildlands. We have passed up a chance of a lifetime." He could not believe that they would "throw away the chance to recover a $30-million asset."

The House gave the coup de grace the next week, but not without a last-ditch stand. Ezra Briggs was in fine fettle as he led the floor fight. The bill was being defeated by the power and influence of the paper industry, he alleged. "I shall not rest until the grass and timber cutting rights have been returned to their rightful owners—the people of Maine." The bill went down, 70 to 61, nonetheless.

"We came so close! I couldn't believe how close," recalled Herb Hartman wistfully forty years later. The result was far closer than it looked at first glance. Senator MacLeod's switched vote deprived Richardson of a majority from his committee and sowed just enough doubt. Too many people disliked one part of it just a bit more than they could embrace another. A committee member who voted against it, Republican Rep. Lynwood Palmer, captured the pervading ambivalence. "Once this bill is defeated, reasonable men will sit down and work out the problem whereby the land will come back to the people." Palmer was a little over-optimistic. The immediate fallout of the grand plantations debacle was a civil war, mostly between its Republican and Democratic supporters. The struggle would leave the nascent BPL stripped of almost all its funding, and the political futures of its director and the conservation commissioner in jeopardy.

The previous summer, when the legislature approved Ken Curtis's Department of Conservation and the BPL within it, Harry Richardson had stated his usual blunt opinion to a reporter. The new commissioner should be "somebody with a lot of zing. . . . But if he's a harmless old dud, we'll be back where we started." Donaldson Koons had "zing," as did Richard Barringer at the BPL. Zing has much to recommend it, but it carries a political risk that "harmless old duds" do not. Commissioner Koons had already crossed swords with James Haskell, habitually referred to as the "controversial director" of LURC. LURC was now in the Department of Conservation, making Haskell one of Koons's department heads. Koons had in fact asked for his resignation over his position on the grand plantations bill. Haskell refused, being retained in his position by the narrowest vote of the LURC commissioners.

Haskell had the backing of an even more powerful politician, House Minority Leader John Martin. Martin had made no secret of his opposition to the appointment of Donaldson Koons, a Republican, to head the Department of Conservation, nor of his belief that another could do the job better. He didn't much like the recent transplant from Cambridge and Harvard, Richard Barringer, either. Despite having introduced LD 1812 in the regular session, Martin was against the grand plantations idea. One of the earlier bill's provisions that survived its enactment was to fund the new BPL from revenues produced on the eighty thousand acres of Public Lots to which the state had clear title. These were lots on which the timber and grass had never been sold or where the rights had reverted after a township was organized. In the past, the interest they generated had gone to the respective plantations. Four of these were in Martin's district, and he feared the people who lived in them would "rise up in arms" if they no longer got the money (a slight 1.5 percent, "in keeping with Maine conservatism," the *Maine Times*'s Cole noted wryly). With that, he and Republican Roswell Dyar (whose bill to tax landowners for posting their lands had such a spectacular rise and fall a year before) introduced a bill to change the funding formula. The *Maine Times* calculated that every $10,000 the bureau would have received under the original law was reduced to $40.

Barringer urged Governor Curtis to veto Martin's bill, but in vain. Larger political issues were clouding the picture. If the House went Democratic, as was expected, John Martin would be the speaker. Ken Curtis, some said, wanted to protect Barringer from the future speaker's wrath. If a Democrat won the Blaine House—George Mitchell was the expected candidate— Republican Koons would be out, and the betting was that he would be replaced by Haskell. The governor withheld his veto, and the BPL limped into the world with a budget of $30,000, less than a third of what it had been promised.

The new bureau had little more than a mission statement. "No direction as to how, to what purposes, or with what means to manage the Public Lots over which it had jurisdiction," recalled Richard Barringer. "Or to retrieve those over which it did not." He had no staff, until Forestry Commissioner Fred Holt assigned forester John Walker, and forest fire ranger John Hinckley to the BPL, along with a desk and a vehicle. So as he ensconced himself in what John Cole called his "one-desk office," Barringer was free to start applying his intuitions as a resource economist. Here was an opportunity to increase economic and social options for Mainers. The sky was the limit; a new town might even be forged, centered in a Public Lot and thriving thanks to the industrial and recreational opportunities all around it. Even more transformative, several Public Lots might be consolidated into one parcel. This was a version of the paper companies' "magic cities in the wilderness," updated to serve all the people of Maine.

One of *A Maine Manifest*'s key planks was a Maine land bank. "The idea," Barringer wrote, "is simple enough: land acquisition, land planning, and land use in the public interest, on a permanent basis." The windfall of four hundred thousand acres of state-owned land might be the way to get it started. With grand plantations no longer on the horizon, the BPL director convened a group of experts to "design a socially desirable resource conservation and development strategy for Maine." They would be applying the *Manifest* on the ground.

The study was a revelation to Barringer and his small staff, who were at this point all CETA-funded employees.[406] Maine, they discovered, was a leader in "innovative regulatory legislation" as attested by such vehicles as shoreland zoning and the Land Use Regulation Commission. Local initiatives could be more effective than a land bank implemented in and decreed by Augusta. Instead of a heavy-handed, regulatory agency, an Office of Resource Conservation and Development in the Executive Office would develop appropriate strategies and identify opportunities for implementing them around the state.[407] A case in point was the town of Dover-Foxcroft in central Maine, which was trying to stem the loss of jobs and young people. An "integrated wood processing facility" on the drawing board would combine sawmill, drying kiln, power generation, and so forth in one facility. Before committing to such a financial investment, a dependable wood supply was essential, and paper companies would not make a long-term contract to supply wood to a competing industry. Thousands of acres of Public Lots could provide an endless source, and Barringer started to work with the town manager at once.

Looking back, Harry Richardson credited the grand plantations bill—even though it didn't pass—with shaking up the paper companies and precipitating a change of attitude about the Public Lots. "Trading desirable sites for less desirable sites," he thought, might be worth it "to extinguish any claim the state might have to grass and timber rights." The issue was not going to go away—not in the legislature, nor in the courts—and the landowners knew it. They also knew that a thousand-acre tract here and there was a blip in their huge ownerships. One acre in twenty-four equaled only 4 percent, and only their land in the Unorganized Territories was affected. For a multinational company with forestland all over the country and even the world, the "risk" might be as little as one half of 1 percent.

Another seemingly arcane issue out of Lee Schepps's report—but an "explosive thing," he called it in retrospect—had begun to sink in: the reality of sharing 150,000 common and undivided acres (the "unlocated" lots) with a suddenly engaged State of Maine. Under partnership law, the owner of even a twenty-fourth of the township had right of access to the whole thing. So long as there was no commercial gain (which would have to be shared) the state could go anywhere it liked on an undivided township, and the state was over a million people. "So my little 4 percent interest," explained Schepps, standing in for the state, "could be used to almost nullify your [the landowner's] right as private property."

"So you come to me and say, this is ridiculous. You're allowing all these people to come on our land. . . . Or you want to build a logging road on our land. Where are you going to put it? You need your partner's consent. Fine! The remedy is you go to court and ask the judge to divide it so I get my one thousand acres, you get your twenty-three thousand. We have to find out where those thousand acres are." Schepps stopped for dramatic effect. "Every township is a separate lawsuit. Every township involves an examination of *all* the assets involved, all of it . . . I mean it will be endless. How do we calculate the value of lots on a mountainside, versus lakefront, versus this or that? It's a real barrel of terrible problems."

The paper companies continued to express their confidence that they would win in court, but there were plenty of reasons to want to get "the state out of their hair," as Schepps put it. Barringer concurred. "They'd like sure as hell to see us out of the way." Endless conflict with the state was a no-win solution, especially when a company had just invested millions of dollars in its mills. For corporations, predictability—knowing what would be coming at them in the future—was the most valuable commodity of all.

Like a logjam on one of the old river drives cleared by a driver with a deft peavey and a stick of dynamite, the situation called for daring intervention. Shortly after the legislature went home for the year, the president of Great Northern Paper Company, Robert Hellendale, quietly approached Governor Curtis with an offer to try to come to terms regarding the Public Lots on his company's lands. The fact that one of the leaders of the state's forest products industry was breaking with his fellows was dynamite indeed. With over two million acres, Great Northern was the largest landowner in Maine. The large private landowners viewed Hellendale's action as a "profound betrayal," recalled Richard Barringer, to whom Curtis assigned the negotiations. Great Northern, however, had a number of concerns at the time, ranging from loggers organizing to public reaction to the company's aerial budworm spraying; Hellendale did not need another controversial issue.

He and Barringer set out to exchange the located Public Lots on Great Northern lands for consolidated tracts of equal value. They had two main objectives: for state and company to "get out of each other's way;" and to "consolidate" Maine's interest into a few large tracts of land. At Hellendale's suggestion, prospective "land swaps" were to be determined on a strict value-for-value basis, taking into consideration the different values of timber stands, water access, and other notable features. For instance, mountain slopes and shorefront were worth less for timber but more for public uses. This was particularly important, Hellendale explained, in order to convince Great Northern's board of directors that he was acting prudently and in the company's best interest, and that it was being treated fairly by the state. Accordingly, the two sides established average prices for all timberland, lakeshore, or other features that might be traded between "The Northern" and Maine.

In a series of closed meetings, Barringer and Hellendale worked out the overall scope of the agreement. Great Northern would trade the grass and timber rights on about sixty thousand acres (roughly two-thirds of its Public Lots) for consolidated land of equal appraised value for commercial logging. There remained thirty thousand undivided acres, some held "in common" with other landowners. These were set aside to maintain the company's standing in the court case, still pending. Schepps also knew that in any future trades, undivided lots would give Maine greater leverage.

With this framework in place—and while the nation watched the rapid disintegration of the Nixon presidency—Barringer and his staff worked through the summer identifying tracts of exceptional public value in Great Northern's ownership. Lee Schepps was the bureau's lawyer, and forty years later, he still got animated speaking of that time, recalling "every single piece of land that came to the state, and why it was picked." Herb Hartmann, who had memorably introduced Schepps to Mount Katahdin and who was one of Barringer's CETA employees, wanted Deboullie Township. Barringer thought they should have Squapan because it was strategically located to the populated areas of Aroostook County. Schepps himself argued for T6R11 (site of the famous Telos Canal) between Baxter State Park and the Allagash Wilderness Waterway. It had never been cut with a chainsaw, Schepps told them, and the bureau needed all that timber to pay its bills.

The bureau's deliberations were not confined to maps on a table. Barringer and his staff made forays into the forest to see for themselves. A couple of college interns, Vicki Parker from Colby College and Elizabeth Swain from Hampshire College, spent the summer traveling the state, prospecting for land-swap options. They were aided enormously by John Walker and forest ranger John Hinckley, on loan from the Forest Service.[408] Walker and Hinckley had worked together resurveying the Public Lots and marking their boundary lines in the 1960s. Their knowledge of the Unorganized Territory, as well as Maine timber markets, was unsurpassed. Barringer described John Walker as "one of those old-fashioned Maine people who could do anything." A licensed pilot, Walker flew Parker and Swain all over Great Northern's lands, getting a sense of the value of the standing timber and its long-term potential.

The night on Gero Island, in the middle of Chesuncook Lake, has a special place in the early annals of the BPL. The group—which included Nancy Ross, Lee Schepps, and Herb Hartman—was making a canoe reconnaissance of the West Branch. Barringer had made a pot of chili for the expedition, but it got left in the car. That night Hartman made biscuits from an old woods-man's recipe. The next morning, Schepps showed his appreciation for their texture by making him a special plate of rocks covered with jam for breakfast.

By early fall, a proposal had been fashioned to acquire fifty-eight thousand acres in five large blocks of outstanding "multiple use" value. Negotiations within Great Northern proceeded quickly. On December 11, in the closing days of his administration, Governor Curtis and Robert Hellendale met again to sign the agreement. "Probably the most important land transaction to take place during this century," said Richard Barringer in announcing the deal to the press. Although it was a value-for-value exchange in principle, Great Northern considered the lands the state requested amounted to an extra $100 per acre, and it counted about $6,000 as a charitable gift to Maine. This was risky, as it assumed the paper companies would win the legal battle. If they didn't, Great Northern would have some explaining to do to the IRS. But, said a happy Barringer, "for the state, it's a no-lose proposition."

Barringer gave Robert Hellendale most of the credit. "This agreement happened because Hellendale wanted it to happen," he told the press. "He showed great leadership." In negotiating a separate peace for his company, its CEO had made a significant, and difficult, break with the rest of the paper industry. Moreover, some of the trades were held in common with other landowners. The Pingree heirs, for instance, owned 25 percent of Deboullie Township. When Brad Wellman found out that Great Northern had negotiated away its 75 percent without telling him—he put it bluntly—"we were kind of pissed."

Bob Hellendale was more of a statesman than the other landowners, said a future CEO of one of Maine largest companies, who was just beginning his own career at the time. He could see the big picture, which let him break through the "iron curtain" of denial that prevailed in most of the industry. Two years later, Hellendale gave his own insights into his thinking. "We were convinced that we could win in the courts, but we were also convinced that the legislature might legally take away that victory," he said at a ceremony held by the Appalachian Mountain Club's Maine chapter to honor him and other paper companies and state officials for "distinguished service." He went on to say that, when he first suggested a possible deal, he thought the chances were "about a hundred to one." Getting his board of directors on board was "one of the most challenging jobs I ever had to do."

Receiving a similar citation on the same occasion, Richard Barringer noted that for the first time, Maine and the paper companies had negotiated "as truly independent equals. . . . If my reading of history is right, this is truly a dramatic and basic change." He also praised the contribution of environmental organizations to the process, saying there was "no substitute for expressions of interest from organizations like AMC."

At last, Maine had won a decisive victory in its quest to reclaim its Public Reserved Lands. As important, a precedent had been set that might return almost a half-million acres of land to the people of Maine. As early as mid-summer, a number of other paper companies were said to be considering an approach to the state. By year's end, preliminary talks had begun with three of them—International Paper, Georgia-Pacific, and Brown Paper Company—for, if all went well, seventy thousand acres more. The value-for-value approach developed with Great Northern would be the basis for all these settlements.

Chapter Twelve

Trades, Raids, and Sovereign Immunity (1975–1980)

The only hurdle left to complete the land swap negotiated with Great Northern was ratification by the legislature. A bill to do so was presented at a public hearing before the Public Lands Committee on February 26, 1975. A dozen people spoke; no one opposed it.[409] Conservation Commissioner Donaldson Koons hailed the deal as a huge step toward recovering the timber and grass rights belonging to the state. Linwood Palmer, a leading Republican legislator who had voted against the grand plantations bill, echoed what he had said on that occasion: "Reasonable people sitting down and negotiating could solve this problem." He especially congratulated Bureau of Public Lands Director (BPL) Richard Barringer for making it happen.

Even Ed Sprague, the early agitator on behalf of the Public Lots, allowed himself to be positive. He could not resist declaring, "After three years of hopeful waiting, I now have the pleasure of standing before this committee and saying to doubters and opponents I told you so." Still, the swap was the "best and most practical" option available, and it was a good template for getting back all the Public Lots.[410] "My gut feeling is that I should be very much a proponent of the bill," said a man at the hearing, Gardiner Defoe, who leased three lots for a boys' camp. Before committing himself, however, he asked about the new dispensation's impact on lease-holders. Barringer reassured him: as a current lease-holder, meet "reasonable regulations," and you'll get a lifetime lease. Barringer took the opportunity to share his optimism about the public lands' potential to earn their keep. The bureau had "no intention of taking [all] these lands out of forest production." Stumpage from the lots already under state control could be expected to bring in $100,000 per year.

The next week, by a wide margin, the legislature approved the agreement, and on March 18, 1975, the bill was "quietly" signed by the new governor,

James B. Longley.[411] It was an "excellent example of the spirit of cooperation needed between private industry and state government," said Longley, whose campaign promise had been to bring a business approach to Maine's problems. Having been blessed by legislature and governor, the Great Northern lands were formally conveyed to the state in the fall. (A strike by independent woodcutters and truckers against the paper companies caused a brief delay. Corporate management felt the transfer would be "inappropriate" while the dispute continued.)

What Maine and its people had gained was astounding. Five magnificent parcels had replaced sixty or so thousand-acre tracts scattered across the map. Fifteen thousand acres in Holeb Township—in Somerset County almost on the border with Quebec—included a stretch along the Moose River, a canoeist mecca, and thousand-acre Holeb Pond. Seventy miles to the northwest, in Piscataquis County, the Chesuncook Village tract included three-thousand-acre Gero Island in the middle of Chesuncook Lake.

In Aroostook County within thirty miles of Maine's northern boundary, Maine acquired Great Northern's two-thirds undivided interest in Deboullie Township, including seventeen ponds (four containing critical populations of the rare blue-back trout, *Salvelinus alpinus oquassa*) and stunning talus-strewn mountains.[412] According to Richard Anderson, any list of the most spectacular areas to acquire in Maine would have Deboullie Township at the top. "It's all low mountains and fantastic ponds," he described it with eyes gleaming.

West of Greenville on Moosehead, the state's largest lake, an eight-thousand-acre block stretched from Little Squaw Mountain to the lake itself. (In 2011, Little Squaw Mountain was renamed Little Moose Mountain out of respect for Native Americans.) Finally, twenty thousand acres in Township T6R11, site of the Telos Cut, connected Baxter Park and the Allagash Wilderness Waterway. The tract was closer to Great Northern's mill in Millinocket than a lot of the company's lands, and it retained the right to cut wood on T6R11 for several years. It paid the BPL at market rates, and the income would become a mainstay during the bureau's early years.

Altogether, the lands traded by Great Northern included sixty miles of shoreline on some of Maine's most iconic lakes and streams. It was "a happy solution to an immense problem," acknowledged Harrison Richardson. Still, in his view, it simply whittled an "enormous rip-off" of the public down to "a major rip-off." Feisty as ever, the former chairman of the Public Lands Committee did not intend to let up on the paper companies; they had held and, with the exception of Great Northern, continued to hold the Public Lots without either the "legal or moral right to do so."[413]

Not only did the land swap with Great Northern provide an example for other companies to follow. The parcels Maine acquired had been carefully chosen as nuclei that could be enhanced by further trades. Behind these choices had been the passion of a trio of public officials: Richard Barringer, whose strategic sense and political savvy ensured that the deals were as good as they could be; Lee Schepps, advocate for as much shoreline as possible and attention to the bottom line; Herb Hartman, champion of the distant mountaintop and remote pond. Their complementary skills and concerns would be brought to bear on all the negotiations for the next three years.

Already the momentum was building. In addition to the three that had already come forward (International Paper, Georgia-Pacific (GP), and Brown Paper Company), five more companies were showing various degrees of interest in finding a solution.[414] If all these negotiations came to a happy close, nearly half the Public Lots could be back in state control by the end of 1975 or the beginning of 1976.

With Great Northern's acres in hand, Barringer's bureau needed, as he put it, to "make effective use" of them. Besides conservation and public recreation, here was an opportunity for a more diversified and productive woods economy. But, to provide wise management for hundreds of thousands of acres, the BPL had to be put on a firmer foundation. So far, it existed merely at the discretion of the commissioner of conservation.

One of Barringer's early hires at the BPL was a young Bangor-bred attorney just out of Boston College Law School. David Flanagan knew something about the politics surrounding Maine's forests.[415] While earning his law degree, he had written pleadings for the suit against the Baxter Park Authority when it allowed Great Northern to violate the terms of its deed in the park's "scientific forestry" section. He had also been a Democratic aide in the state legislature. But being in-house lawyer for the fledgling BPL—at a princely $11,000 a year, thanks to a CETA grant—was Flanagan's first real job, and his first task was to construct a legal framework for the bureau as a permanent state agency.

"Planning" and "management" would be its watchwords, and they would be informed by the principles of multiple land use. Its objective was "a sustained yield of products and services in accordance with both prudent and fair business practices." The bureau would be responsible for all lands belonging to the state.[416] Barringer wanted to be sure the legislation would "require us to manage the public land under our own income." Any surplus would be placed in a Public Reserved Lands Acquisition Fund to be used exclusively to "purchase and assemble" more public land. In managing its assets for a financial return, the BPL had more in common with the State Liquor Commission than any other state agency.

Those assets—the land the state would be acquiring—might reach $6 million in value. Flanagan felt sure that the BPL could manage the resource as efficiently as a private entity. In his mind, the bureau was "an experiment in rational, competitive economic enterprise." Looking for ways state land could return a profit appealed to his entrepreneurial spirit too.[417] Together with Lee Schepps—still at the attorney general's office representing the Department of Conservation—Flanagan set to work drafting the bill.[418] Parts of it were new, but a lot of it consisted of amendments to existing law. In particular, wherever the Bureau of Forestry was named in the new bill, "Forestry" was struck through and replaced by "Public Lands." It was "mechanical stuff, but it was unprecedented," Flanagan recalled.

"An Act to Improve the Management of the Public Lands" was presented to the Maine House in March by Democratic Representative Neil Rolde. The title was familiar, but in making the BPL independent of the general fund—even turning it into a profit center—it "represents a philosophical departure for the state," Barringer told legislators. The bureau would have enough money, responsibility, and legal power to start correcting Maine's reputation for poor land stewardship. Transactions of up to four thousand acres would be handled with the consent of the governor and executive council. Larger deals would need legislative approval. Legislators would receive a financial account at the end of each year.

By this time, return of the Public Reserved Lands was part of the official Democratic platform, but LD 930 had bipartisan support. John Martin and Lynwood Palmer were cosponsors. This didn't mean it had no opposition. The casus belli was obvious in the amendments to existing law. The Public Reserved Lands had always been the purview of the Forestry Department. The timberland managers had no desire to see the BPL made permanent, still less to strengthen its powers. It was, they testified, a duplication of effort that wasted public resources. It should be eliminated, and charge of the Public Lots returned to the men who had let their companies treat them like private lands for over a century: the foresters and land managers of the Forestry Department. The Public Lot controversy hasn't ended, wrote Bob Cummings that year. The big question now was "Who'll Control Them?"

The Forestry Department hadn't been a Land Office since the turn of the century, countered Barringer and his supporters. Its primary function was to assist the forest products industry. Its resources went first to preventing forest fires and controlling insect infestation. It advised small woodlot managers and provided general information about forestry to the public. The BPL's mission was different, and it would get lost among all these very necessary activities. Finding an appropriate balance for multiple-use management required a bureau independent of traditional timber-harvesting concerns. When LD 930 passed, there was no question in Barringer's mind whom to thank for it. Rep. John Martin was the key. "It would never have happened without him. John Martin is the most skilled legislator in Maine history." In fact, it became law without the governor's signature. When the bill reached his desk, Governor Longley refused to sign it, although he refrained from a veto. Longley had gotten off on the wrong foot with the state agencies, from whose department heads he had demanded undated letters of resignation; they had refused. He wasn't finding the legislature any easier to work with.

That something extraordinary was happening in Maine was apparent in a September 1975 headline in the *New York Times*: "Maine to Recover More Forest Land." That the origins of the Public Lots were unfamiliar outside Maine was clear from the piece's misleading reference to "a 396,000-acre wilderness reserve the state let fall into the hands of private landowners a century ago." Otherwise, the report was accurate, taking a broad brush to the main sequence of events: from the original sale of the timber and grass rights to the battle over the grand plantations; the lobbying against Harrison Richardson's run for governor to the negotiations now ongoing with eight paper companies. The reporter ended with the Damoclean sword that hung over them: if progress had not been made by the time the legislative session started in January, "there will be no shortage of legislators ready to resume the fight. Few observers are predicting that the big landowners can prevail the second time around."

When Donaldson Koons resigned later that month, Governor Longley tapped Richard Barringer to succeed him as conservation commissioner. His confirmation hearing before the executive council was businesslike and generally friendly. No one testified either for or against his appointment.[419] Instead, it became an appraisal of the BPL. As its director, said Barringer, his first job had been to convince the companies that the "state is not playing games" and that "we were determined to assert the public interest" and get the Public Lots back. He was optimistic that 210,000 acres would soon be returned to state control. Having consolidated them into large blocks, "we want to manage these lands wisely." The BPL, Barringer told the council, provided a rare chance to put together "a model land management agency."

Evidently one of the council members heard this as code for the ideas Barringer had put forward in *Maine Manifest*, especially the public land bank (which the *New York Times* article had also mentioned). It proved to be the only contentious part of the hearing. "Have you changed your mind about anything you wrote in this book?" inquired the councilor. Barringer stood his ground, diplomatically. In general, he continued to believe what he had written; however, he had come to understand the difficulties involved in carrying them out. In the balance between ecology and economics, environment versus development, there were no easy answers. Barringer was confirmed as commissioner of conservation two weeks later, and his position as BPL director was filled by Lee Schepps.

At the *Maine Sunday Telegram*, Bob Cummings was assiduously keeping tabs on the negotiations. By mid-November, four paper companies—St. Regis, GP, Brown, and Diamond International—were close to a deal. Preliminary proposals were being exchanged with four others: International Paper, Scott, Huber, and Dead River. These "eight-way" talks would soon return the 210,000 acres Barringer had promised the executive council, wrote Cummings. The immediate return was more like 44,000.

As the new year, 1976, and the special session began, executives of J.M. Huber Corporation scrambled to complete its deal with the state in time to be included in the company's 1975 tax returns. In return for 12,100 acres of Public Lots, Huber was giving up 14,000.[420] When it was approved and signed into law in March, Maine received another superb package of lake, mountain, and commercial forest, part exchange and part gift. The largest parcel in the swap was Huber's two-thirds ownership of half of Squapan township, 6,000 acres around Squapan Lake in the St. John River watershed and worth $1 million. (Squapan was changed to Scopan in 2011, at the same time, and for the same reason, as Little Squaw became Little Moose.) The gift was 5,119 acres along the western ridgeline of Bigelow Mountain, including North Horn.

"Many hikers consider the view from North Horn among the most spectacular of the entire two thousand-mile Appalachian Trail," wrote an ecstatic Bob Cummings. With six high peaks stretched over twelve miles, the whole Bigelow range was one of the trail's gems, and Huber's gift included half of them. There were nine miles of hiking trails, with campsites and lean-tos already maintained by volunteers from the Appalachian Trail Conference and the Appalachian Mountain Club in Maine. To provide access to the new state land, Huber added a right-of-way on two trails through its property.

It was not only thru-hikers who prized the Bigelows. A battle over their fate—one of Maine's early struggles between environmentalists and developers—had been brewing for several years.[421] At the beginning of 1976, it was approaching its climax.

What put Bigelow in the crosshairs of public controversy was Maine's abortive bid to host the 1976 Olympic Winter Games, the centerpiece of which was a proposal for a multimillion-dollar ski resort there. In January 1967, the New England Governor's Conference endorsed the proposal over several other candidates in the region. Maine's new governor, Kenneth Curtis, promoted the Bigelow plan tirelessly. However, the fundraising goal of $5 million remained elusive, and at the end of the year he withdrew the application, leaving open the possibility of reviving the bid when the project might be further advanced.

The developers, a Boston syndicate, continued to promote and flesh out their proposal and in 1969 purchased eight thousand acres stretching from the shore of Flagstaff Lake (created by Central Maine Power Company's dam) up the north slope of Bigelow Mountain. They then asked the Maine legislature to create a new town called Flagstaff and give its "inhabitants" the benefit of the Public Lots and all revenues accrued since the cutting rights were sold.

"It was routine legislation except for two things!" scoffed Bob Cummings. The town had zero inhabitants, still less the twenty-one generally required for incorporation; and it was conditional on the Federal Aeronautics Administration approving construction of an airport. Not funding or building an airport, mind you, stressed the solons; approval was all that was needed to proceed. Should an airport be built, Uncle Sam would pay up to 80 percent of the cost if it were a public airport. A companion bill, the Mountain Resorts Air Port Authority, provided for just such an eventuality. The whole situation was ripe for imaginative language, and Peter Mills, Republican senator from Farmington, rose to the occasion. "I take a dim view of incorporating the rocks and the hills and the lakes without any inhabitants except the porcupines and the bear," he said. Even so, Mills bowed to the clamor for jobs the development would bring to the region and voted with the majority. It was left to Bob Cummings to answer the questions that none of the legislators appeared interested in asking. The town of Flagstaff was to comprise two townships, include 1,960 acres of Public Reserved Land, and snap up the $46,480 they had earned for the Unorganized Territory's school fund now sitting in the state treasurer's office.

Three years later, the Flagstaff Corporation's plans had expanded to a $200 million, four-season luxury resort with an airport for private jets, as well as the accoutrements of an upscale skiing center. The company had already sunk $1.75 million into the project. When Lawrence Stuart's Parks and Recreation Commission (still floating free as one of the two-hundred-odd agencies that comprised Maine government before 1972) began to negotiate with landowners for a thirty-seven-thousand-acre state park around Bigelow, the stage was set for a pitched battle between business and conservation interests.

What one side touted as the "Aspen of the East," Ezra Briggs, the legislature's venerable environmental warrior, deemed a "bunny club for Boston billionaires." At one hearing, a developer confronted Briggs with the question, "Who's ever seen the backside of Bigelow anyway?" It became "one of Jim's ironic mantras," recalled Nancy Ross.[422] The Flagstaff Corporation promised a model high-end resort that could be emulated elsewhere in Maine and bring 3,200 jobs to the area. Opponents saw increasing traffic and strip development, higher taxes, a stampede of "No Trespassing" signs, and most of those jobs going to folks from away. Flagstaff argued that their investment would benefit neighboring locally owned ski mountains. Those local owners tended to see competition instead. Whichever it might be, the Maine Mountain Planning Commission, whose chair was King Cummings (also an owner of the nearby Sugarloaf ski resort), urged the legislature to put the brakes on mountain development in Maine, starting with Flagstaff.

Flagstaff's proposal came before LURC in October 1973. The LURC board was a Who's Who of state and private conservation leaders: Lawrence Stuart, Fred Holt, and Philip Savage—heads, respectively, of Parks and Recreation, Forestry, and State Planning; Clinton "Bill" Townsend from the board of the Natural Resources Council of Maine; and Dead River Company's Christopher Hutchins (the grandson of the company's founder). The chair was the commissioner of conservation, still Donaldson Koons. A sign of the complicated considerations at stake was the notable crossovers in the two opposing camps. A former assistant attorney general, who had worked with Lee Schepps and written most of the LURC statute, represented the Boston team. Home-grown ski resort and condo developers were siding with environmentalists. Even the usually opinionated editor of the *Maine Times*, John Cole, admitted to being ambivalent. The company was only developing eight hundred of its eight thousand acres and had agreed to set aside the rest for conservation. (He was less ambivalent about the drab room—crowded and uncomfortable—where what turned into a fifteen-hour hearing was held. It "failed miserably as a setting for so momentous an event. But then, that is so typical of Maine.")[423]

Behind the finer legal arguments, much of the opposition to the Flagstaff project came from a sense that "we have to stop somewhere" before all Maine's backcountry was developed. LURC, however, had only two options, and drawing the line was not one of them. It could zone the land for either "development" or "management." The first would give thumbs up to Flagstaff Corporation's plans, the second thumbs down. But even if the company was unable to develop a resort, nothing would prevent it from logging or subdividing the eight thousand acres it owned, a Pyrrhic victory to those seeking to protect Bigelow Mountain.

Initially, LURC decided in Flagstaff's favor. Ten days later, meeting in executive session, the commissioners reversed themselves and denied the permit until a comprehensive plan for the region could be completed. The decision effectively imposed a moratorium on development in the Unorganized Territories, a policy LURC had resisted until then. Flagstaff sued, accusing the board of being "arbitrary and capricious." It had just allowed Sugarloaf to expand, only to have its owner, in his capacity as head of a state planning committee, recommend a halt to further mountain development. The company also charged various LURC commissioners with irregular behavior during the process: strong-arming other members, bias against Flagstaff, and violation of Maine's right-to-know laws.

The rights and wrongs of LURC's decision, however, were soon over-taken by a public campaign. Activists in the area formed a group, Friends of Bigelow, to save the mountain for the people of Maine. In February 1974, they hiked the ten miles to its peak, bearing, in the poet Longfellow's words, "through snow and ice, a banner with a strange device." The device read not "Excelsior" but "Save Bigelow," and they left it, unfurled, at the summit. The next year, a bill to establish a preserve around the mountain was brought before the legislature. When it failed to pass, the Friends launched an army of volunteers to gather signatures to place the question on the ballot as a citizen's initiative. Forty-five thousand voters signed the petition, and a vote on Bigelow's future was scheduled for June 1976.

The chamber of commerce was against it; so was the legislature, which voted down the original bill. It would be too expensive, said Governor Long-ley, and would "deny money in the future for the elderly, our students, and to an unknown extent to the opportunity to bring quality jobs to Maine." How-ever, when the BPL acquired the Huber land on Bigelow—more than 10 per-cent of the proposed preserve—the Friends of Bigelow got a powerful boost. As a gift, it opened the door for Maine to apply for matching federal funds up to $500,000 towards purchase of the rest. It also forced Flagstaff, which had hoped to buy some of the same land for a ski run, to redesign parts of its plan.

The Huber Corporation was not completely out of the picture; it still owned land on Bigelow's lower slopes. On Beaver Cove, it had shown that a tim-berland company could double as a real estate developer. By turning Stratton Brook into a lake, it could create an attractive site for a similar project. It wasn't economically feasible at the moment, but Huber's planners were keep-ing an eye on Sugarloaf's fortunes, should its expansion produce "the market we need to develop."

In June, the people of Maine voted 51–49 percent to preserve the Bigelow range, putting an end to all such plans. Under the Bigelow Preserve Act, the state could acquire up to forty thousand acres on and around the mountains. The land was to be "retained in its natural state for the use and enjoyment of the public," which included "hiking, fishing, and hunting." Timber harvesting would be allowed, but it must be "consistent with the area's scenic beauty and natural features." Along with the Flagstaff Corporation's eight thousand acres, the state would take over the only part of its plans the company suc-ceeded in building, the Flagstaff Lodge.[424]

The Bigelow Preserve Act had no fiscal note or appropriation attached to it. It was implemented in the first place with the BPL's land exchanges. Boise-Cascade provided five thousand acres including the two highest peaks in the range, the land next to the Huber parcel on the west and the Flagstaff Corpo-ration's to the north.[425] Across from Bigelow's northern flank, on Flagstaff Lake, Diamond International ceded four thousand acres of prime timberland.

Several years later, in 1980, GP added another nine thousand acres within the preserve boundary.[426] In the meantime, through the BPL and the Bureau of Parks and Recreation, Maine bought out the Flagstaff Corporation for $3,294,500, about two-thirds of which came from the federal Land and Water Conservation Fund. Forty years later, Barringer still thought the deal "Very clever!" And after it was struck, the Boston developer told him, "Well, now I can at least send my kids to college."

Bob Cummings liked to tell the story of a call he got from the conservation commissioner one day at about that time. "Barringer says, 'Bob,' he says, 'Brown Paper Company wants to settle. What do we want that Brown has?'" Cummings replied without a moment's thought. "The Mahoosucs!" The Mahoosuc Mountains are the famously rugged section of the Appalachian Trail with glacial boulders and chasms so deep that ice lasts in them all year round. The Appalachian Mountain Club, of which Cummings was an ardent supporter, had set a goal of protecting the range as a fitting celebration of its centennial in 1976. "Well the anniversary came and went, and not an acre of the Mahoosucs was protected," Cummings recalled. So when Barringer called him, it must have seemed like the answer to a prayer.

In return for its 11,200 acres of Public Lots, Brown Paper ended up giving Maine 15,300 acres strategically located around Grafton Notch State Park. International Paper added another 10,000 acres shortly afterwards. By the end of 1977, state-owned land around the Mahoosucs and Grafton Notch, which had been established in 1963 with 3,000 acres, totaled 27,600 acres, with twenty-three miles of the Appalachian Trail running through it.

Water bodies were the BPL's other priority. In addition to the Mahoosucs, Brown gave up shoreline on two impressive lakes: Chain of Ponds, part of the trail celebrating Benedict Arnold's heroic march to Quebec; and a one-third ownership of Kennebago Lake, famous for the size of its brook trout. The company also had a one-third ownership on nearly ten thousand acres of timberland between Mooselookmeguntic and Upper Richardson lakes.[427] With these and a relatively small tract on Four Ponds (where the Appalachian Trail nudges westwards after the Mahoosucs), Brown Paper gave Maine an impressive holding in the Rangeley area. The Four Ponds Reserve Lands were augmented a year later with two thousand acres from International Paper, which elsewhere yielded land on Scraggly Lake, northeast of Baxter Park, and Rocky Lake, north of Machias in Washington County—two remote ponds famous for their fishing and rich in wildlife and ecological interest.

Besides its lands on Bigelow, Diamond International added to other A-list locations as well. In northern Hancock County, Maine already owned 5,300 acres on Duck Lake, popular for its white sand beaches and salmon fishing.

Diamond added 2,600 more acres, which with parcels from Dead River Company (1,520 acres) and St. Regis Paper Company (11,468 acres) gave the state control of a block of 24,558 acres. This included all the shoreline of Duck and four other lakes of breathtaking beauty and sport for anglers and paddlers. Diamond also gave up forest between Baxter Park and the Allagash, the area Lee Schepps had singled out from the start, and where Maine had already acquired land from Great Northern in its groundbreaking deal.

More "out-of-court settlements," as Bob Cummings had taken to calling them, yielded land around other renowned lakes. Seboeis—dead center of Maine and a recreational favorite for Millinocket and its environs—was part of separate swaps with Boise-Cascade and St. Regis, returning a block of 9,800 acres. Nineteen miles, or two-thirds, of the lake's shoreline was now open for public recreation. On Squapan in the St. John River valley, St. Regis added 2,000 acres to the Huber Corporation's trade, giving the state a total of 8,000 acres around that curious boomerang-shaped lake.

Altogether, a clutch of deals with four paper companies were approved during the legislative session, adding thirty-two thousand acres to Maine's public lands. Commissioner Barringer particularly complimented the companies' woods managers, praising "the grace, high-mindedness and goodwill with which these men conducted the negotiations."[428] The significance of the moment was well expressed by State Senator Andrew Redmond from Somerset County. It was, he told his colleagues, "a historic turning point. We are creating, in these trades and the others to come, a system of State Forests. It is and will be the greatest public trust which we pass on to future generations. . . . I believe this is an exciting time in Maine. We shall be a witness in the next few years as the State begins, for the first time, to manage significant areas of forest lands exclusively for public benefit."[429]

On Christmas Day, Bob Cummings announced in the *Maine Sunday Telegram* that the year had seen a total of 44,000 acres actually returned to Maine, with another 26,500 acres in the pipeline and waiting to be conveyed. One by one, negotiations with the paper companies were bearing fruit, as was the BPL's methodical selection of the tracts it wanted. Maine was well on the way to clawing back 145,000 acres, or almost half what it was seeking from the paper and land-owning companies. BPL director Lee Schepps was hopeful that all the remaining lots could be negotiated amicably. Failing that, he warned, he would not hesitate to pursue Maine's claim through the court or the legislature.

Whatever agreements the paper companies negotiated with the state had no effect on the lawsuit they and the landowners brought in 1973. Any land swaps now being arranged with the BPL were entirely voluntary and separate. Another factor keeping all the companies interested in the case was that if they lost, they would lose the tax deductions they had taken for what they had claimed as gifts.

To start the judicial process, a preliminary hearing had been scheduled in December 1975, but it was postponed by mutual agreement to give both sides more time to prepare. Their attorneys were grappling with a hundred years of forestry practices, forest species, and the laws that applied to them, all of which had continually evolved as the years marched on. Besides the timber rights themselves, there was the question of what the old deeds meant by the term "timber." Was it limited to the large-diameter pine, oak, or spruce trees that were generally harvested a century ago? Or did it include any form of fiber, as became the practice with the advent of the paper industry, and as redefined by the legislature in 1903?

"With so many facts and circumstances pertaining to the issues," explained Gerald Amero, the Pierce Atwood attorney representing the landowners, "it would have been tremendously difficult to present your case, all through witnesses." The trial time needed would create a traffic jam in the court's schedule. With the agreement of both parties, the Superior Court appointed a highly respected former senior justice of the Law Court, Donald W. Webber, as a referee, or special master, to "try the above case and make a report of his findings of fact and conclusions of law to the Court as soon as may be."[430]

The task of assembling the relevant evidence fell to Amero and Martin Wilk, then deputy attorney general. The two lawyers toiled mightily to compile an agreed stipulation of fact on which the case would be adjudicated. Together they reviewed in great detail the origins of the Public Lots and the history of their conveyancing, mostly between 1850 and 1875. In the final document, which was some thousand pages, the parties agreed that the facts it contained were "true and correct but make no agreement as to the weight to be given them nor to the relevancy or materiality thereof."

"Marty and I pretty much lived together for two or three years," Amero recalled. "We spent hours, days, weeks and months sitting across the table, going over draft paragraphs, and fine-tuning and honing them." There were "moments of shouting at each other," he admitted, but only occasionally, such as "Friday afternoons getting close to closing, after a whole week of discussion, and we were both running out of patience." Each lawyer ended up with great respect for the other.

It was not until June 1978—five years after the landowners and paper companies had filed suit against Attorney General Jon Lund—that the trial held its first public hearing. By that time, the attorney general was Joseph Brennan. Although he was now in private practice, Martin Wilk continued to handle the case for the state. Through two days of testimony, June 29 and 30, the only witness was a history professor from the University of Maine, David C. Smith, who was a specialist in the history of lumbering.[431] A recital of the professor's credentials, noted one reporter, took fully twenty minutes. After that, the court was treated to a veritable seminar on nineteenth-century forestry.

Forest management didn't exist, explained Smith. Lumber operators didn't consider managing for future growth. Why did they need to, when the forests of Maine were still considered an "exhaustless merchandize," in the words of Massachusetts' first governor? "They cut and got out. . . . They were frontiersmen moving on to new forests to the north and west," Smith told the judge. Cutover acres, to the extent the woodsmen thought about it, would become agricultural land. The implication was clear: cutting rights, when sold, carried no expectation of being used more than once.

As to the term "timber," it was a "term of restriction" in the mid-nineteenth century, stated Smith. It meant species with commercial value: pine, spruce, and oak for construction; later it included birch and maple that could be made into furniture. But fir—the forest's main commercial product since the turn of the century—was considered a trash species until chemical processes were invented that could break it down to make paper. By that time all the rights to cut "timber" on the Public Reserved Lands had been sold.

That the deeds were silent on these two points, Professor Smith concluded, was because they had no need to stipulate the obvious. No one at that time would have thought of making a second cut, or cutting anything but what they considered to be "timber." Smith's testimony, reported Bob Cummings, "generally supported the state's contentions."

In November, the two sides presented their legal briefs—"in excess of 400 pages"[432]—and Justice Webber began his examination of the facts. He had seemed to be impressed by the witness. Professor Smith demonstrated "enough familiarity with the history of the time" that his opinion should be admissible as evidence, Webber stated on one occasion as he overruled an objection by Amero, the companies' attorney.

With the Public Lots coming back in negotiated out-of-court settlements by drips and drabs, and with attorneys Wilk and Amero preparing their legal briefs for Justice Webber, at least a part of all this "new," "free" land became the target of a takeover bid. The attempt came from a surprising quarter, a case that in several ways had a parallel with the Public Reserved Lands themselves.

At about the time Bob Cummings first alerted readers of the Portland newspapers to the Public Lots, a young lawyer named Tom Tureen began a series of litigations that would culminate in the final settlement of Indian land claims in Maine (and other New England states).[433] As with the Public Reserved Lands, the underpinning legal argument went back to when Maine

was part of Massachusetts. In the case of the claims of the Penobscots and
Passamaquoddies, this was the federal Non-Intercourse Act of 1790. Signed
by President George Washington himself, it stated that no Indian land could
be sold without the consent of the U.S. Congress.[434] Specifically:

> That no sale of lands by any Indians, or any nation or tribe of Indians within the
> United States, shall be valid to any person or persons, or to any state, whether
> having the right of pre-emption to such lands or not, unless the same shall be
> made and duly executed at some public treaty, held under the authority of the
> United States.

The act was, coincidentally, largely the work of Henry Knox, inheritor of
the Waldo Patent and at that time Washington's secretary of war. The Indians
he had in mind were those to the west, beyond the Appalachian Mountains,
into whose territory the new country was expanding. Nearly two centuries
later, however, Tureen turned to the Non-Intercourse Act to force the secretary of the interior to sue Maine to recover the lands its tribes had lost. The
case was such an audacious long shot that at first none of Maine's elected
leaders took it seriously. According to Neil Rolde, when Tureen first briefed
Governor Longley on it, he fell asleep. However, the potentially devastating
impact of such a suit soon made itself felt.

"The Indians may legally own two-thirds of Maine," began a news item
in the *New York Times*.[435] The venerable Boston law firm Ropes & Gray
refused to certify municipal bonds within the twelve and a half million acres
affected and recommended its clients not buy them in Maine. Some 350,000
homes, to say nothing of paper company and timber lands, were thrust into
legal limbo.[436] "It's preposterous," Attorney General Joseph Brennan fumed
to the *Times*. "You just don't undo 200 years of history that readily." Suddenly he and Governor Longley were scrambling to find a solution. Observed
the Penobscot leader, Nicholas Sappiel, in a sardonic response to this sudden
change of attitude, "Now they're getting a few gray hairs. You've never seen
so many lawyers, reminds you of a cartoon."[437]

A prolonged legal struggle threatened dire economic, political, and social
consequences for Maine. Existing titles to vast areas of land were potentially
worthless. The only alternative was to negotiate a federally sponsored settlement. Said Attorney General Brennan, "Whatever ancient claim the American Indian has to land must be the responsibility of the federal government,
not innocent citizens who bought and farmed, settled or developed land in
good faith over the last 100 or 200 years."

Enter Georgia Supreme Court Justice William B. Gunter, President Jimmy
Carter's special representative to the negotiations. At a press conference on July
15, 1977, the judge recommended compensating the tribes with $25 million in

cash from the U.S. government, and one hundred thousand acres from Maine (valued by Bob Cummings at $15 million).[438] The judge did not mention the Public Lots by name, but his intention was transparent: "The state reportedly has in its public ownership in the claims area in excess of 400,000 acres."

Cummings reacted as would a mother bear when her cub was threatened.[439] In an opinion piece in the *Maine Sunday Telegram*, he readily admitted that the Indians were owed compensation "a sorry history of murder, exploitation, land thefts and destruction of a culture"—but he bridled at the suggestion that Massachusetts (on behalf of its District of Maine) took the lands without the congressional consent stipulated in the Non-Intercourse Act. There was never any secret about Massachusetts' dealings with the Indians; and when Congress granted statehood to Maine, it required Maine to carry out the provisions of "Massachusetts' allegedly illegal treaty." At most, it was a technical illegality. Asked Cummings, dripping with irony, "Does anyone doubt that had Massachusetts asked permission to steal Indian land Congress wouldn't have gone along?"

He continued: "It is unconscionable that a quarter of Maine's 400,000 acres of Public Lots be given to a quarter of one percent of the state's citizens." Once more, he laid out what the public lands represented and the unique gift they offered to late-twentieth-century Maine: the chance to design for the future without having the politically impossible task of undoing the land-use decisions of the past. Maine produces paper, but not books; fine hardwood, but not furniture. The Public Lots are an opportunity to change this, even to stipulate that wood from them must be processed in Maine. So much had been already recovered; so much would be lost "if suddenly a quarter of them are wrenched away." Everyone, including the Indians, Cummings concluded, would lose if Congress considered the Public Lots like a "windfall" that could be plundered without loss or pain to the citizens of Maine.

When Gunter's proposal pleased nobody, the president sent a three-person negotiating team to Maine. It took another three years to reach an agreement, but Maine's Public Reserved Lands were off the table. On October 11, 1980, President Jimmy Carter signed the Maine Indian Claims Settlement Act, by which they relinquished all claims to land in Maine.[440] Neither side was happy, but, according to Joseph Gousse, fear was the great leveler.[441] Maine feared that if it lost in federal court, its territory could be decimated, with catastrophic results for its citizens. The Indians feared that if Ronald Reagan became president, he "would make good on his promise to exterminate their federal claims altogether." (A month after the bill was signed, Reagan won the election.) Both sides were unnerved by the rising "paranoia and outrage," which had all the signs of "preparation for a land war that the tribes had neither threatened, nor desired."[442]

The apparent windfall of land long forgotten prompted raids from other quarters as well. "While one state agency struggles to force the return of Maine's 400,000 acres of public lots, another agency wants to turn some of the acreage over to a paper company," wrote a perplexed Bob Cummings early in 1978. The special master was still striving to come to a reasoned solution when the Maine Guarantee Authority (predecessor of the Finance Authority of Maine) quietly sold some Public Lots to a paper company. After a prolonged struggle, the Kennebec Pulp and Paper Company had gone bankrupt, despite a $7 million loan from the Maine Guarantee Authority to save it. To salvage what it could from its investment, the authority intended to sell the assets—the mill and timberlands—to Madison Paper Corporation. Included in the land was about a thousand acres of Public Lots.[443] Lee Schepps had first learned of the proposed sale the previous spring, and it presented a problem for the BPL. The state was claiming in court that paper company rights to timber and grass on Public Lots no longer existed; it followed that those once "owned" by the defunct Kennebec Pulp and Paper could not be part of the Maine Guarantee Authority's deal with Madison. To include them was to damage the state's case. Schepps asked the authority to give him a fortnight's warning before taking further steps. Instead, the authority went ahead on its own, only notifying the BPL director six days after. Pleading his board's responsibility to "get the most economic value out of the land to recover our losses," the authority's manager offered a barely civil comment. "They allege their position would be hurt. We allege that we don't see that it does." Schepps had the support of Attorney General Brennan on the grounds that so small a portion of the land would hardly affect the deal with Madison. Conservation Commissioner Barringer, however, decided that discretion was the better part of valor and agreed not to fight the Guarantee Authority's decision.

A potentially more ominous threat to the future of the Public Reserved Lands started with the town of Osborn, population fifty-three. Organized as a plantation since 1895, Osborn was incorporated as a town in 1976. The selectmen of the new town expected that the 960-acre Public Lot within its bounds would be turned over to them, as would have been done in the past. However, the bill that created the BPL left the Public Lots in the care and custody of the state. Osborn petitioned the legislature for a special exception, but the request was denied. The attorney general ruled, a year or two later, that "Osborn's claims of ownership or uncertainty of state title were invalid."[444] Not to be thwarted, the town then tried to halt a BPL timber operation on its Public Lot. The judge dismissed the case as unlikely to prevail.

By this time, Osborn's Public Lot had become a cause célèbre for local control, always a heated issue in Maine. "Win or lose, we do not plan to let this injustice to Maine rural people be swept under the rug," wrote a selectman in a feisty call to rally other towns. They were all victims of a coup d'état, engineered in Augusta behind the backs of local citizens. Aided and abetted by the Hancock County Planning Commission, the town introduced another bill, asking the legislature to correct a "legislative travesty." The commission's executive director, who was also an Osborn selectman, stridently decried the "liberal, urban oriented legislature and governor" that treated rural communities as "hillbillies."[445] He was none other than James Haskell, former director of LURC.

The "liberal" governor, Joseph Brennan, sympathized with Osborn, but he felt that the town's needs could be met without contravening the law, "which has proven to be wise and forward-looking."[446] Barringer—reappointed as conservation commissioner when Brennan took office the year before— agreed. He found it "regrettable" that town officials had shown no interest when he tried to work with them on a solution.

On the face of it, Osborn's position was reasonable enough. A fiercely independent community, its residents relied on firewood for heat all winter. They wanted to make the Public Lot a town forest as a sustainable fuel supply. At the bill's hearing before the legislature's Energy and Natural Resources Committee, town officials pointed to a history of sound forest management, unlike the paper companies, which they understood was the reason for the state taking over the Public Lots. They also charged that BPL's skidders had damaged Osborn's forestland. This was unfortunately true, admitted Lloyd Irland, by then the BPL's third director. The ground had frozen later than expected, but the skidders were pulled out as soon as he saw what was happening. "Past mismanagement is a reason for doing better in the future, not for giving the land away," commented Robert Gardiner, executive director of the Natural Resources Council of Maine, by then one of Maine's major environmental organizations. The chair of the Energy and Natural Resources Committee, however, was Sen. James McBrearity, a long-time foe of the BPL. He was quick to whip up support for Osborn from other towns organized post-1973 and did his best to add two of them to the Osborn bill.

If that bill passed, wrote Cummings in dismay, the precedent would strip away far more than 960 acres. Any town being incorporated would expect the same treatment. With half a dozen new towns since 1973, "the state would lose control over nearly 6,000 acres of its public domain this session alone." He estimated as much as 40,000 acres could be at risk over the long haul. In the end, the town accepted a compromise offered by the BPL, and the bill was voted down. Osborn would receive 50 percent of the stumpage from its Public Lot, and town officials were given a voice in its management through a fifteen-year renewable lease.

In early May 1979, the Maine Superior Court's special master, Justice Donald W. Webber, delivered his decision on the Public Reserved Lands. He came down on the side of the landowners and paper companies and recommended that the Superior Court do the same. The deeds granted between 1850 and 1875, Justice Webber declared, conveyed "the right to cut timber which was in existence at the time of the grant as well as the right to cut timber thereafter coming into existence," and they included the "right to cut all sizes and species of trees."[447] The "statutes and conveyances"—the first authorizing the sale of timber and grass rights, the second effecting such a sale—were quite clear. They could only be terminated by the incorporation or organization of a township.

David Smith's court testimony the year before had been widely considered favorable to the state, and at the time Webber had seemed impressed with the professor's ideas. Now, however, his reasoning went along altogether different lines. Over the years, he wrote, the legislature, "though fully aware of the way the statutes and conveyances were being interpreted, made no effort to voice its displeasure." It made no attempt to "limit the cutting rights of the purchasers." As to the type of tree the old deeds might have assumed, "the word timber has always had a meaning broader than that assigned by Dr. Smith," Justice Webber maintained. Those ancient legislatures knew perfectly well what they were doing. They had but a single goal, he reminded the parties: to find a way of keeping the forest safe from fire and theft until such time as it would legally be the problem of the people who had come to live there. Feeling "helpless and frustrated in the face of depredations," they took the only option open to them if they were to conscientiously "discharge their obligations."

Webber understood, he said, how more recent legislators might see things differently. "In these modern times of an awakened public interest in conservation of the Maine wilderness, recreation and good forest management," it was easy to see why they might question their predecessors' intentions in giving away "so much to the wild land owners"; but nothing, he added, is "so effective as 20-20 hindsight." A week later, Judge Daniel Wathen, on behalf of Kennebec County Superior Court, accepted the special master's decision. The return of the 141,000 acres that remained in dispute had just become much more difficult.

"State Loses Battle in Public Lands War," read Bob Cummings's headline in the *Portland Press Herald*. Both sides filed motions, the plaintiffs to accept the referee's report. The state appealed the case to the Maine Supreme Judicial Court. In his objections, Martin Wilk cited erroneous conclusions of law (specifically whether the 1850 law authorized the sale of rights to cut timber not yet in existence, as well as the use of the term "timber") and erroneous findings of fact (such as the likelihood that towns would or would not spring up, and whether future tree growth was anticipated by either the land agent or the legislature).

Cummings did his best to cast the judge's decision as a temporary setback, a lost battle in a winnable war. It had no effect, he pointed out, on the deals the BPL had already negotiated, 179,000 acres, most now consolidated into large blocks of awe-inspiring land. Only 20,900 acres of Public Lots, voluntarily returned by Scott Paper Company, remained as scattered tracts. Even if the state lost its appeal to the Law Court, there could be a silver lining. All these acres would be counted as gifts that could trigger matching federal funds—as had the Huber Corporation's gift on Bigelow—for further purchases of public land.

Maine could continue to negotiate for the voluntary return of the Public Lots, he pointed out in a follow-up article under the headline, "Basic Facts Seen Aiding State Position." If that didn't work, it could try to organize the wildland townships again. There could be another grand plantations bill, but townships could also be organized piecemeal, as had happened when the town of Carrabassett expanded into an adjacent unorganized township. The Public Lot came back to Maine, and there were plenty of existing municipalities within the Unorganized Territories that could expand in the same way. Above all, Maine had "a bargaining chip it didn't have when the first Public Lots bill was filed nearly six years ago." At that time, the public had never heard of them, but it had now, and there was a BPL managing them. Under these new circumstances, companies might well prefer to give up their Public Lots voluntarily and take a tax deduction before the opportunity went away. "Sooner or later some legislature will pass a general wildlands organization bill—an updated version of the grand plantation scheme of 1974," concluded Cummings.

As it happened, the day after Judge Webber announced his decision was Lee Schepps's last day at the BPL. Schepps was returning to Texas to take over a family business following the death of his father. Two weeks earlier, he had outlined his thoughts on the BPL's future in a confidential valedictory memo to Barringer. In it, he offered a handful of tactical options should the referee rule against the state.[448] A lawsuit might recover a particular Public Lot in as many as fifteen situations—what he called "discrepancies": deorganized plantations where the timber and grass rights were never reclaimed; towns or plantations that had been organized across a township line. In fact, if a town surrounded by three unorganized townships were to spread its municipal boundaries by a thousand acres into each of them, Maine would recover three Public Lots. The Law Court had ruled that only part of a township needed to be incorporated to terminate the cutting rights on all of it. "Numerous such opportunities exist," advised Schepps.

He also suggested that the BPL's new director contact Pingree heir Brad Wellman. If Wellman were persuaded that the state meant business when it came to recovering the remaining 150,000 acres of Public Lots, Schepps was sure he would be amenable to an agreement for Seven Islands's 35,000 acres, if it included the right to cut a specified amount of timber for a few more years. Such a deal could set a precedent for others. In general, Schepps recommended a slow-down—not a stop—to land exchanges. In just three years, the BPL had acquired 200,000 acres, and it needed time to digest them.[449] He noted that considerable mineral exploration was going on in the wildlands, which made it a risky time to trade. With only so many acres to exchange, "it would not hurt to take a few years to make the remaining trade decisions."

Most of all, he wrote, be "extremely cautious about future land exchanges where the State gives up good timberland for recreational property." Lloyd Irland, Schepps's successor at the BPL, went even further. "I see my principle role as producing raw materials for the Maine economy, while protecting recreational uses, and wildlife," he told the *Maine Sunday Telegram.* Irland was a forest economist from the Yale School of Forestry who had been overseeing the Maine Forest Service's spruce budworm control program since 1976.

One major trade was still in the works. It involved widely separated parcels in different counties, which was unusual, and was also the reason the exchange was one of the few deals that became controversial with the public. The northern slope of Bigelow Mountain had been acquired by GP when the company purchased Hudson Pulp and Paper Company in the early 1970s. In return for adding these nine thousand acres to the Bigelow Preserve, GP held on to the Public Lots in eastern Maine, its core land base. Fearing their interests were being sold out, activists in notoriously independent Washington County protested the swap. When it came before the legislature, they asked for more study before making a decision. "No one wants to use those tracts" (the GP Public Lots), one of the solons said in approving the BPL's plan. "All they want is more time to organize."

In fact, the public was losing very little of significance. The most sensitive part of the trade was Rocky Lake, a popular smallmouth bass fishery. It was adjacent to GP land, and the company wanted it. Irland's priority had to be Bigelow, so, with Barringer's approval but not that of some of his staff, he reluctantly hived off the end of the township and gave it to GP. "It's probably better to avoid this conflict now," Barringer offered, "and try and resolve it in the negotiations that remain to be done, with other landowners." The BPL did indeed acquire all of Rocky Lake in subsequent trades approved by the legislature.

On October 1, 1980, the Conservation Department advised Governor Brennan in a briefing paper, "It is probably safe to assume that there will be no further large land exchanges until Cushing vs. Cohen is decided."[450] Lloyd Irland turned his attention to managing the 250,000 acres of forest (as well as submerged lands and islands) he was now responsible for. A big help was the contract with Great Northern on T6R11 in the northwest corner of Baxter Park, the "cash register," Irland called it, years later. "It somewhat took pressure off the crew to get moving on active management of several other large pieces." His immediate goal was to turn his bureau into a profit center that would generate its own income after the Great Northern contract was completed.

The Public Lots were stocked with overmature trees. Overmature trees "just take up space in the forest," said Irland. They don't grow. His immediate priority would be to "harvest this low-grade wood so the forest will be healthier." Where the bureau had been on average cutting about a thousand acres a year, Irland increased it to seven thousand acres, "raising timber production to a level commensurate with maintaining the productivity of the resource base." By 1981, the BPL had increased its revenues from $300,000 to $800,000 per year, with projections to reach $1,000,000 or more by 1985.[451]

That caught the legislature's attention and early in 1981, the Energy and Natural Resources Committee held hearings on a bill to share the wealth with the general fund.[452] The line-up was familiar: Irland and Maine Audubon Society on one side, Senator James McBrearity and the Maine Forest Products Council on the other. Irland stressed that the state was just gearing up for efficient management of the public lands. "To disrupt it now would be a tragic and irreparable mistake." The Senator thought it was up to him and the Legislature to decide how much the state should spend on forest management. The situation had a certain irony, which Bob Cummings was quick to hone in on. When the BPL was set up in 1973, it was McBrearity among others who had demanded that it fund itself so as not to become "an expensive albatross." Instead, consolidation of 250,000 acres of public land had allowed for efficient management at last. "Possibly too efficient as it is turning out," Cummings added.

The other source of income for the Bureau was the leases for camp lots. Although it was not leasing any new ones, the Legislature had ordered the BPL to maintain the existing ones. Irland, however, had raised the rates, and this was another bone of contention with some legislators. Donald R. O'Leary, a Democrat from Caribou, was working with McBrearity on a bill to take away the BPL's authority to set rates for leases. "Don't spend the camp lot money. You may not have it long," he told Irland. The BPL director countered that he was only charging what the paper companies were charging, and that he could hardly do less in granting exclusive access to the public's land.

By the session's end, Irland had succeeded in fending off the lawmakers on the question of the BPL's income from forestry. One day, perhaps the Public Reserved Lands might generate a million dollars for the state to do what it liked with. But right now, the surplus was a modest $200,000; the BPL needed it if it was to bring all its lands into production. He was, however, not so successful with the camp leases. From now on, lease fees would be established by the Bureau of Taxation. "The public lands are now 'taxed,' rather than leased," wrote a caustic Bob Cummings. Cummings took the opportunity to castigate the public for its lack of interest in the Public Lots with the result that it was losing them bit by bit. The BPL had lost its ability to set fair fees for leases. "Why? Because 200 leaseholders showed up at the legislative hearing—while only a handful of speakers urged the public rights to its lands be protected."

It was soon evident to Irland that it would take decades to prepare a management plan for every tract, one at a time. His solution was to divide the state up into three administrative regions with field offices, so that BPL land managers would be in closer contact with the land and, as importantly, the people who lived there. Each region was made up of a number of "districts," which included one or more of the twenty-seven consolidated trade land parcels. Each of these large management units formed a hub around which unconsolidated Public Lots formed smaller satellites. Everything worked better, including the public meetings which could now discuss a district rather than a lot of separate smaller units.

For management plans to be successful at this larger scale, the BPL's fifteen service foresters needed to adjust, as well. Their background was in managing woodlots, and not landscape-scale tracts extending for thousands of acres. They were applying the same prescriptions they had used for forty-acre parcels, mostly improvement cutting to make up for years of high-grading. "All this small scale forestry applied to large scale tracts was putting BPL in danger of running out of money," Irland recalled. Meanwhile, biologists from the Department of Inland Fisheries and Wildlife were complaining that good wildlife management required more diversity, even small clear-cuts.

To learn to look at an entire pattern of land instead of a woodlot and to calculate the allowable cut required a major cultural shift. Irland got the U.S. Forest Service to assign a forester to the Bureau, to design a silvicultural program for multiple-use. Bernard Schruender, from Jefferson National Forest in south-west Virginia, started with undertaking an inventory of the BPL lands. He also began to hold "prescription meetings," bringing the foresters in from the field to Augusta. "Foresters love to argue about forestry," said Irland, and the results of these all-staff meetings soon showed results.

Meanwhile, the Law Court's decision had been expected as early as the first half of 1980; then while there was still time to begin land appraisals before snow started to fly, hoped Herb Hartman, now at the Bureau of Parks. On October 7, 1980, the Justices spoke. They vacated the Superior Court's decision and sent the case back for further consideration. The problem was "sovereign immunity," under which the state (or sovereign) is immune from civil suit. The "continuing refusal, or at least reluctance" to deal with the issue by everyone involved in the case was "a fundamental problem," stated Justice Sidney Wernick. As a result, the lower court's decision could only be dismissed. Bob Cummings thought the Justices were trying to "duck the issue."

Neither side was happy to see the case bounced back on what seemed like a technicality. All agreed on the urgent need for a decision on the Public Lots, Attorney General Richard Cohen explained to the legislative leadership. This could only be accomplished by waiving the state's sovereign immunity. The Legislature promptly passed a Resolve expressing their judgment that in the Public Lots case, sovereign immunity did not apply, and even if it did, the need to adjudicate the matter as speedily as possible was paramount.[453] As an emergency bill, it became effective immediately, February 11, 1981. The question of the Public Lots was once more on track for a definitive ruling.

Acreage Swaps Between Maine and Paper Companies Before the Law Court's Decision

Year	Company	Given to Maine	Received from Maine
1975	Great Norther Nekoosa	58,726	59,983
1976	J.M. Huber Corp.	14,021	12,162
1977	Boise-Cascade (Oxford Paper)	10,323	10,732
	International Paper	32,577	32,577
1978	Brown Paper	15,358	11,677
	Dead River	1,520	1,520
	Diamond International	8,109	8,109
	St. Regis	15,944	18,135
1979	Scott Paper	20,900	0
1980	Georgia-Pacific	9,358	10,496*

*included 4,000 acres of state-owned Public Lots; therefore net gain to state from GP trade was less than 6,000 acres.

Chapter Thirteen

"To the Surprise of Everyone in the World . . ."
(1981–1984)

When Bob Cummings's office phone rang on August 24, 1981, it was Martin Wilk, the state's lawyer, at the other end. "And I will always remember his words," said Cummings, a quarter century later. "To my dying day. He says, 'Bob,' he says, 'to the surprise of everyone in the world including me, we won.'"

Cummings immediately called the Bureau of Public Lands (BPL), where Bernard Schruender had just taken over from Lloyd Irland, now the state economist. "Our spirits are on a high that just won't come down," Schruender told him.

By a vote of three to one, Maine's Supreme Judicial Court had voted to overturn the lower court decision in *Charles R. Cushing et al. versus the State of Maine*.[454] Maine had prevailed and had recouped the timber and grass growing on the Public Lots. The BPL had title to another 150,000 acres, worth an estimated $30 million. Governor Joseph Brennan called it a victory "of historic proportions for the people of Maine."

Writing for the majority, Justice David Roberts was at pains to emphasize "the narrowness of the issues before us." The court had concerned itself with simply two questions: When, between 1850 and 1875, the state sold the rights to harvest grass and timber on the Public Lots, did it intend to sell future forest growth as well? And, did the right to cut include any species and size of tree, or only those considered to be commercial at the time? These were the questions "framed by the parties and the Referee." All other issues—"such doctrines as estoppel, acquiescence, waiver, laches, or prescription"—were off the table.[455] "We consider only whether the Superior Court erred in accepting the Referee's determination of what was conveyed to the original grantees during the period from 1850 to 1875."

Almost everything connected to lumbering had changed since those days. In trying to sift out contemporary assumptions from the ones prevalent in

1875, the logic of Judge Roberts's opinion started at a different point than had the Special Master, or Referee as he was referred to in his ruling. It was a forensic masterpiece.

Judge Webber's opinion had been founded on the 1850 statute, the language of which he had thought "clear and unambiguous." The right to the timber and grass on a Public Lot existed until the township was organized. That the Legislature had done this intentionally was apparent from the subsequent actions of the landowners and the land agent. Without specific reference to "standing timber," there was no reason to assume any limitation on cutting until a town might be incorporated.

Justice Roberts, however, based his reasoning not on the statute but on real estate law, starting with the "instrument of conveyance," the standard deed issued by the Land Agent. All it said was that the buyer had the "right to cut and carry away the timber and grass from the reserved lots," and that he could continue to do so until the township was incorporated. The deed said nothing about trees that might grow in the future. The absence of restrictive language, for example, "only standing timber," was no basis for assuming additional rights. The deeds did not "clearly and unambiguously" convey future growth; they were therefore "ineffective to convey an interest in any timber that was not in existence."

That, Webber the Referee had suggested, might be because what was being purchased was the right to cut the timber, not the timber per se. This, Roberts ruled, was splitting hairs; the court was "unable to find any practical or legal distinction" between the two. Nor could it find a precedent for presuming that cutting "second, third, and successive growths" was authorized without explicitly saying so. In suggesting that a continuous right to cut might be assumed since the township might not be incorporated for a long time, if ever, the Referee had erroneously mingled two separate threads in the case: the scope of the grant and its duration, "'what may be cut under the grant' and 'when the right to cut may expire.'"

Although fully convinced of their interpretation of the deeds' legal implications, the three justices agreed with the Referee that they were dealing with an exceptional situation, "indeed a case of novel impression." They knew of no "facts or circumstances even roughly analogous" to it. Everything—the history, the statutory language, the deeds themselves—was "unique." They therefore had gone the extra mile and, following the Referee's lead, examined the "extrinsic surrounding circumstances."

The plaintiffs had made much of the Legislature's instruction to the land agents to sell timber and grass rights on unlocated Public Lots to the purchaser of the township "at the same rate per acre."[456] An acre in fee ownership could, *ipso facto*, be harvested again and again; if the right to cut an acre on a Public Lot cost the same, surely it must extend to future harvests as well. Not necessarily, responded the high court. Equating the "value of the timber in existence at the time of purchase" on the two acres was even more likely.

The court's position was strongly originalist. It all depended on divining the realities and perspectives of landowners and officials a hundred years ago. Unquestionably, the state intended to transfer to the private sector the headache of guarding the Public Lots against trespass. Less clear was whether the state saw trespass as a permanent problem, requiring perpetual action. The Referee had taken the plaintiffs' view that the need would last until a township was incorporated. The court found the defendants' position more persuasive: it was the standing timber that had to be protected; "once the right to cut that timber was sold, there would be nothing left to steal from the State."

For the same reason, the land agent would have had no need of the "veritable army of foresters," conjured up by the Referee, to ensure that only trees standing at the time of conveyance were being cut. Such a need would not have arisen for decades. Moreover, to surmise that the Legislature had given any thought to it at all "begs the question" that it actually envisioned "future generations of marketable timber." The trees still being cut in 1850 were hundreds of years old, and there was little reason to assume they would ever be replaced by a crop as valuable. Ideas about sustainable forestry were half a century away, as was the pulpwood industry that would eventually provide a market for younger trees.

There remained the fact that the state had allowed successive owners to treat the Public Lots as if they were their own. What subsequent owners and office holders thought about it was irrelevant, the Law Court declared. Only the parties involved in the original transactions could answer for their intent. Also irrelevant was the fact that the state had never tried to resell the rights or challenge the landowners and for the same reason. "We are not deciding the present rights of the parties in light of their conduct and that of their predecessors over the past 130 years," wrote Roberts.

In a suit between private individuals, there would be no inference of intent if it was not written into the deed. The justices were "all the more reluctant" to do so in a case involving the State and its constitutional obligation to hold the Public Lots in trust for the people of Maine. The ultimate flaw in the Referee's case, they said, was an exclusive focus on *"the State's desire to reach a solution to its management problems," to the neglect of its responsibility as trustee of the Public Reserved Lands*.

"The proper interpretation of the timber and grass deeds," the majority wound up, "leads to the conclusion that the State conveyed only the right to cut trees in existence on the date of the conveyance." This opinion rendered moot what size and species of tree were conveyed since, as both sides agreed, there were no longer (in any commercial sense) any trees that had been standing when the deeds were purchased.[457] As to what options the state might have as a result of its decision, the Justices remained silent.

To Jerry Amero, the landowners' attorney, the interesting thing was that both sides cited the clarity of the language in the evidence as the basis for their (opposite) positions. Having digested the stipulation of fact prepared by Wilk and himself, they said the same thing: "You don't have to look at anything else but the language."

Thirty-five years later, Amero hadn't changed his mind about the language in the deeds: it had to include future crops of timber and grass. How could the single crop argument possibly have applied to grass? Grass produces a new crop every year, which the lumbermen "cut and carried" to feed their horses and oxen. As to the question of "standing timber," there were cases in the stipulation of fact where land agents used the term to limit a harvest to the timber in existence. "And that phrase is not found in the timber and grass deeds," Amero insisted.[458] Be that as it may, he conceded, "based on an argument that I think was difficult to follow, three respected justices concluded otherwise."

All in all, six respected judges left their mark on *Cushing et al. vs. Maine* as it wound its legal way from the Special Master to Maine's Supreme Judicial Court. Three of them found in favor of the private owners: Judge Donald Webber, the Referee who wrote the opinion; Judge Daniel Wathen (while on the Superior Court, where he accepted Webber's report three years before); and Justice David Nichols, the lone dissenter on the Law Court. The three justices siding with the state, however, made up the majority: Justices Sidney Wernick, who had precipitated the flurry over sovereign immunity; David Roberts, who wrote the majority opinion; and former Dean of the Maine Law School, Edward Godfrey.[459]

The reaction of the paper companies and landowners was one of shocked surprise. "We were quite angry," recalled Seven Islands's Brad Wellman, with masterful understatement. "Our first reaction was to fight." Having only just gone to work for his family's company, Baskahegan's Roger Milliken had yet to develop the same emotional investment as those of his peers who had spent a lifetime in the woods. Still, he was baffled by the court's decision. While the deeds might not have exactly promised the rights "as long as the river shall flow and as long as the sun shall shine," the language sounded pretty permanent to Milliken. "They weren't buying one year's worth of hay," he said, echoing Amero.

The companies' immediate complaint was that the case had been heard by only four of the Law Court's seven justices. Three judges whose votes could reasonably have been expected to change the balance had recused themselves.[460] Arguing that a case of this magnitude deserved the attention of the full court, Great Northern petitioned for it to be re-heard. The appeal was denied.

Another path to consider was to accept the Law Court's ruling but claim that the State had lost its rights to the lands by neglecting them for a hundred years. Most came to the conclusion that it was unlikely to prove a winning strategy for the landowners. On the state side, Martin Wilk didn't think it realistic that a judge would "now come in and say that even though the court has declared the cutting rights are exhausted, Maine can't now assert those rights." Perhaps as significant, after more than eight years of litigation, there was little appetite for another extended lawsuit. "Even lawyers are getting tired of this case," Amero was quoted as saying, although he did not forswear the possibility.

The final option was an appeal to the U.S. Supreme Court. But what were the odds of success? Two of the three potential outcomes—besides finding for the state, the Justices could refuse to hear the case, thus letting the Maine judgment stand—would go against the paper companies and landowners. In the end their lawyers decided it was too risky a gambit. At the same time, from the state's point of view, though its chances looked better, there was still the possibility of the Supreme Court overturning the Law Court's ruling. It was this uncertainty, Roger Milliken felt, that ultimately "pushed both parties to find someplace in the middle." Mutual risk would make room for compromise.

That the Supreme Court was even considered showed how staggering the financial jeopardy might turn out to be. The customary penalty for timber trespass was triple damages. If the Supreme Court found that the state had owned all the timber after the first cutting, sometime between 1850 and 1875, it would add up to a century of trespass. There could easily have been a second cut in the 1890s, another in the 1920s, another in the 1960s. Multiply the value of all that timber by three. Then add nearly a hundred years' worth of interest for the 1890s harvest, fifty years' worth for the 1920s, etc. "It all added up to a really big number, really fast," explained Milliken.

Another factor to be considered was the one Lee Schepps had raised since the beginning.[461] In townships where the Public Reserved Land was undivided—like most of northern Maine, the heart of Seven Islands's and Great Northern's ownerships—the state could cause them a real headache as a "tenant-in-common." The Forest Service could, for example, refuse to sign permits or agree to prices. "A tenant-in-common can gum up the works pretty quickly," mused David Carlisle, grimly. "We had the discussion: would they go through with it, would they tie us up?" Carlisle didn't think "they"—the State—would do so deliberately, but there was always the possibility. At Seven Islands, Sarah Medina, the company's land-use director, was less sanguine. Based on internal discussions, she was in no doubt about a threat to prohibit harvests in townships with unlocated lots. Either way—and regardless of the court case—there was every reason to get the state out of the private ownerships. Consolidating the lots just might be the silver lining.

Absent an appeal or countermove from the landowners, Maine officials had to make one major decision. What would be an appropriate and reasonable level of restitution, beyond compensation for the lost timber, to impose on timberland owners for cutting on state's forests without authorization for some hundred years? The justices had been definite: they had nothing to say on the matter. The state would have to decide on its own.

For now, however, the BPL was not waiting on the future. The landowners heard from Director Schruender within a month of the court's decision. He requested that "all private parties" halt harvesting operations on located Public Lots (now unequivocally the property of the state.) On unlocated lots, revenue agreements must be formalized with the State. In the meantime, account of all the income from located and unlocated lots, retroactive to August 24, was to be forwarded to the BPL, as well as a list of all their Public Lots.

Richard Barringer, by this time, was no longer conservation commissioner. Governor Brennan had persuaded him to join the executive department as director of State Planning.[462] To replace him as conservation commissioner, Barringer recommended Richard Anderson, a fisheries biologist and the former Maine Audubon director, as his successor. Barringer, himself, continued to be attentive to his old Department's care and together, he and Anderson took up the task of crafting a final settlement.

The obvious solution, a huge financial payment starting with triple damages, would be a nightmare for the landowners. But what if the state asked to be compensated with land instead? Even 400,000 acres was but a small percentage of what they held in all. And from the state's point of view, these lands had the potential to be turned into some truly magnificent—even priceless—public reserves. The two officials decided they must persuade Governor Brennan to go for acres rather than dollars.

Before he became governor, as Attorney General in the Longley administration, Joseph Brennan had pushed the case against the timber companies. Before that, as a State Senator, he had been appalled at the defeat of the grand plantations bill. Persuading now-Governor Brennan that the Law Court had given Maine, in Anderson's words, "a wicked opportunity" turned out to be surprisingly easy. Barringer and Anderson were smart, dedicated public servants who "believed what they were saying and knew what they were doing," he said later.

In a conciliatory letter to the landowners and paper companies, the governor urged them to pick up the negotiations from before the court's final decision.

Past land swaps had resulted in consolidating Public Lots and private lands into "more contiguous blocks, thereby easing problems of ownership and management to all participants." He invited them to join in a further process of "thoughtful deliberation" that would produce "lasting benefit to both the public and private sectors."

To drive the state process, Governor Brennan set up a blue-ribbon panel with himself as chairman. It included Anderson, Barringer and David Flanagan, now the Governor's legal counsel. Martin Wilk was the group's special counsel and chief spokesman. Brennan also deputed one of his own staffers, Annee Tara, who later became Anderson's deputy at Conservation and, at the time, the only woman among the key players on either side. Just before Christmas, 1981, the panel began the work of identifying the best places for Maine to acquire from each ownership. These would be presented as a proposal to the landowners to get the "thoughtful deliberation" going.

Anderson, Barringer and Tara had all spent a lot of time in the woods, and they knew which areas would be most valuable for public use. They considered a combination of factors—timber as well as recreation and wildlife—but the process owed as much to their personal experiences, mostly recreational, as to scientific methodology. "We literally sat around the table with a map and brain-stormed," Annee Tara later recalled.

They quickly put together a list they knew would be "pretty scary" to the landowners. Further refinement produced one that was "fairly rational, fairly realistic," though still "aggressive." It was a "best of all possible worlds" list for public ownership, Tara admitted, but it was not going to obstruct or interfere seriously with the landowners' primary interest, timber growing and harvesting. For one thing, the places of highest value for recreation—mountains with steep slopes and the shores of lakes—were harder to log and therefore potentially less valuable to a company feeding its mills.

The other piece of the puzzle was to come up with a dollar figure on which the state could base its claim for damages. While the others were drawing circles on maps, Martin Wilk and Lloyd Irland, now the state economist, started running calculations on how much Maine had lost in timber revenues from the Public Reserved Lands over the last century. Bob Cummings was not shy about putting forward his own back-of-the envelope calculations. By the forest industry's rule of thumb, an acre produced half a cord per year. 320,000 acres would have produced 160,000 cords; at $5 per cord for fifty years, the state's claim would be $40 million. Even taking industry claims that an acre generated a mere $2 per year, the resulting figure was $32 million, still a big number.

Richard Barringer was aiming for a slightly higher level of precision. Maine needed to determine "what was cut, where, [and] under what conditions." On top of that, there was the question of the penalty. It was, said Barringer, the natural resource economist, "an extraordinarily interesting problem." Lloyd Irland's training as a forest economist made him just about the only man in state government who could develop an approach that involved law, economics and mathematics from scratch. Not only did he have to figure out how many times a lot had been harvested after the cut specified in the deed. He also needed to calculate the value of the timber cut each time. There were no public records of the actual transactions, so Irland combined the total acreage of the Unorganized Territories with stumpage prices, for which he calculated an average per decade going back to 1875. It was certainly not a highly refined number, but the best they could do short of going through the harvest and sales records of all the companies for the past eighty years.

Having worked out approximately how much the state should have been paid for all that timber—plus interest over different lengths of time from about 1900 to 1980—a penalty for cutting without a permit all that time had to be assessed. In the end, Wilk and Irland came up with a formula: the landowners would surrender two dollars' worth of land for every dollar's worth of Public Lots, based on present value. (In the early 1980s, timberland was worth about $110 per acre.[463]) From the state's point of view (if not the landowners), it did not represent full compensation—triple damages for timber trespass—but was a compromise, recognizing that if it came to litigation another win for Maine was not assured. It still added up to a big number.

With the ideal lands identified and an approximate dollar value for the landowners' liability exposure arrived at, it was left to Barringer and Anderson to compile it all into a document that could be disseminated to the paper companies and landowners for maximum effect. This was a matter of grave importance to Maine. Rather than a loose sheaf of maps of the individual ownerships, they put together a professionally-designed brochure like a corporate annual report, printed on high quality paper. It consisted of a statement by Governor Brennan and a list of the criteria used in selecting the particular lands. "As you will see," wrote the governor, "the proposal is aimed principally at filling out and building upon the Public Reserved Land Management units we have put together in past exchanges with you." The rest of the booklet was made up of maps of the parcels the state wanted from the various landowners. If a picture is worth a thousand words, a map is worth even more, and there was no need for further written commentary.

To further reinforce the gravity of the occasion, Governor Brennan agreed to release it at a ceremony in the Blaine House, the governor's residence in Augusta. Brennan personally invited the heads of all the companies involved. Martin Wilk prepared the governor's remarks. His message would be that the Law Court had decided in the State's favor; the grass and timber rights sold to the landowners had expired. It had been a very lengthy litigation. Rather than start a new, potentially equally drawn-out and expensive legal battle, the State would like to settle once and for all with a negotiated exchange of land.

On the morning of May 4, 1982, despite the early summer beauty of the day, the mood was at once somber and tense, and filled with anxious anticipation. As Governor Brennan approached the podium, a hush settled over the Blaine House reception room. He looked up from the three-ringed binder containing Wilk's notes.

"Welcome, fellow Democrats," he said. Martin Wilk looked around the silent room. "Everybody was stone-faced," he recalled. "There was not so much as a hint of a smile."

As described at the beginning of this book, the meeting was not a long one. Having staked out the State's position, Governor Brennan handed out the document his team had assembled. He did not get into specifics, owner by owner. He stuck to the general theme of working together to accomplish a result that would be in the best interests of Maine. Its citizens would get significant blocks of desirable public land; the paper companies and other owners would get total control of their holdings rather than having the state, as a 1/24 interested party, interfere in their future management decisions. And they would avoid heavy restitutions and penalties, now and forever. His overall appeal was simple and direct: that they all resolve the matter through good faith negotiation rather than litigation.

The meeting at the Blaine House set the stage for another set of prolonged negotiations. Particularly affected were the large, non-industrial landowners—led by Seven Islands and Prentiss & Carlisle—none of which had participated in the voluntary land swaps. Of the paper companies, the only one that had remained above the fray was Irving Pulp & Paper.

Even before the Blaine House meeting, some eyebrows had been raised at the undeniable fact that a small group of officials were making decisions of long-term importance to the public and negotiating the results behind closed doors. Mistrust spilled into the public eye in early 1982. In exchange for over 457.5 acres of prime timberland, the Coburn Land Trust handed over 545 acres to the BPL, including four miles of river frontage on the Moose River, a popular canoeing stream.

"The people I've talked to say that trade was a disaster," the Natural Resources Council's Rob Gardiner told the *Maine Times*. He also thought the BPL was placing too much importance on consolidating public lands within a township. (The Coburn land abutted the 16,000 acres already put together in Holeb Township.) Cantankerous as ever, Ed Sprague, accused the BPL of bungling the negotiation by using Tree Growth Tax valuations, which, he alleged, were widely regarded as misleading. What the state saw as valuable river-front, Sprague saw as bog. In fact, he argued, it was already under LURC protection as a deer yard, so why acquire it at all?

The critics were "mesmerized by the current standing crop of timber," retorted Lloyd Irland, who had negotiated the deal while still at the BPL; they should take a longer view of how the land could be used in fifty years' time. Ever philosophical, Irland appreciated that the question of balancing timber value against recreation was tricky and needed to be brought "into a very bright focus." In this case, he had taken "an opportunity to add land to an existing large unit, plus add a desirable river-scape."

The bigger problem for Gardiner was the lack of public input in the sites being chosen and the decisions being made. There should be a "mechanism" to ensure that the public interest was being served. He and Sprague started pushing for some sort of citizen advisory board to oversee closed-door negotiations. The companies they were negotiating with, countered Richard Anderson, were under no obligation to deal with the state. "They're accustomed to privacy," said the conservation commissioner. It was very hard to negotiate "when you don't know if what you say will appear in the papers the next day." He did not see that citizen oversight would serve the public interest, and it had the potential to bring everything to a halt.

Anderson and Gardiner were in fact old friends. In the early 1970s they had worked together on a television series called *Up Country*, a tribute to Maine's wilds. They made a great team—Gardiner, the television producer, and Anderson, the man who knew all the topics, all the places, and all the people to talk to—and the series was successful beyond their wildest dreams. A decade later, with Gardiner prodding the BPL to be more transparent, Anderson's solution was to ask him to head up the agency.[464]

The BPL's new director—a "Rock Hudson figure," recalled one of the team—arrived just as the post-court-decision negotiations were beginning. To Rob Gardiner, the lands the BPL had picked in the first round showed a distinct bias toward recreation. "They said, 'I'd love that mountain, I'd love that promontory along the Allagash Waterway, I'd love that lake and all the surrounding lands.'" There were, too, "an awful lot of bogs." Bogs—Gardiner made the word sound like a dull thud—are amazing ecosystems, he agreed; "little environmental storehouses, little treasuries," of great interest to Maine's Critical Areas Program. But they were an easy lift from the landowners' perspective. Giving up an acre and a half of bog for an acre of timberland was a steal. Gardiner didn't question the places protected so far. However, in proposing new parcels for acquisition, he was mindful of Lee Schepps's last recommendation that the BPL's long-term financial health would depend on timberland, not just scenic and recreational gems.[465] It didn't need to be highly-stocked when it was acquired.

In fact, Maine could get more acres by trading for cut-over lands. The forest would grow back.

The BPL's recommendations were fed to Martin Wilk, the state's chief negotiator.[466] Wilk's basic position was no-nonsense: We won. We want the land you have been overusing for generations. We also want land in compensation. And we're going to get it. His tactic was to ask for a lot, then make the other side talk. He did it with a smile, but as one negotiating from strength. Said Gardiner, "Marty knew when to leave the room, have a side conversation, come back another day. He wasn't into marathon meetings. He would lay his idea on the table, and let the other side figure out how they were going to respond."

At one prep session for a meeting with a landowner, Gardiner recalled making various suggestions, throwing this or that argument on the table. "Marty just turned to me and said, That's not the way we are going to do this. We're going to just go in and make this request, and do it in a way that exudes such confidence that this is the answer we are going to end up with, that we don't have to get into the details of why. Sometimes you just put something on the table and stop talking." Gardiner "learned more about negotiating from Marty Wilk than any other three people in my life."

Wilk had the patience to allow each negotiation to set its own pace. Mostly, his dealings were with the attorneys: Don Perkins at Pierce Atwood for the paper companies and Edward "Ted" Leonard at the Bangor law firm of Eaton Peabody for the non-industrial landowners. (As the process continued, Perkins took over the general management of the negotiations.) Inevitably some negotiations took longer than the task force had hoped. "There were certain things that the private landowners had to digest, and they couldn't digest it in big chunks, they had to take little bites," Wilk would explain to his colleagues. Occasionally, Richard Barringer or Annee Tara expressed impatience about a particular negotiation. "Some things just were going to take more time," Wilk had to reassure them. To push any harder, in their counsel's opinion, would be a mistake. In the long run, he was indomitable.

"Marty was the maestro. He was terrific as a negotiator and terrific dealing with people," said Paul Stern, looking back to when as a young lawyer he was assigned by Attorney General James Tierney as a liaison with the negotiations.[467] Stern had come to Maine from Washington DC the year before, dismayed at the political handcuffs put on his efforts at the Environmental Protection Agency. In Maine he was "allowed to accomplish things." Working with Wilk would prove to be one of the most fulfilling points of his career. Perhaps because of his own frustrations at the EPA, Stern particularly admired the way Wilk was able to let various bureaucratic entities think they were more in charge than they were. "A small group of people, including some with large egos," he recalled, "were led by Marty—they didn't know they were being led—to get the best possible results." From Stern's point of view, his own job was as much to "hold the AG at bay" as it was to ensure the negotiations went according to Hoyle.

Stern also had the task of drafting the agreements, which were finicky in the extreme. Deeds for even the tiniest fractions could be thirty or forty pages long. He also wrote the bills that had to be submitted to the Legislature, one for each deal. It was "not sexy stuff," just a myriad of complex little issues, but Stern liked working hard—long days, nights and even weekends—to get the job done. So he was particularly riled at Don Perkins's advice to his clients that he would always call at 4:30 in the afternoon, because state workers were so lazy they would give him a better deal, just to get home on time. "NO! NO! NO!" was what Paul Stern had to say about that.

This misconception aside, he considered Perkins a distinct asset to the negotiation process. Each paper company had its own strategy and concerns, and their attorney's marching orders varied accordingly. By providing a common thread, Perkins was able to minimize the amount of old ground each negotiation had to revisit, which was helpful to both sides.

The first of the landowners to settle were the Heirs of David Pingree, whose approximately million acres were managed by Seven Islands Land Company. They had stayed out of the earlier negotiations, partly because Brad Wellman—as president of Pingree Associates—was sure that the landowners would win in court. Also, according to Sarah Medina, the Pingree ownership was a trust, and by law the trustees could do nothing that diminished its value, which precluded any negotiation. The court decision in favor of the state changed all that. "It could have brought business to a screeching halt," she said ruefully.

Even so, Wellman was initially inclined to challenge the state. The court had not decided whether the timber rights had been limited to commercial timber or not; the question was irrelevant if the rights had expired. "We thought that if the state had meant merchantable, they could have written merchantable," Wellman explained. But if that was all it meant to grant, then the "first and obvious defense" was to go through the company's records for each township and sort out the species that had been cut. It soon became clear that the expense of researching a hundred years of timber harvests would be outrageous. Beside the dollar cost, the effort would have been "so destructive to our ability to properly manage the balance of the land," Wellman recalled.

The fact that the Public Lots in so much of the Pingree land were undivided further weakened the company's position. The only way to extricate itself from having the state as a tenant-in-common would be through a court-ordered, or hostile partition of the Public Reserved Lands in each township. It was another expensive and drawn-out prospect that left Wellman with little choice but to negotiate. Acre for acre, the exchange worked out with the Pingree heirs was about 2 to 1.[468] In return for 19,950 acres of scattered Public Lots, Maine received 41,364 acres in large blocks, mostly in northern Aroostook County. Nearly thirty-one miles of shoreline included prime waterfront around Eagle Lake (17,000 acres) and the Deboullie ponds (1,600 acres), the eastern shore of Squapan (now Scopan) Lake (3,500 acres), and the Allagash Wilderness Waterway (2,500 acres).

"Substantial frontage" on Richardson and Mooselookmeguntic lakes (17,000 acres) was perhaps the most difficult part of the whole deal. David Pingree's "empire" had started in western Maine, and his heirs did not want to part with land on either lake. "They'll never give that up in a million years," said Richard Anderson when he saw it on the BPL's wish list. "Well, Dick," Barringer replied, "It's a great place and we must ask for it." Issues within the Pingree family made it possible. Pingree heir Bessie Phillips wanted to complete a preserve begun by her deceased husband on Mooselookmeguntic's western shore.[469] Wilk offered a compromise, noting that without frontage there, "I am afraid that the entire exchange would become jeopardized." The trade with Mrs. Phillips allowed Wellman to negotiate giving up a smaller portion of Pingree's Western lands.

Barringer remembered hiking Deboullie Mountain with Brad Wellman at about that time. As they sat talking at the top of the mountain, the incredible landscape below them, Barringer "saw a side of Brad I hadn't seen before." He felt that Wellman was resigned and at peace with the settlement. He had succeeded in overcoming considerable opposition from some of the Pingree heirs, and he had freed them from the threat of further court action. During a meeting with Martin Wilk and his attorney Ted Leonard, Wellman planted his forefinger on the middle of his forehead and said, "I deserve a gold star right here."[470]

At a press conference on October 6, 1983, Governor Brennan announced the successful completion of negotiations with Seven Islands and urged the Legislature to approve it. Maine would receive "outstanding recreational lands and excellent timber management opportunities." By including compensation for cutting after the initial grant expired, he pointed out, the exchange was "a clear departure from the earlier transactions and represents the kind of cooperation and public-minded action that is to be congratulated."

The agreement was a major milestone and set the terms of the exchange—two acres to Maine for every acre of Public Reserved Land—as the basis for subsequent negotiations. The other companies and landowners were less than pleased. Wellman saw the terms as having been "forced upon," rather than negotiated by his company. "Is there a difference between those two things?" asked Baskahegan's Roger Milliken. "He acquiesced one way or another. He may not have volunteered, but he established the precedent. Once Seven Islands settled, it felt like the die's cast and we'll just all surrender together."

Baskahegan Company's ownership was about a tenth the size of Seven Islands'. "We were the little guys, just waiting to see what would happen," said Milliken. The heart of their ownership was northern Washington County where promises of outstanding farmland had been luring settlers for over a century. Most of the Public Lots had, therefore, long been located, unlike on Seven Islands land. (At least one had been located and then forgotten as its boundary lines disappeared.) Some of the townships had been populated so long they had three reserved lots of 360 acres each—one for the church, the minister and the school—dating their settlement back before 1831 when Maine started to reserve its public land in thousand-acre lots. Baskahegan had no interest in holding onto most of these. However, he suspected that the BPL would want more notable places than the low saucer-shaped topography of glacial lakes slowly filling in, which made much of his land, in Milliken's words, "plain-vanilla."

When he sat down with Wilk, it was the first time Milliken had represented his family in a business deal, and he soon realized that he wasn't going to have much say over the outcome. "Marty was sitting behind his desk, and it was like he had a big club in a corner of the room. And every now and then, we'd both kind of look over and know that that club was there. And it kept the conversation very civil and productive and moving forward." Having swapped land, acre-for-acre, for the only Public Lots he wanted to keep, Milliken covered the penalty from a 10,000 acre outlier in Baskahegan's land base where the Reserved Lands had never been located. Milliken's grandfather had bought T3R7 in the 1920s. It was spectacular land through which Wassataquoik Stream flows out of Baxter Park and into the East Branch of the Penobscot. To let it go was not an easy decision. A Yale forester who had been a consultant to the family for thirty years put it this way, Milliken recalled: "You look at that land, and your head says, Yeah, that's what we should trade, and your heart whispers, Noooooo." But the head was right. The state was not going to be satisfied with a plain vanilla diet, and these acres were anything but. They included some of the last stands of old-growth pine anywhere in Maine. Not coincidentally, the timber was also difficult to access, and an old bridge over the gorge would have been very expensive to maintain. In the end Baskahegan gave up 3,000 acres as settlement for trespassing.

The negotiations with Prentiss & Carlisle offered a different set of challenges. Founded by David Carlisle's grandfather in 1924, the company had been offering forest management services to private clients—among them some of the original families who invested in Maine's forests—for over fifty years. In 1982, the company managed a total of 950,000 acres, including 28,166 acres of Public Reserved Lands, some located, others not. Because of the company's conservative management, there were still a few trees growing that had obviously been standing when the grass and timber deeds were written. When the Justices' verdict came down, the Carlisles' first instinct was to identify how many of these there were. After a cut on a Public Lot, David Carlisle explained, "we'd go to each pile, and we'd see one [old trunk], and we'd hack off a 'cookie.'" In the end, the number of these Methuselahs was too small to make a difference.

Once negotiations over damages—Carlisle preferred the word to "trespass"—started, Prentiss & Carlisle joined the process. He sensed that "the values were closing" as it wound on. Rather than giving up two acres, the company could maybe "swap an acre for 1.25 acres; and that .25 was maybe worth it to get [the state] out of the unlocated public lots; and if there were any damages maybe it was worth it to mitigate that."

First, however, the parties had a major bone of contention to clear up. Maine and its negotiator were considering Prentiss & Carlisle's land as one ownership when it actually belonged to about eighty different landowners. With some effort, Carlisle and his father, George, finally convinced Wilk that this wasn't going to work. Unless trades were made with separate owners, it would be impossible to match up the Public Lots with land the state wanted in a way that was fair to them. If a tract was 8,000 acres but the owner had only a thousand-acre Public Lot to swap, what then? "We said you can come after us; we're not going to give you 8,000 acres in exchange for 1000," Carlisle recalled.

In the end, Prentiss & Carlisle submitted some eighty individual proposals. Unsurprisingly, "that frustrated the dickens out of [the state]," Carlisle noted. It was scarcely easier for the company. Frequently, multiple members of a family had to sign off on a single agreement; in the case of the descendants of J.P. Webber, there were more than twenty-five signatures.

To round out important trades they had already executed, Barringer and Anderson wanted several parcels in which Prentiss & Carlisle had a minority interest. Even a negotiator of Wilk's caliber had to take less than 2-for-1 to get them. Two such tracts—David Carlisle thought they were the best in terms of conservation—were T12R13 and T10R4. The Allagash flowed through the first, and Maine had already secured International Paper's majority interest. T10R4 included shoreline on Squapan (Scopan) Lake, much of which had been acquired from St. Regis and Huber Corporation. In both instances, said Carlisle, the state was "willing to take an acre for acre swap there, and we were willing to give an acre there to get rid of them in an un-located Public Lot."

"I'd say that half of it worked out pretty quickly and pretty smoothly," Carlisle conceded. But the other half dragged down the process. "We were probably the last one to settle, close to it, and it made it pretty contentious at times." Overall, he found the whole situation "one of the *worst* experiences that I've had." Carlisle guessed that the state ended up accepting some plain vanilla just to close out the negotiation. "The wish list that we got [from Governor Brennan] wasn't the land that they ended up with," he said.

Wilk had the most difficult time with Great Northern. In the wake of the grand plantations bill, its then-president, Robert Hellendale, had been the first to volunteer to negotiate a land swap. At that time, the company had held on to its common and undivided interest in 30,000 acres of Public Lots, in order to maintain legal standing in the judicial process. Now, Hellendale was gone, Robert Bartlett was in charge, and Great Northern was taking a very hard line with those 30,000 acres. Bartlett was a former woodland manager who was always a foe of the Public Lots settlement. "Very standoffish and negative" was how Martin Wilk described him.

He explained to attorney Don Perkins that if his client "didn't want to play, they don't have to play. We'll just exclude them for now." There were enough negotiations going on with the other companies and families to keep him busy, said Wilk. He couldn't understand how Great Northern's executives thought it was going to enhance their position. Being at the tail end of the deal-making was unlikely to strengthen their hand. Perkins realized that this was not in Great Northern's best interest. Among other things, he warned all the members of his "Public Lots Coalition," the State was "pressing very hard to get things together" in time for the legislative session. It had set a deadline for the negotiations to be completed by January 1, 1984. Without "a satisfactory result" at that time, and it "may not execute new permits … for cutting on townships where the Public Lot is unlocated." The result would be "a termination of operations in January with severe consequences in many instances."[471] Great Northern came to the table.

At the beginning of September, 1984, a special session of the Legislature approved the last major deal in the case of the Public Reserved Lands. Maine received 99,260 acres consolidated into a dozen blocks of useful, often very beautiful public land in exchange for 73,786 acres of scattered small Public Lots. Nearly three quarters of it came from Great Northern (38,225 acres) and Prentiss & Carlisle 33,084 acres). The rest included two other paper companies, International Paper (11,961 acres) and Scott (10,132 acres) and a smattering of smaller tracts from among others, Baskahegan and Coburn Land Trust. In value, this last deal represented an extra $5 million to the state, bringing the total additional value of the Public Lots to $60 million.

One landowner was still refusing to come to the table. At the governor's meeting in the Blaine House, Jim Irving had quipped about the part of the horse they would all get in any deal with the state. Since then, his company, Irving Pulp and Paper, had continued to resist.

Finally, Anderson and Barringer had had enough. Their only option, they told Governor Brennan, was to take the Canadian company to court. For the first time, Brennan baulked at one of his lieutenants' suggestions concerning the public lands. Don't do that, he told them. Let me invite Jim Irving to lunch. Irving accepted the invitation at once and flew to Augusta for a private lunch at the Blaine House. Neither Barringer nor Anderson was invited, but they were waiting outside when the meal was over. As the governor and his guest came out of the dining room, it was obvious from their demeanor that it was all done.

In return for their Public Lots, Irving gave up 17,000 acres, including 12,000 around Jackman and Attean Pond. Reminiscing more than thirty years later, Joseph Brennan could not remember exactly how he had persuaded Irving, other than to say that when a governor points out that his state has always had a mutually beneficial relationship with a company, the CEO of that company is apt to listen.

"It didn't occur overnight," reflected Martin Wilk, who had returned to full-time private practice the year before. "We completed all the negotiations eventually. Some were much more difficult than others. But in the end, they were all successful, and Maine ended up pretty much with what it wanted." Bob Cummings had already touted the imminent conclusion of the epic tale, with which he had been so closely tied, in dramatic cadences posted on June 4, 1984.

> It's a tale of neglect of responsibility by some state officials and of extraordinary dedication by others.
>
> It's a saga that had its beginnings with the first land grants by English kings three centuries ago—a saga that will largely be played out by the end of summer.
>
> It's the story of Maine's public lots.

Chapter Fourteen

Putting the Public into
the Public Reserved Lands
(1984–1987)

"The challenge now," said Rob Gardiner, "is to bring these lands under the kind of management that public lands deserve." Bob Cummings was more dramatic. "Maine faces an opportunity and challenge unprecedented in modern times," he wrote in *Appalachia*, the journal of the Appalachian Mountain Club.[472] Four hundred and fifty thousand acres of former Public Lots were back in the care and custody of the State, specifically the Bureau of Public Lands (BPL). Of these, 300,000 acres were already consolidated into twenty blocks of stupendous public preserves. The rest, still scattered across Northern Maine, awaited further trades; a few were suitable for timber production or wildlife protection on a limited scale. Large and small, the BPL's charge was to manage them "in a manner consistent with the principles of multiple land use."[473]

If multiple-use, defined broadly, meant managing the forest for timber, wildlife, and recreation equally, quipped Cummings, then the BPL's policies were like Orwell's *Animal Farm*: some uses were more equal than others. In 1983, a paltry $30,000—out of a $665,000 budget—was set aside for public recreation, meaning that "for most of the land there was no recreation management at all." The Bureau's planners, the reporter felt, were still in thrall to the idea that the Public Lots were a chance to earn millions through timber sales and new woods industries. The money was made by timber harvesting, so it was being plowed back into timber harvesting.[474]

Cummings was not unsympathetic to the BPL's problems. A small, young agency had spent its first half-dozen years wrestling with land swaps and consolidating them into the gems of public land they were now charged to manage. Much time and energy still went into "fighting the brush fires of controversy," he pointed out. And in the Bureau's short history, Rob Gardiner was already its fifth director. All this might explain why the public remained mostly oblivious to what a triumph the return of the Public Lots was for them. Not that people were ignoring the land. Cummings documented the increasing numbers hiking through the Mahoosucs, paddling down the Allagash, hunting and fishing in Deboullie. But they often had no idea that it was public land. Many old industry property signs were still standing, and no new state signs had been posted. Neither were trails being laid out, while the camping grounds were overcrowded to the point that "they can best be described as wilderness slums," wrote Cummings.

Being a "best-kept secret" had a political cost, too. "The Public Lots have no constituency," Richard Anderson lamented. No one knew that better than Cummings, who continued to cover every public hearing connected with them. Every legislative session, he watched the lawmakers comply with requests to nibble away at that priceless 400,000 acre legacy. "Why?" he fumed over and over again. "Because no one shows up to object." As yet, he decided, "the Public Lots are an opportunity waiting to be taken."

To "make the public lands truly public," the BPL needed to put more effort into improving the experience for hunters and fishermen, campers and hikers. A brochure was soon in the making, the first step to promote public use of the land. It was a hymn to the wonders of such places as the Bigelows and Mahoosucs, where "cold shadows of windswept granite push skyward and then topple toward the distant horizons." In Deboullie Township, "close-set mountains, steep slopes harboring ice caves, form bastion walls around a network of remote glacial lakes, deep and cold." Trail-work was begun in the summer of 1984, on Little Squaw (now Little Moose) Mountain. Campsites and access roads started to be improved as well, first around Duck Lake.

In April 1985, the Public Lots—their opportunities and challenges—were the subject of a weekend conference at the Augusta Civic Center to celebrate Earth Day. Only New York's Adirondack Park could rival them in beauty and wildness, asserted Lloyd Irland in his remarks. He emphasized *wildness*, not wilderness, a distinction that would become more controversial in the next few years. At the time, however, there was no discernible constituency for wilderness or "preservationist policies." What the public wanted, said Irland, was "a managed landscape producing forest products, wildlife and recreation." Rob Gardiner said he expected less than 10 percent of the land base would be off-limits for harvesting, which was music to the ears of the paper and forest products company reps.

Maine's conservation groups had not expressed so much interest in the Public Lots since the Bowdoin meeting in the wake of Bob Cummings's first article. The Appalachian Mountain Club spoke up for recreation, although its spokesperson recognized that some places might be in danger of "being loved to death by people like me." The Nature Conservancy stressed the presence on many of the Public Lots of rare and endangered species—orchids, alpine plants, the blue-back trout, for example—that needed special protection. The Sportsman's Alliance of Maine wanted to ensure that sportsmen had access to all the public lands, but not build "a network of roads that lead to every brook or pond"; it was "virtually impossible to please everyone," he admitted.[475] Conflicting interests, the conference warned, would bring tremendous pressures as the Public Lots became better known and used more widely.

Multiple-use forest management had been a buzzword ever since it was first enshrined in the federal act of 1960.[476] It was expressly mandated by—and defined in—the law that created the BPL in 1973, LD 1812.[477] A practical understanding of the concept, however, was still fuzzy around the edges, and it had yet to be properly applied in Maine. When BPL staff looked around for a model from other states or the U.S. government, they came up empty. "We have not found an entire system that we would want to copy," Gardiner had told a gathering of foresters and wildlife experts in March. In forging its own approach, he thought, the BPL had a unique opportunity to make multiple-use "a little more tangible, a little more concrete" by defining it on the ground.

Up to this point, most of the BPL's field staff were foresters. Under Bernard Schruender's guidance, their expertise had expanded from woodlot management to landscape-scale forestry. At all-staff meetings several times a year, one of them would make a presentation and receive feedback on how he was managing his particular unit, but these would be silvicultural treatments and would be critiqued accordingly. It was not that the staff didn't care about wildlife or recreation, but they were largely unversed in those fields.

The experience of one man in particular gave him a broader view. Before joining the BPL, Leigh Hoar Jr. had been a planner in the Parks Department and the first Supervisor of the Allagash Wilderness Waterway. For whatever reason, the BPL turned out to be a much more satisfying fit for Hoar, and he thrived. "Leigh Hoar, more than anyone else, was responsible for implementing the multiple-use program on the public lands," according to Richard Barringer. Gardiner also hired a full-time recreation specialist and a wildlife biologist. The latter was a staffer at the Department of Inland Fisheries and Wildlife who was detailed to work exclusively on public lands. The bureau picked up his salary and in the process acquired a positive liaison with a powerful Commissioner. With these new positions, a serious multiple-use program could be implemented.

The statute mandated "a sustained yield of products and services in accordance with the principles of sound planning."[478] Sound planning started with an inventory. Which lands should be protected for wildlife, managed for recreation, or harvested to support the bureau's operation? Unlike a corporation, the BPL did not have to maximize its timber profits. The goal was a diverse forest, pleasing to wildlife and recreationists, as well as foresters. The BPL, Gardiner announced symbolically, had even "resolved to peacefully co-exist with beaver on public lands." (Beaver damming activity notoriously destroys valuable timberland by flooding it.)

The BPL's timber product was large diameter, high quality logs. To guide it in putting together a harvesting program consistent with multiple-use principles, the bureau created an advisory committee that would "reflect as diverse an aggregation of interests and expertise as possible and an extensive public constituency."[479] The land's "ecological requirements" dominated the group's priorities, as did the "need to resolve or mitigate conflicts" between differing interests. Foresters, ecologists, representatives of Maine's conservation community (including Maine Audubon and Gardiner's former organization, the Natural Resources Council) all participated.

As part of developing management policies, Gardiner suggested a "planning exercise." Like almost everyone, he could only describe Deboullie in superlatives; in the whole North Maine Woods, "you couldn't find a Township with more scenic and recreational value." To quantify this "gut" valuation systematically, he asked the staff to identify every acre that should be managed for these values alone. In "a gem of a township" like Deboullie, Gardiner guessed it would be 35 percent at least. He was "stunned" when the data came back. Deboullie's beauty and recreational opportunities were based on only 15 percent of the land. Timber could be the priority on the other eighty-five percent. On most of the other public lands, fractions needing special protection for their recreation or scenic value would be even smaller. Harvest levels needed to support the BPL's operations could be achieved without sacrificing anything. "You *can* have your cake and eat it too," Gardiner concluded.

The BPL adopted its "Planning Policy for the Public Reserved Lands" on the last day of 1985. The draft had survived three public hearings and extensive public comment with "a lot of little changes, but no sweeping revisions." Its innovation as a prescription for multiple-use lay in two guiding concepts: dominant use and sub-dominant, or secondary, uses. Instead of user groups competing for every acre, reserves would be divided into sub-units, each of which would be managed for a dominant use or value (timber, wildlife, recreation, scenic beauty, etc.) based on what was on the land. The Deboullie exercise had shown that if wildlife habitat and scenic recreation priorities were identified first, there would be more than enough working forest left to support the BPL.

The same subunit was often important for other uses as well; for instance, timberland might have value for wildlife or recreation. These secondary uses would be protected by special management objectives, such as harvesting standards or best management practices.[480] Even visually important areas could be harvested, if the cut was carried out sensitively, so that "recreationists won't see the difference," said Gardiner.

One potential use where the "difference" would be very visible was mineral extraction. "A gravel-pit is a pretty poor multiple land use," Gardiner told a *Maine Times* reporter.[481] It wouldn't be prohibited, he said, but it would hardly be favored. As for mining, were a valuable mineral lode to be discovered, it would trigger a major revision of the management plan including agency reviews with public hearings and comment.

One way to reduce conflict with forestry was to limit areas where recreation was the dominant use to those providing "dispersed and primitive" activities, for example, high mountains and along waterways. The public lands were for "primitive recreation that stresses self-reliance." Campsites were isolated, approachable only on foot or by canoe. Boat launches were designed for canoes, not power boats. Elsewhere, tracts of "back-country"— "wilderness" was becoming an "emotionally-charged word," and it was deliberately avoided—were defined as 100 acres or more where a unique mix of features lent it a wild character. Here the recreation expert would ensure that harvesting operations left plenty of diversity.

As "a practical and cost-effective system for public land management," the planning policy was a major advance. "No one else has defined as precisely what multiple-use means and how it will be applied," Rob Gardiner stated with justifiable pride. It was also a far cry from the days when Bernard Schruender was beating back attempted raids on BPL resources with arguments from his experience in the U.S. Forest Service, where the National Forests spent $2 for every $1 earned. The BPL had a million dollar surplus.

With lands identified for their dominant uses, a management plan for each of the twenty consolidated units, ranging in size from 3,000 to 30,000 acres, could be developed.[482] To ensure broad participation in the process, the advisory committee was expanded into a larger stake-holder group. Members were chosen for their particular expertise and asked to work in the spirit of consensus, rather than lobby for their institution's position. "We started with the principles and then worked down to our specific management plans and as [the group] saw those principles being applied in the management plans, they were very supportive," Gardiner recalled. Applying the dominant use concept was a "classic illustration" of letting the facts on the ground speak for themselves *before* joining battle. If 90 percent of a piece of land were free of conflict, it was "just crazy to spend all your time arguing about the remaining ten percent," he reasoned.

Instead of the long struggle Gardiner had anticipated over philosophy and principle, disputes were reduced to a few points that could be easily overcome with a little magnanimity. For example, deer yards, the forested areas deer depend on to survive snow and freezing temperatures in winter, had been a perennial bone of contention between ecologists and foresters. Through the lens of dominant use, the amount of land the deer required turned out to be inconsequential. With little debate, the dominant value for deer yards became wildlife habitat.

Another controversial issue on which the BPL now had a position was the presence of off-road vehicles, especially ATVs (all-terrain vehicles). At the conference, snowmobilers had presented a strong case for being allowed on public lands. Snowmobiles operate on frozen ground. Once the ground thawed, the snowmobile was no longer there, nor was there much evidence that it ever was. Gardiner had made it clear that he had no intention of keeping snowmobiles out of the public lands. ATVs were different, even if the recreational experience was somewhat similar. They only functioned where the ground was soft, and riders had a penchant for streams and wet areas, making a mess of the land and destroying streambeds. The BPL became one of the first landowners to ban ATVs, although the policy allowed a limited area for research into their impacts.

The Planning Policy also finally tackled the thorny issue of leasing private camp lots on public land. Early on, the nascent BPL had sought to phase the program out, but the Legislature stymied its efforts. A few years later, Lloyd Irland tried to increase the rental fees—camp owners were still paying a hundred bucks a year; instead the Legislature took away the BPL's authority to set them and kept all fees at the old level. During Bernard Schruender's time as BPL director, Sen. James McBreirity tried to lower them, saying that a campsite's value resulted from improvements made and paid for by the leaseholders. On the contrary, they inevitably have the best sites—rocky shores and beaches—leaving the public with access to muddy or marshy shorefront only, Schruender told the Senator.

"Weeks are spent in every legislative session warding off efforts …. to get the bureau to reduce their rents or to sell them the land under and around their camps," wrote Bob Cummings. Most recently it was a rush of camp-owners who had been leasing their site from one or another of the paper companies for years and years. Suddenly they found that the land had been traded, and their leases were now with the State. At a public hearing later that session, a hundred leaseholders showed up to support a bill (surprisingly co-sponsored by Neil Rolde) allowing them to buy their camps.[483]

Under "Special Uses," the BPL's new policy started to set some limits. No new private leases for camp lots would be executed. Case by case, the bureau would reassess "continuation of certain leases, as opportunities permit." Any future developments would have to demonstrate "significant public benefits."

Backed by his commissioner, Richard Anderson, Gardiner also started the process of stepping up the rents. These campsites, he pointed out, were worth far more than the token $100 a year most people were still paying. The owners of the land—the people of Maine—needed to get fair value. Most of the other landowners soon followed suit.

Being the only state agency to generate a surplus gave the BPL its own set of problems. The Legislature started to see it as a cash cow. Back when they created the BPL, skeptical lawmakers had made its budget dependent upon the revenues it produced. Now, the drafters of the Planning Policy deemed it prudent to reinforce that decision with a "firm declaration" prohibiting the Public Reserved Lands from being "exploited to support unrelated uses and programs." Based on their origin in the Articles of Separation, they argued, it would be unconstitutional for Public Lots revenue to go into the general fund.

Nonetheless, Gardiner was constantly on guard against attempts to amend the restrictions on his agency's income. Beyond maintaining a cash balance of half the annual expenses as a rainy day fund, Gardiner's rule was never to have "too much loose cash sloshing around" lest it be "too obvious and too tasty" for the legislature to resist. When there was extra money, "we would squirrel it away in different places." There were plenty of legitimate opportunities for spending that would benefit the public, and the bureau created special-purpose funds, such as installing boat launches on lakes.

The BPL was now the tenth largest landowner in the state, and it was suggested that it join the University of Maine's Cooperative Forestry Research Unit (CFRU). The primary research center on the impacts of logging on Maine's forest, CFRU's activities were funded by the large landowners based on the acreage they owned. "Nobody begged BPL to become a member," said Gardiner, but he thought that it was the right thing to do. It proved to be a turning point in the BPL's relations with the landowners. The prevailing attitude that the state was the enemy of the private sector had gained extra weight in the forest products community during the court case and its aftermath. With the BPL contributing financially to CFRU—the same as all the other landowners—that attitude began to soften. Instead of an adversary that "had squeezed them so badly when they were negotiating the lands," the bureau was becoming a partner, Gardiner said. He remembered particularly how impressed David Carlisle was. Further cooperation followed, such as mutual agreements for hauling timber across each other's lands and using each other's logging roads. Becoming a member of CFRU had "a big positive impact."

By the end of Governor Joseph Brennan's second and final term, the heavy lifting in terms of management plans for the Public Reserved Lands had been accomplished. Two maps succinctly told the story from 1963 to 1987. The first, included in Austin Wilkins's report, was spattered with little black rectangles—each marking a Public Lot that could be found on a map—thickest in western and eastern Maine, then thinning out as they went farther north. Here speckled squares—townships where the lots had not been divided—predominated. Twenty-four years later, the BPL map was dominated by a score of large green splashes, identified with names like Deboullie, Telos, Mahoosucs. Not all the Public Lots were consolidated, and they came in handy as private, nonprofit organizations began to play an increasing part in land conservation.

In early 1986, The Nature Conservancy announced a campaign to purchase Maine's last vestige of virgin forest, Big Reed Pond and Reed Mountain, north of Baxter Park, from the Pingree heirs. The 3,800-acre parcel represented "the one-tenth of 1 percent of Maine's 17 million acres of forestland that has never been touched by human hands," as Mason Morfit, the Conservancy's Maine director, put it.[484] That it had never been cut was due to its distance from a waterway when river-driving was the only means of getting the logs to the mills. That it never would be cut was due to the legendary Seven Islands forester, John Sinclair. When a road was being laid out to salvage some stands hit by spruce budworm—according to Edwin Meadows, who worked for Seven Islands—he put his hand down on the map and said, "Stop there." In keeping with his reserved style, Sinclair's only comment about protecting this gem was, "It's the right thing to do." Now a three-way transaction brought in the BPL, which agreed to sell six surplus Public Lots to The Nature Conservancy to trade with the Pingrees in exchange for Big Reed Pond. At the same time, the bureau gave the Pingrees several scattered lots in return for some high-value scenic and recreational lands around Allagash and Eagle lakes.

By the time the deal came to fruition, Republican governor John McKernan had succeeded Brennan in the Blaine House.[485] Gardiner had remained as BPL director "just long enough to think that maybe my head wouldn't be chopped off."[486] However, six months into the new administration, McKernan appointed his own director, Edwin Meadows. Gardiner had arrived at the bureau as the final round of negotiations began, and he was not "in the room where it happened," he quipped, quoting Aaron Burr's hit song from the musical *Hamilton*. However, his thoughtful analytical approach created a multiple-use protocol for forest management that has since won national acclaim. Earning around $1.5 million a year, the Public Reserved Lands were finally a fact of life.

Chapter Fifteen

A Unique Agency Takes Its Place (1987–2000)

Apart from a couple of isolated interventions, Maine's environmental groups had little to do with reclaiming the Public Lots. Bob Cummings frequently bemoaned the absence of the public at committee hearings. From time to time, Maine Audubon and the Natural Resources Council of Maine took supportive positions, but the issue was never their priority. In fact, NRCM's board of directors voted not to get involved, because they wanted to set their own agenda. At least in the beginning, the detachment of Maine's conservation organizations probably owed as much to a lack of the resources needed for a prolonged legal struggle.

The decade during which the Public Lots case unwound was a time of transition for the environmental movement. Early campaigns—against the Dickey-Lincoln Dam, in support of the Allagash Wilderness Waterway and the Bigelow Preserve—relied heavily on ad hoc volunteer efforts. As the decade after Earth Day gave way to the 1980s, the scope of environmental activism—both goals and resources—expanded by leaps and bounds. Supported by increasing public awareness, organizations like Maine Audubon and the Natural Resources Council of Maine began to flex their public policy muscles. The Public Lots themselves might have departed the front pages, but the forests hadn't, and the paper companies were continually in environmentalists' crosshairs. For the next quarter century, while the BPL quietly got on with the job, the North Woods were the center of a succession of environmental storms that roiled the state. The first was over a spectacular five-mile stretch of rocks and rapids on the West Branch of the Penobscot River.

At about the time Governor Brennan's Public Lots Task Force was negotiating with the large landowners, one of them, Great Northern, announced plans to build a hydroelectric dam on the Big Amberjackmockamus Falls, or "Big A" as it became known. An extraordinarily acrimonious struggle ensued, pitting the paper company—Maine's largest landowner and second-largest employer—against a coalition of environmentalists, sportsmen, anglers, and outfitters, led by the Natural Resources Council and Maine Audubon. The fight, at least in the company's rhetoric, was over "payroll versus pickerel," either jobs or the environment. Finally, in March 1986, Great Northern abandoned its plans. The Big A was saved, but an abiding bitterness between environmentalists and the forest products industry, especially the paper companies, would taint the forest debate in Maine for a decade or more. [487]

While environmental attorneys from Audubon and the Natural Resources Council were becoming fixtures at hearings before the legislature and the regulatory boards, a "kinder, gentler" strain in Maine's efforts to protect its natural resources was also evolving. Less controversial than policy or advocacy, land conservation appealed to a wider constituency and attracted much larger contributions. The $1.1 million raised by The Nature Conservancy to purchase Big Reed Pond was a record at the time. Another organization, the Maine Coast Heritage Trust, originally founded to protect and preserve Maine's islands, was also building an impressive portfolio of conservation achievements and high-level donors. Both groups were ideally placed to make the most of an idea born in the waning days of the Brennan administration that would continue to augment Maine's Public Reserved Lands.

A rising economy was heating up the market for second homes, and it was beginning to alarm much of the public. They saw wildlands threatened with fragmentation, and access to treasured fishing holes and hunting stands lost to vacationers from away. One citizen of Aroostook County wrote to Governor Brennan, asking him to convene a special commission to assess the threats to Maine's outdoor heritage. With only months before he left office, Brennan said yes. A Who's Who of Maine's most celebrated outdoorsmen and women made up the Special Commission on Outdoor Recreation for the State of Maine. It was "a wicked list of people," said conservation commissioner Richard Anderson, who took charge of the project. [488]

Throughout the fall of 1986, the special commission held public hearings all over the state. With the administration's days counting down, it drafted thirty recommendations. One of them—a $50 million bond issue for land acquisition—was too much for some. Leon Gorman (L.L. Bean's grandson and president of the company), for one, thought it would distract the public from the commission's larger goal. [489] After a concerted lobbying effort by Anderson and Richard Barringer, however, the bond was included in the commission's final recommendations. Between the election of the new governor and the year's end, they drafted a bill for the bond that would create the Land for Maine's Future (LMF) program.

McKernan's transition team requested a copy of the bill, and Anderson gave the only other one to Democratic State Representative Pat McGowan, a member of the legislature's Appropriations Committee.[490] When the new administration asked for a $5 million bond for land acquisition, McGowan sponsored a competing request for $50 million, which passed, although at the last moment, $15 million was syphoned off to an economic development project.[491] Thus, in November 1987, the ballot included a request for a $35 million bond to secure "the traditional Maine heritage of public access to Maine's land and water resources or continued quality and availability of natural resources important to the interests and continued heritage of Maine people." Its sole aim was to purchase land when it was available. In Anderson's words, "You could figure out what to do with it afterwards."

The LMF bond was the biggest nontransportation bond in state history, which "seemed a little bit off the charts," recalled the Maine Coast Heritage Trust's president, Jay Espy. Although previously shunning the spotlight of the political arena, Espy and The Nature Conservancy's Mason Morfit now found themselves leading a high-voltage political campaign. They would have to be more outfront, according to Morfit, if they were going to "jazz up the electorate" and get them to vote for the bond. With Maine Audubon and the Natural Resources Council, they formed a coalition to spearhead the campaign, Citizens to Save Maine's Heritage.

The campaign received broad public support. At the press conference announcing the acquisition of Big Reed Pond, Governor McKernan gave it a boost, saying, "We have to have a statewide effort to preserve our wilderness areas." On the same occasion, Brad Wellman of the Pingree heirs went further, saying, "Everybody should recognize that the $35 million bond issue is just a drop in the bucket."[492] On Election Day, 1987, the Land for Maine's Future bond passed by a margin of two to one.

With $35 million in hand, the LMF board (including state officials and private citizens) consolidated the state's land acquisition process in one place. Before LMF, land acquisition was driven by different agency priorities. With LMF, the public—from local land trusts to statewide organizations like the Maine Coast Heritage Trust—selected the places it wanted; the board weighed their proposals based on established criteria and provided funds accordingly. LMF could not be accused of being some out-of-control, out-of-touch bureaucracy "cramming proposals down people's throats," said Irland. And the fact that year after year it received more proposals than it could fund—and that they came from the bottom up—put the lie to the claim that Mainers thought they had enough public land.

Putting LMF in perspective, said Richard Anderson, "There's nothing that even compares to the Public Lots consolidation as an astounding case of public policy and land acquisition. But the other big deal was the LMF." And when it started to make deals for conservation land, surplus Public Lots that had never been consolidated were frequently available to sweeten them. Ed Meadows had become director of the Bureau of Public Lands shortly after the legislature passed the original bill for the LMF bond. (As head of government affairs at Seven Islands, he had testified in favor on behalf of the Maine Forest Products Council.) Confident that the referendum would pass as well, he started gearing up to implement it almost at once. When the public approved the bond in November, the administrative machinery was pretty well ready to roll, and public hearings on how the LMF program should operate began early in the new year.

That there were still wild places in Maine in urgent need of acquisition if they were to be preserved was demonstrated almost immediately. At the end of 1987, nearly a million acres of forestland—all Diamond Occidental's holdings in northern New England and up-state New York—were put on the block. The Anglo-French corporate raider Sir James Goldsmith had acquired them in a hostile takeover five years before. When he sold them to a French telecommunications company, it promptly put them back on the market. It was the largest sale of forestland in nearly fifty years, and 790,000 acres were in Maine.

Maine's conservation groups were already tracking the spread of second homes in the wildlands. The sale of the Diamond lands confirmed their worst fears. The forest products business was changing radically. The boardrooms of old Maine-based industries were migrating to Wall Street. Hugh Chisholm's model of a single company feeding its mills from its own forests was being overtaken by new economic realities resulting from the Tax Reform Act of 1986.[493] Paper manufacturing companies were either seeking to maximize their returns by cutting the forest harder, or divesting themselves of it altogether. As those lands came on the market, an old real estate appraisal term, highest and best use, gained new currency. Using the HBU concept, land with lakeshore was far more valuable for building house lots than for growing trees.

In the event, most of the Diamond lands in Maine were bought by another paper company, James River. At the national level, Diamond had meanwhile offered The Nature Conservancy a chance to review all their holdings, essentially giving the NGO first dibs on tracts they might wish to buy for conservation. In Maine, one such was a ridge in Hancock County including Black and Caribou mountains. Separating the white sand beaches of Donnell Pond to the west from the forested shoreline of Tunk and Little Tunk lakes to the east and south, the top of Black Mountain has among the most glorious views in Maine. When The Nature Conservancy's Kent Wommack expressed his organization's interest in purchasing it to Ed Meadows, he knew it could be the keystone for a most ambitious project the two end pieces of which were already in play.

Donnell Pond had been on and off the radar for possible public acquisition since Acadia became a national park. In the 1940s or 1950s, Prentiss & Carlisle, the land management company, had bought it in a deal with Oxford Paper Company.[494] During his last year at the BPL, Rob Gardiner had started negotiations with the Carlisles for a fifteen-hundred-acre tract, but nothing came of it. The following year, 1987, the company signed a purchase agreement with the Patten Corporation, a Vermont-based real estate development company, instead. Patten's plan was to place 150 house lots on the pristine shoreline. Without waste of time, advertisements appeared—in red, white, and blue—for the Great American Land Auction, to be held July 4, 1988. That "raised a howl of protest" from people living in the area.[495] Throughout the fall, Meadows tried to negotiate with Patten, but the talks invariably broke down. By year's end, they were still several million dollars apart.

It would seem to have been an inauspicious moment for Kent Wommack to propose adding Black Mountain to the pot. However, at that point, Meadows received an urgent call from Robert Bryan, founder of the Quebec-Labrador Foundation.[496] Bryan's family had long been dedicated to protecting Tunk Lake, which among other things was where Admiral Richard Byrd, the Antarctic explorer, summered for the last twenty years of his life. Now Bryan felt he had the family's backing for a bargain sale to the state. In March, the Bryans offered to sell three miles of shorefront on the southwest part of the lake.

At the same time, at Meadows's request, Mason Morfit and Wommack started another round of discussions with the Patten Corporation over Donnell Pond. Within a week, the outline of an agreement emerged around the idea of a limited development at the northwest end of the pond: no more than eight lots with strict setbacks from the shore and a conservation easement to be held by the BPL. A couple of days later, the parties were within striking range of a financial deal. The state would get Prentiss & Carlisle's land around Donnell Pond and return some twelve thousand acres in miscellaneous Public Lots it had accepted from the company as part of what David Carlisle had called the "premium," following the court case. It was more acreage but similar value, given Donnell Pond's HBU potential.

On April 1, 1988, contracts on all three tracts were signed. Amazingly, it was the first time the various parties—Diamond, Prentiss & Carlisle, Patten, the Bryans—discovered that their negotiations had been part of a much larger effort. From the first fifteen hundred acres on Donnell Pond, the deal had expanded until it protected nearly five times as much, including sixteen miles of pristine lakefront and two mountaintops. Those "plain vanilla" Public Lots that Martin Wilk had had to accept from Prentiss & Carlisle, David Carlisle reflected, "turned out to be very fortunate for things like Donnell Pond."

Not included in the mix were funds from LMF, which did not become operational until later that year. In the fall, however, the LMF board asked The Nature Conservancy to go back to the negotiating table with Diamond Occidental and James River. Southwest of Baxter Park, Nahmakanta Lake and its surrounding forest—"embroidered with magnificent lakes, streams and wetlands"—was generally admitted to be the most diverse and scenic tract of Maine's wildlands as yet unprotected.[497] Thanks to Wommack's negotiating stamina, not to mention the good faith of "no fewer than eight public agencies (and at least as many private parties)," 31,500 acres in Nahmakanta and Rainbow townships were added to Maine's public lands.

When he passed the baton to Ed Meadows, Rob Gardiner had told him, "It's one of the best jobs you could ever have." Meadows discovered that Gardiner was right. The BPL was still settling into its curious position as a business enterprise within the government. Just how curious Meadows found out soon enough when he was summoned by the Maine Bureau of Purchase, which wanted to know: when the BPL put a contract out to bid, why did it not award it to the low offer, as government policy dictated? It was a contract for stumpage on the public lands, Meadows explained. We don't want the low bid; we're selling, not buying.

Some challenges were more complicated. McKernan's conservation commissioner, Robert LaBonta, had spent his career as a paper company forester and manager. LaBonta was quite frank with his BPL director that he considered backcountry recreation elitist and that he was unconvinced of the silvicultural benefits of long-term rotations. Meadows had to keep explaining the different economic realities between private and public timber harvesting. Without the pressure of stockholders and rates of return, BPL could let trees grow longer so that they could get bigger and become more valuable. Whether or not he was persuaded, severe ill health forced LaBonta to resign in October 1988. Governor McKernan appointed Meadows to succeed him. Reluctantly, Meadows gave up the "best job you could ever have" and turned it over to his deputy, Tom Morrison.

At the Earth Day conference on the Public Lots in 1985, Dr. Malcolm Hunter, a wildlife scientist at the University of Maine in Orono, had urged that small five-hundred-acre parcels be preserved throughout the forest as "untouched natural laboratories" for scientists to study. By the end of the 1980s, discussions among ecologists at the university had progressed far enough for the State Planning Office to prepare a report on "Establishing a System of Ecological Reserves in Maine." Ecological reserves would be areas set aside to maintain one or more ecosystems representative of a region as a baseline for scientific study, not least silviculture (which ultimately persuaded the forest industry). These reserves had to be relatively undisturbed or well along in recovery from human disturbance, and they had to be large enough for their natural processes to survive in the long term.

The report formed the basis of a legislative resolve introduced by the Natural Resources Council in 1989—calling for the state to study the need for such a system in Maine. When a financial crisis forced the study's funding to be withdrawn, The Nature Conservancy stepped up with the cash. By 1992, an inventory of potential ecological reserves had been completed. Legislation to implement it was drafted, but it became clear that Maine's forest products community was not yet on board. It took five years of facilitated discussion among environmentalists, representatives of the industry, and the relevant public agencies.

The Maine Forest Biodiversity Project was not explicitly brought together to prepare the way for an ecological reserve system, but it was a top priority for the group, which met from 1994 to 1999. Participants had different reasons to worry about eco-reserves taking away access to land on which they were pursuing their interests or livelihoods. The forest industry's attitude was: Don't come looking on our land until you've seen what you can do on yours.[498] Maine's sportsmen were also on the defensive, lest hunting be banned. The BPL had its own concerns: in the inventory, over 160,000 acres of Public Reserved Lands were identified as potential ecological reserves; to take them out of timber production could have a significant impact on the bureau's financial sustainability.

The BPL's commitment was unexpectedly finessed by Independent governor Angus King, who had been elected in 1994.[499] At the same time the Forest Biodiversity Project was seeking consensus, a citizen's initiative to ban clearcutting in Maine inaugurated an altogether different political process. Conservation policy was enmeshed in the ban campaign's divisiveness for the next three years. In search of a path between a rock of green absolutism and a hard place of industry overreaching, a group of foresters and conservationists began negotiating in early 1996.

The talks were excruciating; the landowners called the meetings "the house of pain." A breakthrough at the table would be followed inevitably by back-bencher rejection from one side or the other. Nevertheless, inch by inch, the gap was getting smaller. But there came a meeting in the Blaine House—put at the negotiators' disposal by Governor King to facilitate the process— where the final step appeared impossible.

Kent Wommack, by then an interested observer, recalled the appearance of the governor himself. He addressed the environmental team: if they would accept what they had won so far, the BPL would sweeten the pot by designating Maine's first ecological reserves on some of the public lands. It broke the stalemate. The next day Governor King, the negotiators, and the heads of all the paper companies took part in a press conference to announce support for the Compact for Maine's Forests as an alternative to the clear-cutting ban.[500]

The Maine Forest Biodiversity Project wrapped up its work by publishing an inventory of potential ecological reserves on Maine's public and private conservation lands. Lengthy discussions followed at the BPL, especially around the question of what public uses—such as hunting and snowmobiling—might have to be regulated on public lands designated as ecological reserves. In 2000, as part of the first revision of the BPL's ten-year plan and the Integrated Resource Policy, "ecological reserve" was added as a potential use allocation, along with "recreation, wildlife, and timber."

All that was needed now was authorization for the BPL director to designate specific ecological reserves. As the process moved to the legislature, The Sportsman's Alliance of Maine was for making every designation subject to legislative approval. The Snowmobile Association was on the fence until existing snowmobile trails were grandfathered. The Maine Forest Products Council was leaning against any ecological reserves at all. What was established on public lands today "might become regulation on private land tomorrow."

The bill passed, after amendments capped the proportion of the Public Reserved Lands that could be designated as ecological reserves at 15 percent, and the percentage of "operable timberland" at 6 percent.[501] According to The Nature Conservancy's Barbara Vickery, Roger Milliken single-handedly persuaded the Maine Forest Products Council not to oppose the bill. When it testified in favor, the council's own staff were astonished.[502] The next year, 2001, thirteen ecological reserves, encompassing some seventy thousand acres, were identified. They constituted 12.5 percent of the public lands and 5.4 percent of the timberland.[503]

During the decade it took to set up ecological reserves, the BPL had been through its own share of ups and downs. Tom Morrison had begun working at the bureau just as the last land-swap agreement—with Irving—was completed. By 1989, all the consolidated units with significant public use had management plans, and their first ten-year cycle was being implemented. On many of them, the priority was to improve the composition of the forest. In identifying the lands they wanted in exchange for the Public Lots, past BPL directors had taken the long view: if they could get more acres of a cut-over forest, the state would have the time to let the trees grow back. Now contractors took off the low-quality trees and let a high-value forest develop. It meant belt tightening in some years, Morrison remembered. "Sometimes we were concerned about making payroll." Meanwhile, the quality of the forest on Maine's public lands steadily improved.

In 1992, the same statewide fiscal crunch that deprived the initial ecological reserve study of its funding saw an attempted raid on the Public Reserved Lands Management Fund. It was part of a sweep of all the government departments to reduce their expenses across the board. Public Lots funds, as Morrison remembered it, had been identified to fill a $525,000 gap in the budget of the Department of Inland Fisheries and Wildlife. Attorney General Michael Carpenter advised against the constitutionality of such a course of action. Instead, lawmakers levied a charge on the BPL of the same amount in lieu of excise tax on its lands. Never mind that no other agency was paying such a tax, nor that the amount was calculated or ever justified by a stated rate. Once the dust cleared, Morrison assumed that there was a general feeling among legislators that this was not a road they wanted to travel again.

When Angus King became governor, he appointed another career paper company executive to be conservation commissioner. Like LaBonta, Ron Lovaglio's outlook reflected his career at International Paper, and he was skeptical of the BPL's multiple-use mission. Over time, Lovaglio developed a better understanding of the public lands' special opportunities for growing bigger, more valuable logs. At the beginning, however, he watched every timber sale like a hawk. He also took the lead in combining the bureaus of Public Lands and Parks.

One of Governor King's mantras was efficiency in state government. Without hurting the quality of services they provided, could any agencies be combined? In the Conservation Department, three bureaus dealt with land management; could they be refigured into two? Having considered how the BPL's mission might mesh with that of the Forest Service, Lovaglio and his staff decided it made more sense to combine it with the Bureau of Parks. This was never about funding one or other of the bureaus with Public Lots revenues, stressed Tom Morrison. Morrison became head of the new Bureau of Parks and Lands, with Herb Hartman, who had been head of parks, as deputy director.

Especially in the wake of the clear-cutting referenda, third-party audits were becoming more and more regarded as the cost of doing business in the forest. Like the independent financial audit, a forestry audit examined operations on the ground against a set of standards. The Bureau of Parks and Lands began the certification process in 2000. At the time there was considerable debate over the merits of two audit programs: the Sustainable

Forestry Initiative (SFI), preferred by forest products companies, and the Forest Stewardship Council (FSC), considered more rigorous and effective by environmentalists. Morrison decided BPL should be certified by both systems, "so as not to look like taking sides." BPL successfully completed its certification the following year, although the effort, together with a sluggish market, resulted in an exceptionally low balance in the management account. With ecological reserves added to the Integrated Resource Policy, and its forest practices certified, the bureau would enter the new millennium with a clear mission, clear operating instructions, and an organizational structure to fulfill them.

Chapter Sixteen

"Quiet Darlings" No More— Into the Twenty-First Century

"For decades, the half-million acres of Maine Public Reserve Lands have been the quiet darlings of the state conservation system," wrote Christine Parrish in 2013. "Operating largely under the radar," the system had worked. Parrish was a reporter for a weekly newsprint magazine serving Maine's midcoast, *The Free Press*. As well as being a guide to local goings-on, the paper had an impressive roster of writers, and the publisher allowed them to tackle interesting issues of more than local concern.

One way or another, the "quiet darlings" had been in the capable hands of Tom Morrison since 1988. As director, he had overseen the revision of the Integrated Resource Policy in 2000, among other things adding ecological reserves to it. The process had provided the Bureau of Public Lands (BPL) with an important opportunity to check in with stakeholders and the public. The result had been good for wildlife and recreation, and allowed sustainable logging that over the next decade saw standing timber on public lands increase by 10 percent.

In 2003, the new Democratic governor, John Baldacci, appointed David Soucy, an attorney from Aroostook County, to head the BPL.[504] Morrison became the bureau's operations manager. Much of Soucy's tenure was spent dealing with management issues in the Allagash Wilderness Waterway, threading the needle between environmental concerns and those of the local folks who used it most. The waterway, Soucy pointed out, had been the subject of "vigorous political debate and controversy" since it was first conceived nearly fifty years before. He likened the controversy to "a frothy standing wave," an appropriate simile.[505]

With Governor Baldacci running for reelection, the "standing wave" started to take on a political dimension. In 2006, the last year of his first term, the governor convened a working group to consider how management

257

and oversight of the Allagash Wilderness Waterway might be improved and conflict reduced. Having won a second term, he signed the group's recommendations into law in January 2007. They included a telling final "Observation." No progress could be made without "a return to the civility and respectful discourse" of the waterway's early years. What was needed was "a new beginning of careful listening, respectful communication, and energetic collaboration among all persons and groups with a stake in the future of the Allagash Wilderness Waterway."

This, 2006, was also the year when the exchange of some of the remaining unconsolidated Public Lots helped complete Percival Baxter's dream. In his lifetime, Baxter could never persuade Great Northern to sell him Katahdin Lake on the park's eastern edge.[506] Irving Woodlands subsequently bought the land, putting it up for sale again in 2003. The Department of Conservation tried to buy it but was outbid by the Gardner Land Company, which at once started logging the largest and oldest trees.[507] In 2005, after over two years of tough negotiations, a national land protection organization, the Trust for Public Land, and the Conservation Department secured an agreement to buy it from Gardner.[508] A year was spent raising the price tag's $14 million, "the largest amount of money raised in the shortest amount of time" for a conservation project in state history, asserted Conservation Commissioner Patrick McGowan. In December 2006, Governor Baldacci announced that Katahdin Lake and four thousand acres of old-growth forest were now a part of Baxter State Park. It was "another milestone on our journey to keep the special places in Maine special," said the governor.

Raising the millions was the easy part. More difficult was the task of reconciling a number of conflicting interests. Though Katahdin Lake was always part of Percival Baxter's vision, the Baxter family needed to be reassured that his legacy would in no way be diluted by the first parcel purchased for his park with others' funds. Some people resented the trade or sale of 7,385 acres of Maine's remaining Public Lots, after they had been carefully tended by the BPL for so long. Writing as elder statesmen in an op-ed in the *Maine Sunday Telegram*, Richard Barringer and Rob Gardiner made the argument for Katahdin Lake as a "truly exceptional" case; but "the time is now over" for trading away any more Public Lots, "once and for all."[509] The deal also set aside funds for the BPL to purchase additional lands in counties that supplied the Public Lots lost in the acquisition.

Then there was the inevitable consequence of adding land to "forever wild" Baxter Park. There would be no more hunting or snowmobiling around Katahdin Lake. The pitch of the argument over "traditional uses" reached a level that nearly wrecked the whole project. Eventually, there was agreement that the hunting opportunities around Katahdin Lake were fairly meager, and an additional block of two thousand acres to the north was included in the purchase to be managed for multiple use without any of Percival Baxter's restrictions.

At the beginning of Governor Baldacci's second term, Will Harris, a twenty-plus-year veteran of the Conservation Department, succeeded Soucy as director of the Bureau of Parks and Lands. It fell to Harris, working with the new Allagash Wilderness Waterway Advisory Council, to make the new law work. Another notable achievement was the creation of a new program in response to Richard Louv's book *Last Child in the Woods*, which drew national attention to what the author called "nature-deficit disorder." The BPL's program, "Take It Outside," used Maine's public lands and state parks as a way of reconnecting children and families with nature.

All this while the trees on Maine's Public Reserved Lands—and their value at the stump—were getting bigger and bigger. In an April 2012 interview, Tom Morrison described the BPL as a successful agency that knew what it was doing and was confident in its mission. It made nearly $5 million a year, all but a million of which came from timber sales. Noting that "management has been stable and consistent," he said the major change over the past quarter century had been the bureau's access to ever-increasing amounts of data. It made the planning process "much more sophisticated," Morrison told the reporter.[510] With the public lands (double) third-party certified and the continued close involvement of the foresters, forest scientists, and ecologists on the BPL's silvicultural advisory committee, Morrison was optimistic about the future. A year later, he and Harris discovered that unbeknownst to them—or anyone at the BPL—the goalposts had been abruptly moved.

In 2011, when Republican Paul LePage succeeded Governor Baldacci, his choice to head the Maine Forest Service was Doug Denico, a career forest manager who had worked for five paper companies.[511] In a confidential memo to the governor, dated October 22, 2012, Denico proposed a massive increase in the cut on Maine's public lands. Bureau foresters and the silvicultural advisory committee had set the annual allowable cut for 2013 at 141,500 cords per year, based on the Integrated Resource Policy. Denico wanted to up it to 227,732 cords, a 61 percent increase.

Such a major change in policy would reverse decades of dedicated multiple-use forest management. However, unlike the public process that had previously defined and benefited bureau policies, Denico had not consulted the BPL, let alone offered up his proposal for public comment. "The planned increase in logging was developed by Administration officials who have no legal authority over Maine's public lands," wrote the Natural Resources Council of Maine's Catherine Johnson in a report.[512] Neither did the Maine Forest Service, she added. "That authority rests with the Bureau of Parks and Lands."

BPL director Harris finally learned about the Forest Service plan six months after Denico's memo. Based on a number of documents—memos, drafts, and emails—to which it gained access through formal requests, the Natural Resources Council deduced that over a couple of days in April 2013 "a major negotiation took place between the Maine Forest Service, the Bureau of Parks and Lands, and the Governor's Office." The title of a Maine Forest Service memo—"Areas of Compromise/Conflict Between BPL and MFS Reports"—suggested what took place. The "compromise" was a questionable increase in the harvest to 180,000 cords per year for twenty years. Denico's goal was to reduce the standing inventory on the public lands—which had now reached 23 cords per acre, thanks to years of committed effort by BPL foresters—to 21.5 cords per acre.

An outcry from some of the BPL's top professional foresters was to no avail. Reluctantly, Harris signed off on the deal. He did so, wrote Catherine Johnson, "apparently knowing that BPL had, at least, been able to head off the more harmful proposed increase contained in the original MFS proposal." However, the change was enough to alarm the Forest Stewardship Council. The BPL, it stated in its annual audit, must address the questions of "public participation in harvest plans" and "sustainable harvest levels," or risk losing its certification.

Johnson's analysis of what had happened was forceful and succinct.

> The state's policy for managing our public forest lands was radically altered during a 48-hour period in April 2013, upending a three-decades-old policy to increase the amount of standing timber and grow bigger, older, more valuable trees.

The Public Reserved Lands were back in the headlines. As it happened, Christine Parrish, *The Free Press* reporter, was a professional forest scientist. She was reading "a dull copy of the Maine Public Lands annual report" when a couple of paragraphs "deep in the middle of it" caught her attention. The Bureau of Parks and Lands seemed to be increasing the amount of timber cut on public lands, regardless of other, multiple-use values. "They weren't planning anything so dramatic as a clear-cut," Parrish recalled, "but devaluing something doesn't tend to happen in a rush. . . . It happens step by step until we accept the new normal." According to bureau foresters, "off the record," Governor LePage's administration had been steadily increasing timber harvests at the expense of recreation and wildlife efforts. The silvicultural advisory committee had already increased the annual allowable cut by 20 percent (to 141,500 cords). Even so, the Public Reserve Lands Trust Fund was "below the level necessary to support all program needs," and the bureau needed "to reduce costs and increase revenue . . . to maintain financial viability," Parrish was told.

At about the time that Doug Denico negotiated the new "compromise" allowable cut with the BPL, the governor's office asked for information on how much additional revenue could be realized by increasing the harvest on the public lands to industry sustainable standards.[513] The Maine Pellet Fuels Association had a plan that called for using the extra funds for what Parrish aptly described as a "Cash for Clunkers" program. The clunkers were old, inefficient home-heating furnaces; they would be replaced by energy-efficient wood pellet boilers paid for with a cash rebate generated from the public lands. Once again, a raid was being attempted on funds from land and timber held in trust for all the people of Maine for an unrelated purpose that would benefit only a segment of the population.

In June 2013, in the waning weeks of the 126th Legislature, the Energy and Public Utilities Committee took up the association's bill, LD 1468. The committee did make some significant changes. It gave back to the Public Lands $200,000 for "the building of infrastructure for land management and public access opportunities." Meanwhile, $500,000 was directed to get the "cash-for-clunkers program" off the ground. But was it legal under Maine's constitution? Attorney General Janet Mills didn't think so.[514] The question about dipping into the Public Reserved Lands Trust Fund had been asked before, most recently in 1992, when Attorney General Carpenter barred the use of BPL revenues to meet a shortfall in the state budget. As written, LD 1468 would certainly face a legal challenge. Having already voted to support the bill, the committee found itself in a difficult spot. Now that they knew, over half of the "yeas" said they would have voted differently. However, it was too late in the session to rework the bill. It was sent to the floor, where the full legislature voted it down.

That, wrote Parrish, "fanned a conversation about neglected dollars standing on the stump, waiting to be turned into boards and cords." During the summer, her contacts led her to a seemingly innocuous meeting of the Flagstaff and Bigelow Preserve advisory group. The agenda suggested it would be a routine discussion about trails and recreation on the mountain. Then a public lands employee raised the issue of rumors that an increased cut on the public lands was coming. Evidently the "compromise" cut of 180,000 cords a year had still been under wraps. It was no longer. Parrish followed up by asking if timber was becoming the priority over wildlife and recreation. "Some might think so," a bureau forest manager waffled. As for public review, aside from meetings such as this every five years, the public could find the facts in the Conservation Department's annual report and complain when they saw a timber operation they didn't like.

Nor had the governor given up on his plan to log the public lands harder and divert the extra revenue to the Energy Office. Its director had noticed the Public Reserved Lands Trust Fund had a surplus once again and "wanted as much as I can get." At the beginning of 2014 and the legislature's second session, LePage submitted an emergency bill, LD 1838, "An Act to Expand Affordable Heating Investments with Maine's Public Resources." It would encourage homeowners to switch from oil to cleaner energy sources like natural gas, biomass, and heat pumps. Once again, the money for rebates—$1 million plus—would come from an increased cut on the public lands, which had been "under-harvested."

At the bill's hearing before the Agriculture, Conservation and Forestry Committee, several professional foresters testified that "under-harvested" was an inappropriate term in the circumstances. It ignored that the public lands were meant to be managed to a higher standard than private ownerships and had to provide for wildlife habitat and recreation. Minimum sustainability standards were not enough. The bill was voted out of committee, "ought not to pass." It was said that the governor took out his frustration at the failure of his bill on Parks and Lands director Will Harris personally.[515] For Harris, the writing was on the wall. Four years of weathering the storms of the LePage administration, trying to keep his bureau afloat and true to its mission, was enough. He retired in June 2014.

Tom Morrison found himself head of the Bureau of Parks and Lands, if only as acting director, once more. He too was increasingly uncomfortable with the shape of things to come. Paul LePage had won a second term as governor, and in his 2015 State of the State address, he used the fear of an imminent eruption of spruce budworm to justify cutting still more in the Public Reserved Lands. Robert Seymour, forestry professor at the University of Maine and one of Maine's most respected forest scientists, took issue in no uncertain terms. Seymour had been on the BPL's silvicultural advisory committee since its inception. He labeled the governor's rationale an unnecessary scare tactic to hide his real objective, to bring in more revenue for his favored purposes. Forestry on the public lands "has been an extraordinary success story at no cost to the people. Why change it?" asked Seymour. A retired BPL forester, George Ritz, pointed out that the threat of spruce budworm was "greatly exaggerated," especially since fir (actually the budworm's preferred species) "composes only about 9% of public lands."

But LePage wanted an even bigger change. He was also proposing to dissolve the Bureau of Parks and Lands and split its responsibilities between the Bureau of Conservation (Parks) and the Maine Forest Service (Public Lands).[516] Having "all the foresters under one roof" made sense, said Doug Denico. It would "ensure uniform management of Maine's forest," added

Agriculture, Conservation and Forestry Commissioner Walter Whitcomb, overlooking the principal point of the BPL, which was to support exemplary forestry beyond that available to private industrial ownerships.

The governor's plans reflected a fundamental difference in silvicultural philosophy. The public lands were not being harvested frequently enough, Denico stated. Trees were being left to rot. "You are never going to be shaping a forest as you should be if you are only going to touch that land every forty years," he said. (He seemed to use "touched" and "harvested" interchangeably.) Fifteen to twenty-five years was more like it. The implicit suggestion that "Public Lands foresters were not minding the store" did not sit well with the foresters, most of whom had dedicated decades to the care of their particular patches. Aside from any number of record-keeping reasons that might inflate the forty-year figure, "touched" and "logged" should not be confused. BPL foresters inspected their forests, thinning when necessary, every twenty to twenty-five years, and the result was that they were growing large trees whose value at the stump increased. Said Seymour, the state of the public's forest "should be celebrated, not criticized."

Maine's Public Reserved Lands had not had so much public attention for decades. Not only was the professional forestry community engaged. The Environmental Priorities Coalition—a partnership of thirty-four environmental, conservation, and public health groups—made stopping the governor's bill to merge the BPL with the Maine Forest Service one of its top goals. The proposal reached the legislative oversight committee in March 2015, during the routine annual report on Maine's Public Lands. Its members were skeptical, all the more so because Denico, not Acting Director Morrison, was delivering the report. They were further exasperated by the recommendation, once again, of an allowable annual cut of 180,000 cords, which ignored the concerns they had already expressed about overharvesting. On top of that, the governor was back seeking approval to take the proceeds—this time, $5 million—to convert older home furnaces to more efficient heating systems, even though they had turned down a similar request the year before. In this "Groundhog Day" atmosphere, with "tensions occasionally flaring," the committee took up the governor's proposal.[517]

Whether or not he had been instructed not to attend the committee hearing—when asked, Denico said he didn't know—Tom Morrison concluded he could no longer remain at the agency where he had spent most of his career. He was clearly being forced out, but he was tired of trying to ameliorate the effects of the orders he received, especially harvest levels. He felt that if he couldn't "follow the leader, he should get out of the way." Governor LePage at once put his Forest Service chief in charge of the BPL, bypassing legislative and public input. Management on the Public Reserved Lands was now more like a paper company's than the "exemplary" standards of the past. Relations between the governor and the legislature went from bad to worse.

Faced with an unyielding Agriculture, Conservation and Forestry Committee, LePage announced that unless the transfer of $5 million from Public Lands to the Energy Office was approved, he would refuse to sell bonds, approved by Maine voters, to support the Land for Maine's Future program. (A technicality required the governor's signature for them to be sold.) At that, the committee voted unanimously to direct the BPL to stick with the annual allowable cut supported by Seymour and other professional foresters, 141,500 cords. And instead of endorsing the governor's reorganization plan, they attached legal language protecting the Bureau of Parks and Lands from interference by the Forest Service.

Undaunted, Governor LePage introduced a bill to authorize transfer of "revenues from the increased harvest of timber" in Bureau of Parks and Lands forests to Efficiency Maine "to assist rural Mainers with heating costs." In a letter, he reminded the committee that LMF bonds would not be released "until this timber harvest legislation is sent to my desk." In addition to resorting to hostage-taking and blackmail, the governor's plan "runs against the nearly 230-year history of Maine's public lands," declared an editorial in the *Bangor Daily News*.

Late in the state budget process, and by way of a compromise, the annual allowable cut was quietly increased to 160,000 cords. Wearing his Appropriations Committee hat, Representative John Martin admitted the number had no rationale for it. "We had to pick something. We picked 160." Otherwise, the governor's efforts came to nothing. The loss was subsumed in a fight LePage had picked with virtually the entire legislature when, earlier in the summer, he vetoed sixty-five bills in a fit of pique. Characteristically, LePage announced that he was done with the lawmakers. The lawmakers, editorialized the *Bangor Daily News*, should "return the favor" by standing firm on the public lands.

As well as increasing the allowable cut, the legislature ordered a timber inventory to establish if the new level was sustainable. It also set up a commission to consider the management policies of the public lands and to review once again how the revenue they generated should be spent. Its report to the Agriculture, Conservation and Forestry Committee was due by the end of the year. Members included legislators, stakeholder representatives, as well as Commissioner Whitcomb and the head of the BPL, Denico.

Three years of increased timber harvests had left the BPL in the best financial shape ever. When the Commission to Study the Public Reserved Lands Management Fund met in early September 2015, the big number was $8 million. The big question was how to spend it. Doug Denico argued it should be used to build bigger and better logging roads. Will Harris and Tom Morrison, the former directors, recommended putting it into maintaining and building new trails and meeting already identified recreation needs. The commission was soon deep in technical discussions ranging from scientific forestry to recreation to wildlife management. Little to no enthusiasm was left for expenditures on anything but public lands.

As expected, Attorney General Janet Mills sent a written opinion regarding the legal risks of raiding a constitutionally protected trust fund. A definitive answer would have to come from the Law Court, but based on the 1992 case, she considered that the governor's proposal "would likely meet great skepticism." Public Lands dollars spent on state parks (an idea that had been raised as well) would replace general fund monies, "effectively making trust money interchangeable with General Fund revenue, which is not permitted." However, a proposal to acquire new lands subject to the same management protocols as the Public Reserved Lands "would have a decent chance to pass constitutional muster."

The importance of the commission's deliberations was underscored in a letter drafted by Lloyd Irland and signed by five former conservation commissioners (including Anderson, Barringer, Meadows, Lovaglio, and McGowan). "It is not our habit," they began, "to look over the shoulders of our successors in office, or to offer unsolicited advice." However, the issues at stake "compel us to speak." Surplus revenues "must adhere to their long-term trust requirements," and the commission should be guided by the attorney general. Beside the legal question, they noted, the public lands had "only in recent times yielded revenue surpluses," and this should be spent on what the writers understood was an overall backlog of $55–60 million needed in capital improvements. Regarding "agency realignment," from their combined experience, they found "no virtue," nor any "administrative gains, cost savings, or public benefits" from giving responsibility for the public lands to the Forest Service. The annual allowable cut of 141,500 cords, they agreed, was appropriate and should be maintained until a new inventory could inform a future decision.

With recommendations for basic operations beginning to coalesce, the question remained how the bureau might spend surplus revenues, now and in the future. Getting the word out about what the Public Reserved Lands offered had to be a priority. The general public still had little idea what or where they were. This was amplified by several people's testimony that, though they frequently hiked on the public lands, they rarely saw anything to indicate they were walking on "their" land. Suggestions for getting the word out ran the gamut from basic signage to forestry demonstrations to training qualified loggers.

The commission released its report and recommendations in December 2015. Mindful of the attorney general's warning, money for Efficiency Maine was not among them. The BPL should maintain a cash operating account of $2.5 million a year against unexpected costs. A forest inventory should be undertaken the next year and every five years thereafter. BPL foresters should make decisions on harvest levels, subject to ACF committee oversight.

"There was an awful lot of discussion about the remaining recommendations, including a list of uses for BPL surplus funds," wrote George Smith in his column in the *Bangor Daily News*.[518] Smith, the former head of the Sportsman's Alliance of Maine, had attended all four of the commission's meetings, keeping a special eye on how the discussion affected wildlife and recreation issues. [519] The list included buying land adjacent to existing public lands, focusing on special wildlife habitat such as deer yards, and increasing public access including ADA requirements. Perhaps the item that raised the most eyebrows was taking $50,000 to train loggers in high schools. George Smith, for one, didn't like it. "It may be legal, but it is not right," he wrote. In the end, the commission voted unanimously to accept the report. One member, Forest Service director Denico, abstained. According to Smith, he left the room just before the vote.

"We doubt the commission's work will persuade LePage to drop his proposal to use [Public Lot] logging revenues for heating systems, but the commission's work should end that debate once and for all," declared the *Bangor Daily News* editorial board. Its fatalism was well placed. Not surprisingly, since the commission was essentially a response to his designs on the Public Lands Trust, Governor LePage attacked the report, and continued to attack the legislative bill that would implement its findings. The legislature passed LD 1629, and the governor promptly vetoed it. He blasted the commission in his habitual hyperbolic terms. Giving the legislature oversight of the public lands was "a complete overreach," wrote LePage. "The Commission's distrust of the State's forestry professionals is insulting and, apparently, knows no bounds." Unfortunately, the vote to override his veto fell nine votes short.

Meanwhile, a remote Public Lot on the eastern edge of Baxter Park—a "sliver" in his words—had caught Doug Denico's attention. In an earlier management plan, the BPL had identified the twenty-five-hundred-acre East Turner Mountain Public Lot as a site where the dominant use should be recreation, and special precautions would be required if it were ever logged.[520] It was said to be a "unique forest type" with 150-year-old sugar maples.[521] Denico, however, opined that there was "nothing unique" about it, and he planned to harvest a third of the timber there in the summer. Perhaps more significantly, the lot was largely surrounded by an eighty-seven-thousand-acre parcel put together by Roxanne Quimby, the cofounder of a personal care products company, Burt's Bees. Quimby's intention was to donate it to the National Park Service, and this considerable conservation achievement, fifteen turbulent years in the making, was nearing fruition, much to Governor LePage's outrage. It was still winter when he announced he was rebuilding a logging road on an old legal right-of-way across Quimby's land to reach the "sliver." The *Portland Press Herald* put two and two together: "Governor steps up land fight" blared the front-page headline; "LePage wants road to slice through federal park idea."[522] When President Barack Obama created the Katahdin Woods and Waters National Monument in August that year, there was a logging road running through it.

Roadwork included installing a portable bridge over Katahdin Stream. So eager was the Forest Service to push the road through to East Turner Mountain, however, a helicopter was pressed into service to get the all-terrain vehicles across, rather than wait for the bridge to be built. An undivided 20 percent of the lot was owned by veteran wilderness advocate Charles Fitzgerald.[523] Before operations could begin, Fitzgerald's property would have to be divided from the state's. In the meantime, he was seeking an injunction on the grounds that logging would irreparably degrade the Wassataquoik Stream, "one of the cleanest and most pristine watersheds in Maine." The lot was not cut that summer, nor had it been harvested when Governor LePage left office. The logging road with two branches to access the East Turner Mountain Public Lot ended at its boundary.

The next year, Sen. Tom Saviello, who had chaired the commission, presented the bill to implement its recommendations again. Again Governor LePage vetoed it. The Environmental Priorities Coalition took up the cudgels, and this time the legislature succeeded in overriding the governor's veto—however, not before the BPL's $3 million surplus had all gone for roads and logging contractors. In 2016, the bureau had built fifty-four miles of logging roads. "That's all about harvesting, guys," said Senator Saviello. He was visibly frustrated.

The new law gave the public the tools and the opportunity to help shape policy on Maine's Public Reserved Lands for the foreseeable future. It mandated a forest inventory every five years and detailed reports on growth and harvest levels to assure public accountability. The land would get better trails and bridges, and improved access, especially for persons with disabilities. Clear signage would at last let hikers, hunters, canoers, campers, and fishermen know where they were and that this beautiful lake, that mountain, the streams here and there, and the forest canopy over all would belong to them forever.

But it would have to wait for a new administration. All $5.5 million that was expected to be generated from harvesting on the Public Reserved Lands in 2018 (the last year of the LePage administration) was "already tagged . . . right down to the last penny," wrote Parrish, $2 million alone being spent on roads.[524]

In January, 2019, Democrat Janet Mills succeeded Paul LePage, becoming Maine's first female governor. By late spring, the BPL had an ecologist, Andrew Cutko, as its new director. Having worked previously for the state (the Maine Natural Areas Program) and The Nature Conservancy, he brought a depth of knowledge about Maine's Public Reserved Lands that was badly needed after the eight-year winter of discontent that was the LePage-Denico administration.

Five months after he became BPL director, Cutko spoke of both short- and long-term goals. Early on, Governor Mills had declared climate change a priority for her administration and set ambitious benchmarks for reducing the state's greenhouse gas emissions.[525] With nearly 90 percent of Maine covered by forest, its capacity to remove carbon from the atmosphere would be a key to reaching the governor's carbon neutral goals. The conservative management of the Public Reserved Lands—where growth typically exceeded harvest—offered a particular opportunity to demonstrate the power of well-managed forestland to sequester carbon.

The Public Reserved Lands, now roughly 625,000 acres, also had a role in protecting flora and fauna from extirpation in the face of climate-induced habitat change. Habitat corridors between BPL Units would allow wildlife to migrate to more favorable terrain as temperatures rise. Cutko said that he and his staff have already been in discussion with other groups about the importance of "habitat connectivity" from south to north. With relatively few acres left in common undivided ownership, trading options may be limited, and success may require acquiring new parcels of land.

In the meantime, the Bureau's priority remained "to get more people out recreating." The time is ripe, Cutko said, with so much renewed interest in hiking, canoeing, hunting and fishing, and other outdoor pursuits. He cited a recent study from the U.S. Bureau of Economic Analysis that placed Maine third, out of the fifty states, in the per capita contribution of outdoor recreation to the economy, which was nearly 5 percent.[526] A visit to the Public Reserved Lands, he said, can promote mental and physical health, "exercise together with the appreciation of Maine's natural beauty."

But it's a balancing act, he admitted. Tumbledown Mountain, a relatively new Unit, is in danger of being "loved to death." Sometimes as many as a hundred and fifty to two hundred hikers are on its trails in a day. Such pressure can degrade both the habitat—in this case, a sensitive subalpine ecosystem—and the experiences of visitors.

The BPL will always be challenged and distracted by flashes-in-the-pan. Earlier in 2019, an issue came before the state legislature for the third time since 2013. Conservationists had consistently opposed efforts by a sporting camp in the middle of the Eagle Lake Public Reserved Land to purchase 12.86 acres. Such privatization of the public's land would set a dangerous precedent considering nine other sporting camps had leases on Public Reserved Land. It would also create an in-holding, contrary to BPL policy. Despite these concerns, the Resolve passed, but only after an amendment requiring the deed to stipulate that, whoever the owners, the sporting camp "will never ask for any changes to the deed and . . . neither ask for nor accept any further grants of land from the State." The amendment ended with a stentorian warning: "A violation of this covenant results in the immediate reversion of the parcel to the State."

In another case, two public lots north of the Forks in Somerset County, leased to Central Maine Power by a previous director, had become part of the controversial New England Clean Energy Connect (CMP). CMP plans to build a 145-mile electric transmission line from the Canadian border across western Maine would benefit Massachusetts.[527] Questions were raised as to whether a lease or easement that does not directly benefit Maine people is consistent with the status of the lands as a public trust; and if the lease could be conveyed without a two-thirds vote of the Maine Legislature. From another perspective, legislators were revisiting the sum that CMP originally paid for its lease.

Nonetheless, as this book went to press, the forecast for Maine's Public Reserved Lands was sunny. Director Cutko is well-equipped to once again take up the banner of managing these natural treasures as they are supposed to be managed: for wildlife, for Maine people, and for a sustainable harvest of wood.

Afterword

The Law Court officially returned the Public Reserved Lands to the State of Maine nearly forty years ago. With the passage of time, much of the bitterness around the struggle has turned to acceptance, even a feeling of satisfaction. Jerry Amero, the paper companies' attorney, overcame the frustrations he felt in the immediate aftermath of the ruling. As part of the ensuing process of consolidation, Amero watched both sides come together on "settlements that produced broad public benefits to the state." In the end, he told me, "I view it as a successful case, in spite of the loss."

"Take away all the resentment and what-not, I think the result has been both good for the land owners and for the state," admits Brad Wellman, long retired as president of Pingree Associates. "Given the irrationality of the thought that any of these towns would be settled, putting blocks of land together for the benefit of 'the state' was probably a pretty good idea. So it's not all bad."

Despite qualms about the legal interpretation of the ancient deeds, Roger Milliken, still president of Baskahegan Company, thinks it ended up "a great thing for the State of Maine." He ticked off some of the highlights: consolidation of the Public Lots, "fabulous and very well done"; the dominant-use policy, "farsighted and an example of Maine leading"; ecological reserves, "never would have happened otherwise." With benefit of hindsight, most of the landowners I talked to agree with Wellman's view that this "strange, archaic piece of legality" was going to surface eventually, making "some sort of arrangement that would consolidate blocks of land in state ownership" inevitable.

For it to happen the way it did, however, just the right elements had to be, if not aligned, in active play, starting with the vision and perseverance against the odds of half a dozen public officials, spurred on by a handful of citizen activists, dedicated journalists, courageous lawmakers, and several governors of Maine. "It happened," says Marty Wilk, the state's attorney and chief negotiator, "thanks to some people who were courageous, smart as can be, and very dedicated. One weak link would have blown it, but there was no weak link." Adds Dick Barringer, "We all believed in the public interest and in government as an instrument of the public good."

The presence of highly motivated state officials like Lee Schepps, Barringer, and Wilk, while surely not unique in the annals of Maine government, provided a rare degree of imagination. A succession of commissioners and bureau directors—Dick Anderson, Lloyd Irland, Rob Gardiner—and their staff were informed by a profound knowledge of the land. They made the most of the chance to create innovative policies to protect it. Governor Joseph Brennan's willingness to back them with his seal of approval, which clinched the final deal, was unprecedented.

On the other side of the controversy, Great Northern's Robert Hellendale matched them in foresight, to which he added considerable moral courage. Breaking with his fellow CEOs in Maine's forest products industry, combined with his sagacity in convincing his board members at corporate headquarters, justify his position as "an unsung hero," in Barringer's opinion. Similarly, Brad Wellman had to grasp the nettle both with his landowner cohorts and with fellow members of the Pingree family. He deserves the "gold star" that he joked about putting on his own forehead.

Steps along the road—some of them, ironically, taken by the landowners and paper companies—helped the process along. If one of them had been different, the process might have stalled. By suppressing the Schepps report, Attorney General James Erwin confirmed that the Public Lots were news: what was he hiding? Had he not drawn attention to it in that way, where would have been the story? Had his successor been more of Erwin's political stripe, the story might well have petered out. Instead, at a time of national questioning and suspicion of "the man" (stirred up by the Vietnam war, Watergate, and the struggle for civil rights, among other things), Jon Lund's decision to release Schepps's report as soon as he became attorney general put positive and negative in stark contrast.

Had the landowners not filed suit, the issue might have died in one or another legislative session. Instead, by taking their case to court, the landowners gave the state the opportunity to countersue and narrow the case to just two issues: whether the cutting rights bought by the landowners included future growth or were limited to timber standing at the time; and whether the term "timber," in the context of the nineteenth century, limited the rights to certain species of tree.

The zeitgeist of the 1970s, particularly, was more favorable to a positive outcome for the state than at any time before, and arguably for decades afterwards. Looking back, Bob Cummings told me, "1972 was the ideal time to have broken this story. Had I written it in 1963 [the year Austin Wilkins's report came out], nobody would have paid any attention. [But] with Earth Day just two years earlier, there was a flurry of interest in land conservation. Had I written it in 1983, the legislature would have voted to give it to the paper companies. It was just this brief moment."

This was the time of the "back to the land" movement, and a new land-use ethic was being born. As environmental concern caught fire nationally, "Maine was punching way above its weight" at the regulatory level, says Lee Schepps. He lists the cutting-edge laws that the Environmental Protection Division of the attorney general's office had put on the books, rules protecting shorelands, streams, and great ponds, LURC, the site-location law.

Politics, too, were different. The same "happy confluence of events and good leadership," to which Republican Harrison Richardson attributed Maine's environmental progress in those early years, hovered over his and Democratic governor Kenneth Curtis's early efforts to respond to Cummings's exposé. Although Curtis always had a Republican legislature to deal with, there was a vibrant centrist group committed to environmental protection that spanned "across the aisle." In general, these people believed that government could make a positive difference in Mainers' lives.

The character of Maine and Mainers surely played a role. Yankee tenacity and empathy for the underdog has been a part of the history of settlement of the state, going back to the days of squatters versus great proprietors. Like the latter, the paper companies and large landowners appeared to be powerful, smug, and arrogant—and they had always had their way. The Public Lots case was the first time they lost.

Perhaps as important as generalities about character, the small size of Maine's population has made lawmakers and government officials unusually accessible to the people. In the well-used phrase, "Everyone knows everyone." By contrast, as Schepps pointed out about his home state of Texas, "Things don't happen in Austin if you piss off the oil and gas men."

Are there lessons here for future conservation? Looked at narrowly, it was an unusual situation and a product of its time, unlikely ever to be exactly replicated. The windfall of four hundred thousand acres of wildland that the state had forgotten it owned was as exceptional as it was totally unexpected. The reclamation of the Public Lots was, more than anything else, a legal issue that started the moment in 1972 when Attorney General Erwin told Schepps to study them. Legislative leadership made forays into the controversy, and the executive branch concluded the matter by backing the negotiations; but for various reasons, the nongovernmental conservation organizations—to become such powerful players in future decades—were not initially involved.

At various times during the 1970s and early 1980s, Barringer and Anderson had successfully fended off calls for citizen oversight, pointing out that negotiations tended to run aground "when you don't know if what you say will appear in the papers the next day." By the end of the decade, they would probably not have been successful. Nor would it have been possible for officials like them or Schepps, Wilk, or Annee Tara to take on the kinds of decisions that they were entrusted to make.

In the State House, conservation had ceased to be a bipartisan issue, with Republicans starting to routinely oppose conservation measures. The advent of advocacy organizations like Maine Audubon and the Natural Resources Council of Maine meant that the public Bob Cummings so often tried to rouse was increasingly engaged and wanting to have its say. However, groups wanting to conserve the same land often had different, even conflicting, ideas about how to do it. In short, the times soon became more complicated.

A hint of exactly how differing conservation agendas could muddy the waters emerged in the deep contention over adding Katahdin Lake to Baxter State Park. Although that campaign was ultimately successful, another effort undertaken by the Department of Conservation at about the same time (2006) was not so lucky. The planners of the Maine Backcountry Project never aimed at anything like the scope or complexity of reclaiming the Public Lots; but the project involved passionate individuals drawing circles on maps of Maine's wild places, among other similarities. The department wanted to identify "long distance, human-powered recreational opportunities" that could be marketed as wilderness destinations for eco-tourism and designated with a new land use: backcountry areas. The people "in the room where it happened," at least initially, all represented environmental or conservation groups.[525] When "traditional" users of the wildlands—hunters and snowmobilers, especially—were invited to participate, a storm of protest ensued, and the project had to be mothballed.

But there is a more positive lesson to be learned. With a broader perspective, the Public Reserved Lands story illustrates ways in which change can be brought about when the right people get together to take advantage of a situation and push the envelope without tearing it. Great things will continue to happen when organizations rally around a common cause and take the time to listen to each other. And, it turns out, surprise opportunities—like what to do with four hundred thousand reclaimed acres of public land—continue to come along.

At the very end of the twentieth century, the state was jolted by another surprise involving huge tracts of land. Even experts such as forest economist Lloyd Irland were caught off guard when, after almost exactly a century of dominating Maine's rural landholdings landscape and economy, the paper companies abruptly started cashing out. In the last twenty years, according to the Natural Resources Council of Maine, 8,955,407 acres of Maine forestland have been bought and sold, amounting to 40 percent of the state. That is about a million acres *more* than the public domain the State of Maine inherited from Massachusetts in 1820.

In just four years, the giants that had launched the pulp and paper industry sold off their lands in Maine. In 1998, Great Northern, bought by Bowater, Inc. in 1991, put most of its two million acres on the market. The same year, International Paper—Hugh Chisholm's pioneering, vertically integrated company—sold 185,000 acres, following it up the next year with the sale of another 245,000 acres, including ten miles nearby the Allagash River. In 2004, IP announced the sale of all its million-plus acres in Maine. So tumultuous a change—selling off—after a century of stability was unsettling enough. The makeup of the buyers compounded it: their goals represented an equally unforeseen shift away from traditional forestry.

"Several landowner types have emerged or expanded in the last 10 years," wrote Irland in 2005.[526] This included financial investors, timber barons, and private "kingdom" buyers. Irland compared ownership by the forestry industry and by financial investors (largely timber investment management organizations and real estate investment trusts) in 1994 and 2005. In 1994, forest products companies owned 60 percent of the large tracts of timberland; the financial investors, 3 percent. In 2005, the industry was down to 15.5 percent (mostly in a single ownership), while the investors were up to 33 percent. Irland noted that, whereas forest products companies conceded that "forest certification was necessary to maintain a social license to cut wood," the new types of owner "are less inclined to participate in a social dialogue on sustainable forestry, such as forest certification." Increasing sales for private "kingdoms" and large-scale developments—exemplified by Plum Creek's proposal for a couple of high-end resorts and a thousand house lots that could affect four hundred thousand acres of remote wildland around Moosehead Lake—reawakened fears of sprawl and fragmentation coming to the North Woods.

Irland completed his list of flourishing landowner types with nonprofit conservation organizations. Hidden in the figure of nearly nine million acres changing hands were some astonishingly creative conservation deals. A very partial list of these successes, which combined trades, purchases, and easements and involved governmental, nongovernmental, and private corporations, includes: in 1998, The Nature Conservancy's purchase from

International Paper of 185,000 acres along the remote St. John River; in 2002,
The Nature Conservancy's partnership with Great Northern to place a conservation easement on 200,000 acres of forest around Mount Katahdin; in 2003,
the Appalachian Mountain Club's purchase of almost 37,000 acres from IP in
the heart of the Hundred Mile Wilderness; the West Branch Project in 2004,
forever keeping 329,000 acres out of development; and Roxanne Quimby's
several purchases that culminated in the creation of the 87,500-acre Katahdin
Woods and Waters National Monument east of Baxter State Park in 2016.
As a result, between 1990 and 2019, the amount of Maine that has been
conserved and protected went from 5 percent to nearly 20 percent, or almost
four million acres.

It is no exaggeration to say that all these conservation successes stood on
the shoulders of the Public Reserved Lands consolidation. The appearance on
BPL maps of large green blocks of land did much to inspire the huge interest
in land conservation that has flourished ever since. Dick Barringer considers
that the Land for Maine's Future was an immediate and direct result. "The
settlement and the long process that led up to [the Public Lot] consolidation
made clear the compelling need for what might be termed 'strategic' land
conservation in Maine," he says.

The Bureau of Parks and Lands itself has played a specific and crucial role
in many land deals. Agreements involving multiple partners often take years
to complete, and BPL staff have spent significant time and energy working
with conservation groups, landowners, the federal government, and Maine's
congressional delegation to make them happen. The BPL has "really rocked
and rolled," as Karin Tilberg (former deputy commissioner of conservation
and now head of the Forest Society of Maine) put it in a recent email; the
staff helped conserve hundreds of thousands of acres of land over the course
of a decade.

Still the most recent experience of eight years of radically conservative
government under Governor Paul LePage has been a timely warning. For
years, directors of the Bureau of Parks and Lands (and of Public Lands,
before them) strove mightily to forestall legislative interference; but it took
a legislative oversight committee to protect the results of three decades of
multiple-use "care and custody" when they were more recently put at risk by
the BPL's own department head. As an agency of government, the bureau
provides an operating structure, but the public lands require constant public
vigilance to ensure its officials are accountable as they fulfill their mission.

This controversy over heavier cutting on the Public Reserved Lands did
have one substantial benefit: it brought them back into the public eye. Far better than depending on the silver lining of a storm's publicity, though, would
be to encourage and enable Maine people to take advantage of these special

places. The recommendations of the 2015 Commission to Study the Public Reserved Lands Management Fund should help the BPL to educate the public about its stake in their management and use.

Part of that education is to remember where they came from. "The Public Reserved Lands lawsuit and land trades were, to a large extent, the creation of 'something' out of 'nothing,'" wrote Lee Schepps recently. The origin of the lots themselves goes back two hundred years and more and is inseparable from the story of the settlement of Maine. Considering the size of the consolidated Public Lots—more than twice as much as Percival Baxter's celebrated gift—it is surprising how uncelebrated they are today. "Ironically, their history remains relatively unknown to the public at large, as do the Public Lots themselves," says Marty Wilk. Other conservation efforts, like some of those mentioned above, have been far more visible.

This book has been undertaken to fill the "information gap" in the hope that the Bureau of Parks and Lands will be able to devote its future energies to the mission rather than being forced to fight *for* its existence. There is more to Maine's Public Reserved Lands than bureaucratic wrangling. They are there to be discovered, visited, and loved.

Acknowledgments

In 2015, after several peaceful decades, Maine's Public Reserved Lands were once again in the news. To widespread dismay—and despite warnings from attorneys general over the years that it would be unconstitutional—Governor Paul LePage announced that he intended to spend revenues earned by these public treasures on programs entirely unrelated to them. That fall, two former state officials, Richard Anderson and Richard Barringer, were discussing the situation over dinner. Both men had been deeply involved in restoring the Public Reserved Lands to full state control and consolidating them into spectacular landholdings to benefit the people of Maine. Most of those people, the two men agreed, had no idea of the strange and wonderful story of how they came to be. Richard Anderson called me the next day to urge me to write a book about it.

I started work on New Year's Day, 2016. My first call was to Bob Cummings, the reporter whose articles in the *Maine Sunday Telegram* first drew public attention to Maine's Public Lots. I discovered that he was in the hospital, but his daughter Brenda passed on my message. He very much wants to speak to you about it, she told me. In fact, she said, he told her the whole saga of the Public Lots right then and there. Sadly, Bob's time ran out before we could talk.

Fortunately, I had interviewed Bob some ten years earlier for a book on land conservation in New England, for which I wrote the chapter on Maine.[527] By far the largest chunk of our conversation had been about how he came to take up the cause of the Public Lots. For the same book, I interviewed two other conservation leaders, both of whom were an important part of the Public Lots story but had passed before I started writing *Up for Grabs*. As majority leader in the State Senate, Harrison Richardson led the charge to reclaim the Public Lots in the legislature. As a legislator and as an aide to Governor Kenneth Curtis, Neil Rolde had significant influence on the issue. Neil also gave me helpful advice and encouragement as I began to outline this book.

As it turned out, not many representatives of the large landowners and paper companies were available for interviews. I am all the more grateful for the frank and helpful spirit of the conversations I had with Bradford Wellman, Timothy Ingraham, and Sarah Medina of Pingree Associates and Seven Islands Land Company; David Carlisle of Prentiss & Carlisle; Roger Milliken of Baskahegan Company; and Richmond Cushing of the Webber family. Gerald Amero, who represented them in court, was a fount of information on the case. One company executive only refused to speak to me about the Public Lots.

I received tremendous cooperation and inspiration from many dedicated men and women whose service in Maine government included all stages of the Public Lots settlement. Governors Kenneth Curtis and Joseph Brennan were most generous with their time. A special thank you goes to Lee Schepps: in the same way his exhaustive legal analysis as assistant attorney general set the course for the eventual return of the Public Lots, his phenomenal memory and support set me on a productive course from the start. Together, he and Martin Wilk, the assistant attorney general who saw the case through to the final court decision, kept me straight with arcane legal doctrines and responded to my requests for this or that detail promptly and patiently. Marty was also chief negotiator during the settlement; his tales together with those of Assistant AG Paul Stern gave me a lively sense of the tenor of the times. Herb Hartman, Nancy Ross, and David Flanagan all provided colorful memories of early days at the fledgling Bureau of Public Lands (BPL). I could never have grasped the complexities of the bureau's development without the insights of its directors, starting with Richard Barringer and Lee Schepps, and going on to Lloyd Irland, Rob Gardiner, Ed Meadows, Tom Morrison, and Tom Desjardin. As conservation commissioners, Richard Barringer, Ed Meadows, and Richard Anderson and his deputy commissioner Annee Tara helped me put the Public Reserved Lands into the wider picture of the goals of Maine's Department of Conservation during the 1970s and 1980s. Jon Lund, the attorney general who released the Schepps report to the public, gave me the benefit of his long advocacy for Maine's Public Lands. Given his unique tenure in the Maine legislature, John Martin's reflections were invaluable.

On whichever side of the controversy they were, all these public lands veterans were extraordinarily generous with both time and memory. I am deeply grateful to all of them and only hope that I have told their stories vividly and accurately. Nor do I forget the Fourth Estate: rounding out the story begun by Bob Cummings, Lucy Martin added the perspective of *The Maine Times*; and

Christine Parrish shared an interesting slant on the most recent vicissitudes of the BPL.

Over the three years of research and writing, Richard Anderson was a never-flagging source of assistance, knowledge, and enthusiasm. Early on, he and I went to see Steve Bromage, executive director of the Maine Historical Society, to plumb his interest in the book. Steve, realizing it would make a fine bicentennial book for the Historical Society, put me together with Jamie Rice, director of library services, whose help was indispensable in multiple aspects of preparing the book for publication, from managing contracts and finances to using the MHS's vast resources to track down historical maps and images. Many thanks go to all at MHS. It has been a great partnership.

One of the great pleasures of my research was the extraordinary helpfulness and interest of the men and women who keep tabs on over two hundred years of resources concerning the State of Maine. The staff of the Law and Legislative Reference Library never failed to find a document I requested. Thank you to all the reference librarians, especially Alex Burnett, Sue Wright, Jessica Lundgren, Elaine Apostola, and Ryan Jones. You made my job so much easier. The same is true of the folks at the Maine State Archives. Thanks especially to State Archivist David Cheever, Helen Tutwiler (archivist I) and Heather Moran (archivist II), who humped big cardboard boxes onto my table. And a special acknowledgment to Abraham Schechter, the Portland Public Library's archivist and guardian of the Portland Room, for unfailing knowledge of where to find what.

I was fortunate to be guided to cartographer Margot Carpenter, who drew the maps that elucidate a few historical events. Cindy Bastey from the Department of Agriculture Conservation and Forestry searched the BPL archives for the color photographs of some of the gems of the public lands that appear in the book. And at the eleventh hour, she and ACF colleagues Kathy Eastman and Gayle Koyanagi did what no one else had succeeded in doing over the previous three years: locate the book of maps that Governor Brennan handed out to the large landowners at the meeting at the Blaine House, an account of which serves as the prologue to this book. Not just this author, but everyone who has had any involvement with this curious tale owes Cindy, Kathy, and Gayle a huge debt of gratitude.

There is a very special talent in delivering editorial and historical advice. I was lucky to have three wonderfully complementary readers: Richard Anderson, who read each chapter as it came off the computer, keeping my spirits up with his encouragement and attention to detail; Richard Barringer, who read the whole book with great care and delivered excellent suggestions, especially on the political and contemporary questions; and Richard Judd, whose expert judgment is especially meaningful, for helping me clarify important historical events. To all three Richards, I am deeply grateful for the time and commitment to reading my manuscript. It goes without saying that their attempts to save me from inaccuracy could only be as good as my understanding. Any mistakes are entirely mine.

I can't begin to enumerate all the people with whom, over the last three years, I have discussed the history of the Public Reserved Lands, adding to my understanding of a very complicated and nuanced matter. I benefited hugely from the recollections, at periodic gatherings over beer or oysters, of some of those who helped reclaim the Public Lots, among them Lloyd Irland and Elizabeth Swain. Particularly, I thank Karin Tilberg, whose love for the Maine woods is equaled only by her knowledge of them; Earl Raymond, who is as able to apply his surveying skills to the past as to the mountain in front of him; Horace "Hoddy" Hildreth, who has done as much as anyone in shaping Maine's environmental rules; and Rosamund Zander, who loves trees and anything that encourages them.

Finally, I thank the person who read every chapter in its every permutation, whose editorial word might as well be the Eleventh Commandment, my wife, Amy MacDonald, to whom this book is dedicated.

Notes

PROLOGUE: THIS LAND IS OUR LAND

1. Townships would later be laid out in squares, generally six miles by six miles, on a grid. A township was between 23,000 and 24,000 acres, of which, at first, 1,280 acres were reserved for future public use, the "Public Reserved Lands."

CHAPTER 1: "EXHAUSTLESS MERCHANDIZE"

2. William D. Williamson, *The History of the State of Maine, from its First Discovery A.D. 1602, to the Separation, A.D. 1820, Inclusive*, Vol. 2, 338.

3. Michael Dekker, *French and Indian Wars in Maine*, 130.

4. Williamson, op. cit., 336.

5. *Boston Evening Post*, June 4, 1759.

6. Federal Writers' Project, *Maine: A Guide Down East*, 36.

7. Names, respectively, after William Duke of Cumberland, the "butcher" of Culloden, and the town in England where Governor Thomas Pownall, the most pro-colonist governor, was born.

8. Colin Woodard, *The Lobster Coast: Rebels, Rusticators & the Struggle for a Forgotten Frontier*, 45.

9. Sir Francis Bernard succeeded Samuel Waldo's friend, Governor Thomas Pownall, in 1760.

10. The recognition of Bernard's distinguished service was not quite what it seemed. The Massachusetts House of Representatives made the grant to the unpopular governor to "occupy a part of his time and . . . divert his interest from the seizure of cargoes and from other customs activities." Though Bernard made annual visits to his land, his plans were never realized. John R. Galvin, *Three Men of Boston*, Thomas Y. Crowell Co. 1976, p. 42.

11. Mrs. Seth Thornton, *Traditions and Records of Southwest Harbor and Somes-ville, Mount Desert Island, Maine,* 16.

12. Edgar E. Ring, *Seventh Report of the Forest Commissioner, State of Maine 1908.*

13. Moses Greenleaf, *Survey of the State of Maine,* 399.

14. Paul Wallace Gates, *History of Public Land Law Development,* 44.

15. Continued by the New England states, these practices were also largely adopted by Thomas Jefferson's committee for the settlement of the new nation's western lands in the Land Ordinance of 1785.

16. **Resolve** *Appointing a committee to examine into all trespasses and illegal entries on the unappropriated lands belonging to this commonwealth, and vesting them with certain powers.* May 1, 1781.

17. **Report** *Of the committee appointed by a resolve of the 28th of October last, to examine into the state of the unappropriated lands in the county of Lincoln.* March 22, 1784.

18. **Resolve** *Giving directions to the committee appointed by a resolve of May 1, 1781, to examine into all trespasses and illegal entries on the unappropriated lands belonging to this commonwealth.* July 11, 1783.

19. **Resolve** *Relative to the unappropriated lands within the three eastern counties, directing the committee appointed May 1, 1781, in this case, and choosing a committee to repair to the county of Lincoln to execute certain business.* October 28, 1783.

20. Roger Milliken Jr., *Forest for the Trees: A History of the Baskahegan Company,* 18.

21. Another factor was the lead plate buried by Governor Pownall on the same day and at the same place that Samuel Waldo died. During the peace negotiations that ended the Revolutionary War, it was agreed that the international boundary would be the eastern border of Massachusetts. The British claimed this was the Penobscot, but citing Pownall's certificate of possession, John Adams argued that since the plate had been buried on the river's eastern bank, the province of Massachusetts Bay had extended to the St. Croix River.

22. Rufus Putnam had had a successful career as an officer in the Revolutionary War. At one point, he proposed what would have been the Army Corps of Engineers. When his proposal was turned down, he resigned.

23. **Resolve** *Directing commissioners for sale of Eastern Lands, and the secretary, to furnish documents, &c. to the agent for managing the claims to boundary between the United States and province of New-Brunswick, &c.* June 18, 1796.

24. "The River herein after particularly described and mentioned to be the River truly intended under the name of The River Saint Croix in the said Treaty of Peace and forming a part of the Boundary therein described, . . . And the course of the said River up from it's said Mouth is northerly to a point of Land called The Devil's-Head, then turning the said point is westerly to where it divides into two Streams the one coming from the westward, and the other coming from the northward, having the Indian name of Chiputnaticook or Chibnitcook, as the same may be variously spelt, then up the said Stream so coming from the northward to it's source." *Declaration of the Commissioners under Article 5 of the Jay Treaty, signed at Providence.* October 25, 1798.

25. The American agent, James Sullivan (1744–1808), would become the first Democratic-Republican governor of the Commonwealth of Massachusetts, as well as the first from Maine. The General Court's foresight in surveying the Commonwealth's eastern boundary some ten years earlier proved to be most fortunate.

26. *Resolve Pointing out a mode to the committee appointed the 28th of October, 1783, for doing the business of their commission, relative to the unappropriated lands in the county of Lincoln, and appointing Rufus Putnam, Esq. surveyor for the purposes mentioned.* November 5, 1784.

27. In 1629, a mere eight years after landing at Plymouth Rock, William Bradford had petitioned the King's Council for more land and had been granted one and a half million acres, "forasmuch as they (the Pilgrims) had no convenient Place either of Trading or Fishing within their own Precincts, whereby after so long Travel and great pains, so hopefull a Plantation might subsist." The Kennebec Claim or Plymouth Patent was for "all of that part of New England in America which lieth within or between and extendeth itself between the utmost limits of Cobbisecontee which adjoineth to the river Kennebec, towards the western ocean and a place called the Falls at Neguamkike in America aforesaid and the space of fifteen miles each side of the river commonly called the Kennebec that lies within its limits." "A Famous Law Suit 1765-1766.—Relating to Bath," *The Maine Historical Magazine,* Vol IX, Bangor, ME, 1894.

28. "Eastern Lands Papers, Records, 1770–1860."

29. Public lotteries were a standard way to raise money for the kind of projects that might today be supported by a bond: highway repair, bridges, even endowments for institutions.

30. *An Act to bring into the public Treasury the Sum of one Hundred and Sixty-three Thousand, and two Hundred Pounds, in public Securities by a Sale of a Part of the Eastern Lands; and to establish a Lottery for that Purpose.* November 14, 1786.

31. *"one lot or prize of a township, two prizes of half a township each; four prizes of a quarter of a township each; six prizes of three miles by two miles each; twenty prizes of two miles by two miles each; forty prizes of three miles by one mile each; one hundred and twenty prizes of two miles by one mile each; four hundred prizes of one mile square each; seven hundred and sixty-one prizes of one mile by half a mile each; and thirteen hundred and sixty-six prizes of half a mile square each; reserving nevertheless, as is in this act before-mentioned; making in the whole, two thousand seven hundred and twenty lots or prizes."*

32. *Resolve On the subject of unappropriated lands in the counties of Cumberland and Lincoln.* March 26, 1788.

33. Amasa Loring, *History of Piscataquis County, Maine: From its Earliest Settlement to 1880,* 28.

34. William Lithgow (c. 1715–1798).

35. In August 1786, Daniel Shays led an armed insurrection of farmers and disgruntled veterans, which was finally put down in June the following year.

36. This was publicized through advertisements in "Adams and Nourse's Independent Chronicle, and in the Cumberland Gazette." As a Boston newspaper, the *Independent Chronicle* went back to 1776. It was bought in 1784 by Adams & Nourse,

which became the General Court's printing house that year. The *Cumberland Gazette*, printed in Falmouth/Portland, Maine from 1786–1791, was Maine's first newspaper.

37. Ibid. *Resolve* March 26, 1788.

38. Lloyd Irland, *The Northeast's Changing Forest*, 27.

39. Gates, *History of Public Land Law Development*, 45.

40. *Resolve Directing the committee for examining into the state of unappropriated lands in the county of Lincoln, &c. and vesting them with certain powers, &c.* July 9, 1784.

41. *Resolve For granting lands to certain soldiers, with directions to the secretary to publish this resolve in the several newspapers within this commonwealth.* March 5, 1801.

42. By the time the General Court started receiving claims for these lots, Rufus Putnam was long gone to the Ohio territory. However, the committee's surveyor was probably partly responsible. As an officer in the Continental Army, Putnam had helped draft a petition to General Washington suggesting that soldiers whose pay was in arrears be compensated with bounty land grants instead. It was not a new idea; George III had offered unsettled land to veterans of the French and Indian wars.

43. Battle of Derne in Tripoli, April–May 1805.

44. *Resolve On the petition of Messrs. Enoch Ilsley, Nathaniel Deering, Samuel Freeman and Thomas Sanford.* March 9, 1791.

45. Frederick S. Allis Jr., ed. *William Bingham's Maine Lands 1792–1820*, Vol. 1, 209.

46. *Resolve On the petition of Monsieur and Madam De Gregoire, granting them the island of Mount Desert, and other lands, upon certain conditions therein mentioned.* July 6, 1787.

47. Two years later, almost to the day, the subjects of his most Christian majesty (Louis XVI, the great-great-great grandson of *le Roi-Soleil*) would start their own revolution that would result in his execution.

48. *Resolve On the petition of Martin Brimmer and others, a committee of the Agricultural Society, granting them a township of land, under certain restrictions, and the Secretary authorised to make and execute a good deed thereof.* March 1, 1805.

49. *Resolve Confirming certain lands to the President and Fellows of Harvard College.* June 23, 1790.

50. Greenleaf, *Survey of Maine*, 401.

51. *Resolve Granting a township of land in the county of Lincoln, to be vested in the trustees of Hallowell Academy, with a proviso.* June 1, 1791.

52. *Resolve Containing directions to the committee for the sale of Eastern Lands.* March 2, 1795.

53. Ibid., 401.

54. *Report On the subject of Academies at large.* February 27, 1797.

55. *Resolve Directing the committee on unappropriated lands in Lincoln county, to provide a minister for the plantations in said county, &c.* July 8, 1786.

56. *Resolve: That there be reserved in each township four lots of three hundred and twenty acres each, for public uses, viz. One for the first settled minister; one for the use of the ministry; one for the use of schools; and one for the future appropriation of the General Court; the said lots to average in goodness and situation with the*

lands in such township, and to be designated in such way and manner as the said committee shall judge proper.

CHAPTER 2: SAGAMORES, SPECULATORS, AND STATEHOOD

57. **Resolve** *On the petition of* Amos Patten, *directing the Hon.* Salem Towne, *Esq to make and execute a deed to* Joseph Inman, *of 150 acres of land in the 9 townships of land purchased of the Penobscot Indians.* February 15, 1805.

58. It was presumably Amos Patten of whom Thoreau was thinking when he noted, "Ktaadn . . . was first ascended by a white man in 1804." *The Maine Woods*, "Ktaadn," p. 2.

59. Massachusetts Provincial Congress, *The Journals of Each Provincial Congress of Massachusetts in 1774 & 1775,* 371.

60. John E. Godfrey, "The Ancient Penobscot, or Panawanskek," 88.

61. Ibid., 91.

62. Allis, *William Bingham's Maine Lands*, Vol. 1, 653.

63. **Resolve** *Upon the report of the commissioners appointed to survey the Penobscot lands.* March 2, 1798.

64. Frederick Goodwin.

65. Micah A. Pawling, *Wabanaki Homeland and the New State of Maine, The 1820 Journal and Plans of Survey of Joseph Treat*, 38.

66. James Sullivan, Democratic-Republican Governor of Massachusetts 1807–1808.

67. Ibid., 47.

68. Ibid.

69. **Resolve** *On the representation of the committee for sale of Eastern Lands, authorizing them to conduct the business therein referred to, as they may judge equitable,* February 11, 1791.

70. Frederick S. Allis, Jr., *William Bingham's Maine Lands 1792–1820*, Publications of the Colonial Society of Massachusetts. The following account of land speculation in Maine owes much to Mr. Allis's masterful edition of the papers and documents around the venture that became known as Bingham's Million Acres.

71. Waldo Lincoln, *Genealogy of The Waldo Family—A Record of the Descendants of Cornelius Waldo, of Ipswich, Mass. From 1647 to 1900.*

72. Allis, *William Bingham's Maine Lands,* Vol. 1, 105.

73. *"Tout le monde malade a bord, jusqu'au capitaine."* Bacler de Leval.

74. Ibid., 154.

75. Ibid., 150.

76. Major William Jackson (1759–1828) was a southerner who had been appointed aide-de-camp to Yankee general Benjamin Lincoln when he took over the southern army and needed a "local" intermediary in his new command. After the war, Jackson had been the secretary to the Constitutional Convention.

77. States and territories were very competitive with each other. During the months that the would-be Scioto settlers waited in Alexandria, the locals made frequent efforts to interest them in land in Virginia.

78. Ibid., 103.

79. Ibid., 183.

80. Ibid., 180.

81. Ibid., 513.

82. Ibid., 515.

83. Ibid., 517.

84. Ibid., 520.

85. Ibid., 527.

86. Ibid., 153.

87. Ibid., 247.

88. Ibid., 154, 236.

89. Jackson's letters included lively reports on the French Revolution—"France at this moment exhibits such scenes as the pencil of Salvator Rosa would have been well employed to delineate, abounding in light and shade, which is at once splendid and awful."—and its wars (from a distinctly pro-French point of view).

90. Baring and Bingham evidently got on well, although Bingham's parsimony grated on Baring. "There is a littleness about the man in trifles that will make him for instance dispute all the tavern bills on the road."

91. Gouldsboro. "The whole of the point is a white rock which presents the most barren object you can imagine."

92. Frederick S. Allis Jr., ed. *William Bingham's Maine Lands 1792–1820*, Vol. 2, 769.

93. Presumably Charles-Alexandre de Calonne, whose last-ditch effort to reform French finances led to his being exiled by Louis XVI in 1787.

94. Allis called this allegation "obviously absurd."

95. Allis, *William Bingham's Maine Lands,* Vol. 1, 648.

96. Allis, *William Bingham's Maine Lands,* Vol. 2, 1174.

97. Hereafter, Jefferson's party will be referred to as Republican, which is common usage.

98. Ibid., 1194.

99. As a symptom of these unsettled times, the Lincoln jail had "heretofore by force been opened and several persons liberated therefrom, who were then confined under a charge of having riotously prevented the running the lines." They had to be locked up in Cumberland instead.

100. The "Kennebeck Claim" was the eight-hundred-thousand-acre tract first granted to the Plymouth Colony, one of those "ancient" claims "so clogged by conditions" of which General Lincoln had cautioned Bingham.

101. **Resolve** *On agents, of Eastern Lands letter, Etc. empowering Lothrop Lewis, Esq. to ascertain and mark the line between the commonwealth and Plymouth Company.* February 15, 1804.

102. Ibid., 1200.

103. Ibid., 1203.

104. Ibid., 1215.

105. Hare bought out Knox's claim to a third of the profits by releasing him from his debts to Bingham, "perceiving that his political and private influence was gone

and therefore that there was no use in being longer connected with him," he reported rather coldly.

106. Ibid., 1214.

107. Hare's calculations: 65,000 acres (King's three townships) @ 25 cents per acre = $16,250; less $5,000 (King's purchase price) = $11,250.

108. Alan Taylor, *Liberty Men and Great Proprietors*, 220–25.

109. *Maine Historical and Genealogical Recorder,* 104.

110. Taylor, *Liberty Men and Great Proprietors*, 209.

111. *Maine Historical and Genealogical Recorder,* 104.

112. "Eastern Lands Papers, Records, 1717–1860."

113. Moses Greenleaf, *A Statistical View of the District of Maine*, iv.

114. Edgar Crosby Smith, *Moses Greenleaf, Maine's First Mapmaker: A Biography*, 111.

115. The asterisk gives an interesting etymological glimpse of an important word in this context. It reads as follows: *We have made frequent use of the word settle, and its derivatives in a different sense from any, that is given in any lexicon, we have seen.* Settle, settlers, *etc. are in common use in this country, when we speak of felling the forest trees, and clearing, cultivating, and peopling the lands in the wilderness.*

116. Greenleaf, *A Statistical View of the District of Maine*, iv.

117. *An Act concerning the separation of the District of Maine from Massachusetts Proper, and forming the same into a separate and independent State,* passed June 19th, 1816.

118. Mark Langdon Hill, "A Memorial of Mark Langdon Hill," 370.

119. The polemic had began: "Politicks have been almost as much abused, by statesmen of modern times, as religion was, by the priests of the dark ages."

120. Walter M. MacDougall, *Settling the Maine Wilderness: Moses Greenleaf, His Maps, and His Household of Faith,* 60.

121. "Eastern Lands Papers, Records, 1717–1860."

122. "These terms and conditions . . . shall *ipso facto* be incorporated into, and become, and be part of any constitution." They "may be modified, or annulled, by the agreement of the legislature of both the said states; but by no other power or body whatsoever." An Act relating to the Separation of the District of Maine from Massachusetts Proper, and forming the same into a Separate and Independent State.

123. Article X, Section 5: "And in all grants hereafter to be made, by either State, of unlocated land within the said District, the same reservations shall be made for the benefit of Schools, and of the Ministry, as have heretofore been usual, in grants made by this Commonwealth." The Articles of Separation are rarely printed but remain part of the Constitution to this day.

CHAPTER 3: TIMBER PIRATES AND BORDER WARS

124. William King, Democratic-Republican Governor of Maine 1820–1821.

125. Greenleaf's total comes to 11,843,200 acres; however, he deducted the following: "about 430,000 acres is reserved for the Penobscot Indians & probably about

45,000 is occupied by a number of French, on the St. John in the county of Hancock, which leaves belonging to the Commonwealth 11,368,200 acres, out of which is to be deducted sufficient for the grants already made & not located, a few townships appropriated to making certain roads, & the remainder, which after these deductions will doubtless exceed 11,000,000 acres constitutes the disposable fund of the Commonwealth in Eastern Lands."

126. Smith, *Moses Greenleaf, Maine's First Map-maker,* 111·

127. John G. Deane, "Report of the Committee on State Lands," 212.

128. Treaty Between Massachusetts and the Penobscot Tribe, June 29, 1818.

129. Micah A. Pawling, *Wabanaki Homeland and the New State of Maine, The 1820 Journal and Plans of Survey of Joseph Treat,* 34.

130. Williams, Chase and Co., *History of Penobscot County, Maine,* 581.

131. Jacques Ferland, "Tribal Dissent or White Aggression?: Interpreting Penobscot Indian Dispossession between 1808 and 1835." *Maine History* 43:2, 149.

132. "Communication from John G. Deane, Esq., January 20, 1830." Quoted in Ferland, 153.

133. Ferland, *Maine History,* 152.

134. "Resolve authorizing the Penobscot Indians to sell two townships of lands and pine timber, Approved March 5, 1830." *Resolves of the Tenth Legislature of the State of Maine,* Portland: Day & Fraser. Printers to the State, 1830, 106.

135. His son wrote that Deane "had a great fondness for all kinds of manly sports; loved to have about him good horses and fine dogs, and was enthusiastic in hunting and fishing. His ardent pursuit of these pastimes led him very often to make long excursions into the then wild regions north and northeast of the town of Ellsworth." (*Biographical Sketch of John G. Deane, of Portland, Maine.* Prepared by, and printed for, his son, Llewellyn Deane, June 1885, For Private Use. R. Beresford, Printer, Washington, D.C., 1887, 4).

136. Pawling, *Wabanaki Homeland and the New State of Maine,* 69.

137. William King, "State of the State Address, January, 1821."

138. Letter from John Deane to Governor Samuel Smith, November 2, 1831, *Resolves of the Twelfth Legislature of the State of Maine,* 490.

139. **Resolve** *relating to the settlement of the boundaries between the State and the British Province,* June 18th, 1820.

140. Prices ranged from 25 cents (typically lots in incorporated towns of which there were about forty-five thousand acres) to 4 cents an acre (the "unlocated lands").

141. Ring, *Report of Forest Commissioner,* Maine 1908.

142. Albion K. Parris, Democratic-Republican Governor of Maine 1822–1827.

143. John G. Deane, "Report of the Committee on State Lands," 1831, 208.

144. Ibid., 213.

145. Lyndon Oak, *A Sketch of the Life of General James Irish of Gorham, Me 1776–1763,* 31.

146. Ibid., 32.

147. The first of many such acts, the Schepps report noted.

148. "There shall be reserved in every township, suitable for settlement, one thousand acres of land to average in quality and situation with the other land in such town-

ship, to be appropriated to such public uses for the exclusive benefit of such town, as the Legislature may hereafter direct." Chapter 280, 8, Public Laws of 1824. Although it was not consulted (or the Articles of Separation amended), the Commonwealth made no objection, and adopted the formula on its own lands in Maine.

149. Deane, "Report of the Committee on State Lands," 1831, 214.

150. Ferland, *Maine History,* 150.

151. Townships (T) were numbered by tiers six miles deep that ran parallel to the monument line; the first tier above the line was number 4, the next number 5, and so on. Ranges (R), also six miles wide, ran perpendicular (north–south) forming the grid as they intersected with the east–west townships; the farthest east was Range 1. Each township was identified by its place on the grid, for instance where Range 9 crossed Townships numbered 6, it was referred to as T6R9, which in due course would become Katahdin Iron Works.

152. By this time, the old yellow-birch tree had gone, but it had been replaced with a sturdier cedar marker in 1817 by the surveyors who tried to solve the same problem under the Treaty of Ghent.

153. In 1821, the holder of a grant from Massachusetts had dutifully reserved the ministerial lot, only to find it taken over by a trespasser, who argued that it didn't belong to the grantee any longer. Maine's Supreme Judicial Court had to agree with the defendant's logic but gave the plaintiff "custody and care" of the lot, pending the arrival of the minister. Shapleigh vs. Pilllsbury, see Schepps, p. 26.

154. Oak, *A Sketch of the Life of General James Irish,* 42.

155. Hiram Chapman, *Annual Report of the Land Agent for the Year Ending November 30, 1863,* 6.

156. Ibid., 216.

157. Enoch Lincoln, Democratic-Republican Governor of Maine 1827–1829.

158. Enoch Lincoln, "Speech of the Governor of the State of Maine to Both Houses of the Legislature, 1828," 621.

159. Richard G. Wood, *A History of Lumbering in Maine 1820–1861,* 20.

160. "Domestic Intelligence," *Boston Daily Advertiser,* October 3, 1818.

161. NBKP: North of Bingham's Kennebec Purchase. The township sold for 30 cents an acre.

162. MacDougall, *Settling the Maine Wilderness,* 59–60.

163. Ibid., 54.

164. Eighty years later, Forest Commissioner Edgar Ring wrote: "It is an interesting bit of history that, when later more money was needed to complete the [State House], lands were bringing such a low price that the legislature would not appropriate any of them, but instead borrowed $25,000 for the purpose." Forest Commissioner's Report, 1908.

165. Deane, "The grants to the Plymouth Company, and to Brigadier General Waldo, are some among many, which the people of this State have abundant cause to deplore." 208.

166. Specifically included were lots in townships owned by Massachusetts; at this point, Maine had "succeeded to all of the sovereignty of Massachusetts for the regulation of the Public Lots." Schepps, p. 12.

167. Elijah L. Hamlin, Maine Land Agent 1838, 1841.

168. Elijah L. Hamlin, "Report of the Land Agent of the State of Maine, January 1, 1839," 29.

169. Later the same year, 1839, Aroostook became a Maine county and nearly ignited war with Great Britain.

170. J. Chris Arndt, "Maine in the Northeastern Boundary Controversy: States' Rights in Antebellum New England," 206.

171. Israel Washburn Jr., Republican governor of Maine 1861–1863.

172. Israel Washburn, "Centennial and Dedicatory Address," 99.

173. Wood, *History of Lumbering in Maine,* 79.

174. Federal Writers' Project, *Maine: A Guide Down East,* 132.

175. Richard Hildreth, *Banks, Banking, and Paper Currencies,* 91.

176. Hamlin, "Report of the Land Agent,1839," 32.

177. TK. Richard Judd, *Aroostook: A Century of Logging in Northern Maine,*

178. James Elliott Defebaugh, *History of the Lumber Industry of America,* Vol. 2, 88.

179. Henry Burrage, "Maine and the Northeast Boundary Controversy" (citing *Resolves of Maine II,* p. 77–79), 156.

180. The meeting had been called under a warrant from Penobscot County Justice of the Peace William D. Williamson, Maine's second governor. As speaker of its House of Representatives, he had fulfilled most of William King's term when the latter resigned.

181. Lincoln, "Speech of the Governor 1828," 622.

182. Samuel E. Smith, Democratic Governor of Maine 1831–1834; Message to the Legislature, January 9, 1832.

183. Charlotte Lenentine, *Madawaska, A Chapter in Maine-New Brunswick Relations,* 42.

184. Robert P. Dunlap, Democratic governor of Maine 1834–1838.

185. Edward Kent, Whig governor of Maine 1838–1839; 1841–1842; John Fairfield, Democratic governor of Maine 1839–1841; 1842–1843.

186. Rufus McIntire was "unquestionably a man of ability and integrity. He was a lawyer and had represented his district in Congress four terms," wrote John Francis Sprague. McIntire had also run for governor two years before he became the land agent.

187. According to another account, McIntire and three men "proceeded down the river to the house of one Fitzherbert, in what is now Fort Fairfield village, under appointment to meet the British Land Warden, though it was reported by his Whig enemies that he had gone there in order that he might have a feather bed to sleep on!" The rest of the story stays the same, only adding that the prisoners were "carried on an ox-sled." *Maine My State,* The Maine Writers Research Club, 1919.

188. Michael T. Perry, "'Maine and *her* soil, or BLOOD!': Political Rhetoric and Spatial Identity during the Aroostook War in Maine," 81.

189. William P. Parrott, "Report of William P. Parrott," 78.

190. Joseph Porter, "The Aroostook War, and the Volunteer Troops Therein," 121.

191. Arndt, "Maine in the Northeastern Boundary Controversy," 218.

192. Ring, *Report of Forest Commissioner, Maine 1908*, 83.

193. Robert V. Remini, *Daniel Webster: The Man and His Time*, 556.

CHAPTER 4: "FOLLY OF EXAGGERATION" VS. "WANT OF JUST APPRECIATION"

194. David Bergquist, "Head of Tide."

195. Oak, *A Sketch of the Life of General James Irish*, 31.

196. According to Thoreau, writing in 1846, "There were in 1837, as I read, two hundred and fifty saw-mills on the Penobscot and its tributaries above Bangor . . . and they sawed two hundred millions of feet of boards annually."

197. Henry David Thoreau, *The Writings of Henry David Thoreau: The Maine Woods*, 3.

198. C. T. Jackson, *Second Annual Report on the Geology of the Public Lands belonging to the two states of Maine and Massachusetts, 1838*, viii.

199. Neil Rolde, *The Interrupted Forest*, 253.

200. Levi Bradley, Maine land agent 1842–1847, at that time a record in longevity.

201. In 1832, Audubon made an excursion through the Maine woods. He was impressed by the "lumberers," whose lifestyle he described in some detail.

202. Samuel Cony, Maine land agent 1847–1850; Republican governor of Maine 1864–1867.

203. "When the tree is cut down, it is lined off for *squaring*, and the 'round' outside of the lines is what is called beaten off on the four sides. The wood thus beaten or slashed off in preparation for hewing by the broadax is the prime part of the tree, from which the best class of clear lumber is obtained when the timber is taken in the round to a saw-mill. Besides the destruction of timber of the finest texture and greatest value, there is the upper portion of the tree near to and partly into the top, which would yield lumber of an inferior quality, it is true, but suitable either for domestic use or for export to the American market . . . ; but the upper part of the tree is rejected by the square-timber manufacturer, and left in the woods, with the fine wood beaten off, to rot and become material for feeding forest fires." From the 1879 report of the Commissioner of Crown Lands for the Province of Ontario; referenced in "Report upon Forestry," prepared under the direction of the Commissioner of Agriculture, in pursuance of an act of Congress approved August 15, 1876, by Franklin B. Hough Vol. II, Washington, DC: Government Printing Office, 1880.

204. The legislature had designated the first five ranges as "settling lands" in 1824.

205. On the same trip, Thoreau compared Coffin's and Greenleaf's maps of Maine. Coffin's, he decided, was "the only one I have seen that at all deserves the name." He had found Greenleaf's on the wall of a public-house in Mattawamkeag and described copying it. "So, dipping a wad of tow into the lamp, we oiled a sheet of paper on the oiled table-cloth, and, in good faith, traced what we afterwards ascertained to be a labyrinth of errors, carefully following the outlines of the imaginary lakes which the map contains" (*The Maine Woods,* 16). Greenleaf himself offered a caveat when his map first appeared in 1815. It gave a "tolerably correct" idea of Maine's

"extensive interior, which has hitherto been but little explored, except occasionally by individuals" but without "a new survey of the whole, corrected by celestial observations, under the immediate inspection of persons properly qualified for the purpose . . . a *perfect* Map of Maine *cannot be obtained*."

206. Thoreau, *The Maine Woods,* 7.

207. Samuel Cony, "Annual Report of the Land Agent of the State of Maine, December 31, 1847," 7.

208. This was the area to which Moses Greenleaf referred in his assessment of the District of Maine in 1813: "probably about 45,000 [acres] is occupied by a number of French, on the St. John in the county of Hancock." See note 42.

209. Levi Bradley, "Report of the Land Agent of the State of Maine, December 31, 1844," 12.

210. Thirty-five years later, a commission on settlement was less impressed. Its report on the French colony in Madawaska was scathing. The progress of which Levi Bradley had been so proud had long since atrophied. Having itemized state funds spent on schools and teachers over the years, it found they had been "in great measure frittered away," if not actually spent *"in violation of the law."* Its conclusion: Madawaskans must be made to contribute to their schools like any other Maine town, and their community must be "Americanized."

211. Myron H. Avery, citing Dr. George Thurber's report of the Aaron Young Botanical Survey in "The Keep Path and Its Successors," 133.

212. Cony, *Annual Report of the Land Agent, 1849,* 7.

213. John W. Dana, Democratic governor of Maine 1847–1850.

214. Anson P. Morrill, Maine land agent 1850–1854; Republican governor of Maine 1855–1856.

215. Upon organization, the plantation would receive 6 percent of the accumulated fund each year.

216. Stephen Wheatland, "History of Pingree Heir Timberland Ownership," 119.

217. Lucius L. Hubbard, *Woods and Lakes of Maine, A Trip from Moosehead Lake to New Brunswick in a Birch-Bark Canoe,* 76.

218. Hubbard described life at Chamberlain Farm further: "The farm, which has grown to large proportions, is now owned by Hon. E. S. Coe of Bangor, and on it are raised yearly large numbers of cattle and sheep, and also potatoes, grain, and vegetables. So well do sheep thrive there, that a short time before our arrival one became so fat that, in the words of the superintendent, Mr. Nutter, they 'had to kill him to save his life; couldn't lug himself around.' Mr. Nutter also told us, that, when the season was not backward, he raised just as good corn as grew anywhere in the State of Maine. Good apples grow there, as we proved to our entire satisfaction."

219. Ibid., 221.

220. According to Lucius Hubbard, "They blocked up the outlet with hemlock trees, and when the other loggers, with their "drivers," came along, they were surprised and chagrined to find themselves outnumbered and powerless. Finally, all agreed in writing to pay the required toll, and their portion of the expense of the hundred guards." Ibid. Hubbard, p. 222.

221. "Appeal of Rufus Dwinel to the Legislature of Maine Against an application to that body to take from him his private property and transfer it to others," *The Telos Canal*, Maine State Library 386.W.31R.ME Coll, 3.

222. Tom Burby, "The Sarcophagus of Rufus Dwinel."

223. Robert E. Pike, *Tall Trees, Tough Men*, 221.

224. Anson P. Morrill, *Annual Report of the Land Agent of the State of Maine, December 31, 1850*, 9.

225. John Hubbard, Democratic governor of Maine 1850–1853. Hubbard was a farmer's son who had become a doctor, then served in the U.S. Senate. His opponent for governor was E. L. Hamlin, the land agent.

226. John Hubbard, "Governor John Hubbard's Message to the Legislature, May 19, 1851," 13.

227. The governor had been well briefed by his land agent who spelled out what Massachusetts was up to in rather more detail. "The law that separated Maine from Massachusetts proper . . . provided that the lands belonging to Massachusetts shall not be liable to taxation by this state, while the fee is in that state. But it could not have been contemplated, that under this provision, her lands would be held free from taxation, after she had really sold and parted with all interest in them that is of any value: to wit, the timber standing and growing upon them. This is accomplished by granting permits, operating as a perpetual lease of the lands, or extending forward many years, enabling the lessee to occupy, own and use, the entire value of the lands, and still be subject to no taxes, or be compelled to contribute anything to support the government of the state, that protects him in his business, and gives him facilities for carrying on his operations. The pretense to avoid taxation is, that the state has not sold the soil, and therefore it cannot be taxed; the fee being in the state. This position may be technically correct, but I submit that, justice and a proper liberality protest against such an interpretation of the law. Moreover, when sales of the soil are actually made, and notes given for the payment of the sum agreed on, in several annual installments, it is contended that Maine has no right to tax these lands, until the last dollar of the last payment be paid; which by the consent of parties, may frequently be extended for years, by which operation the lands are held from taxation, in violation of right and equity, if not in open violation of a fair construction of the letter of the law."

228. Morrill, *Annual Report of the Land Agent of the State of Maine, December 31, 1851*, 4.

229. "Our true policy in connection with the public domain has, heretofore, been overruled, and diverted to wrong purposes by the untoward influences of the claims of Massachusetts and those holding titles under her and us." Ex-Governor Hubbard to the legislature, January 1853; also Governor John Hubbard, Message to the Legislature, May 14, 1850.

230. Thirty-Second Legislature, Extra Session: Public Lands. Jos. Titcomb, Chairman.

231. "KNOW ALL MEN BY THESE PRESENTS, That I . . . Land Agent of the State of Maine by virtue of authority vested in me by an act of the Legislature of this State, entitled 'An Act in relation to lands reserved for public uses,' approved August 28, 1850, and in consideration of . . . paid by . . . the receipt whereof I hereby

acknowledge, have granted, bargained and sold, and do by these presents bargain and sell unto the said . . . his heirs, executors, administrators and assigns, the right to cut and carry away the timber and grass from the reserved lots in Township . . . excepting and reserving, however, the grass growing upon any improvements made by an actual settler, said right to cut and carry away said timber and grass to continue until the said township or tract shall be incorporated or organized for Plantation purposes, and no longer."

232. The law reinforced the original intention behind the Public Reserved Lots by stating: "Authority to sell the soil was not and could not be given."

233. Isaac R. Clark, Maine land agent 1855, 1864–1868, 1879.

234. Parker P. Burleigh, Maine land agent 1868–1876.

235. "Bragg vs. Burleigh," *Reports of Cases in Law and Equity, determined by the Supreme Judicial Court of Maine,* Vol. 61, 450.

236. Morrill, *Address of Governor Morrill to the Legislature of the State of Maine, January 6, 1860,* 3.

237. Governor Morrill continued: "The ratio of decennial increase of population was, from 1820 to 1830, thirty-three per cent.; from 1830 to 1840, twenty-six per cent.; from 1840 to 1850, sixteen per cent.; and from 1850 to 1860, will probably be found to be about the same as for the latter period."

238. John Hubbard, "Message to the Legislature 1851," 9.

239. Lot M. Morrill, Republican governor of Maine 1858–1861

240. Governor Morrill tended to be stoic about the situation, and positively puritan in placing the blame. "This overpowering national impulse finds its gratification, also, in corresponding private and social *displays*—in elegant mansions, costly furniture, splendid equippage, and, divested of high aims, takes on the more questionable character of indulgence in mere trappings; and thus the habits of domestic and social life become changed from those of simplicity to those of extravagance."

241. George C. Getchell, Maine land agent 1854.

242. B. W. Norris, Maine land agent 1860–1863.

243. Noah Barker, Maine Land Agent 1857-1860.

244. At war's end, Benjamin White Norris went to Alabama as an agent for the Freedmen's Bureau, supporting redistribution of land to former slaves. "They sent him to Congress in 1868 [when Alabama was readmitted to the Union] to get the land for them. He told them that they had a better right to the land than the masters had. 'Your work made this country what it is, and it is yours.' Ala. Test., pp. 445, 1131." Note and quote from *Civil War and Reconstruction in Alabama,* Walter Lynwood Fleming, Columbia University Press, 1905.

245. Hiram Chapman, Maine land agent 1863.

246. Chapman, *Report of the Land Agent, 1863,* 40.

247. In 1845, Poor braved frostbite and a blizzard to beat Boston agents to Montreal to convince its Board of Trade that rail connection with Portland would provide access to an ice-free port nearer Europe than Boston.

248. "European" because connecting Portland (and Boston) to Halifax, the closest Atlantic port to the Old World, would make it "the short route to Europe."

249. Joshua L. Chamberlain, Republican governor of Maine 1867–1871.

250. Parker P. Burleigh, "Annual Report of the Land Agent of the State of Maine for the Year Ending November 30, 1874," 10.

251. In 1855, a legislative resolve establishing the office of land agent was "approved by the people, amending the Constitution of the State to provide that 'the Land Agent and Attorney General shall be chosen annually by joint ballot of the senators and representatives in convention.'" Forest Commissioner's Report 1927–1928.

252. Neil L. Violette, *State of Maine Seventeenth Biennial Report of the Forest Commissioner 1927–1928*, 13.

253. Edwin C. Burleigh, Maine land agent 1876, 1877–1879.

CHAPTER 5: TROUBLE BREWING: A TREMENDOUS ISSUE REGARDED FROM ANY POINT OF VIEW

254. These reports were published as *The Meddybemps Letters* (named presumably for the lake about thirty miles north of Machias), together with the equally scathing *Maine Hall of Fame*. Original copies are rare to nonexistent because, it is said, the men celebrated in its pages burned all the copies they could put their hands on. Pattangall would later run, unsuccessfully, for governor against Percival Baxter, and would retire as chief justice of Maine's Supreme Judicial Court. He remained a Democrat for most of his life, but with FDR's "New Deal," he said "the Democratic Party has left me." He became a Republican once more (Quoted by Raymond Fellows in *William R. Pattangall of Maine, Lawyer, Politician, Jurist*, 1954).

255. Raymond Fellows and Edward J. Conquest, compilers, *William R. Pattangall of Maine: Lawyer, Politician, Jurist; A Compilation of Facts Relating to a Busy and Interesting Life together with The Meddybemps Letters, The Maine Hall of Fame, Anecdotes and Speeches*, 36.

256. Of the twenty-two governors of Maine between 1857 and 1911, all but two were Republican.

257. Charles F. Oak, "of the International Paper Company," was also clerk and treasurer of the Maine Lumbermen and Landowners' Association. *The Paper Mill and Wood Pulp News*, Vol. XXVI, No. 27, 1903.

258. Ibid., 206.

259. John Stevens Cabot Abbott and Edward Henry Elwell, *History of Maine*, 569.

260. "Canadian Public Lands," 60.

261. Austin Cary would make his name as the "father of southern forestry," but in 1906 he was still in his native New England, angling for a job with Gifford Pinchot's new U.S. Forest Service.

262. Austin Cary, "Maine Forests, Their Preservation, Taxation and Value," 182.

263. Lloyd Irland, *The Northeast's Changing Forest*, 79.

264. Lee Schepps, "Report on the Public Lots," 55–58.

265. *An Act to make certain the meaning of the language 'timber and grass' relating to the public lots.* 1903.

266. Defebaugh, *History of the Lumber Industry of America*, Vol. 2, p. 31.

267. *Leading Manufacturers and Merchants of the City of Boston, and a Review of the Prominent Exchanges,* 332.

268. The Legislative agenda for 1869 includes this item:

ROUTE No. 87.
From Princeton to Houlton, 70 miles and back, three times a week.
Bidder's name.   *Sum per annum.*
Henry Drew.........................$4,400.
F. J. Littlefield.........................1,487.
Martin Cone and Weston Haycock...........990.
Orman F. Lathrop ....787.
Varney W. Putnam and Horace M. Brackett ... 775.
Henry H. Putnam.......................743.

accepted April 20, 1869.
Contract made with Henry H. Putnam, of Houlton, Maine, dated April 20, 1869, at $743
per annum.
By an order dated June 18, 1869, service curtailed to commence at Topsfield, saving 16
miles and $170 per annum, from July 1, 1869.
Leave Topsfield Monday, Wednesday, and Friday at 7 a. m.; arrive at Houlton next days
by 6.30 a. m.
Leave Houlton Monday, Wednesday, and Friday at 7 a. m.; arrive at Topsfield next days
by 8 a. m.

269. By 2016, the pendulum had swung back. "We're now more into lumber than we are pulpwood," Wellman mused that year. "We've gone back to lumber and by-products. Whereas a hundred and fifty years ago, we were long logs and tanning bark; now it's chips." There were only six paper mills left operating in Maine.

270. Abbott and Elwell, *History of Maine,* 568.

271. S.D. Warren Company was bought out by Scott Paper Company in 1967, and then again by the South African paper company SAPPI in 1995.

272. Hugh J. Chisholm, "History of Papermaking in Maine and the Future of the Industry," 163.

273. Rolde, *The Interrupted Forest,* 282.

274. *A Brief History of Papermaking in Maine.*

275. *The World's Paper Trade Review.*

276. Rolde, *The Interrupted Forest,* 284.

277. Ibid., 286.

278. Ibid., 287.

279. Chisolm, "History of Papermaking in Maine," 164.

280. Rolde, *The Interrupted Forest* (citing the Maine Commission of Industrial and Labor Statistics, 1903), 280–81.

281. This informal contract accounted for Maine ranking forty-seventh out of fifty in public land as a percentage of total area as late as the 1990s. See chapter 9.

282. Set to music by the end of the century, it was made popular by Frank Crumit. Osborne's poem appeared in anthologies of light verse. He was presumably the Louis Shreve Osborne who became an Episcopal priest.

283. "In 1891, the Bangor and Aroostook Railroad (BAR) was incorporated as it combined the Bangor and Piscataquis RR and the Bangor and Katahdin Railroad. In 1893, a BAR train operated to Houlton. One year later, the main line reached Caribou and the branch to Fort Fairfield was completed. By 1905, connections were made to Patten, Limestone, Ashland, and Van Buren." *History of Railroading in Maine*, Maine DOT.

284. "Massachusetts Man the Largest of Land Owners," *The Tribune* (Seymour, Indiana), February 7, 1911.

285. In 1988, Brad Wellman made a similar point to the author. In 1980, Maine's Department of Inland Fisheries and Wildlife started an annual lottery for permits to hunt moose. Because of its forest management, Seven Islands's million acres had much of the best moose habitat. "But nobody asked us," Wellman observed.

286. Frank Putnam, "What's the Matter with New England? Maine: A Study in Land-Grabbing, Tax Dodging and Isolation," 532.

287. Since 1846, Maine had been the national leader in the movement to prohibit alcoholic beverages. The Democratic governor John Hubbard was an early prohibitionist, but it subsequently became a Republican issue, though divisive. It is thought that James G. Blaine ultimately lost the 1884 presidential election because the Prohibition Party took away enough Republican votes.

288. Charles Evans Hughes (1862–1948), was governor of New York at the time and would be the Republican candidate for President in 1916. As a progressive lawyer, he had recently made his name investigating the utilities and the insurance industry.

289. Thomas Brackett Reed (1839–1902), legendary speaker of the U.S. House of Representatives.

290. At this time, Llewellyn Powers (1836–1908) had been in the Maine House on and off since 1873. In 1876, the legislature passed his bill outlawing the death penalty in Maine. He was governor from 1897 to 1901.

291. William T. Cobb, Republican governor of Maine, 1905–1909.

292. An editor's note prefaced the first of Liberty Dennett's articles. "How [its public domain]was lost to the people of Maine is a narrative of absorbing interest which will appear in this and subsequent issues; and of even greater interest will be a discussion of what may now be done in the way of legislation, so that the people may recover somewhat of their lost patrimony," a premonition of editorials that would appear sixty-five years later.

293. Dennett's observations regarding the funds set aside for education from the Public Reserved Lands were as withering. After seventy-five years, the fund (in 1907) amounted to some $450,000. The annual payment of 6 percent contributed an "utterly insignificant" $27,000 to a school budget of almost $600,000 (which was itself scandalously low). "Think of it, fellow citizens of Maine," cried Dennett. This was all there was to show for the loss of "the magnificent empire of forests which our fathers owned."

294. Nelson Dingley Jr., Republican governor of Maine 1874–1876.

295. Edwin C. Burleigh, Republican governor of Maine 1889–1893.

296. Burleigh, "Annual Report of the Land Agent of the State of Maine for the year ending November 30, 1874," 15.

297. Dennett's evocative vision of panic is worth a footnote: "the wildlanders were thrown into a state of panic, not quite so intense as a stock panic in Wall street, and it did not manifest itself in such violent gesticulations, or frenzied exclamations, but it was a genuine panic confined to the wildlanders of the legislative session of 1903, and instead of noise and bluster, it was hist! hush! be still! this question of an increase of the tax of our wild lands must not get into the House."

298. Putnam, "What's the Matter with New England?," 525.

299. Christine I. Hepler, "Researching Initiatives and Referenda: A Guide for Maine," 100.

300. Manly Hardy; William B. Krohn, ed., *Manly Hardy: The Life and Writing of a Maine Fur-buyer, Hunter, and Naturalist*, 100.

301. Cary, "Maine Forests, Their Preservation, Taxation and Value," 180.

302. Chisholm, "History of Papermaking in Maine," 161.

303. Defebaugh, *History of the Lumber Industry of America*, Vol. 2, 95.

304. James Lewis, "Honoring America's First Forester on His 150th Birthday," 4.

305. Cary, "Maine Forests, Their Preservation, Taxation and Value," 180.

306. For all these reasons, Cary regretted how carelessly Maine had thrown away its "magnificent heritage of public land." But it was no good "crying over spilled milk."

307. Chisholm, "History of Papermaking in Maine," 167.

308. In fact, sawmills were declining, as pointed out by James Elliott Defebaugh: "With the present immense diversion of timber to the pulp mills there would seem to be little chance of an increase in the products of the sawmills, and the wonder is that the latter have held their own against the new log-eating octopi the grinders and the digesters." "Present Timber Conditions," *History of the Lumber Industry of America*, Vol. 2, p. 18.

309. An Act creating the Maine Forestry District and providing for protection against forest fires therein.

310. Alluding to this possibility in his fundraising letter, J.P. Bass reassured his correspondents that the committee would suggest it only "as a last resort that it will be the only way to defeat the other measure."

311. Violette, *Report of the Forest Commissioner 1927–1928,* 14.

312. Chisholm, "History of Papermaking in Maine," 167.

313. The circumstances around Indian township caught Liberty Dennett at his drollest, although he put it in Aroostook County: "How the landgrabbers missed getting title to this township is more than I can learn. Perhaps they left it in the State's hands as a practice ground for the making of forestry experiments at public expense, and for their own chief ultimate benefit. At any rate, the State still miraculously owns it."

314. Frank E. Mace, Maine forest commissioner 1911–1913

315. Neil L. Violette, Maine forest commissioner 1923–1935.

316. In 1933, the appropriation for managing the Public Lots was reduced to $100.

317. Percival Baxter, Republican governor of Maine, 1921–1925.

318. Earl Raymond, former chief operating officer of Sewall Company, Old Town, Maine.

319. Jon Lund would allude to this battle royal in his defense of the grand plantations bill—see chapter 11.

320. *Paper, A Weekly Technical Journal for Paper and Pulp Mills*, 164.

321. Interview with Percival Baxter, *Portland Press Herald*, May 3, 1937.

CHAPTER 6: CRASH, WAR, AND RECOVERY—MUDDLING THROUGH

322. Waldo N. Seavey, forest commissioner, 1935–1939.

323. "These areas, Bradbury Mt., Lake St. George, Mt. Blue, and Sebago Lake State Parks are operated for the recreational use and benefit of the general public. Forestry practices shall be of such character as to maintain the forest lands in a productive condition. The land shall also be maintained to effectuate a balanced wildlife population." Report of the Forest Commissioner for the Biennium 1939–40.

324. Raymond E. Rendall, *Twenty-Fourth Biennial Report of the Forest Commissioner, State of Maine 1941–42*, 60.

325. St. Croix, Oxford, Penobscot Development, Hollingsworth & Whitney, St. Regis and Atlas Plywood Companies. *Ten Million Acres of Timber: The Remarkable Story of Forest Protection in the Maine Forestry District (1909–1972)*, Austin Wilkins, TBW Books, 1978.

326. Out of an estimated total of $6,571,934 and 9,657,914 man-hours, Development of State and Community Forests requested $343,200 (80,000 man-hours); Boundary Line Survey requested $210,560 (346,552 man-hours).

327. State Forestry Department, "Report of Legislative Interim Committee on Public Reserve Lots."

328. The conflict was reflected in a series of monumental battles between environmentalists and the paper companies even though they were not all directly related to forest practices, for example, the Allagash Wilderness Waterway, Bigelow Preserve, the Big A (standing for Ambejackmockamus) Dam, and the Ban Clearcutting referendum and Compact for Maine's Forests.

329. Immediately after the war, the annual appropriation for the Public Lots increased from $1,000 to $5,000.

330. Macwahoc plantation, the southernmost township in Aroostook County.

331. The other was Eastern Pulp Wood Company's plans for a log dam on Tomah Stream, which would flood some of the Public Lots in Codyville Plantation.

332. The commissioner included the following tabulation in his report:

State Mineral Rights	Acreage
Public Reserved Lots—Timber and Grass Sold	160,236
Public Reserved Lots—Owned in Fee	19,775
Public Reserved Lots—Undivided Interest	About 140,000

333. In 1959, the Forestry Department's annual appropriation for the Public Lots had been upped to $10,000, to be taken from the "annual interest on the accrued principal from the unorganized townships fund."

334. The report's summary, or "Recapitulation," is reproduced on Page X. Although they varied slightly from year to year, the numbers of the public or school lots—as they were as often called in the reports of successive forest commissioners—were broadly consistent. For instance, from the following reports: *1939–1940*—"There are 401,410 acres of public reserved lots, of which the timber and grass on 325,958 acres has been sold." *1941–1942*—"Timber & grass privately owned" 326,778 acres, out of 402,230 acres "Public Lots reserved for school purposes." *1951–1952*—"Timber & grass sold": 320,674 acres out of 390,493. *Austin Wilkins's report (1963)*—Timber & Grass sold: 318,890 acres, out of 397,547 acres.

335. The lots in question were 45 and 48 in Sheridan, near Ashland (1,053 acres), and 31 and 42 in New Sweden (216 acres), all in Aroostook County. Stumpage sold off them, Wilkins noted, went to the state's general fund, although the amount (whether he meant acres or dollars is unclear) "may be small and itinerant." A third lot, 102 in St. Agatha on the Canadian border, was also "uncovered" but had been sold ten years earlier for $251.

336. Violette, *Twentieth Biennial Report of the Forest Commissioner, State of Maine. 1933–1934,* 123.

337. "Report on the Proposed Allagash National Riverway," 7.

338. Author

339. Kenneth Curtis had become governor in 1967, Horace Hildreth and Jon Lund were in the legislature, and Richardson himself was Senate majority leader at the time.

340. Bob Cummings, "Lots of Confusion," 100.

CHAPTER 7: A TALE OF GIVEAWAYS AND NEGLECT

341. Peter Cox, *Journalism Matters,* 188.

342. The Portland papers then included *Portland Press Herald, Evening Express,* and *Maine Sunday Telegram.*

343. Lund served in the Maine legislature for eight years before becoming attorney general in 1973.

344. In 2016, just before Cummings's death, Lund had a bill introduced in the Maine legislature to name one of the townships in the Unorganized Territories Cummingstown.

345. Bob Cummings passed away just as I began writing this book. When I phoned to make an appointment, he was in hospital, but his daughter told me he was very eager to talk to me about the Public Lots as soon as he returned home. Sadly, he ran out of time. However, I interviewed him extensively on the topic in 2006.—TAU

346. See chapter 1.

347. Cummings, "Public Lots: Maine's Chance To Right a History of Wrongs."

348. Wilkins, *Report on Public Reserved Lots,* 10.

CHAPTER 8: WANTED: SOME ASTUTE HORSE-TRADERS

349. Kenneth M. Curtis, Democratic governor of Maine 1967–1975.

350. Quote from Caldwell's obituary. Caldwell arrived at the Portland newspapers in 1965, just two years before Cummings.

351. The legislature officially endorsed leasing camp lots on public lands in 1965, although some of the 389 existing leases dated back much further.

352. Wilkins, "Guest Privilege: Forest Commissioner Answers Telegram," *Maine Sunday Telegram,* April 2, 1972.

353. In his March 12 story, Cummings wrote: "[The state] has recently embarked on a new policy of selling away its public lots for as little as $400 an acre. Sales have been completed for big chunks of the public lots in the Carrabasset Valley near Sugarloaf for an average price of 11 cents an acre and other sales are pending."

354. The map in Wilkins's 1963 report shows the Public Lots in each township. Where ownership was common and undivided, the Public Lot is represented by a dot.

355. Portland attorney Richard Spencer was one of Nader's raiders working on a report of paper company abuses in the Maine woods, which became *The Paper Plantation.* Stumbling upon the Public Lots, he wondered about their greater potential than fodder for paper mills; he recalls mentioning them in a talk he gave to the Natural Resources Council of Maine in 1971 and suggesting the state might have a shot at reclaiming them.

356. Morris R. Wing was also chairman of the Maine Forestry District Advisory Committee.

357. Edmund S. Muskie, Democratic governor of Maine, 1955–1959.

CHAPTER 9: SUPPRESSED: AN HONEST REPORT BY A COMPETENT, CONSCIENTIOUS YOUNG LAWYER

358. Edward D. Murphy and Beth Quimby, "Trailblazing Maine Environmental Reporter Bob Cummings Dies at 86," *Portland Press Herald*, January 23, 2016.

359. Phyllis Austin took her dedication to investigative reporting to the *Maine Times* as its environmental reporter the next year, a position she held with great distinction until the paper ceased publication in 2002.

360. Phyllis Austin, "Public Lots Report not Ready for Public: Erwin," *Portland Press Herald,* October 25, 1972.

361. Cummings, "Law Professor Claims Erwin Suppressing Lots Scandal," *Maine Sunday Telegram*, October 29, 1972.

362. The attorney general's embargo had put Gibbon in a personally awkward situation. He owed a copy of the report to the foundation that had supported his work. As matters stood, he had nothing to show it.

363. After graduation, Tom Gibbon had hoped to join the environmental protection division in the AG's office. With this no longer an option, he got a job as attorney for the Maine Public Utilities Commission where he shook things up for the benefit of Maine ratepayers, before moving on to Washington, D.C.

364. Cummings, "Public Lots: Maine's Chance To Right a History of Wrongs."

365. The 106th Legislature opened on January 3, 1973.

366. Cummings, "Public Lots May Be Lost By Inaction," *Portland Press Herald,* December 31, 1972.

367. In his government reorganization, Governor Curtis proposed a Department of Conservation. The inclusion of LURC (Land Use Regulation Commission) was, in part, against Republican determination to split up LURC's functions "to quiet its outspoken executive director." Cummings, *Portland Press Herald*, January 11, 1973.

368. Dr. John F. Sly's Report on Taxation (1960).

369. *The Paper Plantation: Ralph Nader's Study Group Report on the Pulp and Paper Industry in Maine.*

370. "The Nader Study."

371. Wilkins, *Ten Million Acres of Timber: The Remarkable Story of Forest Protection in the Maine Forestry District (1909–1972)*, 21.

CHAPTER 10: PUBLIC LOTS REPORT: LIKELY AMMUNITION IN THE SPRING

372. Maine's first state park was Aroostook State Park, which started with one hundred acres *given* to the state by Presque Isle citizens in 1938.

373. Jon Lund became the first full-time attorney general in Maine history. He had actually put himself up for the post two years before, on the understanding that James Erwin, who was already the incumbent, was running for governor. To do so, Lund had felt obliged to give up his own seat as a state senator; Maine's attorney general is elected by the legislators, and they don't like having to get a replacement elected on the fly. When Erwin lost his gubernatorial race, he tossed his hat into the ring for AG, regardless. Lund always assumed that Erwin got the job as a "reward for his past party efforts," but after being shut out, he hadn't been one of "Jim Erwin's admiration crew" at that point, although the two men subsequently enjoyed a cordial relationship.

374. "If the State has the unilateral power to modify the details of the original plan of Massachusetts by diverting land and funds intended to benefit the ministry and ministers to schools, then that same power would authorize the diversion of land and funds intended to benefit schools to another public use." Schepps, p. 34.

375. "Accordingly, the rights conveyed under the Grass and Timber Deeds may have expired. The reasoning is based essentially on the facts that (i) the Grass and Timber Deeds do not clearly and explicitly convey future or successive growths of timber, (ii) there are factual and logical reasons why the state may not have intended to convey successive growths, (iii) time and history and not the unequivocal intent of the State expressed in the clear and explicit language of the Grass and Timber Deeds has awarded successive growths on many of the public lots, and (iv) the duration of the cutting rights provided in the Grass and Timber Deeds is so indefinite as to amount, in fact and in law, to a purported conveyance of a perpetual right to cut timber." Schepps, p. 85.

376. Lucy L. Martin, "Maine Can Have its Public Lots Back," *Maine Times*, February 9, 1973.

377. Kenneth Curtis's government reorganization was going into its second year. He had given up on a Department of Natural Resources, which the legislature had voted down (Maine sportsmen were adamant that the Fish & Game Department remain independent lest they lose control over revenue from fishing and hunting licenses) and now proposed a Department of Conservation. Included would be any bureau that emerged to manage the public lands. *Portland Press Herald*, January 31, 1973.

378. The Land Policy and Management Act reached the Senate in 1972, where it languished for four years.

379. "Timberland Owners Offer Public Lots Study Help," *Portland Press Herald*, June 7, 1972.

380. Martin, "The Landowners View their Land," *Maine Times*, March 9, 1973.

381. Familiarly, and now officially, known as Pierce Atwood.

382. According to the Town of Beaver Cove fact sheet, it "actually won an award for the best new community design of the year!" The FAQ goes on, "Difficult economic times during the 1970's resulted in Huber still having half their lots unsold. Much of this unsold land was given to the [two civic/owner] associations as common land/greenbelt, giving added benefits for the residents. . . . In 1973, existing lot owners who were able to get their friends or families to purchase land in the community were rewarded with their choice of a color television or birch bark canoe."

383. Jerry Bley, "LURC's Challenge: Managing Growth in Maine's Unorganized Territories," 94.

384. Martin, "Private Land and Public Use: a Collision Course?" *Maine Times*, March 16, 1973.

385. Cummings, "Public Lots: Maine's Chance to Right a History of Wrongs," *Maine Sunday Telegram*, November 26, 1972.

386. John Cole, "Outsiders Are Taking away our Land," *Maine Times*, March 2, 1973.

387. Bob Cummings, for one, scoffed at it. "The grand total from a century and a half of stewardship of nearly a half-million acres of public lands," he wrote with heavy irony, "now stands at $2.8 million—approximately what a typical community of 15,000 people spends for education in a year."

388. Cummings, "Public Land Sold and Given Away," *Maine Sunday Telegram*, March 12, 1972.

389. This process is authorized by article VI, section 3 of the Maine Constitution.

390. The Webber family was once second only to the Pingrees in forest ownership.

391. During one debate when Richardson was a freshman legislator, he was rebuked for announcing, "As far as I am concerned, any corporation that does not want to comply with our environmental law should move out, and I will meet them in Kittery [Maine's southern border] with a brass band."

392. Austin, "Maine Land Use Regulation Commission: Past, Present, and Future."

393. "Unclean hands" is a defense to a complaint, which states that a party who is asking for a judgment cannot have the help of the court if he/she has done anything unethical in relation to the subject of the lawsuit. Thus, if a defendant can show

the plaintiff had "unclean hands," the plaintiff's complaint will be dismissed or the plaintiff will be denied judgment. One of the plaintiffs representing a relatively small family ownership, Charles Richmond Cushing, was a dentist by trade whose patients included all Jon Lund's sons. "What I remember about the court case," he reminisced with a smile, "was that the deposition read, 'And now comes Cushing with unclean hands.'" After that, when treating the young Lunds, he made a point of washing his hands in front of them.

394. Such "an ingenious resolution of the public lot issue" would address an even longer-running conservation battle. The Dickey-Lincoln dam had divided Maine since Congress authorized it in1965 and continued to do so for another decade. "A Study of the Dickey-Lincoln Hydroelectric Project and its Impact on the Resources of the Upper Saint John River Valley," Rosemary M. Manning, Sierra Club, New England Chapter, 1973.

395. In the biennium 1973–1974, the special session was still strictly for lawmakers to consider emergency bills or those held over from the regular session. It wasn't until the 1980s that the special session became the second regular or short session and could deal with anything.

396. John E. McLeod, *The Northern, The Way I Remember.*

CHAPTER 11: GRAND PLANTATIONS AND GRAND NEGOTIATIONS

397. LD 2545, "AN ACT to Organize the Mainland Unorganized and Deorganized Territories of the State into Grand Plantations." 106th Legislature, First Special Session.

398. Ross would become executive director of the Maine Organic Farmers' and Growers' Association. Herb Hartman became director of the Maine Bureau of Parks and Lands.

399. "Maine's Forest Slums," *Portland Evening Express,* September 19, 1973, 10.

400. Clear-cutting—instead of selective cutting—can cause erosion. In 1973, the only company harvesting its forest using clearcuts was Scott, although the other companies all defended the practice as economically efficient and silviculturally legitimate. Most of them would begin clearcutting a few years later to salvage timber when a major outbreak of spruce budworm started to decimate Maine's forests. Continued heavy cutting led to forest practices regulation in 1989 and, in the 1990s, an attempt to ban clearcutting completely.

401. Peter Kyros's plan to use the Public Lots as a buffer to protect the wilderness character of the St. John River was also presented officially at this meeting.

402. *A Maine Manifest* might never have been written, Barringer wrote in his foreword, "without the gentle hammering and dogged persistence of John N. Cole."

403. "The Curtis style was to identify key problems and bring people together who had ideas and recommendations for solutions. Numerous formalized task forces were evidence of this style," *The Curtis Years 1967–1974,* Ed. Allen Pease.

404. *The Paper Plantation* was the name of the published version of the Nader report.

405. This was the ironic sense in which the Nader report used the term in its title.

406. CETA, the Comprehensive Employment and Training Act, was a federal program signed into law by President Nixon on December 28, 1973, to train workers and provide them with jobs in the public service.

407. Interesting to note that *The World Conservation Strategy* (International Union for Conservation of Nature, United Nations Environment Program, and World Wildlife Fund), which defined "sustainable development," was still half a dozen years in the future.

408. Walker became director of the Maine Forest Service; Hinckley became manager of Bigelow Preserve.

CHAPTER 12: TRADES, RAIDS, AND SOVEREIGN IMMUNITY

409. Harrison Richardson was no longer chairman. He had returned to private practice, having lost the Republican nomination for governor to James Irwin. Richardson's defeat was attributed to his support for grand plantations. It is also true that with an increasingly quizzical citizenry, his strongly held convictions militated against him. After accompanying the candidate on a fact-finding tour, Richard Barringer was unsurprised when Richardson lost. "Harry didn't listen to people," he said. Richard Barringer, personal communication.

410. At this point the status of the Public Reserved Lands the state was trying to recover, in rough numbers, broke down as follows: In total there were almost 400,000 acres, of which Maine had had full control of 80,000 from the start. This would be increased to 140,000 acres by the deal with Great Northern.

411. James B. Longley, Independent governor of Maine 1975–1979, Maine's first Independent governor; scored an upset win, with 39 percent of the vote, over Democrat George Mitchell and Republican James Irwin (who came in third).

412. The Pingree heirs held the balance of the undivided ownership. See chapter 9.

413. Great Northern still held thirty thousand acres in common and undivided ownership. See chapter 11.

414. Diamond International Corporation, Scott Paper Company, Dead River Corporation, St. Regis Paper Company, and the J.M. Huber Corporation.

415. Flanagan went on to become legal counsel and unofficial chief of staff to Governor Joseph Brennan, and later president of Central Maine Power.

416. "Including the public reserved lands, the subtidal lands, unconveyed islands, and public lands not assigned by law to another agency of government. At present the provisions [in the Department of Conservation] are inadequate for the management of these lands in accordance with the principles of sound land use and sound business practice." Statement of Fact, LD 930.

417. His colleagues used to tease Flanagan (who would become president of Central Maine Power Company) for carrying The Little Red Book around with him. He insisted that he was no Communist but was interested in some of Mao's ideas that could be used in management. Nancy Ross, David Flanagan, personal communication.

418. Years later, Flanagan recalled his job at BPL as an opportunity to "let Schepps teach me how to practice law." David Flanagan, personal communication.

419. The executive council, which went back to Maine's original Constitution, would be abolished the next month by a statewide referendum; the legislature had voted to end it during the past session, but as a constitutional amendment, the question had to go to the people.

420. At the time, one of the company executives, David Huber, was a Maine state senator. He recused himself and took no part in the negotiations.

421. Maine's conservation history is marked by a succession of epic battles between environmental organizations and corporations absorbing enormous financial and human resources on both sides. A partial list includes: Allagash Wilderness Waterway, Bigelow Mountain Preserve, Big A Dam, and Clear-cutting Referendum.

422. Nancy Ross, personal communication. During a site visit to the future preserve, Briggs took a photograph of the beautiful ridgeline and heights of Bigelow from the "wrong" side. He gave it to Ross for Christmas. Below the picture, he had written, "Who's ever seen the backside of Bigelow anyway?"

423. Despite the cramped conditions, a general courtesy hovered over the room. The company men especially were "soft-spoken, modulated and observing whatever rules of order were requested," noted John Cole. "These were not the hard-shirted, impatient, barber-shopped men who argued for permission to put 40 houses on 20 acres."

424. Bigelow Preserve Public Reserved Land, covering thirty-six thousand acres in 2018, is probably the only park in the country created by a popular vote.

425. Boise-Cascade had recently bought out the Oxford Paper Company of Rumford.

426. In fact, the state only added six thousand acres to the total Public Reserved Lands returned; the ten thousand acres it gave Georgia-Pacific in return included four thousand acres of Public Lots the state already owned. It also caused some dismay in Washington County.

427. The other two-thirds was owned by Seven Islands. The printed Legislative Resolve transferring Brown's share to Maine was the first that Brad Wellman knew of the deal. As with Great Northern and Deboullie, he was "pissed."

428. Cummings, "Historic Swap Marks Turn in State Land Policies," *Portland Press Herald,* May 3, 1977.

429. Legislative Record—Senate, May 12, 1977.

430. Order Appointing Referee, Kennebec Superior Court, October 8, 1974.

431. David Clayton Smith, author of *A History of Lumbering in Maine, 1861–1960*, University of Maine Studies No. 93, 1972.

432. Motion to Report Case to Law Court, May 15, 1979.

433. *Passamaquoddy Tribe v. Morton*; the First Circuit Court of Appeals upheld the decision, December 23, 1975.

434. *An Act to Regulate Trade and Intercourse with the Indian Tribes*, July 22, 1790.

435. John Kifner, "Maine Indian Suit for Land Halts Bond Sales and Endangers Title," *New York Times*, October 24, 1976.

436. Joseph G. E. Gousse, "Waiting for Gluskabe: An Examination of Maine's Colonialist Legacy Suffered by Native American Tribes Under the Maine Indian Claims Settlement Act of 1980," 546.

437. Kifner, op. cit.

438. Jimmy Carter, "Public Papers of the Presidents of the United States: 1977 Book II," 1759.

439. Cummings, "Why We Shouldn't Give *any* Public lands Away," *Maine Sunday Telegram*, July 24, 1977.

440. The Penobscots and Passamaquoddies each received $26.8 million; the Houlton Band of the Maliseets received $900,000. Two funds were set up: The Indian Claims Settlement Fund, $27 million held in trust by the United States to generate income; the Maine Indian Claims Land Acquisition Fund, to purchase three hundred thousand acres.

441. Gousse, op. cit., 548.

442. Gousse quotes Neil Rolde that "gunshops were emptied of weapons" by an apprehensive citizenry.

443. Although the standard public lot was 1,000 acres, Kennebec Paper's were in two tracts: 320 acres on Mount Abraham, near Kingfield, and 700 acres near Pierce Pond on the Upper Kennebec River. Cummings, *Maine Sunday Telegram*, February 26, 1978.

444. Austin, "New Twist on Public Lots," *Maine Times,* February 29, 1980.

445. Ibid.

446. Joseph E. Brennan, Democratic governor of Maine 1979–1987.

447. The special master's verdict read: "1. The public lot cutting rights now owned by plaintiffs which were granted by the State of Maine during the period 1850-1875 related to and conveyed the right to cut timber which was in existence at the time of the grant as well as the right to cut timber thereafter coming into existence, and 2. That said cutting rights related to and conveyed the right to cut all sizes and species of trees."

448. Lee Schepps, "Timber and Grass Rights; Trades," 55–58.

449. Since the BPL was created in 1973, the land under its control had jumped from 56,000 to 250,000 acres.

450. The legal name of the Public Lots case changed with each new attorney general, representing the State of Maine. The AG was now Richard Cohen.

451. In Irland's testimony to the committee he reported selling stumpage on fifty thousand cords cut on six thousand acres in 1980, and projected cutting on twelve thousand acres for one hundred thousand cords by 1984. At $10 a cord, the BPL would earn $1 million, and he estimated that stumpage prices would rise to $15 a cord.

452. As one former official told me, "Money in government is handled very strangely. There is such a difference [with business] in the way decisions are made and money is treated. In government, money is there to steal. It's like con artists. If it's there you got to use it."—TU

453. *A Resolve, Concerning the Authority of the Attorney General to Seek Adjudication of the Nature and Scope of Cutting Rights Claimed by Private Parties on Public Lands of the State of Maine.*

CHAPTER 13: "TO THE SURPRISE OF
EVERYONE IN THE WORLD . . ."

454. The lawsuit over the Public Reserved Lands changed its title with each change in attorney general. What was initially *Cushing v. Lund* was now *Cushing v. Tierney*, James Tierney being the AG at the time.

455. "We express no opinion on the question of the effect, if any, the parties' subsequent conduct may have under such doctrines as estoppel, acquiescence, waiver, laches, or prescription, which are by the parties' agreement not at issue in this proceeding." Estoppel and laches are legal doctrines. The state can be estopped from claiming damages at this late date. The doctrine of laches is based on the maxim that "equity aids the vigilant and not those who slumber on their rights" (*Black's Law Dictionary*). The outcome is that a legal right or claim will not be enforced or allowed if a long delay in asserting the right or claim has prejudiced the adverse party. Under the doctrine of laches, even though the landowners may not technically have had the right to cut, the state would not be able to recover any damages because it basically encouraged that activity.

456. See chapter 4.

457. In fact, a few trees standing in 1982 had almost certainly existed at the time the rights were sold. "It wasn't huge," said David Carlisle, "but there was a percentage that the court would agree were our trees." Roger Milliken explained how it might have happened on his family's land. "When the pulpwood cuts swept through the Baskahegan land base [in the 1920s], I bet they were cutting trees 8 inches DBH (diameter at breast height) and higher to run down the streams to the pulp mills." Trees of lesser size grew into the openings left by the removal of the other trees. "These were all partial cuts of one form or another, using horses, so a lot of trees of this diameter were left behind and would have just perked along." Justice David Nichols, dissenting, addressed this anomaly. "A few trees may obviously be that old. Vastly more trees may obviously be young growth. In between stand trees the age of which is not so apparent and which may well be the subject of controversy. These are difficulties which would be avoided under the judgment of the Superior Court."

458. The majority opinion did refer to a deed from 1850—the year sale of cutting rights on the Public Lots was authorized—that granted "all the pine and spruce timber standing on said Township." This was subsequently interpreted to include any "increase" that occurred "between the conveyance and the cutting," but not the trees that might have "sprung up" in the meantime,that is, only the standing timber.

459. When the Schepps report was under wraps in Attorney General James Erwin's office, Dean Godfrey had cautioned—to no avail—his student, Thomas Gibbon, the intern, against spilling its findings to the press.

460. Vincent McKusick, the chief justice, had been a partner at Pierce Atwood, which was representing the paper companies; Judge Gene Carter had a conflict of interest in that his son worked for Seven Islands; and Daniel Wathen, who had just been appointed, had accepted the special master's opinion while on the Kennebec

Superior Court. There might have been an empty seat, had President Jimmy Carter won the 1980 election. He had nominated David Roberts to a U.S. district judgeship. Ronald Reagan won instead and Roberts's name was withdrawn.

461. See chapter 11.

462. At first, Barringer resisted leaving the Conservation Department, but Brennan insisted, saying at one point, "You just don't want to give up your air force," a reference to the Forest Service's fleet of aircraft. Barringer relented. At the State Planning Office, he and a talented staff addressed pressing long-term issues, including education reform, public finance, economic and community development, as well as land conservation and, closest to his heart, rivers protection. Richard Barringer, personal communication.

463. Prentiss & Carlisle, "1984: P&C celebrates its 60th anniversary. Timberland sells for $110 an acre."

464. Bernard Schruender, still on loan from the U.S. Forest Service, had been running the BPL since the aw court's decision, continuing to build up the expertise and confidence of the staff.

465. Waterfront was also desired by the state for its high recreation value. Shoreland protection rules limited the timber it could generate, but valuation became more complicated as landowners began to realize its potential for future real estate development.

466. Wilk's official title was Special Counsel to the Governor's Task Force on Public Lands. Commissioner Richard Anderson did not like this title. "You're the negotiator, that's what you are, you're the negotiator," he would say. "Call me whatever you want," Wilk told him. Martin Wilk, personal communication.

467. When the state was being represented by a private attorney, it was standard procedure to have someone from the AG's office to be a liaison and to make sure things proceeded properly.

468. In terms of value, it was closer to 2.5 to 1. Maine received land worth $8,812 million in return for $3.657 million. Sarah Medina, personal communication.

469. Stephen Phillips Memorial Preserve Trust.

470. Dick Barringer told me about the hike up Deboullie Mountain, which Brad Wellman did not recall. Wellman did, however, recall his remark about the gold star and reenacted it for me.—TAU

471. Donald W. Perkins, "Public Lots Coalition," Pierce-Atwood memorandum.

CHAPTER 14: PUTTING THE PUBLIC
INTO THE PUBLIC RESERVED LANDS

472. Cummings, "Lots of Confusion," 97.

473. 12 MRSA ss 551.

474. The BPL budget was based on a ten-year allowable timber harvest level calculated for "optimum production of forest products." Annual revenues—mostly timber sales, but also camp leases—were deposited in the Public Reserved Lands

Management Fund. Proceeds of land sales—including from a few smaller landowners who settled their court claims in cash, for example, Megantic Manufacturing ($164,491); James A. Pierce Estate ($55,000)—went into a Land Acquisition Fund for the Public Reserved Lands system.

475. Spokespersons included: William Plouffe (AMC), Barbara Vickery (TNC), David Allen (SAM).

476. Multiple-Use Sustained-Yield Act of 1960. An Act to authorize and direct that the national forests be managed under principles of multiple use and to produce a sustained yield of products and services.

477. "Multiple use" shall mean the management of all of the various renewable surface resources of the Public Reserved Lots, including outdoor recreation, timber, watershed, fish and wildlife and other public purposes; it means making the most judicious use of the land for some or all of these resources over areas large and diverse enough to provide sufficient latitude for periodic adjustments in use to conform to changing needs and conditions; it means that some land will be used for less than all of the resources; and it means harmonious and coordinated management of the various resources, each with the other, without impairment of the productivity of the land, with consideration being given to the relative values of the various resources, and not necessarily the combination of uses that will give the greatest dollar return or the greatest unit output.

478. 12 MRSA ss 551.

479. *Planning Policy for the Public Reserved Lands of Maine*, "Introduction."

480. Full list of objectives as they occurred in the document is attached.

481. Jeff Clark, "Managing Public Lands," *Maine Times,* November 22, 1985.

482. *Planning Policy for the Public Reserved Lands of Maine*, 8.

483. A bemused Bob Cummings noted that one lease-holder recalled the halcyon days when Scott Paper Company owned the land and how secure he felt in his holding. Now that the state had it, he wanted to buy. But Scott simply gave up its Public Lots, without negotiating a trade, the only company to do so. In other words, this particular campsite had always belonged to Maine.

484. John Hale, "Nature Conservancy, State Acquire Wilderness Areas for People of Maine," *Bangor Daily News*, July 21,1987.

485. John R. McKernan Jr., Republican governor of Maine 1987–1995.

486. When it was, Gardiner became president of Maine's Public Broadcasting Network.

CHAPTER 15: A UNIQUE AGENCY TAKES ITS PLACE

487. Seven Islands' Brad Wellman told the author that although he couldn't prove it, he believed that after the Big A, "the directors of Great Northern said, we're done with the state of Maine." He added, "They didn't give up on Maine after the Public Lots."

488. It included: Leon Gorman (1934–2015, grandson of L.L. Bean and president of the company), Ralph "Bud" Leavitt (1917–1994, legendary Maine outdoor sports

writer), Angus King (Maine governor 1994–2002), and Joan Benoit Samuelson (Olympic marathon gold winner and conservationist).

489. Gorman came to see it as a good outcome. "The people who really knew what could be done in Augusta focused on the money, which turned out to be correct," he later commented.

490. Future commissioner, Maine Department of Conservation.

491. Clinton "Bill" Townsend recalled stopping at Pat McGowans's Canaan store one morning in 1987. McGowan told him he was going to submit a bill for a $5 million land acquisition bond. "And I said, 'Pat, that's insane, it should be $50 million.' The words just absolutely exploded out of me. And Pat looked at me and said, 'Yeah, you're right.'"

492. Ibid.

493. Cliff Hickman, "TIMOs and REITs."

494. It was not uncommon for timberland owners like Prentiss & Carlisle to ask a paper company to put up the money to buy a township, in return for which they would get a share of the wood cut on it.

495. Maine Guide's joke from the time: What's the difference between a dead skunk and a dead developer on the road? There are skid marks in front of the skunk.

496. Bryan's other claim to fame was as half of "Bert and I," the epitome of Maine humor that he created with his Yale classmate, the late Marshall Dodge.

497. "The Nature Conservancy and State Sign 40,000-Acre Purchase Agreement," 2.

498. Barbara Vickery, "Timeline of events leading to eventual establishment of Ecological Reserves in Maine," 1.

499. Angus King Jr., Independent governor of Maine, 1995–2002.

500. In the end, neither initiative won a plurality at the polls. However, the public debate brought favorable attention to third-party forestry audits, which quickly became almost universal.

501. Language was included exempting from these calculations any lands that might be acquired by the bureau specifically as additions to the ecological reserve system.

502. Ibid., 2.

503. Ecological reserves were part of the following units: Spring River Lake, Donnell Pond, Salmon Brook Lake Bog, Bigelow Preserve, Rocky Lake, Duck Lake, Deboullie, Cutler Coast, Mt. Abram, Gero Island, Nahmakanta.

CHAPTER 16: QUIET DARLINGS NO MORE—INTO THE TWENTY-FIRST CENTURY

504. John E. Baldacci, Democratic governor of Maine, 2003–2010.

505. David Soucy, "Running the Allagash: River Drivers Find the Channel," *Maine Fish and Wildlife.* 19.

506. The artist Frederick Church built a camp on Katahdin Lake, as well.

507. Austin, "Deal Would Realize Percival Baxter's Dream."

508. Said Conservation Commissioner Patrick McGowan of the negotiations: "We've seen a lot more valleys than peaks. Our mantra was never give up." Phyllis Austin, *Maine Environmental News*, January 24, 2006.

509. Richard Barringer and Rob Gardiner, "Katahdin Lake Well Worth Selling Some Public Lots To Acquire," *Maine Sunday Telegram*, November 19, 2006.

510. Joe Rankin, "Maine's Public Lands: Recreation, Wildlife Habitat, Timber."

511. Paul R. LePage, Republican governor of Maine, 2011–2018.

512. Catherine B. Johnson, "Maine's Big Old Trees at Risk from Administration's Plan to Increase Logging on Maine's Public Lands."

513. Christine Parrish, "Christine Parrish—Leaving Free Press for Wilderness Job in VA," *The Free Press*, May 17, 2018.

514. Janet Mills (Democrat) succeeded Paul LePage as governor of Maine in 2019.

515. George Smith, "Political Hack or Professional Manager—Who Will Governor LePage Appoint as Parks and Lands Director?"

516. The Department of Conservation had been merged with the Department of Agriculture and became the Department of Agriculture, Conservation and Forestry in 2013.

517. Kevin Miller, "Maine Forest Service Official Grilled over Logging, Public Park Management," *Portland Press Herald*, March 11, 2015.

518. Smith, "Legislature's Public Lands Commission Slams Forest Door on Governor's Demands."

519. George Smith, who had been the longtime executive director of the Sportsman's Alliance of Maine, wrote regular blogs as well as columns about Maine wildlife issues.

520. Nick Sambides Jr., "Landowner Seeks Injunction Stopping State Harvesting," *Bangor Daily News,* March 18, 2016.

521. Parrish, "Maine Woods Legislative Update," *The Free Press,* March 10, 2016.

522. Miller, "Governor Steps up Land Fight," *Portland Press Herald*, February 13, 2016.

523. Determined to save Nahmakanta Lake when Diamond Occidental put it on the block, Fitzgerald put up and lost his $1 million deposit. Nahmakanta was subsequently acquired by the state. See chapter 15.

524. Parrish, "State Park Cuts, the Maine Public Lands Takeover, and $3 Million Missing," *The Free Press,* March 30, 2017.

525. Governor Mills' statutory goals, approved by the Legislature, would reduce statewide greenhouse gas emissions by 45 percent by 2030 and by 80 percent by 2050; and increase the amount of electricity from renewable sources from the current 40 percent to 80 percent by 2030 and 100 percent by 2050. Addressing participants at the United Nations Climate Summit on September 23, she further announced an Executive Order committing Maine to "strive to achieve a carbon neutral economy no later than 2045." "Maine won't wait," Mills told the delegates. "Will you?" Colin Woodard, *Portland Press Herald*, September 23, 2019.

526. Only Hawaii and Montana placed higher.

527. The New England Clean Energy Connect would bring electricity generated by Hydro-Quebec in Canada to Massachusetts via the New England electric grid.

AFTERWORD

1. Twenty-six groups were represented, seven of them from out of state or national organizations.
2. J. M. Hagan, L. C. Irland, and A. A. Whitman. Changing timberland ownership in the Northern Forest and implications for biodiversity. Manomet Center for Conservation Sciences, Report # MCCS-FCP2005-1. Brunswick, ME: 2005, 25 pp.

ACKNOWLEDGMENTS

1. Twentieth-Century New England Land Conservation, A Heritage of Civic Engagement, ed. Charles H. W. Foster, Harvard University Forest, 2009.

Bibliography

Abbott, John S. C., and Edward Henry Elwell. *History of the State of Maine.* Second edition. Augusta, ME: Brown Thurston Company [for E. E. Knowles & Co.], 1892.

Allis, Frederick S. Jr. *William Bingham's Maine Lands 1792–1820.* Publications of the Colonial Society of Massachusetts Vol. 36. Portland, ME: The Anthoensen Press; Boston: The Colonial Society of Massachusetts, 1954.

Arndt, J. Chris. "Maine in the Northeastern Boundary Controversy: States' Rights in Antebellum New England." *The New England Quarterly* 62, no. 2 (June 1989): 205–23.

Austin, Phyllis. "Maine Land Use Regulation Commission: Past, Present, and Future." Maine Environmental Policy Institute website, April, 23, 2004. Accessed March 22, 2019. http://www.meepi.org/files04/pa042004.htm.

———. "Deal Would Realize Percival Baxter's Dream." *Maine Environmental News* (January 24, 2006). Maine Environmental Policy Institute website. Accessed March 24, 2019. http://www.meepi.org/files06/pa012406.htm.

Avery, Myron H. "The Keep Path and Its Successors." *Appalachia* (December, 1928): 132–47.

Bergquist, David, "Head-of-Tide." *Life on a Tidal River.* A project of Maine Historical Society in partnership with Maine Memory Network. Accessed March 22, 2019. http://bangor.mainememory.net/page/1366/display.html.

Berry, Peter Neil, "Nineteenth Century Constitutional Amendment in Maine" (1965). Electronic Theses and Dissertations. Accessed March 22, 2019. http://digitalcommons .library.umaine.edu/etd/2385.

Bley, Jerry. "LURC's Challenge: Managing Growth in Maine's Unorganized Territories," *Maine Policy Review* 16 (2007): 92–100.

Bradley, Levi. *Report of the Land Agent of the State of Maine, December 31, 1844.* Augusta, ME: Wm. T. Johnson, 1845.

A Brief History of Papermaking in Maine, Maine Pulp and Paper Association. Accessed March 25, 2019. https://web.archive.org/web/20050320132934/http://www .pulpandpaper.org/html/history_of_papermaking.html.

Burby, Tom. "The Sarcophagus of Rufus Dwinel." June 21, 2015. Strange New England. Accessed March 25, 2019. http://www.strangenewengland.com/2015/06/21/the-sarcophagus-of-rufus-dwinel/.

Burleigh, Parker P. "Annual Report of the Land Agent of the State of Maine for the Year Ending November 30, 1874." *Public Documents of Maine: Being the Annual Reports of the Various Public Officers and Institutions for the Year 1875.* Vol. II. Augusta, ME: Sprague, Owen & Nash, 1875.

Burrage, Henry S. *Maine in the Northeastern Boundary Controversy.* Portland, ME: Marks Printing House, Printer for the State, 1919.

"Canadian Public Lands." *Portland Daily Press*, July 18, 1907; quoted by Liberty B. Dennett in "Maine's Wild Lands and Wildlanders." *Pine Tree Magazine* 8, no. 1 (August 1907): 53–61.

Carter, Jimmy. "Public Papers of the Presidents of the United States: 1977 Book II." Washington, DC: Office of the Federal Register, National Archives and Records Service, General Services Administration, 1977.

Cary, Austin. "Maine Forests, Their Preservation, Taxation and Value." *Twentieth Annual Report of the Bureau of Industrial and Labor Statistics for the State of Maine 1906.* Augusta, ME: Kennebec Journal Print, 1907, pp. 180–93.

Chapman, Hiram. *Annual Report of the Land Agent of the State of Maine for the Year Ending November 30,1863.* Augusta, ME: Stevens & Sayward, 1863.

Chisholm, Hugh J. "History of Papermaking in Maine and the Future of the Industry." *Twentieth Annual Report of the Bureau of Industrial and Labor Statistics for the State of Maine 1906.* Augusta, ME: Kennebec Journal Print, 1907.

Cony, Samuel. *Annual Report of the Land Agent of the State of Maine, December 31, 1847.* Augusta, ME: Wm. T. Johnson, 1847.

———. *Annual Report of the Land Agent of the State of Maine, December 31, 1850.* Augusta, ME: William T. Johnson, 1850.

Cox, Peter. *Journalism Matters.* Thomaston, ME: Tilbury House, 2005.

Cummings, Bob. "Lots of Confusion." *Appalachia* (Winter 1986–1987): 96–104.

Deane, John G. "Report of the Committee on State Lands." *Resolves of the Eleventh Legislature of the State of Maine.* Portland, ME: Todd and Holden, 1831.

Defebaugh, James Elliot. *History of the Lumber Industry of America* Vol. 2. Chicago: American Lumberman, 1907.

Dekker, Michael. *French and Indian Wars in Maine.* Charleston, SC: The History Press, 2015.

"Eastern Lands Papers, Records, 1717–1860." Secretary of the Commonwealth of Massachusetts website. Accessed March 26, 2019. https://www.sec.state.ma.us/arc/arcpdf/eastland.pdf.

Federal Writers' Project of the Works Project Administration. *Maine: A Guide Down East.* Boston: Houghton Mifflin, 1937.

Fellows, Raymond, and Edward J. Conquest, compilers. *William R. Pattangall of Maine, Lawyer, Politician, Jurist: A Compilation of Facts Relating to a Busy and Interesting Life together with The Meddybemps Letters, The Maine Hall of Fame, Anecdotes and Speeches.* Self-published, Bangor, ME, 1954.

Ferland, Jacques. Citing "Report on Indian affairs/Petition of John Neptune and Joseph Socbasin, Penobscot tribe," Council Report no. 17, 1831, *Indian Affairs Documents from the Maine Executive Council.* Quoted in "Tribal Dissent or White Aggression?: Interpreting Penobscot Indian Dispossession between 1808 and 1835." *Maine History* 43:2 (August 2007) 149–52.

Gates, Paul W., and Robert Swenson. *History of Public Land Law Development. Written for the United States Public Land Law Review Commission.* Washington, DC: Wm. W. Gaunt & Sons, 1987.

Godfrey, John E. "The Ancient Penobscot, or Panawanskek." *The Historical Magazine and Notes and Queries Concerning The Antiquities, History, and Biography of America.* Third Series 1, no. 2; Whole Number 21, no. 2. (February 1872), Morrisina, NY: Henry B. Dawson: 85–92.

Gordon, Nancy M. "Protecting the Public Interest: Land Agents vs. Loggers on the Eastern Frontier, 1820-1840." *Enterprise & Society* 3, no. 3 (September 2002). Cambridge University Press: 462–81.

Gousse, Joseph G. E. "Waiting for Gluskabe: An Examination of Maine's Colonialist Legacy Suffered by Native American Tribes Under the Maine Indian Claims Settlement Act of 1980." *Maine Law Review* 66, no. 2 (June 2014): 536–68.

Greenleaf, Moses. *A Statistical View of the District of Maine; More Especially with Reference to the Value and Importance of its Interior.* Boston: Cummings and Hilliard,1816.

———. *Survey of the State of Maine, in Reference to its Geographical Features, Statistics and Political Economy.* Portland, ME: Shirley & Hyde,1829.

Hagan, J. M., L. C. Irland, and A. A. Whitman. *Changing Timberland Ownership in the Northern Forest and Implications for Biodiversity.* Report # MCCS-FCP2005-1, Manomet Center for Conservation Sciences, Brunswick, ME, 2005. 25 pp.

Hamlin, Elijah L. "Report of the Land Agent,1839." *Documents Printed by Direction of the Governor and by Order of the Legislature for the Year 1839 Vol. 1.* Augusta, ME: Smith & Robinson, 1839.

Hardy, Manly. *Manly Hardy: The Life and Writing of a Maine Fur-buyer, Hunter, and Naturalist.* Compiled and introduced by William B. Krohn. Orono, ME: Maine Folklife Center, 2005.

Hepler, Christine I. "Researching Initiatives and Referenda: A Guide for Maine." *The Haworth Press* 26, no. 3–4 (2008): 97–112.

Hickman, Cliff. "TIMOs and REITs." Unpublished internal report. March 19, 2007. Accessed March 25, 2019. www.fs.fed.us/spf/coop/library/timo_reit. pdf.

Hildreth, Richard. *Banks, Banking, and Paper Currencies.* Boston: Whipple & Damrell, 1840.

Hill, Mark Langdon et al. "A Memorial of Mark Langdon Hill and Others." *North American Review and Miscellaneous Journal* 3, no. 9 (1816). Boston: Wells and Lilly, 362–425.

Hodgdon, John. "Land Agent's Report, January 1, 1835." *Documents Printed by Order of the Legislature, of the State of Maine. 1835.*

Hubbard, John. "Message of Governor Hubbard to Both Branches of the Legislature of the State of Maine, May 19, 1851." *Documents Printed by Order of the Legislature of the State of Maine during its Sessions A.D. 1851–2.* Augusta, ME: William T. Johnson, 1852.

Hubbard, Lucius L. *Woods and Lakes of Maine, A Trip from Moosehead Lake to New Brunswick in a Birch-Bark Canoe.* Boston: J. R. Osgood and Co., 1884.

Irland, Lloyd C. "Rufus Putnam's Ghost, An Essay on Maine's Public Lands, 1783–1820." *Journal of Forest History* 30, no. 2 (April 1986): 60–69.

———. *The Northeast's Changing Forest.* Petersham, MA: Harvard University Forest, 1999.

Jackson, C. T. *Second Annual Report on the Geology of the Public Lands belonging to the two states of Maine and Massachusetts.* Augusta, ME: Luther Severance, 1838.

Johnson, Catherine B. "Maine's Big Old Trees at Risk from Administration's Plan to Increase Logging on Maine's Public Lands." Unpublished internal report by the Natural Resources Council of Maine. March 2014. NRCM website. Accessed March 22, 2019. https://www.nrcm.org/wp-content/uploads/2014/03/MainesBig OldTreesatRisk.pdf.

Judd, Richard. *Aroostook: A Century of Logging in Northern Maine.* With research assistance by Patricia A. Judd. Orono, ME: University of Maine Press, 1989.

King, William. "State of the State Address," January, 1821. Maine State Archives. Accessed March 27, 2019. https://www.maine.gov/sos/arc/collections/williamking .html.

Leading Manufacturers and Merchants of the City of Boston, and a Review of the Prominent Exchanges. Boston: International Publishing Company, 1885.

Lenentine, Charlotte. *Madawaska, A Chapter in Maine-New Brunswick Relations.* Madawaska, ME: Madawaska Historical Society, 1975.

Lewis, James. "Honoring America's First Forester on His 150th Birthday." *Peeling Back the Bark:* Exploring the collections, acquisitions, and treasures of the Forest History Society. August 11, 2015. Accessed March 2109. https://fhsarchives .wordpress.com/page/4/.

Lincoln, Enoch. "Speech of the Governor of the State of Maine to Both Houses of the Legislature, 1828." *Resolves of the Eighth Legislature of the State of Maine.* Portland, ME: Thomas Todd, 1828.

Lincoln, Waldo, ed. *Genealogy of the Waldo Family—A Record of the Descendants of Cornelius Waldo, of Ipswich, Mass. From 1647 to 1900.* Worcester, MA: Charles Hamilton, 1902.

Loring, Amasa. *History of Piscataquis County, Maine: From its Earliest Settlement to 1880.* Portland, ME: Hoyt, Fogg & Donham, 1880.

MacDougall, Walter M. *Settling the Maine Wilderness: Moses Greenleaf, His Maps, and His Household of Faith.* Portland, ME: University of Southern Maine's Osher Map Library and Smith Center for Cartographic Education, 2006.

Maine Historical and Genealogical Recorder Vols. 1–2. Portland, ME: S. M. Watson, 1884.

Massachusetts Provincial Congress. *The Journals of Each Provincial Congress of Massachusetts in 1774 & 1775.* Boston: Dutton & Wentworth, 1838.

McLeod, John E. *The Northern, The Way I Remember.* Condensed from a history by John E. McLeod. Millinocket, ME: Great Northern Paper Company, 1982.

Milliken, Roger Jr., *Forest for the Trees: A History of the Baskahegan Company.* Augusta, ME: R. Milliken, 2013.

Morrill, Anson P. *Annual Report of the Land Agent of the State of Maine, December 31, 1850.* Augusta, ME: Wm. T. Johnson, 1852.

Morrill, Lot. *Annual Report of the Land Agent of the State of Maine, December 31, 1851.* Augusta, ME: Wm. T. Johnson, 1852.

Morrill, Lot. *Address of Governor Morrill to the Legislature of the State of Maine, January 6, 1860.* Augusta, ME: Stevens & Sayward, 1860.

"The Nature Conservancy and State Sign 40,000-Acre Purchase Agreement." *Maine Legacy* (June 1990). Published by the Nature Conservancy.

Oak, Lyndon. *A Sketch of the Life of General James Irish of Gorham, Me 1776–1863.* Boston: Lee & Shepard, 1898.

Osborn, William C. *The Paper Plantation: Ralph Nader's Study Group Report on the Pulp and Paper Industry in Maine.* New York: Grossman Publishers, 1974.

Paper, A Weekly Technical Journal for Paper and Pulp Mills 31, no. 26 (April 18, 1923).

Parrott, William P. "Report of William P. Parrott." *Documents printed by order of the Legislature, of the State of Maine, during its Session A.D. 1840.* Augusta, ME: Wm. R. Smith & Co., 1840.

Pawling, Micah A., ed. *Wabanaki Homeland and the New State of Maine, The 1820 Journal and Plans of Survey of Joseph Treat.* Amherst, MA: University of Massachusetts Press, in conjunction with Penobscot Indian Nation, 2007.

Perry, Michael T. "'Maine and *her* soil, or BLOOD!': Political Rhetoric and Spatial Identity during the Aroostook War in Maine," *Maine History* 47, no. 1 (January 2013): 69–93.

Pike, Robert E. *Tall Trees, Tough Men.* New York: W.W. Norton & Company, 1967.

Planning Policy for the Public Reserved Lands of Maine. Bureau of Public Lands, Maine Department of Conservation, June 11, 1985.

Poor, Laura Elizabeth, ed. *The First International Railway and the Colonization of New England: Life and Writings of John Alfred Poor.* New York: The Knickerbocker Press, 1889.

Porter, Joseph W., ed. "The Aroostook War, and the Volunteer Troops Therein." *The Bangor Historical Magazine* 2 (1886–1887). Bangor, ME: Joseph W. Porter, 1887: 121–24.

Putnam, Frank. "What's the Matter with New England? Maine: A Study in Land-Grabbing, Tax Dodging and Isolation." *New England Magazine* 36, no. 5 (July 1907): 515–40.

Rankin, Joe, "Maine's Public Lands: Recreation, Wildlife Habitat, Timber." *Fresh from the Woods* (April 26, 2012). Forests for Maine's Future web site. Accessed March 27, 2019. http://forestsformainesfuture.squarespace.com/fresh-from-the-woods-journal/maines-public-lands-recreation-wildlife-habitat-timber.html.

Remini, Robert V. *Daniel Webster: The Man and His Time*. New York: W.W. Norton & Company, 1997.

Rendall, Raymond E. *Twenty-Fourth Biennial Report of the Forest Commissioner, State of Maine 1941–42*. Augusta, ME: State of Maine Forest Service, June 1, 1943.

"Report on the Proposed Allagash National Riverway." Bureau of Outdoor Recreation, U.S. Department of the Interior. July, 1963.

Ring, Edgar E. *Seventh Report of the Forest Commissioner, State of Maine 1908*. Waterville, ME: Sentinel Publishing Co., 1908.

Rolde, Neil. *The Interrupted Forest*. Gardiner, ME: Tilbury House, 2001.

Schepps, Lee. "Report on the Public Lots." Maine State Attorney General's Office. Unpublished typescript. September 12, 1972.

———. "Timber and Grass Rights; Trades." Internal memorandum. April 24, 1979. Maine State Archives.

Smith, Edgar Crosby. *Moses Greenleaf, Maine's First Map-maker*. Bangor, ME: Printed for the De Burians by C. H. Glass & Co., 1902.

Smith, George. "Political Hack or Professional Manager—Who Will Governor Le-Page Appoint as Parks and Lands Director?"*George's Outdoor News*, June 6, 2014. *Bangor Daily News* website. Accessed March 27, 2019. http://georgesoutdoornews .bangordailynews.com/2014/06/06/maine-woods/political-hack-or-professional -manager-who-will-governor-lepage-appoint-as-parks-and-lands-director/.

———. "Legislature's Public Lands Commission Slams Forest Door on Governor's Demands." *George's Outdoor News*, December 1, 2015. *Bangor Daily News* website. Accessed March 27, 2019. https://georgesoutdoornews.bangordailynews .com/2015/12/page/3/.

Soucy, David. "Running the Allagash: River Drivers Find the Channel." *Maine Fish & Game Magazine*, 46, no. 2 (Summer 2004). *Inland Fisheries and Wildlife Magazine*. Book 100. Maine Department of Inland Fisheries and Wildlife.

State Forestry Department. "Report of Legislative Interim Committee on Public Reserve Lots." State of Maine. 1947.

Taylor, Alan. *Liberty Men and Great Proprietors*. Chapel Hill: University of North Carolina Press, 1990.

Thoreau, Henry David. *The Writings of Henry David Thoreau: The Maine Woods*. Boston and New York: Houghton Mifflin and Company, 1906.

Thornton, Mrs. Seth S. *Traditions and Records of Southwest Harbor and Somesville, Mount Desert Island, Maine*. Auburn, ME: Merrill & Webber Company, 1938.

Violette, Neil L. *State of Maine Seventeenth Biennial Report of the Forest Commissioner 1927–1928*.

———. *Twentieth Biennial Report of the Forest Commissioner, State of Maine. 1933–1934*. January 5, 1935.

Washburn, Israel. "Centennial and Dedicatory Address." *1774. 1874. Centennial Celebration and Dedication of Town Hall, Orono, Maine, March 3, 1874*. Portland, ME: Bailey & Noyes, 1874.

Wheatland, Stephen. "History of Pingree Heir Timberland Ownership." *Biennial Report of the Forest Commisioner, 196--1970.* Augusta, ME: Forest Commissioner. 1970.

Wilkins, Austin. *Report on Public Reserved Lots.* Prepared by State Forestry Department, State of Maine, 1963.

————. *Ten Million Acres of Timber: The Remarkable Story of Forest Protection in the Maine Forestry District (1909–1972).* Oakdale, CA: TBW Books, 1978.

Williams, Chase and Co. *History of Penobscot County, Maine.* Cleveland: Williams, Chase and Co., 1882.

Williamson, William D. *The History of the State of Maine, from its First Discovery A.D. 1602, to the Separation, A.D. 1820, Inclusive.* Hallowell, ME: Glazier Masters and Co.,1832.

Wood, Richard G. *A History of Lumbering in Maine 1820–1861.* Orono, ME: University of Maine, 1935.

Woodard, Colin. *The Lobster Coast: Rebels, Rusticators & the Struggle for a Forgotten Frontier.* New York: Viking, 2004.

The World's Paper Trade Review 39. (February 13, 1903). London: W. John Stonehill & Co.

Index

Commission, 301n363; Public Lots
study by, 150
Godfrey, Justice Edward, 225
Goldsmith, James, 250
Gorman, Leon, 248, 310n488
Grand Plantations: Martin, J., on, 193–
94; Richardson on, 180–81, 188–89,
195, 305n409
grass rights, *See* timber and grass rights
Gray, Norman, 121
Great American Land Auction, 251
Great Northern Paper Company, 103,
116-17, 128, 157, 174, 176, 178;
Public Lots on land of, 196
Greely, Ebenezer, 65
Greenleaf, Moses, 20, 60, 82, 93, 125,
166, 287n125; on academies, 16–17;
maps by, 291n205; publications of,
38–39, 84; on public lands, 42–43; as
surveyor, 54, 56–57; on taxation, 6
de Gregoire, Marie Theresa, 15, 25–26
Gunter, William B., 212–13

Hamilton, Alexander, 23, 61
Hamlin, Elijah L., 59–60
Hancock, Governor John, 6, 8, 28
Hancock County Planning Commission,
215
Hand, Lynwood, 170, 175
Hardy, Manly, 112
Hare, Charles Willing, 35–36
Harris, John, 10, 51
Harris, Will, 259–60
Hartman, Herb, 150, 180, 192–93, 221,
255; on land swaps, 201
Harvey, Sir John, 65, 67, 69
Hary, Edith, 151
Haskell, James, 145, 156, 159, 167, 172,
193; at LURC, 189
Hellendale, Robert, 237, 270; Barringer
and, 196–98
H.F. Eaton Company, 61
Hildreth, Horace, Jr., 166, 167
Hinckley, John, 194, 197
Hoar, Leigh, Jr., 241

Hobbstown, 121
Holeb Township, 200, 230
Holland, Park, 15
Hollingsworth and Whitney, 120–21
Holt, Fred, 174, 181, 183-84, 206,194
Homestead Act, 92
Houlton, 77, 101
Howland, 45
Hubbard, Governor John, 84–86,
297n287; on homesteaders, 89; on
public domain, 293n229
Huber, David, 306n420
Hudson Pulp and Paper Company, 218
Hughes, Charles Evans, 106, 297n288
von Humboldt, Alexander von, 57
Hunter, Malcolm, 252–53
Hutchins, Christopher, 206

Indian Township, 114
Initiative and Referendum Act, 111
Inland Fisheries and Wildlife,
Department of, 220, 241, 297n285
Inman, Joseph, 19, 22
Inman, William, 19
Interdepartmental Committee on Public
Lands, 148, 152, 156, 161
International Paper Company, 98,
128, 145, 190, 198, 204, 273,
274; as landowner, 172; on local
populations, 174; value of, 102
Irish, James, 49–52, 58, 62
Irland, Lloyd, 14, 215, 218, 222,
240, 270; on management, 219;
management plans of, 220; on
nonprofit organizations, 273–74; on
rental fees, 244; on timber revenues,
228–29
Irving, J. D., xi; Brennan and, 238
Irving Pulp & Paper, 230

Jackman Pond, 238
Jackson, President Andrew, 63
Jackson, Charles T., 72–73, 75
Jackson, General Henry, 24, 27, 31
Jackson, Major William, 27, 31, 285n76

334 *Index*

P110. *See* Paper Industry Information
Office
Palmer, Lynwood, 193, 202
Panic of 1857, 90
Panic of 1873, 94
Paper Industry Information Office
(P110), 145, 165, 185
The Paper Plantation, 304n404
paper production, 102, 166;
environmentalism and, 299n328;
industry value of, 128; Richardson
on, 174–75
Parker, Vicki, 197
Parks and Recreation Department, 144,
168, 205, 208
Parris, Governor Albion K., 48, 49
Parrish, Christine, 257, 260–61
Parrott, William, 68–69
Passamaquoddy Tribe, 212
Pattangall, William R., 98, 99, 107,
111–12, 114; on Democratic Party,
295n254
Patten, Amos, 19–20, 285n58
Patten Corporation, 251
Pearl Harbor, 120
Penobscot Log Driving Company, 82
Penobscot River, 6, 8, 13, 18–20, 26,
35, 37, 43–44, 53, 55, 72, 99, 103,
112, 212, 235; mills on, 290n180
Penobscot Tribe, 3, 4, 33, 44, 287n125,
307n440; territory of, 21–22
Perkins, Donald, 190, 232, 237
Phillips, Bessie, 234
Pierce Atwood, 176, 210, 232, 308n460
Pine State Magazine, 107
Pingree, David, viii, 79–83, 102, 128,
233
Pingree, David, Jr., 83, 105
Pingree Associates, Inc., 233, 269
Piscataquis Canal and Railroad
Company, 56
*A Plan of the Public Lands in the State
of Maine* (Coffin), 73

plantations, 87, 118–19, 190–91;
Schepps on, 78–79. *See also* Grand
Plantations
Plymouth Patent, 283n27. *See also*
Kennebec Claim
Poor, John A., 56, 85, 86, 93, 94, 95
Portland and Rumford Falls Railroad,
103
Portland Press Herald, 160, 163, 216–
17, 267
Post War Planning Commission, 121
Powers, Llewellyn, 108–9, 297n290
Pownall, Governor Thomas, 3, 4, 20,
281n7, 282n21
Preble, William Pitt, 64, 70
Prentiss & Carlisle, 172, 174, 230, 251–
52; negotiations with, 235–36; Public
Reserved Lands of, 236
Presumpscot River, 102
public domain, defining, 71–72;
Greenleaf on, 42–43; early
management of, 48–49; for
settlement or timber, 52; problems
with Massachusetts regarding, 83-86
Public Lands Committee, 170, 180, 183,
186, 190, 199; on LD 1812, 177
Public Lots, *See* Public Reserved Lands
public recreation, 181; Gardiner on,
243; waterfronts and, 309n465
Public Reserved Land Management
units, 220, 229, 243
Public Reserved Lands, viii, 7, 58, 96,
179; Acquisition Fund, 125, 201;
campsites, leases of, 147-48, 219,
244; categories of, 127; "legislative
interim committee" (1947) study on,
121–22; consolidation of, 144, 196,
217, 246; Cummings on, 138–39,
142, 151, 157, 179, 191, 238, 239;
Curtis on, 145, 148; defining, 143;
division of, 226; early history
of, 18; Dyar bills on, 169–70;
evolution of, 173; hostile partitions

Washington, President George, 212
Washington County, 78, 114, 218
Wassataquoik Stream, 235, 267
Water Improvement Commission, 184
Wathen, Justice Daniel, 216, 225, 308n460
Webber, Justice Donald W., 210, 211, 223; on Public Reserved Lands, 216; on Smith, D. C., 216
Webber, J. P., 100, 101, 102, 236; family, 174
Webster, Daniel, 32, 69
Webster-Ashburton Treaty, 69, 71, 73, 75, 83
Wellington, Duke of, 67
Wellman, Brad, viii, 78, 102, 174, 175, 185, 249, 310n487; Barringer on, 233; at BPL, 218; on Great Northern, 198
Wernick, Sidney, Justice 221, 225
West Branch Driving and Reservoir Dam Company, 103–4
West Branch Project, 274
Wheatland, Richard, 79
Wheatland, Stephen, 189
Whig Party, 65–66, 290n186
Whitcomb, Walter, 263, 264

Wild and Scenic Rivers Program, 129
Wilk, Martin, x, 144, 145, 181, 210–11, 216, 228, 270, 275; BPL and, 232; Gardiner on, 232; on land rights, 226; on Public Lots, 210; on timber revenues, 228
Wilkins, Austin, 6, 96–97, 121, 123, 126–27, 130, 143, 246; as Forest Commissioner, 182; on natural resources, 147; on Public Lots, 139–40; on Public Reserved Lands, 136; retirement of, 160; on Schepps, 160–61
William I (King of the Netherlands), 62–63
Williamsburgh, 38, 55, 56
Williamson, Governor William, 5, 290n180
Wing, Morris R., 145–46, 175, 185, 189
Wommack, Kent, 250–51, 254
Woodlands, Irving, 258
World War II, 120–22
Wyman, Walter, 117, 125

Year Without a Summer, 40, 47
Yom Kippur War, 186